Understanding
Unemployment

Understanding Unemployment

Lawrence H. Summers

The MIT Press
Cambridge, Massachusetts
London, England

This book was set in Palatino by Asco Trade Typesetting Ltd., Hong Kong, and printed and bound by Halliday Lithograph in the United States of America.

Library of Congress Cataloging-in-Publication Data

Summers, Lawrence H.
  Understanding unemployment.

  Bibliography: p.
  Includes index.
  1. Unemployment—Collected works.   I. Title.
HD5707.5.S85   1987   331.13'7   87-3866
ISBN 0-262-19265-9

To my parents—whose example has meant so much

Contents

Contents

List of Tables

Preface

This book collects papers written over the last decade about the economics of unemployment. They share an increasingly controversial premise that unemployment is an analytically meaningful and useful concept and that the extent of unemployment represents a serious and potentially remediable social problem. The current (August 1989) strength of the world economy should not blind us to the huge unemployment problem that remains. The number of unemployed in the nations of the OECD is 60% greater than in was in 1979 when the first of the essays collected here was written, and is 150% greater than it was in 1973. During the 1980s unemployment problems have been particularly serious in Europe. But even in the United States unemployment has increased sharply, with the male unemployment rate rising from an average of 4.3% in the 1950s and 1960s to an average of 7.4% during the 1980s.

Do unemployment statistics measure anything meaningful? It is unfortunate but true that an economist's book on unemployment written in the 1980s requires a defense of the concept. An increasingly fashionable body of economic thought holds that there is little information to be gleaned by studying unemployment, that the proper approach to understanding labor market fluctuations involves articulating theories of labor demand and supply that track observed movements in employment and wages. The question of what those who are not working are doing with their time is, in this view, a matter of subsidiary importance.

The relevance and importance of unemployment as an analytic concept is suggested by a simple comparison. The share of the American adult population that was employed was greater in 1982 when the economy suffered its worst postwar recession than it was in 1968 at the height of the Vietnam boom. Clearly there were greater labor market problems in 1968 than in 1982, problems that took the form of persons without jobs who wanted them—the problems manifested in an unemployment rate nearly three times as high in 1982 as in 1968. Variations in the taste for work are a problem that is analytically separable from the issue of whether markets function in such a way as to allow all those who want to work at going wages to do so. This is the primary issue involved in the study of unemployment.

Much ink has been spilled debating the meaning of the concept of involuntary unemployment. At some wage it is true that the unemployed could surely find employment, if only by selling apples on street corners. In modern economies where wages are set by employers, not employees, this bit of argument is of minimal relevance. As long as firms set the wages of workers, and as long as workers with characteristics similar to those who are looking for work are receiving a set wage, the concept of the "going wage" is perfectly explicit. And, as the Current Population Survey illustrates each month, the question of whether people are or are not searching for work is one they find meaningful. Of course, as several of the papers in this book make clear, there are ambiguities in defining unemployment. But this is not to say that economic analysis should step away from the problem of studying why the extent to which people who want jobs cannot get them differs so strongly from place to place.

The papers in this book seek to measure, describe, and explain unemployment. Their focus is heavily empirical. Before one can explain a phenomenon or solve a problem, one has to understand its scope and variations in its extent. It is no accident that the empirical work in the papers included here is not generally preceded by development of a full-blown optimizing model. I believe that at this stage in our understanding of unemployment (and most other phenomenon as well), our goals should be modest. The establishment of a reasonably robust collection of stylized facts is as much as empirical work can hope to accomplish.

Most of the papers collected in this book are coauthored. My coauthors deserve a disproportionate share of the credit for anything that is good in them. Reading them over, I am struck by how frequently the passages that I now regret were inserted at my insistence. My greatest intellectual debt is to Kim Clark with whom I coauthored five of the papers included in this volume. It was Kim who sparked my original interest in unemployment and contributed as much as anyone to my graduate education. I am also indebted to Olivier Blanchard, Gregory Mankiw, James Poterba, and Julio Rotemberg for contributing so much to my education as well as for permitting me to reprint our joint work.

I have been fortunate in having the opportunity to work in the uniquely stimulating Cambridge economics environment, initially as a graduate student at Harvard, then at MIT, and finally back at Harvard. Of special importance has been the privilege of maintaining a base of operations at the National Bureau of Economic Research for the last twelve years. Martin Feldstein's example and good advice have shaped my career as an economist. The wonderful environment he has created at the NBER has nourished it. I hope the many research assistants who worked (at all hours of the day and night) on the papers collected here got something out of the process. I owe them a great deal.

The first paper included here was published at about the time I first met my wife Vicki. She has made the intervening ten years very happy ones. And her gentle nagging helped bring this book to fruition.

The remainder of this preface briefly summarizes and reflects on the chapters that follow. The papers in the first section of this book address the issue of unemployment dynamics. Both the social consequences of unemployment and the types of policy that are potentially efficacious depend on whether unemployment is comprised largely of a small group of hard-core unemployed who are out of work much of the time or whether it largely reflects rapid turnover as workers move from job to job and new workers enter the labor force. At the time when the first two chapters were written, the latter view was becoming increasingly fashionable. In part, this reflected the increasingly conservative temper of the times. In part, it reflected the assimilation of new statistical research on unemployment durations.

With just what initial goal I cannot now recall, Kim Clark and I began working with the BLS gross flows data in 1978. After a while we became convinced that the turnover view of unemployment to which we had been exposed as graduate students greatly overstated the degree of turnover among the unemployed. The problem was not so much with the Current Population Surveys that underly our unemployment statistics; rather it was with the way in which these statistics were interpreted.

Chapter 1 highlights four main problems with the conventional view that since estimated mean durations of unemployment are short, most unemployment must be short term and relatively innocuous. First, there is the question of whether one wants to measure the duration of the average spell of unemployment or of the spell that contains the average week of unemployment. This distinction turns out to make a great deal of difference as the relatively few long spells of unemployment contain a large fraction of total weeks of unemployment. For example, in 1974, a year when the unemployment rate averaged 5.8%, the mean duration of completed spells of unemployment was one and a half months, but half of all unemployment was due to spells lasting three months or more.

Second, there is the issue of how unemployment spells end. In the surveys used to measure unemployment, 45% of all unemployment spells withdrawal from the labor force rather than job finding. Labor force withdrawal reflects discouragement and the abandonment of search in some cases. In other cases it reflects the inherent ambiguity associated with any definition of the labor force. As chapter 3 demonstrates, in other cases it reflects reporting errors. A proper measure of the duration of unemployment needs to take account of those spells that appear short only because they involve a brief period of labor force withdrawal between two intervals of job search.

Third, there is the reality that the same people tend to experience multiple spells of unemployment separated by only brief periods of employment. We estimate that in a typical year close to half of all unemployment is tracable to a small fraction of the workforce that is out of work for more than half the year. Looking over longer periods of up to four years, the phenomenon of concentration in unemployment is even more pronounced. Finally, there are difficulties associated with the standard classification of the unemployed by reason for unemployment. It turns out that much of the reentrant unemployment category is made up not of the long-term unemployed but of those completing relative brief spells without jobs.

These observations and other evidence developed in the paper call into question the relevance of search and temporary layoff models in thinking about unemployment. They suggest the appropriateness of models that instead focus on the question of why a small group of workers come to be unemployed a substantial fraction of the time. We highlight in the conclusions of our paper the observation that most of the unemployed profess to have reservation wages that are rather close to prevailing wages. This may have a great deal to with the question of why they remain unemployed for long stretches.

Chapter 2, coauthored with Kim Clark, applies the same type of analysis found in chapter 1 to the problem of youth unemployment. It is striking that half of the unemployed in the United States are under the age of 24. Again our analysis highlights the potential seriousness of the problem. While it is true that the vast majority of young people find jobs very easily, and move in and out of the labor force without great difficulty, this group does not account for a large fraction of observed unemployment in the

United States. Problem unemployment is confined to a relatively small group that is out of work a large fraction of the time.

Rereading the last half of chapter 2, I am struck by the strength of our emphasis on the importance of aggregate demand. We note that demand fluctuations across both time and space seem to have a very large impact on the level of unemployment, particularly for disadvantaged workers. And we emphasize evidence suggesting the presence of rationing in youth job markets. At the time the paper was written, I interpreted evidence of rationing as suggesting that policies that operated on the supply side without affecting labor demand would have little effect on employment. Today I am much less confident. Supply side policies may affect the level of wages even in models where wages are set in such a way that jobs are rationed. The efficiency wage models in Shapiro and Stiglitz (1984) and Bulow and Summers (1986) provide one example of a setting where supply side policies that affect the cost of becoming unemployed can affect the wage rate at which jobs are rationed.

In working with longitudinal data on unemployment, it became clear to Clark and me that the raw data greatly overestimated the amount of labor market mobility because of reporting errors. Errors in reporting labor market status cancel out in measuring the unemployment rate at a point in time, but they do not cancel out in measuring mobility. Chapter 3 reprints a study coauthored with James Poterba that seeks to correct these errors and generate more realistic estimates of transition rates between labor force states. Our approach is to use data generated by the CPS Reinterview Survey to gauge the extent of reporting error and then to estimate corrected transition matrices based on this information.

The results are quite striking. Particularly in the case of transitions in and out of the labor force, it appears that the raw data greatly overstate by as much as 80%. As a consequence the length of spell durations is greatly underestimated. Our estimates suggest that taking account of reporting errors raises estimated unemployment durations by more than 50% for some population subgroups. Because our corrections are much more important for adult population groups than for teenagers, they serve to accentuate the differences between population groups found in standard data.

At the time that the essays in the first section of this book were written, I had given little thought to the problem of unemployment outside the United States. In graduate school I had absorbed the belief that it was unfortunate that the United States did not have the desirable labor market institutions that permitted Europe to have such a low natural unemployment rate! Even after our efforts to correct standard figures and high-light the concentration of unemployment in the United States, the extent of concentration in the United States has been small compared to that in Europe. To cite just one example, Olivier Blanchard and I estimate in chapter 8 that whereas those out of work for two or more years accounted for 8% of American unemployment in 1984, they accounted for 65% of British unemployment in the same year. The message that theories of unemployment need to account for its concentration is valid all over the world.

The papers in the second section address the issue of cyclical unemploy-ment. Chapter 4, coauthored with Kim Clark, highlights an important and underemphasized stylized fact about cyclical variations in unemployment —the fact that most variations occur among "secondary workers." We estimated that only 23% of the cyclical variations in American employment occurred among men aged 26 to 64 years. Given the increase in women's labor force participation, I suspect the share would be even smaller today. This finding reflects the fact that the employment of secondary workers is extremely sensitive to cyclical conditions. For example, the estimates in chapter 4 suggest that a cyclical strengthening sufficient to increase employment of prime age males by 1% increases the employment of black teenagers by 6%.

The finding that secondary workers' employment is so sensitive to economic conditions is a consequence of our focus on changes in labor force participation as well as unemployment. The observation that the unemployment rates of some population subgroups remain high even when the unemployment rate of mature men is driven to very low levels does not imply that aggregate demand cannot have an effect on the employment of high unemployment groups. Instead, it reflects important discouraged worker effects; labor force participation, particularly of young women, surges at cyclical peaks.

Chapters 5 and 6 assess in very different ways the intertemporal sub-stitution theory that has been invoked by Robert Lucas and other new classical macroeconomic theorists in an attempt to account for fluctuations in the level of employment without resorting to notions of involuntary unemployment. Chapter 5, coauthored with Kim Clark, contrasts the evi-dence suggesting the importance of "timing effects" on labor supply, which are emphasized by believers in intertemporal substitution, with evidence on the importance of "persistence" or "habit formation" effects. The data strongly suggest the presence of important persistence effects in labor supply but reveal little evidence of timing effects.

The evidence comes from several sources. Perhaps most striking is an examination of the effect of World War II on the labor force participation of women. As has often been emphasized, the increase in employment opportunities for women during the war led to a great increase in their labor force participation. We emphasize the aftermath of this episode as a testing ground for theories of labor supply. If the scheduling effects emphasized by proponents of the intertemporal substitution hypothesis predominate, participation after the war should have been lower than it would have been had the war not taken place. On the other hand, if habit formation effects were dominant, one would expect at least a semipermanent change in labor supply as a consequence of the war experience. The latter view is supported empirically. Further evidence of the importance of persistence effects comes from U.S. time series data and from a cross-sectional analysis of the relationship between state unemployment and labor force participation.

Although the paper was written without reference to the European unemployment problem, it references Phelps (1972) and refers to the possibility of downturns having hysteresis effects on subsequent output and employment. The idea that not working can be "addictive" plays an important role in some views of the current European unemployment problem. It is difficult to extrapolate from the findings a judgment about just how large are persistence effects in labor supply, but the findings certainly suggest that they are a more important than the timing effects emphasized by modern theorists.

Chapter 6, coauthored with Gregory Mankiw and Julio Rotemberg, is written in a much more modern, and in my view, less satisfactory idiom. It seeks to take seriously and rigorously test the intertemporal substitution hypothesis by estimating the Euler equations that characterize the behavior of the American economy's representative consumer. The fact that the tests decisively reject the theory comes as little surprise. I never assigned a very high probability to the possibility that failure to allow for nonseparabilities with leisure accounted for rejections in tests of consumption Euler equations. The observation that consumption is procyclical while leisure is countercyclicial, coupled with the observation that the real wage is not strongly procyclical, is sufficient to raise serious questions about the intertemporal substitution theory's explanation of cyclical employment fluctuations.

The third part of the book takes up a number of aspects of structural unemployment. Chapter 7, coauthored with Kim Clark, examines the relationship between unemployment insurance and unemployment. I think we were entirely correct in highlighting the difficulties with partial equilibrium approaches to this problem that focused only on unemployment insurance and a single labor market transition, usually the transition out of unemployment. Our research strategy of examining the effect of unemployment insurance benefits or potential unemployment insurance benefits on each of the possible labor market transitions still seems a more satisfactory approach. Unfortunately, as the paper makes clear, we had great difficulty in obtaining sensible-looking results for some of the transitions. This may be the result of the pervasiveness of erroneous transitions.

The results do, however, suggest that in addition to its behavioral effect, unemployment insurance probably also has an important reporting effect on measured unemployment. Increases in unemployment insurance raise the size of the labor force by inducing people to enter, causing persons who would otherwise withdraw to remain in the labor force in order to collect benefits. The results also demonstrate that unemployment insurance has potentially large effects on transitions out of employment; even apart from temporary layoffs, it appears to encourage job separations into unemployment.

Chapter 8, coauthored with Olivier Blanchard, argues that theories of hysteresis are necessary to account for European unemployment during the 1980s. The basic argument is that the experience of the 1980s suggests that the equilibrium-restoring tendencies of labor markets that have been shocked hard are extremely weak. It is impossible to account for the dramatic increase in the apparent natural rate of unemployment in most of Europe by pointing to supply factors that changed during the 1980s. Unemployment has been too high for too long, with too little impact on inflation for it to be attributable to a cyclical downturn. We argue that the sharp disinflation of the early 1980s raised unemployment and that hysteresis mechanisms caused this shock to have long-lasting effects.

The paper focuses most directly on the possibility of hysteresis arising in settings where insiders have considerable power in settting wages. Shocks that raise unemployment may, by causing layoffs, disenfranchise some workers, whose interests cease being considered in the wage-bargaining process when they become unemployed. With fewer members, unions bargain more aggressively, keeping unemployment high even after the initial demand shock has subsided. We suggest that this mechanism may complement other mechanisms that rely on the loss of human or physical capital.

The central policy question involves the reversibility of the process. Could a series of favorable shocks sharply reduce the apparent natural unemployment rate just as the series of unfavorable shocks in the late 1970s and early 1980s raised it? The answer to this question depends greatly on what theory of hysteresis one adopts. Stocks of physical and human capital cannot be replenished nearly as easily as workers can be reenfranchised. Our reading of the evidence from the U.S. recovery from the Depression is optimistic. It suggests that normal or natural rates of unemployment can track actual rates of unemployment in the downward as well as the upward direction.

Chapter 9 is concerned with American structural unemployment. It was written at a time when unemployment rates in the 5% range seemed unattainable. The first part of the papers demonstrates that in almost every meaningful sense, there was more problem unemployment in the mid-1980s than at cyclically normal time periods in the 1960s or 1970s. Although it was not apparent to me at the time, with hindsight it is clear that this reflects the fact that the recovery still had a long way to go in 1985.

The latter part of the paper is more successful. It argues empirically for the importance of transitional unemployment. By transitional unemployment, I refer to unemployment incurred by persons moving between high and low wage jobs. the argument is that any meaningful theory of unemployment must be premised on some notion of labor market segmentation, since some jobs are always available to the unemployed while others that employ workers with the same characteristics are not. When the high wage sector contracts, unemployment increases.

Several types of empirical evidence suggest a link between labor market segmentation and unemployment. First, states where high wage jobs are lost seem to have much more dramatic increases in unemployment than states where low wage jobs are lost. Second, states that are heavily unionized have higher unemployment rates and lower employment—population ratios than states where unions are weak. This conclusion continues to hold even if the composition of employment is controlled for. Third, during the 1970s when the natural rate of unemployment increased sharply, union wage effects rose, as did industry wage dispersion. Significantly, there was a negative correlation between industry wage and employment changes.

I suspect that some of the reduction in the apparent natural rate of unemployment in recent years has to do with reduced transitional unemployment. A sharply falling dollar has led to a manufacturing turnaround. Union power has been eroded by domestic regulatory action and inaction as well as by international competition. More generally, international competition has restrained wage increases in high wage industries. All these factors, as well as a continuing decline in the share of the unemployed who are supported by unemployment insurance, have probably increased the degree of wage pressure at any given level of unemployment from what it was several years ago.

Chapter 10 contains the volume's only theoretical paper, a short comment coauthored with Olivier Blanchard that seeks to expand on the ideas of hysteresis and multiple equilibria put forth in our earlier paper. We suggest the need for theories of "fragile" equilibria that can explain why small changes in conditions can sometimes lead to large changes in economic outcomes. Some mechanisms that can generate fragile unemployment equilibria are suggested.

I

Describing and Measuring Unemployment

1

Labor Market Dynamics and Unemployment: A Reconsideration

with Kim B. Clark

Economists in recent years have come to view unemployment as a dynamic phenomenon. Both theoretical and empirical research have emphasized the role of turnover in understanding unemployment. The instability of employment, the brevity of unemployment spells, and the large flows into and out of unemployment have been central themes of this work.[1] Where the unemployed were once viewed as a stagnant pool of job seekers awaiting a business upturn, today economists describe unemployment in quite different terms. A leading contemporary macroeconomics textbook, after reviewing published evidence on unemployment dynamics, found that "the important conclusion [is] that average unemployment is not the result of a few people being unemployed for a long period of time. Rather unemployment is the result of people entering and leaving the pool of unemployment fairly often"[2] Proponents of the dynamic view interpret a large part of observed unemployment as an indication of "normal turnover" as people search for new jobs. "Problem" unemployment, according to this view, is largely confined to a few demographic groups that display pathological employment instability and leave jobs at a high rate.

The central thesis of this paper is that most unemployment, even in tight labor markets, is characterized by relatively few persons who are out of work a large part of the time. We find that "normal turnover," broadly defined, can account for only a small part of measured unemployment. Much of observed joblessness is due to prolonged periods of inability or unwillingness to locate employment. These conclusions appear to hold at all points in the business cycle for almost all demographic groups. They suggest the need for a reexamination of theoretical models and policy recommendations that feature a dynamic portrayal of unemployment.

Reprinted by permission, with revisions, from *Brookings Papers on Economic Activity* 1: 13–60, 1979. Copyright © 1979 by the Brookings Institution.

During the last decade a major effort has been made to place the theory of unemployment on sound microeconomic foundations.[3] Theoretical research has focused on providing explanations of unemployment that are based on individual maximization. Two primary theoretical paradigms— search theory and the theory of contracts—have evolved as explanations of why persons rationally choose to be unemployed some of the time. Both are, in an important sense, theories of voluntary unemployment. In search models, persons choose to be unemployed in order to engage in productive search. Contract theories explain why workers might choose to sign contracts that insure fixed wages but allow for uncertain employment. The search and contract paradigms provide a coherent account of large flows into and out of unemployment, but they are inconsistent with repeated long spells of joblessness. The plausibility of these theories thus depends on which characterization of unemployment is correct.

The study of unemployment dynamics also has important policy implications. Emphasis on dynamics tends to reduce the welfare significance of unemployment. The implication is that the burden is widely shared and that few individuals suffer greatly. Furthermore, turnover is sometimes seen as socially productive in facilitating an efficient matching of persons to jobs. On this basis it has frequently been argued that reducing unemployment below some "natural" rate would be a step away from economic efficiency.[4] Observed high turnover rates and brief unemployment durations have led many analysts to suggest that appropriate measures to remedy unemployment should be focused on facilitating rapid job search and increased job holding, rather than on increasing the number of available jobs. Even the case for public employment programs is frequently expressed in terms of the problems of high turnover groups.[5] Perhaps most important is the fact that the turnover view has been used to discredit earlier notions of "hard-core" unemployment. The emphasis in employment and training policy has shifted toward improvements in the operation of labor markets rather than the employment prospects of specific individuals.

The first part of the paper examines the distribution of completed spells of unemployment. The apparent brevity of spells has played a key role in supporting the dynamic view of unemployment; it has been used to suggest that, except in weak labor markets, jobs are readily available to most of the unemployed. We challenge this view by demonstrating that only a small part of unemployment is experienced by persons who find a job after a brief spell. In 1974, for example, when the unemployment rate was relatively low, only 36% of unemployment was attributable to persons finding a job within three months.

Almost half of all unemployment spells end by persons leaving the labor force. In the official statistics, movements between unemployment and employment are dwarfed by transitions into and out of the labor force. The second part of the paper examines these transitions in the labor force. We find that the distinction is weak between the categories of "unemployment" and "not in the labor force." Many observed transitions appear to arise from inconsistent reporting of quite consistent behavior. Repeated spells of unemployment separated only by brief periods outside the labor force appear to be common. This strongly suggests that the mean length of individual unemployment spells greatly underestimates the length of time it takes workers to move between jobs. Indeed, we conclude that the average person unemployed at a point in time will experience almost six months of unemployment during a year. The analysis also suggests that the "reentrant" unemployment category is quite misleading. We show that a large fraction of this group is comprised of persons who have recently lost or left jobs.

The interpretation of the frequency of unemployment spells depends on whether they are widely dispersed among the population. This issue is examined in the third part of the paper, which presents evidence on the concentration of unemployment over one- and four-year horizons. Because of the pervasiveness of multiple spells, a large fraction of all unemployment is attributable to persons out of work a large part of the time. Over half of joblessness is traceable to persons out of work for more than six months in a year. The concentration of joblessness is far greater than we would expect from normal turnover. We conclude that normal turnover accounts for at most 1.5 points, or about 25% of unemployment at high employment levels.

The limited importance of short spells in explaining total unemployment has important implications for current theoretical paradigms, which are explored in the fourth section. In light of the finding that most unemployment is attributable to persons with long periods of joblessness, we reevaluate the significance of theories of search and temporary layoffs. Neither appears able to explain a large part of measured unemployment. Survey data suggest that relatively few of the unemployed search in ways that would be more difficult if they were employed. Moreover, most jobs are found by persons who move directly from another job or from outside the labor force. Temporary layoffs do not appear to be of great significance. Using newly available matched tapes from the Current Population Survey

(CPS), we find that only about half of those reporting layoff unemployment return to jobs in the same occupation and industry. Our calculations suggest that at a maximum only about 7% of all unemployment and 14% of unemployment among men aged 25 to 59 can be explained by temporary layoffs. The paper concludes by advancing some suggestions on sources of extensive unemployment.

1.1 The Distribution of Completed Spells of Unemployment

Recent research on unemployment has emphasized the distinction between the frequency and the duration of spells of unemployment.[6] We begin our reexamination of unemployment dynamics by analyzing the distribution function of the duration of completed unemployment spells. The estimated spell distributions provide the basis for estimating characteristics such as the mean duration of a completed spell, which have been the focus of earlier work. The distributions can also be used to calculate a different concept, the fraction of total unemployment attributable to spells of different durations. To see the importance of the difference between these measures, consider the following example. Suppose that, each week, twenty spells of unemployment began lasting one week, and one spell began lasting twenty weeks. The mean duration of a completed spell of unemployment would be 1.9 weeks; but half of all unemployment would be accounted for by spells lasting twenty weeks. In a steady state, the expected length of time until a job was found, among all those unemployed at any instant, would be 9.5 weeks. Focusing on the mean duration of a completed spell would not convey this picture of the underlying unemployment experience.[7]

We calculate the distribution of completed spells using the gross-flow data of the U.S. Bureau of Labor Statistics, which is derived from monthly CPS data. Individuals are included in the CPS sample for four months, then are dropped for eight months, and return for four additional months. By matching individual survey responses in successive months, flows between labor force states can be estimated. These data underlie much of the empirical work in this paper.[8]

The procedure used to calculate the distribution of unemployment spells is briefly described here and detailed in an appendix.[9] Probabilities of withdrawal from the labor force or of job entrance—exit probabilities—within the subsequent month can be computed for persons who have been unemployed for different lengths of time. After fitting a smooth curve relating duration and exit probability, the distribution of completed spells can be derived. Given the spell distribution, the proportion of unemployment due to spells of any arbitrary duration can be evaluated. Because we work directly with the hazard function that relates exit probabilities and duration, our calculation of the completed spell distribution does not depend on the assumption of a steady state. Various features of the completed spell distribution are indicated in table 1.1. The data are presented for male and female teenagers and adults and are based on average transition probabilities in 1974. We chose 1974 because it represents the most recent year for which data are available when the economy operated at high employment levels. The distribution of spells for the total population in 1969 and 1975 are also shown.[10]

The first two rows of figures confirm the traditional conclusion that the typical spell of unemployment is quite short. Sixty percent of all spells in 1974 were completed within a month, and the mean duration of a completed spell was slightly less than two months. In 1975, when the unemployment rate rose precipitously, the mean duration of a spell increased by about a week. The response to cyclical movements appears to be quite asymmetric. Almost 80% of all unemployment spells lasted less than one month in 1969 when the unemployment rate was 3.5%. The finding in previous work that young people have shorter mean durations of unemployment than older persons is also confirmed.

Short spells of unemployment can be the result of either easy entrance into new jobs or high rates of withdrawal from the labor force.[11] These two causes obviously have different implications. The relative importance of spells of unemployment that end in exit from the labor force is examined in the third and fourth rows of table 1.1. In the aggregate, 45% of spells ended in withdrawal in 1974. This proportion varies substantially across demographic groups, from 26% for men over twenty years of age to almost 60% for young women. The high rates of exit from the labor force indicate the inadequacy of the duration of completed spells as an indicator of the ease or difficulty of finding work. The point is well illustrated by comparing young and older men. Adult men have unemployment spells that are about 50% longer than those of teenagers. This differential is largely attributable to the much higher withdrawal rate of teenagers. The fourth row of the table attempts to provide a more meaningful indicator of the ease of finding a job by calculating average durations for hypothetical "indomitable" job seekers. These durations are calculated by finding the average duration of a completed spell, excluding the effect of withdrawal. To do this, we define the probability of exit from unemployment as

Table 1.1
Characteristics of completed spells of unemployment, by demographic group, 1974, and for all groups, 1969 and 1975

	1974					1969	1975
	Males		Females				
Characteristic	16–19	20 and over	16–19	20 and over	All groups	All groups	All groups
Completed spells of unemployment							
Proportion of spells ending within one month	0.71	0.47	0.70	0.60	0.60	0.79	0.55
Mean duration of a completed spell (months)	1.57	2.42	1.57	1.91	1.94	1.42	2.22
Proportion of spells ending in withdrawal from the labor force	0.46	0.26	0.58	0.55	0.45	0.44	0.46
Mean duration for "indomitable" job seeker (months)[a]	2.58	3.45	3.19	4.02	3.37	2.03	4.22
Proportion of unemployment[b]							
By length of spell (months)							
2 or more	0.55	0.80	0.55	0.69	0.69	0.49	0.75
3 or more	0.34	0.63	0.33	0.48	0.49	0.24	0.58
4 or more	0.23	0.48	0.21	0.34	0.36	0.12	0.45
5 or more	0.15	0.37	0.14	0.25	0.26	0.06	0.35
6 or more	0.11	0.28	0.09	0.18	0.19	0.03	0.27
Spells ending in withdrawal	0.47	0.26	0.59	0.58	0.47	0.46	0.48
Spells ending in employment, by length of spell (months)							
2 or less	0.36	0.29	0.28	0.24	0.28	0.42	0.23
3 or less	0.42	0.39	0.33	0.30	0.36	0.49	0.30

Source: Derived from authors' calculations of the distribution of unemployment spells, using gross-flow data from the Current Population Survey of the U.S. Bureau of Labor Statistics. Th‿ ‿e procedure ‿ ‿n is detailed in an appendix available from the authors upon request.
a. Calculated by finding the average duration of a comple‿ ‿red spell, excluding the effect of withdrawal from the labor force.
b. Expressed as a fraction of the total weeks of unemployment w‿ ‿ith in the specific age-sex category.

$$P^*_{ue} = \frac{P_{ue}}{P_{ue} + P_{uu}},$$

which is the probability of finding a job, conditional on not dropping out of the labor force.[12]

A comparison of the durations for indomitable job seekers with the conventional calculations underscores the importance of withdrawal in reducing the length of unemployment spells. When the option of withdrawal from the labor force is removed, the average duration of a completed spell in 1974 rises from 1.94 to 3.37 months. Focusing only on finding a job alters the demographic duration pattern. While the mean duration of a completed spell for female teenagers, for example, is less than that for the total population, the "indomitable durations" for these two groups are very close together. Adult women have spells of average length as conventionally measured, but the calculation for the indomitable job seeker illustrates that this is *only* due to their high rates of withdrawal from the labor force.

The indomitable calculation is merely illustrative; it is not calculated from the actual experience of all persons who never leave unemployment until they obtain a job. It assumes that those who end unemployment spells by leaving the labor force would have the same probability of finding a job if they stayed in as those who actually did stay in. To the extent that more determined persons have higher than average probabilities of finding jobs, it may thus overstate the length of time individuals take to acquire employment.

The fact that most spells are short does not imply that most unemployment is due to short spells or that most unemployed persons at any point in time will leave unemployment soon. If, for example, all the unemployed had a probability of one-half of escaping unemployment in a given month, the mean duration of completed spells would be two months, but three-quarters of unemployment would be due to spells lasting more than two months. Of those unemployed at a point in time, ultimately half would have experienced more than three months of unemployment. If the probability of escape from unemployment declines with duration, the concentration of unemployment in the longer spells would be even more pronounced.

The lower half of table 1.1 weights spells by their length to portray the distribution of months of unemployment. The results present a different picture of unemployment from that suggested by the spell distribution. While 60% of spells in 1974 ended within a month, almost half of all unemployment was attributable to spells lasting at least three months—that is, of all those unemployed at any moment in 1974, half experienced three months of unemployment or more before terminating their spell.[13] The concentration of unemployment in long spells is even more pronounced, among adult men, almost 50% of whose unemployment is contained in spells lasting four or more months. The 1969 and 1975 figures reveal sharp cyclical changes in the concentration of unemployment. While only 3% of total weeks of unemployment in 1969 was found among those who experienced long-term unemployment—spells lasting six months or longer—the share of long-term unemployment rose to 27% in 1975.[14]

The concentration of unemployment in longer spells results from two factors. First, there is a natural tendency for most of the weight in any probability distribution to be found in its tail. Even if all unemployed persons at all points in their spells had the same probability of exiting from unemployment, a disproportionate share or unemployment would be endured by the "unlucky" group who suffered long spells. Second, the tendency toward concentration in longer spells will be exacerbated if the probability of exit from unemployment declines with duration. This occurs because the longer a spell lasts, the longer is its time until completion. Declining exit probability can occur because of either duration dependence or sorting. Duration dependence means that, because workers are unemployed longer periods, their exit rate falls. Sorting refers to the fact that even if individuals have exit probabilities that are constant, the longer term unemployed will be disproportionately comprised of those with a low probability of exit.

Declining exit probabilities appear to be characteristic of almost all demographic groups. In a typical month in 1974, for example, 34% of those unemployed between one and four weeks found jobs, while only 16% of those out of work more than six months did so. In figure 1.1 we indicate the importance of declining exit probabilities for adult women. In the upper panel we contrast the pattern of actual probabilities of exit from unemployment with the constant exit probability implied by a simple Markov model. In the lower panel we compare the distribution of months actually observed with that implied by the Markov model. The Markov model implies that 9% of the unemployment is found in the spells lasting six months or more. In fact, 18% is found in these spells. Thus both the normal tendency toward concentration and declining exit probabilities imply that the focus on the average or median spell is misleading because much of unemployment is contained in the relatively few long spells.

The proportion of unemployment attributable to spells ending in with-

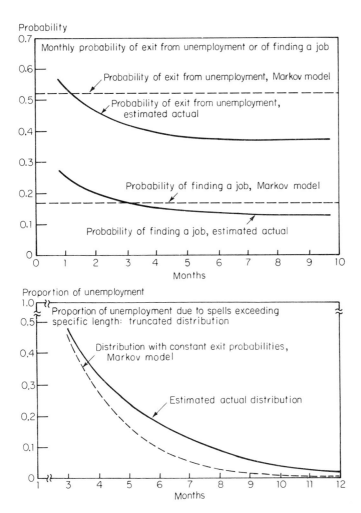

Figure 1.1
Exit probabilities and unemployment distributions, females aged 20 and over, 1974.
Source: Same as table 1.1. The distribution of months of unemployment in the Markov model is based on our constant probabilities of exit from unemployment and of finding a job.

drawal from the labor force is shown in the third row of table 1.1. It is marginally greater than the proportion of spells that end in employment because withdrawal spells last slightly longer than those terminating with a job.

The final rows of the table demonstrate the unrealistic features of the view of unemployment that stresses relatively easy access to jobs after a brief spell of unemployment. For the entire population, only about one-third of unemployment is due to spells ending in a job within three months. The view that most of the unemployed are in the midst of short transitions between jobs is simply wrong. *Even during the strong 1969 peak, less than half of the unemployed found jobs within three months.*

1.2 Patterns of Transition in the Labor Force

Movements into and out of the labor force dominate all other labor market flows, at least as they are measured in the official statistics. According to the gross-flow data from the Bureau of Labor Statistics, almost 70% of persons who enter employment in a given month were outside the labor force in the preceding month.[15] An equally large fraction of persons leaving employment withdraw from the labor force without ever being measured as unemployed. Most movements into and out of employment thus do not involve any measured unemployment. This surprising fact underscores the importance of understanding withdrawal from and reentry into the labor force. Moreover, the sheer size of the flows into and out of the labor force raises serious questions about the distinction between unemployed persons and those not in the labor force. In an average month between 1968 and 1976, the gross-flow data indicate 3.8 million people leaving the labor force and 4.0 million people entering. If each individual had no more than one transition annually, the monthly size of the flows would imply that each year 45 to 50 million people, or half the labor force, enter and another 45 to 50 million leave. The extent of multiple changes in classification by individuals implies that many transitions do not reflect significant changes in behavior.

Various aspects of withdrawal from the labor force are examined in table 1.2. In the first and second rows we contrast the monthly probability of withdrawal from employment and unemployment. The rate of withdrawal from employment might be thought to represent the "normal" rate of withdrawal due to reasons of illness or home responsibilities.[16] This rate is dwarfed by the rate of flow out of unemployment. In total, while only 3.3% of those employed withdraw, over 20% of the unemployed exit from the

Table 1.2
Characteristics of labor force withdrawal and reentry and selected groups outside the labor force, by demographic group, various years, 1974−77

Characteristic	Males		Females		All groups
	16−19	20 and over	16−19	20 and over	
Withdrawal from the labor force					
Monthly probability (1974) of withdrawal					
From employment	0.102	0.013	0.133	0.045	0.033
From unemployment	0.286	0.119	0.318	0.230	0.208
Classification (1977) of those who withdrew from unemployment (proportion of withdrawals)[a]					
Persons wanting a regular job now	0.443		0.469		0.460
Discouraged workers	0.161		0.142		0.150
Selected groups (1974) outside the labor force (ratio to unemployed)[a]					
Persons wanting a regular job now	0.492	0.712	1.044	1.372	0.877
Discouraged workers	0.076	0.089	0.100	0.225	0.135
Persons outside labor force for economic reasons[b]	0.411	0.182	0.435	0.169	0.384
Proportion of withdrawals (1976) who reenter the labor force[a]					
Within 1 month	0.644	0.244	0.407	0.291	0.341
Within 2 months	0.804	0.442	0.526	0.349	0.443
Within 12 months	0.810	0.766	0.813	0.760	0.779

Sources: Data on the probability of withdrawal are annual averages for 1974 based on unpublished tabulations, adjusted by The Urban Institute as described in Jean E. Vanski, "Recession and the Employment of Demographic Groups: Adjustments to Gross Change Data," in Charles C. Holt and others, *Labor Markets, Inflation, and Manpower Policies*, final report to the U.S. Manpower Administration (Urban Institute, 1975), pp. C-1 to C-14. The remaining data on withdrawal from the labor force are annual averages for 1977 and are unpublished tabulations from matched files of the fourth and eighth (departing) groups in the Current Population Survey. The data for categories of persons not in the labor force are annual averages for 1974 and are from *Employment and Earnings*, vol. 21 (January 1975), pp. 159−160, *Employment and Training Report of the President, 1978*, p. 201, and unpublished tabulations. One- and two-month rates of reentry were calculated using the matched file of the CPS for May through August 1976. The twelve-month rate is defined as one minus the ratio of the number of persons outside the labor force who had work experience in the last year to the sum of monthly flows out of the labor force. The data are from the gross-flow data of the CPS or from unpublished tabulations. All unpublished tabulations were provided by the Bureau of Labor Statistics.
a. Expressed as a fraction of the number of withdrawals, or the number of unemployed, for the specific age-sex category.
b. Persons with work experience in the last year.

labor force, suggesting that only a small part of withdrawal from unemployment occurs for reasons independent of being unemployed.

The third row shows that, when asked the reasons for labor force withdrawal, nearly half of those who withdrew from unemployment in 1977 continued to profess to "want a regular job now."[17] The fourth row shows that about one-third of this group gave inability to find a job as the sole reason for not seeking work and were thus classified as discouraged workers. It is likely that many of the remaining two-thirds gave inability to find work as a reason for not searching, but they are not counted as discouraged workers under current definitions. The National Commission on Employment and Unemployment Statistics observes, "The CPS attachment tests are both arbitrary and subjective; they assume that certain reasons for not searching...indicate unavailability for work even if the respondent also cites reasons of discouragement. These reasons for not *looking* for work cannot necessarily be equated with not being available for work if a job were available."[18]

The data suggest that some, but not all, movements from being unemployed to being outside the labor force reflect an inability to find desirable work. While discouragement may account for up to half of the outflow from unemployment, the behavior of the remaining persons who exit requires further explanation. Existing discussions of unemployment have not focused attention on why an individual would actively search for several months, and then neither search nor respond affirmatively to the question, "Do you want a regular job now?" One explanation that has been advanced is that persons remain in the labor force for many months in order to collect unemployment insurance benefits—presumably leaving when benefits are exhausted. While unemployment compensation (and other forms of social insurance) may well have an important effect on the probability of withdrawal for those receiving benefits, it is unlikely to be a dominant explanation of the high overall rate of exit from the labor force. Less than half of the unemployed receive insurance benefits, and a large part of withdrawal occurs among young people and women who frequently are ineligible for unemployment insurance. Most important, the 1975 extension of the benefit period from twenty-six to sixty-five weeks had only a small effect on the overall rate of withdrawal.[19]

It seems likely, however, that some observed exit and entry flows arise from inconsistent reporting of consistent behavior.[20] Careful examination of the way in which the data are generated confirms the ambiguity and arbitrariness of the distinction between unemployment and not being in the labor force. Minor variations in circumstance or the exact construction of the

CPS have a great influence on the classification of persons according to this distinction. For example, being exposed to the survey appears to affect responses. In 1977 the recorded rate of unemployment was 11% higher among those in the first rotation group than it was in the third rotation group.[21] The rate of participation in the labor force was correspondingly lower, while the rate of employment was slightly different. This pattern, referred to as "rotation group bias," is common to all demographic groups in all years.

The ambiguous nature of the concepts used to define unemployment is further illustrated by differences in the reporting of rotation groups that emerged after a slight change in the questionnaire was introduced in 1970. In response to the Gordon Committee report, a variety of questions about the work experience, current activity, and job-seeking intentions of persons outside the labor force was added to the monthly survey in 1967. Originally only persons in the first and fifth rotation groups were asked these questions. In 1970, the procedure was changed so that only persons in the fourth and eighth groups were asked. Following the introduction of the new procedure, the pattern of reported unemployment by rotation group changed precipitously. Unemployment in the fourth and eighth (departing) rotation groups rose 7 to 9%, while unemployment in the first and fifth groups fell by an equal amount.

Differential reporting across rotation groups suggests that "looking for work" is an ambiguous concept. This implies that the distinction between being unemployed and out of the labor force may be arbitrary for a significant number of persons. The clearest evidence of arbitrariness comes from the CPS reinterview program.[22] As part of its validation of the survey, a supervisor from the U.S. Bureau of the Census reinterviews some of those included in the sample. The reinterviews usually take place one week after the initial survey and use the regular questionnaire, modified to refer to the survey week. The responses to the interview and reinterview are then reconciled. Published results of the reinterview program suggest a substantial amount of spurious volatility. Of those measured as unemployed in the original survey, 11% are deemed to be employed or out of the labor force after reconciliation with the reinterview. About 13% of persons who are measured as unemployed in the reinterview survey are recorded as outside the labor force by the initial survey. Another 4% are recorded as employed. Thus the total number of misclassifications is about one-fourth the number of unemployed persons. This figure does not include persons who consistently misclassify themselves and thus do not show up as errors in the reinterview survey.

The likelihood of classification error and the extent of discouragement imply that many of those not in the labor force are in situations effectively equivalent to the unemployed. It should be clear that the majority of those outside the labor force are neither classified incorrectly nor discouraged. However, even a small proportion of those outside the labor force is large relative to the number of unemployed. Some notion of the potential amount of hidden unemployment can be gleaned from the fifth through seventh rows of table 1.2, which indicate the size of selected groups not in the labor force as a fraction of the number unemployed.[23] The fifth row indicates that almost as many people are out of the labor force and want a job as are listed as unemployed. More women are out of the labor force and want to obtain a job than are unemployed. Additional evidence of the functional equivalence of many persons in and out of the labor force comes from the reasons persons out of the labor force give for leaving their last job. A group equal to 38% of the unemployed list economic reasons, such as job loss or slack work, as their reason for withdrawal. This suggests strongly that their withdrawal reflects the available employment opportunities.

These facts, taken together, indicate that a large number of persons out of the labor force are sensitive to job opportunities, and would likely choose to work if a job were available. This implication is confirmed by the strongly procyclical movement of the labor force participation rate. It is also supported by geographic evidence suggesting a large response of participation to economic opportunities.[24]

The last three rows of the table provide more direct evidence on the subsequent behavior of those who withdraw from the labor force. If observed withdrawals do not reflect a change in willingness to accept employment, then the time spent outside the labor force should be relatively brief. Rates of reentry within one, two, and twelve months of withdrawal are presented for each demographic group. The rates for one and two months are based on newly available longitudinal data taken from the CPS in May, June, July, and August 1976. We calculated the percentage of those persons unemployed in May 1976 and outside the labor force in June, who were back in the labor force in July (one-month reentry rate) and in August (two-month reentry rate). These calculations underscore the brevity of withdrawal from the labor force for a substantial fraction of those who exit from the labor force. For the unemployed population as a whole, we find that 34% of those who withdrew in June 1976 reappeared in the labor force in July. By August, over 44% were back in the labor force.[25]

The finding that withdrawal from the labor force is followed by reentry within a short period reinforces the conclusion that many of those classified as not in the labor force are functionally indistinguishable from the unemployed. It is implausible that those seeking work in May and also July or August experienced a substantive change in job-seeking intentions in June.[26] Some of the instances of withdrawal reflect persons who become discouraged and cease searching. Many more reflect the ambiguity and arbitrariness inherent in any definition of labor force activity. We have emphasized the problems with the category of not in the labor force, but those difficulties are mirrored in the unemployed group. Although many persons counted as unemployed are eager for work and sensitive to job opportunities, a significant fraction of the unemployed exhibit only marginal search behavior and do not appear to be committed to finding work.

There can be little doubt that current definitions offer a misleading portrayal of the dynamics of the labor market. It appears that many of those who withdraw experience a brief spell outside the labor force and a further period of "reentrant" unemployment. The official statistics capture two relatively brief spells of unemployment, yet the evidence presented here suggests that the experience might be more appropriately characterized as a single lengthy spell of unemployment.

1.2.1 Reentrant Unemployment

One implication of the view of labor force transitions developed here is that the category of reentrant unemployment may be quite misleading. The welfare significance of such unemployment is frequently downgraded. However, it appears that many reentrants have experienced only quite brief spells outside the labor force. It may be more appropriate to view this group as representing long-term unemployment rather than as turnover in the labor force or transition after a long absence.

In May 1976, a special survey on the job-search behavior of the unemployed was conducted as a supplement to the CPS. This survey provides considerable information about work intentions and work experience, and for reentrants permits a rough calculation of the time spent outside the labor force before reentry. Table 1.3 presents data on the characteristics of reentrants. In the first row we examine the importance of reentrant unemployment for different demographic groups. The data indicate that those groups most likely to end a spell of unemployment by withdrawing from the labor force—teenagers and adult women—are important sources of reentrant unemployment.

Table 1.3
Characteristics of reentrants into the labor force, by demographic group, May 1976

Characteristic[a]	Males				Females				All groups
	16–19	20–24	25–59	60 and over	16–19	20–24	25–59	60 and over	
Reentry unemployment (percent of unemployment)	28.5	24.1	13.1	28.0	25.2	39.1	31.7	33.1	25.1
Time outside the labor force for unemployed reentrants, cumulative distribution (percent of unemployed reentrants)[b]									
3 months or less	19.6	27.4	39.9	30.2	25.6	30.1	16.6	27.5	25.8
6 months or less	28.3	43.3	51.6	42.5	31.6	47.4	24.4	27.5	36.8
9 months or less	61.1	57.6	64.3	42.5	55.9	63.7	33.4	35.9	52.7
12 months or less	73.9	64.7	75.8	65.0	70.6	71.0	37.8	51.3	61.9

Source: Survey of job-search behavior of the unemployed, supplement to the May 1976 Current Population Survey.
a. Expressed as a fraction of unemployment, or of unemployed reentrants, for the specific age-sex category.
b. Time outside the labor force is calculated as the difference between the number of months since the last job and the number of months of unemployment in the current spell. Approximately 3.3% of reentrants failed to provide the necessary information but are included in the base figures. Another 4.4% had a negative value of time outside the labor force. These individuals are included in the category of three months or less.

While the demographic composition of reentrant unemployment is consistent with evidence on propensities to exit and enter presented earlier, it is important to identify how long reentrants have been out of the labor force. We present a cumulative distribution of time between the last job and the beginning of the current spell of unemployment. Because those currently unemployed may have experienced more than one such spell, this measure overstates time spent outside the labor force. Even with this conservative measure, we find that 26% of reentrants have been out of the labor force for three months or less and that 62% return within a year of exit. Similar patterns emerge across demographic groups. Except for middle-aged and older women, the proportion reporting a year or less outside the labor force lies between 65 and 75%.

Overall, it appears that the reentrant unemployment category is quite deceptive. A significant part of the category is comprised of persons who leave or lose jobs and record a brief period outside the labor force in the midst of a lengthy spell of unemployment. Insofar as reentrant unemployment spells are short, this reflects only the CPS classifications and says little about the ease of finding a job. The category combines persons with different experience. Some are suffering long spells of joblessness, while others have no serious employment problems. A more meaningful breakdown could be developed using the length of time since the last spell of employment as a basis for measurement. This is not possible in the regular CPS, which is unfortunate.

1.3 The Concentration of Unemployment

The arbitrariness of the distinction between unemployment and not in the labor force and the resulting frequency of multiple spells of unemployment suggest the importance of analyzing unemployment experience over a long horizon. Retrospective data over a year or longer are less likely to be contaminated by spurious movements into and out of the labor force. Persons are unlikely to recall nine months later that they were unavailable for work for a short period in the midst of a lengthy unemployment spell. Thus retrospective durations may give a more meaningful measure of the length of spells of joblessness. Retrospective reporting of behavior may have the limitation, however, that it is more subject to recall error than contemporaneous response.[27]

The annual work experience survey asks all civilian noninstitutional respondents in the March CPS to describe their work experience and unemployment experience in the preceding year. We have used these data to calculate two measures of joblessness. The first is the official definition of unemployment, the number of weeks spent seeking work or weeks on layoff. This conventional definition is compared with a second concept in which the number of weeks spent searching are combined with weeks outside the labor force for those who list "unable to find work" or "looking for work" as the principal reason for less than a full year of work.[28] This combined concept is referred to as "nonemployment." It is important to note that nonemployment excludes weeks outside the labor force for those citing illness, family responsibilities, or "other" as the principal reason for part-year work. For these persons, nonemployment is defined as weeks of unemployment. In both calculations, persons are excluded from the sample if they did not participate in the labor force or if they listed school attendance as their main reason for part-year work.

The distributions of unemployment and nonemployment for selected demographic groups are shown in table 1.4. Of the almost 94 million workers who were in the civilian labor force and were not in school at some point during 1974, 14.1 million, or 15%, experienced unemployment. The average amount of unemployment for persons with unemployment is fifteen weeks or about three and a half months. Male teenagers have the highest number of weeks per person, while women appear to accumulate fewer weeks of unemployment within a year. There is some cyclical variation in weeks of unemployment, but most cyclical fluctuations appear to be from movements in the number of persons experiencing unemployment.

The number experiencing nonemployment differs only slightly from the number unemployed. However, weeks of joblessness are significantly greater when time outside the labor force is included. Nonemployment in 1974 averaged 19.9 weeks, or about four and a half months. This implies that the average unemployed person spent one month outside the labor force though still wanting a job. Because many persons move directly from unemployment into employment, the evidence suggests that the remainder who withdraw following unemployment will experience significant periods of hidden unemployment.

The second section of the table provides the distribution of unemployed persons and unemployed weeks. The concentration of unemployment emerges as a clear conclusion. In 1974, the 2.4% of the labor force who experienced more than six months of unemployment accounted for over 41% of all the unemployment. The 4.9% of the labor force who experienced more than twenty-six weeks of nonemployment accounts for two-thirds of all nonemployment during the year. Compared with the spell durations of table 1.1, which are estimated from the monthly CPS, a much higher fraction of unemployment and nonemployment is included in spells lasting more than fourteen weeks—73% of unemployment and 84% of nonemployment.

Some significant demographic variations occur in the distribution of weeks of unemployment. Most surprising is the large concentration of unemployment among male teenagers. The importance of extensive unemployment among male teenagers who are not in school is inconsistent with the view that youth joblessness arises from a high rate of movement between jobs with brief intervening periods of unemployment. Over half of all unemployment among this group is attributable to the 8.4% of its members who are unemployed for more than six months during the year. More than three-quarters of all nonemployment in this group is attributable to its members who are out of work for more than six months. The concentration of unemployment is least pronounced among adult women, which indicates their high propensity to withdraw from the labor force. Adopting the alternative nonemployment definition makes a relatively large difference for this group.

There is a strong cyclical pattern in the distribution of weeks of unemployment. The fraction of the labor force unemployed for over twenty-six weeks more than quadrupled between 1969 and 1975, and the share of unemployment accounted for by those persons rose from 35 to 55%. Compared to the analysis of completed spells, the cyclical response of the distribution of weeks of unemployment in the work experience data is much less asymmetric. In terms of weeks per person or the fraction of the labor force with six months or more of unemployment, 1974 lies more or less proportionately between 1969 and 1975, which is not the case in the spell distributions of table 1.1.

There is another way of conveying the evidence on the concentration of unemployment that clarifies its impact and sharpens the cyclical patterns evident in the work experience data. Suppose that one asks the question, "How much unemployment will those currently unemployed experience within the year?" The answer can be obtained by using the distribution of total weeks of unemployment presented in table 1.4. Those data indicate, for example, that 41.8% of those unemployed at any particular moment in 1974 would experience more than six months of unemployment during the year. Using the nonemployment definition, 66.7% would report more than six months of joblessness.

The weighted averages of the distribution of weeks of unemployment are shown in table 1.5. The figures are to be interpreted as the average

Table 1.4
Characteristics and distribution of unemployment and nonemployment, by demographic group, 1974, and for all groups, 1969 and 1975[a]

| | 1974 | | | | | 1969 | 1975 |
| | Males | | Females | | | | |
Characteristic or distribution	16–19	20 and over	16–19	20 and over	All groups	All groups	All groups
Characteristic							
Persons with labor force experience (millions)	2.8	51.3	2.5	37.4	94.0	85.2	94.5
Unemployed persons (millions)	0.9	6.8	0.9	5.5	14.1	8.5	17.4
Average weeks of unemployment per unemployed person	18.6	15.8	14.8	13.9	15.0	12.4	18.8
Nonemployed persons (millions)	0.9	6.8	0.9	5.6	14.2	8.7	—
Average weeks of nonemployment per nonemployed person	25.7	18.9	24.9	18.9	19.9	15.9	—
Distribution[b]							
Unemployed persons (percent of labor force)							
1–4 weeks	6.3	2.5	11.0	5.3	3.7	3.4	3.5
5–14 weeks	9.5	5.1	9.8	5.4	5.3	3.6	5.7
15–26 weeks	8.1	3.4	8.1	3.3	3.4	1.9	4.5
27–39 weeks	4.9	1.3	3.7	1.3	1.4	0.7	2.3
40 weeks or more	3.5	0.9	2.4	0.9	1.0	0.4	2.3
Weeks of unemployment (percent of weeks)							
1–4 weeks	2.6	4.4	5.3	5.5	4.2	5.7	2.6
5–14 weeks	16.2	22.6	18.3	31.1	22.4	27.8	15.6
15–26 weeks	27.4	32.7	32.6	27.3	31.7	31.6	27.0
27–39 weeks	26.3	21.0	22.2	17.4	21.1	19.1	22.3
40 weeks or more	27.5	19.3	21.6	18.7	20.7	15.8	32.5

Table 1.4 (continued)

Characteristic or distribution	1974					1969	1975
	Males		Females		All groups	All groups	All groups
	16–19	20 and over	16–19	20 and over			
Nonemployed persons (percent of labor force)							
1–4 weeks	4.2	2.0	6.9	3.9	2.9	—	—
5–14 weeks	7.4	4.5	7.7	4.2	4.5	—	—
15–26 weeks	5.3	3.0	4.9	2.2	2.8	—	—
27–39 weeks	7.0	2.3	5.3	2.0	2.4	—	—
40 weeks or more	9.2	1.6	11.4	2.7	2.5	—	—
Weeks of nonemployment (percent of weeks)							
1–4 weeks	1.4	2.5	1.8	3.4	2.6	—	—
5–14 weeks	7.5	15.1	7.6	13.7	13.0	—	—
15–26 weeks	11.8	22.8	10.2	15.0	17.7	—	—
27–39 weeks	26.7	29.2	18.3	23.2	25.6	—	—
40 weeks or more	52.2	30.4	62.1	44.6	41.1	—	—

Source: Calculations based on the annual survey of work experience of the civilian noninstitutional population, supplement to the March Current Population Survey, 1970, 1975, and 1976. Figures are rounded.

a. The data exclude those who answered "school" when asked their reason for part-year work. The total for unemployment includes only part-year workers and those without work experience. Full-year workers (50–52 weeks) who may have experienced one or two weeks of unemployment are excluded from the calculations of unemployment and nonemployment, but are counted in the labor force. Nonemployment is defined as weeks of unemployment plus weeks outside the labor force for those giving "looking for work" as the principal reason for part-year work, or "unable to find work" as the principal reason for not working during the year. For those reporting illness, home or family responsibilities, retirement, or something else when replying to these questions, nonemployment is defined as weeks of unemployment.

b. Expressed as a fraction of the labor force, or the weeks of unemployment or nonemployment, for the specific age-sex category.

Table 1.5
Expected weeks of unemployment and nonemployment, by demographic group, 1974, and
for all groups, 1969 and 1975

| | 1974 | | | | | 1969 | 1975 |
| | Males | | Females | | | | |
Category	16–19	20 and over	16–19	20 and over	All groups	All groups	All groups
Unemployment	28.5	24.8	25.8	23.0	25.2	24.1	29.3
Nonemployment	36.0	29.7	31.9	32.6	32.3	—	—

Source: Calculated as a weighted average of total weeks of unemployment and nonemployment, by duration category, as described in the text. The data are derived from table 1.4.

weeks of unemployment and nonemployment accumulated during the year
for persons measured as unemployed in a given month.[29] In a steady state,
this corresponds to estimating, for persons currently unemployed, how
much unemployment they had during the preceding year or will have
during the current or following year. The estimates are extremely large.
Because the 1974 situation closely parallels current economic conditions,
the figures suggest that persons currently unemployed will have experienced an average of almost six months of unemployment by the end of the
year. The demographic differences parallel differences in the distribution of
weeks of unemployment. Unemployed male teenagers experience a somewhat greater number of weeks of joblessness than average, while adults
experience slightly less.

The expected number of weeks of unemployment for those currently
unemployed is not very sensitive to the cycle. Even in 1969, when it is
widely believed that *all* but frictional unemployment was eliminated, the
average person measured as unemployed at a point in time experienced
five and a half months of unemployment. In the 1975 downturn, the
duration approached thirty weeks. No matter what the state of the business
cycle, those who are out of work can expect to accumulate a large number
of weeks of unemployment. Although the average number of weeks experienced by an unemployed individual rises moderately over the cycle,
the data suggest that the primary effect of a decline in aggregate demand is
a sharp increase in the incidence of long-term unemployment. Comparison
of the 1969, 1974, and 1975 distributions (table 1.4) shows that as unemployment rises, the incidence of short-term unemployment increases only
modestly, while longer term unemployment rises precipitously.

1.3.1 The Concentration of Unemployment over Time

Analysis of annual data provides little basis for determining the relative impact of market adjustments and personal characteristics on extensive unemployment. Besides aggregate movements, long-term joblessness could arise from stochastic fluctuations in demand in diverse labor markets. Given the necessity for extensive wage adjustments and possible relocation, it is clear that shifts in demand could produce extensive periods of joblessness for those directly affected. Over long periods of time, however, adjustments are more likely to occur, and so the burden of this kind of unemployment should be fairly equally distributed. In contrast, personal characteristics that may lead to disadvantageous experiences in one year are likely to persist into the future. A persistence of concentration over several years would lend credence to the notion that personal characteristics and not market maladjustments are at the heart of the observed extensive joblessness.

Obviously, both personal characteristics and market maladjustments are likely to be at work in a given situation. Some insight into their relative importance, however, may be obtained through analysis of longitudinal data. Because the CPS provides no data on individuals over a period longer than two years, we used the National Longitudinal Survey (NLS) of men aged 45 to 59 for the 1965–68 period to examine the concentration of unemployment. The NLS provides extensive information on the labor force experience of several thousand men aged 45 to 59. The sample of middle-aged men is chosen for analysis because of the relative importance of prime-aged men in the total labor force and because of the greater welfare significance of behavior within this group. Calculations of weeks of unemployment and nonemployment over the four-year period are presented in table 1.6 for the total sample and for nonwhites. The labor force concepts used in the NLS questionnaire are comparable to those in the work experience survey, and the definitions of unemployment and nonemployment in the calculations are likewise identical to those in our earlier analysis.

The job attachment of middle-aged men and the effect of the sustained economic expansion of the 1965–68 period are evident in the relatively small fraction of the sample experiencing unemployment or nonemployment. In contrast to the experience of groups who move into and out of the labor force frequently, only 21.1% of men aged 45 to 59 experienced unemployment during the four-year period. For those with unemployment, however, the time spent looking for work averaged 20.3 weeks. An ad-

Table 1.6
Characteristics and distribution of unemployment and nonemployment of nonwhite and all
men aged 45 to 59, four-year period, 1965–68[a]

Characteristic or distribution	Total labor force		Nonwhite labor force	
	Unemployed	Non-employed	Unemployed	Non-employed
Characteristic				
Persons experiencing un-employment or nonemploy-ment (percent of labor force)	21.1	21.6	31.8	32.5
Weeks per person experienc-ing unemployment or nonemployment	20.3	21.2	22.7	23.7
Expected total weeks per person with unemployment or nonemployment at a point in time	48.0	51.4	47.3	50.1
Distribution[b]				
Unemployed or nonemployed persons (percent of labor force)				
1–14 weeks	12.0	11.8	16.2	15.8
15–26 weeks	3.8	3.9	5.8	5.6
27–50 weeks	2.9	3.1	5.4	6.1
51–70 weeks	1.3	1.6	2.4	2.8
71–110 weeks	0.7	0.9	1.7	2.0
111 weeks or more	0.2	0.3	0.1	0.2
Unemployed or nonemployed persons (percent of weeks)				
1–14 weeks	17.4	15.7	14.7	13.4
15–26 weeks	18.4	16.8	17.2	15.2
27–50 weeks	24.7	23.5	26.3	26.4
51–70 weeks	17.8	18.6	19.4	19.2
71–110 weeks	14.6	17.1	19.9	22.3
111 weeks or more	7.1	8.3	2.6	3.5

Source: National Longitudinal Survey of Work Experience of Men 45–59 Years of Age,
1965–68.
a. The total labor force over the 1965–68 period was 14.4 million; the nonwhite labor force
was 1.2 million. Nonemployment is defined as weeks of unemployment plus any weeks
outside the labor force if the reason given for not looking was "unable to find work."
b. Expressed as a fraction of the labor force, or the weeks of unemployment, for the specific
category.

ditional week was spent outside the labor force because of inability to find work.

This apparent concentration of joblessness is examined in greater detail in the distributions, by weeks, of unemployment and nonemployment presented in the table. It is clear that an accumulation of brief periods without work is not the dominant source of total weeks of unemployment. For the sample as a whole, only about one-third of all unemployment is attributable to those with less than six months of joblessness during the four-year period. Almost 40% of unemployment can be traced to persons who are out of work for a year or more. The distribution is slightly more concentrated when the nonemployment definition is used. Relatively little difference occurs in the distributions of unemployment for nonwhites. A smaller proportion of nonwhite unemployment is due to persons out of work over two years, but a correspondingly larger proportion is traceable to those unemployed between eighteen and twenty-four months.

The concentration of unemployment is most dramatically shown by the mean amount of unemployment experienced by persons unemployed at a point in time. The figures in the third row of the table indicate that the average unemployed person at any point in the 1965–68 period was out of work for almost a year during the period. These figures, it should be emphasized, apply to prime-aged males in a boom period. There is reason to expect that the duration would lengthen if the calculation were extended to other groups or periods. This suggests to us that much of unemployment, even in a boom period, may be the result of a semipermanent mismatch between the capabilities and desires of workers and the available employment opportunities.

1.3.2 Normal Turnover and Extensive Unemployment

A central conclusion following from the evidence thus far presented is that normal turnover (short spells of unemployment followed by job attainment) accounts for an insignificant proportion of measured unemployment. Robert Hall suggests that normal turnover can be characterized by the assumptions that a person requires, on average, two months to find the first job, but only one month to find subsequent jobs; and that teenagers change jobs every year, young adults every two years, and adults every four years.[30] Our calculations demonstrate that only a small proportion of unemployment is attributable to such turnover. Table 1.4 indicates only 4.2%, or about 0.25 point of measured unemployment in 1974, was due to persons out of work less than one month. Similar conclusions emerge

from the NLS data. Even taking a far broader definition than Hall and regarding all unemployment of those out of work less than three months as
normal turnover, one can account for only about 1.5 points of aggregate
unemployment.

It is instructive to consider reasons for the contrast between our conclusion and Hall's suggestion that 3.3 points of unemployment can be attributed to normal turnover. The principal difference seems to be Hall's
assumption that all workers have this quantum of normal turnover unemployment; in fact, most people do not suffer this much. The concentration
of unemployment among some workers contrasts with the ease with which
most of the labor force finds jobs. More than half of those who change jobs
experience no unemployment at all. Over 70% of labor force entrants find
jobs without being measured as unemployed.[31] The NLS reveals that only
about 20% of mature men experienced any unemployment at all during the
1965–68 period.

1.3.3 Observed Concentration and Predictions from the Markov Model

The concentration of unemployment and the insignificance of normal turnover evident in this section could be deceptive. As we noted earlier, even if
all workers were alike and faced identical constant probabilities of moving
between labor force states, one would expect that a disproportionate share
of unemployment could be attributed to the relatively few "unlucky"
workers who were slow to find jobs. Moreover, Hall's estimates of the
frequency and duration of normal spells could be treated as statistical
averages. It is therefore important to isolate the extent to which the results
in tables 1.4 and 1.6 reflect genuine heterogeneity of workers. We do this
by contrasting the observed distribution of weeks of unemployment with
those that would be generated by Markov models in which all workers had
the same constant probabilities of transition. In particular, we simulated the
distribution of weeks of unemployment that would be generated both by
the actual average 1974 transition probabilities and by a set of hypothetical
probabilities designed to yield Hall's assumptions of normal turnover.[32]
The salient features of actual and simulated distributions of weeks of
unemployment during the year are shown in table 1.7.

The results demonstrate that the actual distribution of weeks of unemployment is much more concentrated than either Markov model would
predict. Consider, for example, the group of males aged 20 and over. Only
27% of all unemployment in this group can be traced to persons out of
work for less than three months. This may be contrasted with the predictions of 58.4% and 83.9%, respectively, from actual and "normal turnover"

Table 1.7
Alternative estimates of the distribution of unemployed persons and of weeks of unemployment, by demographic group, 1974[a]

Distribution[a]	Males		Females		All groups
	16–19	20 and over	16–19	20 and over	
Unemployed persons (percent of unemployed)					
Actual	32.4	13.2	35.0	14.8	15.0
Markov model					
Actual probabilities	57.0	16.2	41.6	13.6	23.3
Normal turnover probabilities	66.2	24.5	66.2	24.5	28.5
Unemployment due to persons with three months of unemployment or less (percent of weeks of unemployment)					
Actual	18.8	27.0	23.6	36.6	26.6
Markov model					
Actual probabilities	66.1	58.4	70.6	60.6	61.3
Normal turnover probabilities	75.0	83.9	75.0	83.9	81.4
Unemployment due to persons with more than six months of unemployment (percent of weeks of unemployment)					
Actual	53.8	40.3	43.8	36.1	41.8
Markov model					
Actual probabilities	3.5	8.7	4.1	8.3	8.0
Normal turnover probabilities	1.4	0.3	1.4	0.3	0.6

Sources: Actual distributions are calculated from the results in table 1.4. The other distributions are based on simulations of a Markov model in which all workers had the same, constant transition probabilities. One simulation used actual 1974 transition probabilities, and the other used a hypothetical set of probabilities designed to yield the normal turnover assumptions in Robert E. Hall, "Why Is the Unemployment Rate So High at Full Employment?" *BPEA*, vol. 3 (1970), p. 390.
a. Expressed as a fraction of the number of unemployed, or the weeks of unemployment, for the specific age-sex category.

Markov models. The differences in the proportion of prolonged unemployment are even more dramatic. Fully 40.0% of unemployment is experienced by men who are out of work over six months, compared to 0.3% predicted by the normal turnover model. The results are quite similar for other demographic groups. These results, if anything, underestimate the importance of heterogeneity. Similar calculations using a longer horizon provide much more striking evidence. Almost 40% of unemployment among men shown in table 1.6 was attributable to persons out of work for more than fifty weeks. If the experiences of those men were characterized by the average transition probabilities of men aged 25 to 59 in 1968, only 0.2% of unemployment over a four-year period would have been attributable to this group! It seems clear, then, that a large part of unemployment cannot be traced to normal turnover, regardless of how elastically it is defined. An explanation of the extensive unemployment of a small fraction of the population is required.

The insignificance of normal turnover in accounting for measured unemployment need not imply that frequent movement between jobs with brief intervening spells of unemployment is unimportant. Extensive unemployment over a year could arise from the tendency of certain members of the labor force to move from one unsatisfactory job to another, as proponents of a turnover view of unemployment have claimed.[33] Some insight into the importance of the "frequent job exit—brief unemployment spell" characterization of the unemployment problem can be gleaned from table 1.8. The table presents data from the March 1975 work experience survey, which show that those with more than twenty-six weeks of unemployment

Table 1.8
Number of spells, weeks employed, and weeks outside the labor force for persons with more than twenty-six weeks of unemployment, by demographic group, 1974

	Males		Females		
Characteristic	16–19	20 and over	16–19	20 and over	All groups
Average number of spells of unemployment[a]	2.0	1.7	1.6	1.4	1.6
Average weeks employed	10.9	11.8	9.4	10.4	11.0
Average weeks outside the labor force	3.4	3.3	5.1	4.2	3.7

Source: March 1975 work experience survey, supplement to the Current Population Survey.
a. Calculation of the average number of spells assumes those with three or more had 3.5 spells.

spent about nine months unemployed, and averaged twenty-three weeks per spell. While the observed brevity of employment may be an indication of serious problems of instability, it is clear that extensive unemployment does not arise through an accumulation of brief spells of unemployment between jobs.

1.4 Alternative Explanations of Unemployment

The preceding tabulations suggest that most unemployment is the result of a relatively small part of the population suffering repeated, extended spells. The unemployment rate is high even at full employment because a few people are out of work for much of the year. The dominant theoretical views of unemployment fail to explain this concentration that characterizes actual experience in labor markets.

According to these theoretical views, unemployment is understood as an optimal response to economic conditions. In search theory, persons choose to be unemployed in order to seek better job opportunities. In contract theory, they enter into implicit or explicit understandings with employers under which temporary layoffs are the optimal response to variations in demand. These views do not recognize equilibrium involuntary unemployment. They exclude the possibility of the labor market failing to "clear" over sustained periods. Such models may explain a great deal of the observed labor market behavior and may fit the experience of many, perhaps even most, workers. But it is not plausible that efficient response, either to the uncertainty of what jobs may be found or to variations in demand, could lead to arrangements in which persons repeatedly spend a large part of the year involuntarily without jobs. In the next part of the paper we examine survey evidence on the behavior of the unemployed to assess the significance of temporary layoffs and of search models in accounting for unemployment.

1.4.1 Temporary Layoffs

Temporary layoffs have played a central role in recent theoretical and empirical research on unemployment.[34] Moreover, the theory of contracts, which underlies research on temporary layoffs, has contributed to our understanding of the persistence of inflation and the response of quantities rather than prices to aggregate demand. Models in which layoffs emerge within an optimizing framework assume essentially permanent attachment of workers to firms. The development of a long-term attachment to a firm is usually explained in terms of job-specific human capital. For a variety of reasons, including risk aversion, unemployment insurance, and difficulties in enforcing contracts, wages are fixed over the contract period and firms respond to fluctuations in demand by laying off workers.

The May 1976 supplement to the CPS is the first nationwide survey of the job-search methods that are used by the unemployed. Because it has been matched to the regular CPS for May through August 1976, we can analyze the subsequent labor market experience of those on layoff. Before examining the results, it is useful to clarify the distinction between the official terminology of the Bureau of Labor Statistics and the popular lexicon. In the CPS, workers on layoff are divided into two categories—temporary and indefinite. Temporary layoff status is reserved for those with a job to which they expect to return within thirty days. Other workers on layoff who indicate a possibility of returning to their original employers sometime after thirty days are placed in the indefinite category. Most persons on layoff are classified in the second group. Following previous research, we use the term "temporary layoff" to refer to both official definitions.

The results of the analysis for the total population and for men aged 25 to 59 are presented in table 1.9. Temporary layoffs do not account for a large fraction of total unemployment and are not a dominant source of job loss. In 1976, they accounted for only 13% of total unemployment. This figure would be even lower if 1976 had not been a year of high unemployment. Among middle-aged men, only one-fourth of the unemployed were on layoff, and over three-quarters of those on layoff did not expect to return to their original job within thirty days. The data further reveal that persons on layoff are a minority of those losing jobs because only 32% of all workers and 42% of men aged 25 to 59 who lost their jobs in 1976 were on layoff.

The significance of temporary layoffs as a distinct category of unemployment depends on whether a high proportion of those on layoff return to their original employer. We have no direct evidence on this question, but some inferences can be drawn from available data.

If some of those on layoff in fact do not return, then the fraction of unemployment due to "true" temporary layoffs is actually smaller than the calculations above suggest. Unfortunately, the CPS does not ask the newly employed whether they have previous work experience at the same firm. The survey does inquire, however, about the occupation and industry of workers and persons who are unemployed. The third through fifth rows of table 1.9 report the proportion of workers returning to the same industry and occupation. We estimate that 51% of persons on temporary layoff

Table 1.9
Unemployment due to temporary layoffs and reemployment and search intensity of all unemployed persons and persons on temporary layoff, males aged 25 to 59 and total population, 1976[a]

Characteristic	Males, 25–59		Total population	
	Temporary layoffs	Total unemployed	Temporary layoffs	Total unemployed
Unemployment[b]				
Proportion of unemployment	0.25	1.00	0.13	1.00
Proportion of job losers	0.42	—	0.32	—
Reemployment[b]				
In same industry	0.68	0.55	0.66	0.36
In same occupation	0.68	0.47	0.66	0.33
In same industry, occupation	0.55	0.38	0.51	0.24
Intensity of search				
Average hours of search per month	23.3	33.9	18.3	24.9
Average number of search methods used	2.6	3.6	2.5	3.4

Sources: Survey of job-search behavior of the unemployed, supplement to the May 1976 Current Population Survey, and matched May through August 1976 Current Population Survey.
a. The category of temporary layoffs includes both persons expecting to be recalled within thirty days and indefinite layoffs. Industry and occupation are measured at the two-digit level used by the U.S. Bureau of the Census. Those who did not search are assigned zero hours and zero methods of search. Search intensity data are tabulated for those with four or more weeks of unemployment.
b. Expressed as a fraction of the specific category.

return to jobs in the same industry and occupation. This fraction is double the corresponding proportion for all unemployed; an approximately equal number of persons change industry and occupation. Almost one-sixth of those on layoff change both industry and occupation.

It seems reasonable to infer that persons who change industry or occupation do not return to their original jobs. The data suggest, therefore, that no more than one-half of those on temporary or indefinite layoff could possibly be returning to their original jobs. If observed reemployment is temporary, and many of those changing industry and occupation eventually return to the original employer, 51% could be an underestimate. By August, the proportion of persons on temporary layoff who had returned to their original industry and occupation was higher than it was in June. The evidence suggests that the return rate to the original industry and occupation may be nearer 60 to 65% than the 50% we estimate without "stopgap" jobs.

On the other hand, two further considerations point toward lower estimates of return rates. First, many workers undoubtedly return to different jobs in the same occupation and industry. Second, the proportion returning to the same industry and occupation is calculated on the basis of persons who return to a job before dropping out of the sample.[35] Thus persons with longer spells of unemployment and those who are recorded as withdrawing from the labor force (56% of the sample) are excluded. It is reasonable to expect a smaller proportion of those with long spells of unemployment to return to the same job. This supposition is supported by the finding that 51% of those on temporary layoff in May who were employed in June returned to the same industry and occupation, while only 29% of persons who first became reemployed in August did so.[36]

These figures seem to contradict previously published results suggesting that between 66 and 85% of workers on layoff return to their original employer.[37] There is an important difference that might well account for much of the disparity. Previous studies have estimated the proportion of workers on layoff who return to the original employer (recall rate) by contrasting rehire and layoff rates in manufacturing from establishment data. That calculation will differ from the CPS results presented here if very short layoff durations coincide with a high probability of recall. In this case, the recall rate estimated from establishment data is likely to overstate the fraction of those currently on layoff who will return because it weights all spells of unemployment equally. If most periods of layoff are short, which seems likely, and are followed by workers returning to their original jobs, but some of those periods are lengthy and are followed by entrance into new employment, a high recall rate can coincide with a small proportion of those currently on layoff returning to the original employer. It is the latter concept, however, that is relevant for determining the fraction of unemployment attributable to returning workers.

We further examine the job attachment of persons on layoff by contrasting their search behavior with the search behavior of other unemployed persons. The May 1976 job-search survey provides several measures of the search intensity of the unemployed. Persons on temporary layoff are contrasted with all unemployed persons in table 1.9. Whether measured in terms of hours per month or number of methods used, the results suggest that persons on layoff search almost as much as unemployed persons in general.[38] It is doubtful that this is traceable to any requirement of the unemployment insurance system. Under many state laws persons on layoff collecting unemployment insurance are not required to search for work. Moreover, many of the search methods used by persons on layoff are not mandated by the unemployment insurance system. Almost 32% answer want ads and over 52% report that they have talked with friends and relatives about jobs. Less than half register with the state employment service, which is surely the most credible way to comply with a search requirement of the unemployment insurance system.

These findings, together with the results on return rates, indicate that the temporary layoff model can account for no more than a small fraction of observed unemployment. Only 13% of the unemployed in May 1976 were on layoff. If more than half of this group did not return to their original jobs, no more than 7% of unemployment, or 0.5 point of the aggregate unemployment rate, is attributable to temporary layoffs. During periods when the unemployment rate is changing rapidly, layoffs are more important: between 1974 and 1975, for example, layoffs accounted for about 30% of the increase in unemployment. Once unemployment stabilized, the importance of layoffs diminished. Between 1974 and 1976, for example, the overall unemployment rate rose by 2.1 points, of which only 13.3% represented layoffs. All the increase in persons on layoff was accounted for by the indefinite category; the number on layoff officially classified as "temporary" actually declined from 1974 to 1976. Because a significant number of persons on layoff do not return to their original employer, no more than 7 to 8% of the increase in unemployment between 1974 and 1976 can be explained by layoffs. Furthermore, no more than 15% of the sharp 1974–75 downturn can be accurately described by the layoff model.

The theory of contracts has raised important questions about the unemployment insurance system. However, it does not appear that the theory can account for a large part of measured unemployment. Only a small fraction of unemployment is due to those grouped in the official layoff category, and an even smaller fraction is due to those on layoff who actually return to their original jobs. The paradigm is not completely accurate even for persons who return because they appear to search seriously for alternative employment. It seems clear that while job attachment and implicit contracts may be pervasive and important for other purposes, explanations for most unemployment must be sought elsewhere.

1.4.2 Search Theory

Another explanation of unemployment is offered by models of job search.[39] According to these models, individuals become unemployed when the return to search exceeds the return to remaining employed or out of the labor force. Unemployed persons continue to search until they receive an offer whose value exceeds the return to continued search or until they decide that the net return to search is negative and withdraw from the labor force. The theory thus offers an explanation of both the flow into and the duration of unemployment.

In search models, time spent searching is a form of investment. Persons invest by forgoing income and becoming or remaining unemployed in order to find jobs with higher wages. The credibility of the theory depends on persons receiving a reasonable return on their investment in search time. The return that is received depends critically on the expected duration of the person's next job. If job tenure is low, the return to search is also likely to be low because higher wages will be received only briefly. Even if tenure is expected to be lengthy, individuals may anticipate that wage differentials will not persist in a competitive market.

In table 1.10 we report estimates of the mean duration of completed spells of employment and completed spells in a given job for various demographic groups.[40] The estimates are calculated using the gross-flow data from 1968 to 1976 and a special 1961 survey of job changers by the Bureau of Labor Statistics. The duration of a completed spell of employment has been calculated as the reciprocal of the monthly probability of exiting from employment. To find the mean duration of completed job lengths, it is necessary to take account of persons who move from one job to another without experiencing unemployment. The survey of job changers includes estimates of the proportion of job changers who experience no unemployment. Because the probability of leaving a job is the sum of the probability of job change without unemployment and the probability

Table 1.10
Duration in employment and duration in a job, by demographic group[a]

Characteristic	Males			Females			All groups
	16–19	25–59	Total	16–19	25–59	Total	
Employment duration							
Probability of leaving employment							
By leaving the labor force	0.116	0.004	0.020	0.143	0.044	0.057	0.034
By becoming unemployed	0.043	0.011	0.015	0.030	0.011	0.013	0.014
Duration in employment (months)	6.3	66.7	28.6	5.8	18.2	14.3	20.8
Job duration							
Proportion of job changers experiencing no unemployment	0.560	0.542	0.528	0.560	0.542	0.565	0.540
Duration in a job (months)	2.8	30.5	13.5	2.6	8.3	6.2	9.6

Sources: The probabilities are estimated from 1968–76 gross-flow data from the Current Population Survey, with adjustments as described in Vanski, "Recession and the Employment of Demographic Groups." The data on job changers experiencing no unemployment are taken from the 1961 survey of job mobility conducted by the Bureau of the Census for the Bureau of Labor Statistics. The data are reported in Gertrude Bancroft and Stuart Garfinkle, "Job Mobility in 1961," *Monthly Labor Review*, vol. 86 (August 1963), pp. 897–906, especially tables 1, 4, and 6. The data on job changers are not available by sex for the specific age groups presented in this table. For men and women aged 25 to 59, data on all persons aged 25 and over are used, and for male and female teenagers aged 16 to 19, all teenagers aged 14 to 19. Applying the same fraction to men and women may lead to a slight understatement of the job duration for women and a slight overstatement for men.

a. Duration in employment is defined as the reciprocal of the sum of the probabilities of leaving employment. Duration in a job is the duration in employment multiplied by one minus the proportion of persons changing jobs with no unemployment.

of leaving employment, it is possible to calculate the probability of leaving a job and its reciprocal, average duration in a job.[41] The average durations are influenced by noneconomic factors such as pregnancy leave, long illness, and return to school. And those durations do not distinguish layoffs with recall from other types of job separation.

The results indicate the implausibility of the search model as an explanation of why people become or remain unemployed. Adult men have the largest potential gains from search because their jobs last longest. Yet they are the group with the lowest unemployment rate. For all workers, the average job lasts less than ten months. For teenagers, the figure is slightly less than three months. A high proportion of persons who change jobs experience no unemployment. The proportion averages 54.0% for the total population, and 56.5% for women. The duration of the average completed spell of employment, as opposed to time at a single job, is also quite short, lasting twenty-one months. Thus the payoff to investment in search is likely to be low even if high wages are "portable" between jobs.

The notion that being unemployed in order to search is a useful activity that characterizes an efficient labor market is also unsupported by evidence. The most important problem is that the majority of the unemployed search in ways that would be possible if they held a job. According to the 1976 job-search survey, the average person unemployed for four weeks or more devoted only seventeen hours a month to search.[42] Furthermore, most jobs are found through channels that do not require the person seeking a job to be unemployed. A January 1973 special survey of successful job seekers conducted as a supplement to the CPS found that 26% had obtained a job through friends or relatives and 14% had used want ads, while only 35% had found a job through direct application to employers.[43]

The feasibility of on-the-job search is supported by the finding noted above—that is, half of job changes occur without intervening unemployment. This finding creates two difficulties for search theories of unemployment. First, it calls into question the theory's explanation of the flow into unemployment: if workers can search for a new job while continuing to work, there is no reason for them to quit for that purpose. Second, if most jobs last only a short time, and workers can search on the job, there is little reason for a worker to reject job offers. Such a worker can continue searching for more attractive offers while working at an inferior job. In fact, it appears that most unemployed accept the first job offer they receive. According to the May 1976 survey, about 10% reported that they had rejected a job offer. Simple explanations based on the search model, which suggest that the unemployed refuse offers until a sufficiently attractive one comes along, do not appear capable of explaining continuing unemployment.

More recent developments in search theory have attempted to account for the dearth of offers received by the unemployed.[44] These models characterize search as a sequential process in which the unemployed seek successively less attractive potential employers, accepting the first offer they receive. This version of the theory explains why unemployed workers report that they have received no job offers. It does not afford an explanation of why workers do not accept a relatively unattractive job and continue to look for a more attractive one. Even ignoring this difficulty, the sequential search model does not offer a reasonable explanation for prolonged unemployment. Given the brevity of tenure in most jobs, unemployed workers could raise their total return from search by looking for less attractive jobs from the beginning.

1.5 Concentrated Unemployment: Explanations and Implications

The discussion above demonstrates that unemployment is high because a relatively small number of workers are out of work a large part of the time, although the remainder of the labor market clears. Even over fairly long periods, the burden of unemployment is highly concentrated. An individual who is currently unemployed can expect to be unemployed six months out of the next twelve, and one year out of the next four years. Conventional search and layoff theories appear to be incapable of explaining this type of unemployment. We now briefly consider some potential explanations of extensive unemployment. The purpose of this analysis is to suggest a number of issues requiring further research rather than to provide final answers.

Although our main focus in this section is on the noncyclical aspects of unemployment, a satisfying explanation of extensive unemployment must also shed light on its fluctuations. The number of persons with more than six months of unemployment rose more than fourfold between 1969 and 1975. Most cyclical variation in unemployment is attributable to changes in the number of persons experiencing extensive unemployment. Little can be explained by changes in the number of persons suffering only a small amount of unemployment during the year. Thus an explanation of extensive unemployment that rests entirely on the characteristics of a subset of the labor force cannot be complete. Such a theory would explain little about the observed fluctuations in the unemployment rate.

The existence of a minimum wage floor is sometimes blamed for extensive unemployment. With rigid wages, the demand for labor could be expected to fall short of the number of available workers at the prevailing wage. While the logic of this explanation is impeccable, its empirical relevance is limited at best. We find concentrated unemployment among adult males, almost none of whom work for near the minimum wage when employed. Studies of changes in minimum wages have typically found relatively small unemployment effects.[45] At a time when the minimum wage was $2.30 only 17% of the respondents in the May 1976 job-search survey who had been unemployed more than fifteen weeks reported a wage on their last job between $2.00 and $2.50. Another 10% were found in the $2.50 to $3.00 range. It seems unlikely, therefore, that a reduction in the minimum wage could have a direct effect on most of the long-term unemployed. The statutory level is too low to affect most persons. Even for those who are potentially covered, a large (licit and illicit) uncovered sector exists in which jobs paying less than the minimum wage can be found.

Welfare payments and unemployment insurance are also candidates for explaining long-term joblessness. In an earlier study, using state data on registrants in Aid to Families with Dependent Children and food stamp programs, we found that welfare registration programs have raised measured unemployment by about 0.5 to 0.8 percentage point. We also estimated that the existence of unemployment insurance almost doubles the number of unemployment spells lasting more than three months.[46]

These results should be viewed with caution. An unknown portion of these influences on measured unemployment merely reflects reporting effects.[47] As we emphasized above, nonemployment rather than measured unemployment is the concept that deserves attention. Furthermore, the concentration of unemployment was evident in 1969, before enactment of work-registration requirements for welfare recipients and before the extension of the duration and coverage of unemployment insurance benefits. Finally, cyclical fluctuations in the incidence of extensive unemployment cannot be traced to changes in regulations concerning social insurance.

Extensive unemployment is sometimes explained as a consequence of "high reservation wages" by the unemployed. Because their reservation wages are close to their market wages, the unemployed "want to be" out of work a significant portion of the time. They show up as unemployed rather than as outside the labor force because they are available for work at some wage and frequently make casual attempts to see whether they can obtain it. This explanation of unemployment could account for some of the behavior described above. Frequent movements between being unemployed and being outside the labor force would be expected of those whose reservation and market wages were nearly equal. One would also expect cyclical upgrading wages and job opportunities to have large influences on these persons. Finally, the near-equality of market and reservation wages would explain casual search because it implies that joblessness is not costly.

This explanation, if correct, has important implications for macroeconomic policy. It suggests that the cost of unemployment to individuals may be quite small. A person whose market wage is equal to his reservation wage is indifferent about whether he is employed. Even if this were true, his unemployment would be socially costly. As Feldstein and Gordon have emphasized, taxes and social insurance drive a large wedge between the private and social costs of unemployment.[48] What direct evidence exists suggests that reservation wages are near market wages. The May 1976 job-search survey found that only 36% of those who seek jobs reported reservation wages below their previous wages. Almost a fourth reported reservation wages more than 20% in excess of their last wages. These results were obtained when overall unemployment was high. One would expect to find even greater excesses of reservation wages over market wages during an average period.

It is difficult to explain why so many persons should have such high reservation wages. For persons with productive or enjoyable home opportunities, high reservation wages are easy to comprehend. Robert Hall has noted that 30% of the unemployed who were not in school reported keeping house as their major activity during the survey week, and 18% listed retirement or "other."[49] It is more difficult to understand the high reservation wages of the 52% for whom being on layoff or looking for work was the major activity. To some extent, they may result from the direct and indirect effects of social insurance and minimum wages. By subsidizing unemployment, social insurance measures raise reservation wages. Minimum wages, by affecting the social definition of a "decent job," may increase reservation wages. This effect will be especially important if workers define "decent" or minimally adequate wages in terms of the amounts others are receiving. Similarly, reservation wages may be high if some workers are unwilling to accept pay cuts under almost any circumstances.

While the high-reservation-wage view explains certain aspects of the behavior described in this paper, it does encounter several difficulties. First, despite using a variety of specifications, we were unable to relate successfully the probability of finding a job within a month to the ratio of the reservation wage to the market wage of an individual. Second, substantial and persistent regional differences in extensive unemployment cannot be explained within this framework. Why should the proportion of persons whose reservation wages are close to their market wages differ substantially across regions?

Extensive unemployment could arise from stochastic demand shocks.[50] Suppose that the economy is comprised of many labor markets, separated either geographically or by occupation and industry. Stochastic demand shocks occur constantly in these markets. If wages were sluggish when negative shocks occurred, some labor markets would be out of equilibrium where long-term unemployment could be observed. In markets where positive shocks are received, vacancies will be observed if wages are sluggish upward, otherwise equilibrium will be restored immediately at higher real wages. Thus in an economy of this type, one might expect to see extensive involuntary unemployment at every point in time, even though wages and prices in individual markets are sluggish but not rigid. While this type of formulation affords an explanation of concentrated unemployment within a year, it is less convincing as a story about persistent joblessness of the type observed in the NLS data on middle-aged men.

Another explanation of extensive unemployment focuses on the high rate of job exit and is implicit or explicit in many recent studies of unemployment dynamics. Frequently proponents of this view attribute the high rates of job exit to unattractive "dead-end" jobs. As we noted above, many people are out of work much of the time because they hold jobs very briefly. But surprisingly, a relatively small proportion of the extensively unemployed report low previous wages. In the May 1976 job-search survey, 38% of persons out of work fifteen weeks or more had previous wages below $3.00 an hour, while more than 33% had previous wages below $3.00 an hour, while more than 33% had previous wages over $4.50 an hour. Among adults with more than fifteen weeks of unemployment, the average wage was $3.88. The average wage of all workers paid on an hourly basis in May 1976 was $4.06. Thus it does not appear that the problem groups are in jobs that are substantially less attractive than those held by the remainder of the population. In any event, the "high exit" explanation of extensive unemployment is more descriptive than analytic. It can describe an important source of difference in the average unemployment rates across demographic groups. But it does not provide an answer to what it is about the labor market that causes some persons within a demographic group to hold jobs for such brief periods.

Each of the explanations for unemployment that we discussed has some plausibility, but there is no solid empirical evidence to support any one, or to aid in choosing among them. No individual's experience can be neatly pigeonholed into one of these categories. Nor is there any reason to believe that a single monolithic explanation should characterize all extensive unemployment. More research is necessary to quantify the importance of these potential explanations and to develop new theories illuminating extensive unemployment. It appears that current theories that emphasize the importance of high turnover of the unemployed population are relevant to only a small portion of all unemployment and a smaller portion of joblessness. An understanding of the reasons for extensive unemployment is a necessary precondition for the design of useful policies to combat it.

This research was supported by the U.S. Department of Labor and Harvard University, Graduate School of Business Administration, Division of Research. We want to thank James L. Buchal, Michael C. Burda, Edward Y. Fu, David G. Golden, Barbara C. Job, Judith E. Lebow, Robert J. McIntire, Morris J. Newman, James M. Poterba, and especially Daniel E. Smith for assistance in various stages of this project. Comments by members of the Brookings panel have led to significant improvements in this paper.

Notes

1. See Hall (1970, 1972), Perry (1972), Smith, Vanski, and Holt (1974), Feldstein (1973, 1975), Kaitz (1970), Salant (February 1977), and Akerloff and Main (October 1978).

2. Dornbusch and Fischer (1978), p. 482.

3. The most notable early contributions appear in Phelps et al. (1970). Other important papers include Baily (January 1974) and Azariadis (December 1975).

4. Perhaps the most well-known statement of this view is found in Friedman (March 1968) pp. 1–17. Hall (1972) argues that the natural unemployment rate is below the optimal level because unemployed workers generate positive externalities by reducing recruiting costs.

5. A menu of policy prescriptions following from a dynamic view of the labor market may be found in Feldstein (1973). Policies derived from a turnover perspective are studied in Holt et al. (1971). Baily and Tobin (1977) argue that public employment programs can be useful in addressing the problem of high turnover.

6. This distinction is emphasized in almost all papers cited in note 1. An additional theme in some of these papers has been the short duration of unemployment spells.

7. None of the concepts considered in this paragraph corresponds to the published statistics on the duration of unemployment. These statistics provide the mean

amount of unemployment already experienced by persons currently unemployed. They thus apply to interrupted rather than to completed spells. In our numerical example the mean duration for those currently unemployed would be approximately five weeks.

8. The gross-flow data have been used in several previous studies of labor market dynamics. Papers other than those previously cited include R. Smith, "A Simulation Model of the Demographic Composition of Employment, Unemployment, and Labor Force Participation," and Toikka, Scanlon, and Holt (1977). Problems in the data are examined in Hilaski (October 1968). One of our main points, the importance of considering nonparticipation in understanding unemployment dynamics, is emphasized in much of this work.

9. The appendix is available from the authors on request.

10. Our calculations do not appear to be sensitive to the choice of years. For example, the results for 1973, which some might regard as more typical than 1974, differ negligibly from the 1974 results. Our calculation of the duration distribution of unemployment spells, which differs from previous estimates (for example, Kaitz 1970), does not depend on the assumption of a constant flow into unemployment. We do not require this assumption because we work directly with the hazard function relating exit probabilities and duration.

11. This point is emphasized in Perry (1972) and Marston (1976). Their discussions emphasize the difficulties that high rates of withdrawal created for interpreting unemployment duration statistics.

12. The P_{ue} and P_{uu} terms are, respectively, the probabilities among the unemployed of finding a job or of remaining unemployed. Alternative treatment of withdrawal is possible. At one extreme, those who withdraw could be treated as identical to those who find jobs, so that the adjusted probability of exit from unemployment would be the measured probability of finding a job. This approach yields durations substantially longer than those reported in table 1.1. A further possibility is to treat only part of withdrawal as indicative of no desire for work. The probability of leaving the labor force from employment, for example, could be taken to indicate the probability of normal withdrawal from unemployment. The results that use this approach are similar to those of table 1.1.

13. This calculation requires the assumption of a constant flow into unemployment during the year.

14. These statistics contrast sharply with published data on the distribution of interrupted spell lengths. In 1974, for example, on average 7.3% of the unemployed had already experienced six months of unemployment, yet almost 20% would do so before their unemployment spell ended.

15. The importance of transitions in the labor force has been a central theme of much work using the gross-flow data. Marston (1976) emphasizes that unemployment for certain demographic groups is characterized by withdrawal from the labor force followed by reentry. Calculations on which parts of this section are

based, which indicate the importance of transitions in the labor force, are presented in Clark and Summers (1979c)

16. This argument was first advanced in Perry (1972)

17. These tabulations were kindly provided by Robert McIntire of the Bureau of Labor Statistics.

18. National Commission on Employment and Unemployment Statistics (January 1979) pp. 65–66.

19. Table 1.1 indicates that 45% of spells ended in labor force withdrawal in 1974, compared to 46% in 1975.

20. Hall (1970) emphasizes the arbitrariness of the unemployment definition. He notes survey evidence suggesting that a high proportion of persons measured as outside the labor force return within a short time. His focus is on the incidence of "hard-core" unemployment rather than on the interpretation of unemployment dynamics.

21. This figure is based on unpublished tabulations provided by Morris Newman of the Bureau of Labor Statistics. Rotation group bias is examined in Bailar (March 1975).

22. This paragraph is based on data provided in Bureau of the Census (1968)

23. We use the term "hidden unemployment" to refer to persons classified as outside the labor force whose behavior is functionally equivalent to that of the unemployed. Many persons who are unemployed are functionally indistinguishable from persons who have withdrawn from the labor force.

24. The cyclical response of participation is documented in Perry (1977) and in Clark and Summers (1979a). Geographic differences in unemployment and participation are considered in Clark and Summers (1979a). For the purposes of this paper it is immaterial whether participation responds to the unemployment rate or to fluctuations in the real wage. While traditional analyses focus on the net difference between the number of "added" and "discouraged" workers, it is the total number of workers falling into either of these categories that is relevant here.

25. These results are not an artificial result of the summer months. Reentry rates have been estimated using the March through June 1976 matched file. In that data the one-month rate is 33.8%, while the two-month rate is 45.3%.

26. It might be argued that the patterns of withdrawal and reentry found in the summer months reflect desires of the unemployed for a one- or two-month vacation. Because the reentry rates in March through June matched file are similar to those in the May through August file, the vacation argument must apply to both spring and summer months. Although vacations from unemployment may be reflected somewhat in these data, they are unlikely to be a dominant explanation. Most activities that fall under the heading of vacation can be carried out while one

is looking for work, particularly given the required frequency (once in four weeks) of search and the kind of activities (answering want ads, talking with friends) that constitute "looking" in the CPS.

27. It should be noted that unemployment in the work experience survey is lower than that implied by the monthly figures (4.9% versus 5.6% for 1974). The discrepancy may arise because of differing definitions (that is, use of a four-week test period in the monthly CPS) or response error. It is interesting to note that weeks of nonemployment are similar in the two surveys. Moreover, the mean length of a spell is significantly greater in the work experience data because the number of spells reported is much smaller. For further details, see Clark and Summers (1979c).

28. The response "looking for work" applies to part-year workers; "unable to find work" applies to nonworkers who searched for work.

29. This concept differs from the mean duration of unemployment for all those experiencing unemployment at some point during the year. By capturing all those unemployed at a given point in time, it weights longer spells more heavily. This is because longer spells are more likely than shorter ones to be in progress at the measurement point. An arithmetic example of the difference between mean duration of a completed spell and expected unemployment duration for the currently unemployed was given before the discussion of table 1.1. These issues are discussed in more detail in Salant (February 1977).

30. Hall (1970) p. 390

31. This figure is a 1968–76 average from the gross-flow data. Little yearly or demographic variation occurs.

32. Hall's turnover assumptions imply for teenagers, for example, a weekly probability of 1/4 of moving out of unemployment and a weekly probability of 1/52 of exiting from employment.

33. Hall (1970) states this view clearly: "The real problem is that many workers have frequent short spells of unemployment" (p. 387).

34. Theoretical developments emphasizing the importance of temporary layoffs include Baily (January 1974) and Azariadis (December 1975). Barro (July 1977) has pointed out a severe theoretical difficulty. He notes that the set of admissible contracts is unduly restricted by Baily and Azariadis. He argues that an optimal contract would mandate a fixed level of employment. Empirical studies include Feldstein (December 1978), Medoff (June 1979), and Lilien (1977).

35. Persons in the third rotation group in May can only be monitored into June, when they leave the sample. Hence, if they do not become reemployed in June, they are excluded from the calculation.

36. Coding errors in the industry and occupation data lead to an offsetting bias. It is difficult to assess its magnitude. Comparison of reported occupations and industries in successive months for the unemployed suggests that coding errors could

bias the 50% estimate by up to 20 percentage points. Even this bias is probably less important than those noted in the text.

37. These figures may be found in Medoff (June 1979) and Lilien (1977).

38. These conclusions are similar to the ones reached in Bradshaw and Scholl (1976). At the time Bradshaw and Scholl were writing, no nationwide sample of the search behavior of the unemployed was available.

39. The search literature originated in Stigler (June 1961). Applications of the model to explain cyclical fluctuations in unemployment include Mortensen (December 1970) and Alchain (1970). Empirical tests are presented in Kiefer and Neumann (February 1979) and Barron and Mellow (forthcoming). An excellent survey of the literature is contained in Lippman and McCall (June 1976). An extensive critique of search theory that first made many of the points referred to here is included in Gordon (1973).

40. Because the probability of leaving a job declines sharply with tenure, the mean duration of a completed spell is much less than average tenure for those currently on a job. The distribution and determinants of job tenure are discussed in Freeman (December 1978).

41. These calculations require a steady state assumption to be strictly accurate. For this reason we used average transition probabilities offer the 1968–76 period. The 1961 survey of job changers provides age-specific data on the number of people who changed jobs at least once, rather than the total number of job changes. The calculations in table 1.10 are thus likely to overstate somewhat the length of a completed job spell. The sampling interval of one month in the gross-flow data also leads to overestimates of spell lengths.

42. Rosenfeld (November 1977), p. 41.

43. Bureau of Labor Statistics (1975), p. 41.

44. See, for example, Salop (April 1973).

45. For an analysis along these lines see Gramlich (1976). Enforcement of the minimum wage is examined in Ashenfelter and Smith (April 1974).

46. These estimates are based on an analysis of transitions out of unemployment, using the May through August 1976 matched file. It should be noted that the estimates are partial equilibrium calculations. A general elimination of the unemployment insurance system is likely to have different effects than would elimination for a single person.

47. For a discussion and empirical analysis of reporting effects, see Clark and Summers (forthcoming).

48. Feldstein (May 1978) and Gordon (1973).

49. See Hall (July 1978).

50. This argument is a central theme in Tobin (March 1972).

2

The Dynamics of
Youth Unemployment

with Kim B. Clark

At any given moment almost 2 million teenagers aged 16–19 are unemployed. Another 600,000 are out of school and neither working nor looking for work. Only about 60% of all teenagers and 25% of black youths who are out of school are employed. These high rates of joblessness have been a source of concern to both economists and policymakers. This chapter seeks to clarify the dimensions of the youth employment problem by analyzing the distribution of unemployment and related patterns of labor force mobility.

High rates of joblessness among young people have been explained in two quite different ways. The traditional view holds that the problem is one of job availability. A general shortage of openings makes it very difficult for some workers to find jobs. It takes the unemployed a long time to find a job. Much of the problem with the traditional view is traceable to a hardcore group who are out of work a large part of the time. The "new" view sees employment instability as the crux of the joblessness problem.[1] It treats the large flow into unemployment rather than the long length of unemployment spells as the crucial symptom of the problem. As Martin Feldstein, a leading exponent of the new view, has written, "The picture of a hard core of unemployed persons unable to find jobs is an inaccurate description of our economy.... A more accurate description is an active labor market in which almost everyone who is out of work can find his usual type of job in a relatively short time.... The current structure of unemployment is not compatible with the traditional view of a hard core of

Reprinted by permission of the University of Chicago Press, with revisions, from Richard B. Freeman and David A. Wise, eds., *The Youth Labor Market Problem: Its Nature, Causes, and Consequences*, Chicago: The University of Chicago Press, 1982, pp. 199–235. © 1982 by the National Bureau of Economic Research.

unemployed who are unable to find jobs." [2] In particular, proponents of the new view emphatically reject the suggestion that the solution to the youth unemployment problem lies in job creation.

The results in this chapter strongly support the traditional view of the youth joblessness problem. They suggest that much of what appears to be evidence of dynamic labor market behavior is in fact a reflection of artifacts in the data. A large proportion of the measured flow into and out of unemployment is made up of quite spurious transitions into and out of the labor force. We also show that even though many unemployment spells are very short, their contribution to total unemployment is negligible. Most of the youth joblessness problem is attributable to a small group of young people who remain out of work a large portion of the time. Inability to find suitable work rather than pathological instability seems to be this group's main problem.

Section 2.1 of the paper presents raw data on labor market flows. Section 2.2 illustrates the long-term nature of "problem" youth unemployment. The role of job shortages and effects of aggregate demand are the subject of the section 2.3. A final section concludes the paper with a discussion of some implications of the findings and directions for future research.

2.1 Characteristics of the Teenage Labor Market

The central difference between the traditional and new views of youth unemployment lies in their conception of turnover. The former emphasizes the infrequency of job finding and the consequent lengthy duration of unemployment, while the latter focuses on the brevity and frequency of unemployment spells. Presentations of both views typically concentrate on flows between unemployment and employment. Less attention is devoted to movements into and out of the labor force. We try to present a fuller picture of the youth labor market by examining in a systematic way movements among all three labor market states (i.e., employment, unemployment, and not in the labor force [NILF]). We extend previous work on the dynamics of the youth labor market by focusing on the differences in behavior between young people who are in and out of school. After presenting the basic data characterizing the dynamics of youth labor markets, we examine the relative importance of transitions into and out of the labor force as well as the duration of completed spells in each of the labor market states.

2.1.1 The Basic Data

The dynamics of the youth labor market are examined in this section using the BLS gross changes data. Individuals included in the Current Population Survey (CPS) are in the sample for four months, then out for eight months, and then in the sample for four months before leaving for good. The data in this study are derived from a special file which matches the March, April, May, and June Surveys taken in 1976. It is possible to follow one rotation group over the entire period and several rotation groups over shorter intervals. From these data it is possible to find the number of individuals who moved, for example, from unemployment to employment during the preceding month. Since there are three possible labor market states, nine monthly flows may be calculated.

We summarize the available information in a 3×3 matrix of transition probabilities and a vector of three stocks. Thus for each of several demographic groups we consider the matrix

$$P = \begin{vmatrix} P_{ee} & P_{eu} & P_{en} \\ P_{ue} & P_{uu} & P_{un} \\ P_{ne} & P_{nu} & P_{nn} \end{vmatrix}, \tag{1}$$

where, for example, P_{eu} represents the proportion of employed workers in a preceding month who are unemployed in the current month. Since a worker must always be in one of the three labor force states, the rows in P sum to 1. Therefore, if any two of the transition probabilities out of a state are known, it is easy to compute the third. In order to calculate aggregate flows between states, we multiply the transition probabilities by appropriate initial stocks. This may be conveniently represented in matrix form as

$$\begin{vmatrix} F_{ee} & F_{eu} & F_{en} \\ F_{ue} & F_{uu} & F_{un} \\ F_{ne} & F_{nu} & F_{nn} \end{vmatrix} = \begin{vmatrix} S_e & O & O \\ O & S_u & O \\ O & O & S_n \end{vmatrix} P, \tag{2}$$

where F_{ij} represents the flow of workers into state j from state i and S_e, S_u, and S_n refer to the stock of workers employed, unemployed, and not in labor force (NILF) respectively.

Since much of the emphasis in this study is on labor force transitions, it will be convenient to define a state L, for labor force, which includes both E and U. It is clear that

$$F_{nL} = F_{ne} + F_{nu}$$

$$F_{Ln} = F_{en} + F_{un}. \tag{3}$$

The transition probabilities may then be represented as

$$P_{nL} = P_{ne} + P_{nu}$$

$$P_{Ln} = \frac{E_{t-1}}{L_{t-1}} P_{en} + \frac{U_{t-1}}{L_{t-1}} P_{un}.$$

(4)

At the outset, it is crucial to acknowledge a major defect of the gross changes data. They are very sensitive to errors in reporting or recording labor force status. While such errors tend to cancel out in estimating stock-based statistics such as the unemployment rate, they cumulate in estimates of labor market flows. Several studies of CPS reinterviews have shown that there is substantial recall and recording error. Indeed, a recent census memorandum concluded that "the results for 1976 and 1977 indicate the gross change rate is at least two to three times as large as the adjusted estimate.... The gross change rate is greatly overstated due to simple response variance."[3] Below we suggest that much of what is called response variance is really a reflection of the arbitrariness of the official unemployment definition rather than recall error.[4] In any event, the estimates we report below using the flows data do characterize persons' actual reported movements in the CPS. It certainly does appear that they may overstate the dynamic character of the labor market. If so, the line of argument developed in section 2.2 is strengthened.

2.1.2 Transition Patterns

In table 2.1 we report average flow rates and transition probabilities for teenagers and mature adults as calculated from the March–April and the April–May CPS. Except for in-school youths it does not appear that the results are seasonally aberrant. For the total of male and female teenagers, the probabilities are consistent with average values for the 1968–76 period.[5]

An important feature of these data is the enormous magnitude of all the flows. For example, the results suggest that about 15% or 645,000 young men withdrew from the labor force within a month. At the same time about 20% of those outside the labor force entered the market.

The differences between persons who are in and out of school are particularly striking. Among young men who were in school, a very large proportion, almost half the unemployed, drop out of the labor force within a month. Slightly more than one-fifth find jobs. Almost one-third of the out-of-school group find jobs, while only 18% withdraw from the labor force. It

Table 2.1
Employment, unemployment, and labor force transitions March–May 1976[a]

Demographic/schooling groups		en	eu	ue	un	nu	ne	nl	ln
M1619	Total								
	P	.105	.042	.272	.307	.074	.129	.203	.147
	F	350.3	147.0	237.3	294.6	253.8	450.5	704.4	644.5
	In school								
	P	.173	.033	.217	.479	.061	.111	.172	.246
	F	241.1	46.0	94.9	209.6	209.1	380.4	589.5	450.5
	Out of school								
	P	.053	.049	.310	.185	.134	.210	.344	.077
	F	109.2	101.0	142.4	85.0	44.7	70.1	114.9	194.0
F1619	Total								
	P	.131	.024	.254	.357	.070	.101	.171	.174
	F	411.2	72.9	185.0	257.2	298.1	438.6	736.6	669.1
	In school								
	P	.209	.023	.163	.515	.057	.090	.147	.272
	F	265.5	29.2	54.3	171.6	201.3	317.8	519.1	437.8
	Out of school								
	P	.080	.024	.333	.218	.105	.131	.236	.104
	F	145.7	43.7	130.7	85.6	96.8	120.8	217.5	231.3

Table 2.1 (continued)

Demographic/schooling groups	en	eu	ue	un	nu	ne	nl	ln
M2559 Total								
P	.009	.010	.323	.081	.053	.082	.135	.013
F	332.3	369.1	685.1	171.8	162.6	251.6	414.2	504.0
W2559 Total								
P	.044	.009	.182	.305	.038	.071	.109	.061
F	1033.8	211.5	293.0	491.1	767.3	1433.7	2201.0	1524.9

Source: Tabulations of the March–April–May–June 1976 CPS Match File. The flows have been adjusted to conform to the stock data. The probabilities are averages of the monthly probabilities for April and May.

a. F indicates flow in thousands; P indicates probability; en indicates employment to not in labor force; eu indicates employment to unemployment, and so forth.

is noteworthy that in the out-of-school group the job-finding probabilities of persons who are out of the labor force are quite close to those of the unemployed. While 32% of unemployed young men accept employment within a month, almost 22% of those outside the labor force find a job. Since the probability of exit from unemployment declines quite sharply with duration, it appears that persons outside the labor force have as much chance of moving into employment as do persons unemployed for a significant period. As one would expect, the labor force distinction appears to be much more meaningful in the case of in-school youths; only 11.1% of the teenagers 16–19 find jobs within a month.

The differences between male and female transition probabilities are quite small. The largest difference is that young women appear to be much less likely to reenter the labor force than young men. When they leave employment they are also more likely to withdraw from the labor force rather than become unemployed. Not surprisingly, there are large differences between youth and adult transition probabilities. While the differences are much less pronounced for the out-of-school group, young people appear to be much more likely to enter and withdraw from the labor force. For example, 14.7% of male teenagers withdraw from the labor force each month compared to 1.3% of mature men. Similarly, 20.3% of teenagers outside enter the labor force contrasted with 13.5% for adults.

It is clear from table 2.1 that observed changes in the participation and unemployment of young people reflect a net of large gross movements into and out of the labor force. The importance of labor force entrance and exit in explaining youth employment and unemployment is documented in table 2.2. The data in line 1 illustrate the importance of flows from outside the labor force in changes in employment. Between 60 and 70% of all entrances into employment occur from outside the labor force. The second line indicates that most teenagers who leave employment leave the labor force rather than becoming unemployed. Among out-of-school women, this pattern is particularly pronounced: over 80% of those leaving employment withdraw from the labor force. Lines 3 and 4 indicate that labor force transitions are almost as important in determining flows into and out of unemployment. A large fraction of unemployment spells appear to begin and end outside the labor force.

These results indicate the artificiality of the not-in-labor-force unemployment distinction for young people. Given the frequency of movements between unemployment and not-in-labor-force, it is difficult to distinguish between these two states. Most of the newly employed did not search long enough to be recorded as unemployed. The evidence suggests the possi-

Table 2.2
Relative flows into and out of not-in-labor-force, March–May 1976 by demographic schooling groups

Flow category	Males 16–19			Females 16–19			Males 25–59	Females 25–59
	Total	In school	Out of school	Total	In school	Out of school		
1. Proportion of flows into employment from NILF $(F_{ne}/(F_{ne} + F_{ue}))$	.655	.800	.330	.703	.854	.480	.269	.830
2. Proportion of flows out of employment into NILF $(F_{en}/(F_{en} + F_{eu}))$	.714	.840	.520	.845	.901	.769	.474	.830
3. Proportion of flows out of unemployment into NILF $(F_{un}/(F_{un} + F_{ue}))$	.530	.688	.374	.584	.760	.396	.200	.626
4. Proportion of flows into unemployment from NILF $(F_{nu}/(F_{nu} + F_{ue}))$	.633	.820	.307	.804	.873	.689	.306	.784
5. Proportion of flows into labor force that result in unemployment $(F_{nu}/(F_{ne} + F_{nu}))$	.635	.645	.610	.591	.612	.555	.607	.651

Source: See table 2.1.

bility that for many teenagers, job search is a passive process in which the main activity is waiting for a job opportunity to be presented. This conclusion is especially true of enrolled young people. Their extremely high withdrawal rate (80%) suggests that their job search is extremely casual. The ease with which most young people enter the labor force, documented in line 5 of the table, supports this view. While only about one-third of the unemployed find a job within a month, almost two-thirds of labor force entrants are successful within a month. This strongly suggests that many people only enter the labor force when a job is presented.

The patterns of entrance suggest that the availability of jobs is an important element in determining movements into and out of the labor force. At the same time, the evidence indicating that most teenagers end spells of employment by withdrawing from the labor force provides some indication that teenage unemployment arises from voluntary turnover. Among unemployed teenagers, the quitting rate is about half the job loss rate. However, it seems reasonable to conjecture that a large proportion of those who withdraw from the labor force following employment are quitters. If, for example, it is assumed that 80% of this group is made up of quitters, it follows that about two-thirds of teenage employment spells end in quitting. The importance of considering labor force transitions is well illustrated by this calculation. Even if movements out of the labor force are in large part spurious, they nonetheless distort unemployment statistics.

2.1.3. Spell Durations

The results on flows and rates of transition in tables 2.1 and 2.2 underscore the dynamic character of the youth labor market. The tremendous volatility in the market behavior of young persons may also be conveyed by examining the mean duration of *completed spells* in each of the states. It should be emphasized that the estimates presented below differ from the mean duration of those *currently* in each state. As Kaitz (1970) has shown, the former concept will yield lower estimates than the latter. Table 2.3 presents estimates of mean duration of completed spells in each state. The brevity of mean durations for most groups is quite striking. Male teenagers, for example, have an average duration of a spell of employment of only about 6.5 months.

Out-of-school young people have longer durations in employment, about nine months, compared to about four months for enrolled teenagers. Since persons can remain employed but change jobs, these figures over-

Table 2.3
Labor market durations[a]

Demographic/schooling groups	Duration category (mean duration in months)			
	D_e	D_{job}	D_n	D_u
M 16–19				
Total	6.80	3.00	4.93	1.73
In school	4.85	2.13	5.81	1.44
Out of school	9.80	4.31	2.91	2.02
F 16–19				
Total	6.45	2.84	5.85	1.64
In school	4.31	1.90	6.80	1.47
Out of school	9.62	4.23	4.24	1.81
M 25–29	52.6	24.1	7.41	2.48
F 25–29	19.9	8.7	9.17	2.05

a. D indicates mean duration; e, n, u represent employment, not-in-labor-force, and unemployment. Mean duration for these states is defined as the reciprocal of the probability of leaving the state. D is the duration in a job and is equal to $D_e(1 - d)$, where d is the fraction of job changes with no unemployment. The values of d used here are the same for men and women. Estimates of d are from Bancroft and Garfinkle, "Job Mobility in 1961," *Monthly Labor Review*, vol. 86 (August 1973), pp. 897–906.

state the expected duration of a job. The only available evidence, from a 1961 BLS survey, suggests that about 54% of teenage job changes occur without intervening nonemployment. Adjusting for this flow yields the estimates of the mean duration of jobs shown in column 2. Young people do not appear to hold jobs for very long. The mean duration of a job for all male teenagers was three months. Even for out-of-school men the average job lasted a little over four months. In interpreting these figures, several factors should be recognized. First, the figures are based on exit probabilities calculated from March–April and April–May transitions. Hence they are unaffected by brief summer jobs. Moreover, the estimates may overstate the mean duration of jobs and employment because of the sampling interval. Individuals who are unemployed for less than a month may never appear as unemployed in the survey, so their employment may incorrectly appear unbroken. Similarly, very brief employment spells which would bring down the average may never be recorded. Second, spurious flows caused by reporting error as discussed above lead to an offsetting downward bias in all of the estimates in table 2.3

Columns 3 and 4 illustrate the brevity of unemployment and out-of-the-labor-force spells. Perhaps the most surprising result is the brevity of spells outside the labor force for out-of-school youths. The average NILF spell for this group lasts three months, which is only slightly longer than the average length spell of the unemployed. This is further evidence that these states are functionally almost indistinguishable. There appear to be relatively small differences between men and women, with somewhat more persistence in withdrawal among women. A striking feature of the results is that the mean duration of unemployment is not much different for teenagers and adults. This is in large part because of the high rate of labor force withdrawal among young people.[6]

2.1.4 Seasonal Variation in Labor Market Flows

Perhaps the most striking evidence of the success of the youth labor market in meeting the needs of most young people comes from evidence on seasonal fluctuations. In table 2.4 we examine the changes over the year in various key labor market rates for males 16–19. Seasonal patterns do not vary much among youth groups, and the male 16–19 group is fairly typical. The first line provides the unemployment rate for the summer months and the remainder of the year. No significant increase in the unemployment rate occurs during the summer months. Indeed, the rates in May, July, August, and September are actually lower than the rate over the rest of the year. Of course, the number of unemployed persons rises substantially because as the second row shows, the participation rate soars. The participation rate in July is amost 40% more than its annual average. As line 3 indicates, a parallel rise in the proportion employed also takes place. Not surprisingly, the vast majority of this increase in employment is due to summer-only workers. In the fourth line of the table, we present the proportion of the population who enter the labor force each month. In June, almost 21% of the male teenage population enters the labor force. This figure represents close to 50% of the NILF category. Another 12% of the population enters the labor force in July. Of course, a certain amount of labor force entrance occurs in all months, averaging about 7% of the population. Contrasting this figure with the entry rates for May, June, and July, one finds that during the summer months about an extra 20% of the population enter the labor force. Note that this is a substantial underestimate of the extent of the increase in youths' labor supply, since many teenagers shift from desiring part-time to seeking full-time work during the summer months. Comparisons of the seasonality in teenage labor market behavior with the patterns observed for other demo-

Table 2.4
Seasonal variation in labor market stocks and flows for males 16–19, 1968–76

Stock-flow category	Average for							
	May	June	July	August	September	Rest of year	Annual
1. Unemployment rate	.129	.182	.152	.122	.149	.160	.155
2. Participation rate	.541	.704	.758	.701	.541	.527	.578
3. Employment ratio	.471	.575	.643	.615	.459	.442	.488
4. Labor force inflow as a percent of the population	.086	.213	.117	.060	.057	.073	.087
5. Labor force outflow as a percent of the population	.077	.054	.067	.118	.217	.071	.086
6. Probability of successful labor force entry (P_{ns})	.711	.655	.670	.676	.630	.622	.641
7. Unemployment inflow as percent of population	.025	.073	.039	.019	.021	.028	.031
8. Probability of finding a job if unemployed (P_{ue})	.269	.332	.386	.312	.280	.249	.277

Source: Unpublished tabulations by the Bureau of Labor Statistics, adjusted by the Urban Institute as described in J. E. Vanski, "Recession and the Employment of Demographic Groups: Adjustments to Gross Change Data," in C. C. Holt et al., *Labor Markets, Inflation, and Manpower Policies*, Final Report to the Department of Labor (Washington, D.C.: The Urban Institute, May 1975).

graphic groups leads us to conclude that about three-quarters of summer entrances are due to school ending rather than to fluctuations in employment opportunities.

Not surprisingly, the rates of labor force entrance in June and July are mirrored by high rates of labor force exit in August and September. During these months, about 33% of the teenage population exits from the labor force. Since the rate of withdrawal in a typical month is about 7%, the extra labor force exits during August and September almost exactly offset the extra entrances in the early summer months. Thus both the flow and the stock data suggest that employment only during the summer months characterizes the behavior of about 20% of male teenagers.

The labor market appears to adapt very well to the surge in those seeking employment. In June, when the inflow is at its peak, about two-thirds of labor force entrants find jobs. This figure is actually greater by about 5% than the rate of successful entry during the remainder of the year. Those who do become unemployed during the summer months fare much better than the unemployed in other months, since the job finding rate P_{ue} in May, June, and July far exceeds the rate in the nonsummer months. The fact that these flow rates are significantly higher during the summer months suggests that the additional members of the labor force may have an unemployment rate much lower than that of full-year workers. Clearly, the average unemployment rate over the summer months is lower than during the rest of the year. This suggests that the summer influx of teenagers actually reduces the average annual unemployment rate, since the additional workers appear to fare substantially better both as labor force entrants and as unemployed job seekers than do other teenagers. This quite striking fact bears further comment.

Undoubtedly, public employment and training policy affects the behavior of labor market flows during the summer months. Over the first six years of the period covered in table 2.4 (1968–73), the federal government provided about 600,000 summer jobs through the Neighborhood Youth Corps. The NYC was eliminated with the enactment of CETA in 1973, but summer jobs remain a component of the decentralized employment and training system. In 1976, for example, just over 820,000 jobs were provided in the CETA summer program. The great majority of participants were classified as economically disadvantaged (95.9%), drawn from the unemployed or from outside the labor force (98.7%), and were full-time students (87.8%).

A comparison of the size of the federal summer program with the average flow into the labor force reveals the relative importance of the summer jobs program. From 1968 to 1976, an average of 600,000 summer jobs were provided through NYC and CETA. The data in table 2.4 suggest that about 3 million teenagers left school and entered the labor market each summer. Given the estimated probability of entering with a job (about .6 of average), on the order of 1.2 million teenagers would have remained without employment if no adjustments had been made. Thus about 50% of this group were moved into employment through the federal jobs program. This calculation is likely to overstate, perhaps substantially, the contribution of public policy. We have assumed that the federal jobs constitute net job creation. It is likely however, that the federal program funds some jobs which would have existed anyway. This is more likely to be the case under CETA, where the program largely is run through state and local government units. Unfortunately, estimates of the net jobs created under the summer programs are not available.[7]

The ability of the labor market to deal with the large inflow of workers in the summer should lead one to question demographic explanations of recent increases in youth unemployment. As table 2.4 shows, the labor market is able to deal with a threefold increase in the proportion of the population newly seeking work without an appreciable increase in an individual's difficulty in finding employment. It is improbable that the same labor market should be incapable of adapting to the easily foreseen, persistent, and much smaller increase in the labor force due to demographic shifts. Indeed, the adjustment should be much smoother because in the case of demographic shifts the time frame is much longer and there is no need to create very temporary jobs. While adaptations such as replacing vacationing workers and work scheduling are less feasible in this case, the longer run should permit much greater flexibility.

Taken together, the results in this section convey a picture of an enormously dynamic labor market. It is apparent that most teenagers move easily between labor market states. More than half of all job changes occur without intervening unemployment. Most labor force entrants find jobs without ever being measured as unemployed and incidents of unemployment are typically quite brief. There appears to be no evidence of a serious problem for most teenagers. Yet we did observe in March of 1976 that almost one-fifth of all young people who wanted jobs did not have them, and that an equal number were out of school and jobless, but had chosen not to search. The key question then is whether these average probabilities, which suggest that movement in all directions is quite easy, are relevant to a large part of nonemployment. The next section offers a negative answer to this question.

2.2 The Experience of the Nonemployed

There are at least three reasons why the picture of the labor market presented in the preceding section may be a misleading guide to the experience of the unemployed population at a given time. First, even if most unemployment spells are short, most unemployment may be contained in long spells. To see this, consider the following example. Suppose that each week twenty spells of unemployment begin lasting one week, and one begins with a duration of twenty weeks. This mean duration of a completed spell of unemployment would be 1.05 weeks, but half of all unemployment would be accounted for by spells lasting twenty weeks. Equivalently, in a steady state, the expectation of the length of time until a job is found among all those unemployed at any instant would be 9.5 weeks. Sole focus on the mean duration of a completed spell could clearly be quite misleading.

Second, as we have already emphasized, there is reason to doubt the salience of the distinction between unemployment and not-in-the-labor-force for young people. Unemployment durations appear to be short in large part because of high rates of labor force withdrawal. The brevity of many spells outside the labor force suggests that many of those who withdraw are in fact sensitive to labor market conditions. Indeed, it appears that our official statistics frequently record two brief spells of unemployment, broken by a period outside the labor force, when a single spell of joblessness would be more appropriate.

The third reason why it is necessary to go beyond the average transition probabilities is the need to study the incidence of multiple spells. As Richard Layard has emphasized, one's view about the welfare consequences of youth nonemployment should depend on its concentration.[8] If the burden is quite evenly dispersed, individuals are unlikely to suffer greatly and the economy may even benefit from a better matching between workers and jobs. On the other hand, if the distribution of unemployment is very uneven, the welfare cost to individuals is likely to be greater, and the social benefit much more dubious.

In this section we shall try to deal with these issues by studying the distributions of unemployment and nonemployment weeks. Basically, we seek to answer two questions. First, how long can we expect the teenagers who are unemployed at a given time to wait before entering employment? Second, how much unemployment and nonemployment can they expect to suffer within the year? It is crucial to realize that we seek to answer these two questions for all those *unemployed at a given time* rather then all those who flow into unemployment over some interval. This procedure gives more weight to long spells than to short ones, since persons suffering lengthy spells are more likely to appear in the sample at a given time. In assessing the nature of the unemployment problem, one wants to study the unemployed population, not the experience of persons flowing into unemployment. This key point is illustrated by the numerical example above in which much of unemployment was due to long spells even though the vast majority of spells were short.

2.2.1 How Long Does It Take to Find a Job?

In table 2.5 we present various estimates of how long it takes young people to find jobs. The first row displays the mean duration of completed unemployment spells. The durations of unemployment, as we have already noted, are fairly short. We have also pointed out that labor force withdrawal makes this figure a very misleading indicator of the ease of job finding. In line 2 we attempt to answer the more meaningful question of how long the unemployed must wait until a job is found. The calculation recognizes the possibility of labor force withdrawal and the attendant decline in the probability of finding a job. The possibility of subsequent labor force reentrance into unemployment is also taken into account. The average unemployed male teenager in March of 1976 could expect to wait 5.4 more months before finding a job. Line 3 notes that the average male 16–19 had been unemployed for 2.9 months. Hence the average unemployed person was in the midst of a spell of over eight months of joblessness. The notion that most of those currently unemployed can and will find jobs quickly is simply false. Most are in the midst of lengthy spells without work.

Even the large estimates above may understate the difficulty of movement into jobs. We have argued that many persons who are out of the labor force behave in ways which are functionally equivalent to the unemployed. In line 5 we report the expected length of time until a job is found for currently nonemployed young people. Doubling this figure yields the mean total duration of joblessness for the nonemployed. The results indicate that it takes most persons a long time to find a job. The average nonemployed young man who is not in school will have been out of work for about 7.5 months before returning to employment. The corresponding figures for women are even larger, reflecting greater persistence of labor force withdrawal. All of the estimates in table 2.5 are conservative since they do not take account of the fact that continuation probabilities decline with duration.

Table 2.5
Alternative measures of the duration of joblessness

Duration category	Demographic groups						
	Males 16–19			Females 16–19			Males 25–29
	Total	In school	Out of school	Total	In school	Out of school	
1. Mean duration of unemployment (months): $1/(P_{ue} + P_{un})$	1.7	1.4	2.0	1.6	1.5	1.8	2.5
2. Expected time until next employment spell for those currently unemployed[a] (months)	5.4	7.2	3.0	6.6	9.4	4.2	4.3
3. Average months of unemployment to date	2.9	2.4	3.4	2.4	2.0	2.7	5.3
4. Expected time between beginning of current spell of unemployment and next spell of employment for those currently unemployed[b]	8.3	9.6	6.4	9.0	11.4	6.9	9.6
5. Mean duration of nonemployment (months): $\left(\dfrac{U+N}{UP_{ue}+NP_{ne}}\right)$	6.4	8.1	3.7	8.2	10.4	5.2	5.5
6. Expected total weeks of nonemployment for those currently nonemployed[c]	—	—	7.5	—	—	10.4	11.1

Source: The probabilities underlying the calculations are taken from tables 2.1 and 2.2.
a. This is equal to $(D_u + P_{ex}D_n)/[1 - P_{ex}(1 - P_{ns})]$ where D_u and D_n are durations in unemployment and nonemployment, P_{ex} is the fraction of unemployment spells that end in labor force withdrawal, and P_{ns} is the probability of entering the labor force with a job.
b. Line 4 is line 2 plus line 3.
c. Line 6 is line 5 multiplied by 2; this concept is only meaningful for the out of school group.

2.2.2 How Extensive Is Unemployment?

While the evidence suggests that joblessness is frequently prolonged, we have not yet considered multiple spells. The annual March Work Experience Survey asks all civilian noninstitutional respondents in the CPS to describe their work and unemployment experience in the preceding year. We have used the Work Experience data to calculate two measures of joblessness. The first is the official definition of unemployment as weeks looking for work or on layoff. This conventional definition is compared with a second concept in which the number of weeks spent searching are combined with weeks outside the labor force for those who list "unable to find work" or "looking for work" as the principal reason for less than a full year of work. This concept is referred to as "nonemployment." It is important to note that nonemployment excludes weeks out of the labor force for those citing illness, family responsibilities, or "other" as the principal reason for part-year work. For these individuals, nonemployment is defined as weeks of unemployment. In both calculations, persons who did not participate in the labor force are excluded from the sample.

The distribution of unemployment and nonemployment for selected demographic groups is shown in table 2.6. Of the approximately 6 million young people with labor force experience, about 1.7 million experience unemployment averaging about three months during the year. The average number of weeks is almost 50% greater for the out-of-school group. While the number of persons experiencing nonemployment is not different from the number with unemployment in this sample, weeks of joblessness are significantly greater when time out of the labor force is included. Out-of-school youths average six months of nonemployment per person becoming nonemployed.

In line 6 of the table we examine the experience of the unemployed population at a given time by focusing on the distribution of unemployment and nonemployment weeks. Because unemployment weeks are captured randomly by the survey, the statements that "x percent of unemployment weeks are suffered by persons with y weeks of unemployment during the year," and "x percent of the currently unemployed will experience y weeks of unemployment during the year" are equivalent. Both the unemployment and nonemployment distributions exhibit substantial concentration, with the preponderance of unemployment attributable to persons out of work more than half the year. Among out-of-school male teenagers, 54% of unemployment and 76% of nonemployment were experienced by persons out of work more than six months. Among young black men who were not enrolled in school, 65.0% of nonemployment was accounted for

Table 2.6
The concentration of unemployment and nonemployment for teenagers, 1974

Note on the table body: for row 6, each demographic subgroup is split into two sub-columns, U (unemployment) and NE (nonemployment). For rows 1–5 a single value applies to each subgroup; it is shown below in the subgroup's U column.

	Males / Total / U	Males / Total / NE	Males / Out of school / U	Males / Out of school / NE	Females / Total / U	Females / Total / NE	Females / Out of school / U	Females / Out of school / NE	Nonwhite Males / Out of school / U	Nonwhite Males / Out of school / NE	Nonwhite Females / Out of school / U	Nonwhite Females / Out of school / NE
1. Total with labor force experience (millions)	5.99		2.82		5.27		2.44		.31		.30	
2. Total with unemployment (millions)	1.71		.91		1.56		.85		.14		.17	
3. Average weeks of unemployment per person with unemployment	12.7		18.6		10.4		14.9		20.1		16.4	
4. Total with nonemployment (millions)	1.71		.91		1.56		.85		.14		.17	
5. Average weeks of nonemployment per person with nonemployment	16.2		25.2		15.4		24.1		29.0		30.3	
6. Distribution of individuals and weeks by duration	U	NE	U	NE	U	NE	U	NE	U	NE	U	NE
1–4 weeks % of labor force	11.2	10.3	6.2	4.2	14.4	12.6	10.9	6.9	7.5	4.6	17.1	9.0
% of total weeks	6.2	4.4	2.1	1.0	9.4	5.5	4.2	1.6	1.6	.7	3.7	1.0
5–14 weeks % of labor force	9.0	7.9	9.7	7.3	8.3	7.2	9.9	7.7	16.5	11.3	17.5	8.0
% of total weeks	24.8	17.0	16.0	9.0	26.8	15.8	19.1	9.1	17.8	8.5	18.8	4.6
15–26 weeks % of labor force	4.1	2.8	8.1	5.3	4.0	2.4	8.2	4.8	6.4	2.2	9.2	4.3
% of total weeks	23.8	12.7	28.2	13.7	27.1	11.0	33.2	12.0	14.6	3.4	20.8	5.3
40+ weeks % of labor force	1.9	4.2	3.6	8.4	1.2	4.9	2.4	10.5	7.5	18.8	7.5	28.2
% of total weeks	24.0	41.3	27.6	47.4	17.1	49.4	21.5	57.2	37.3	65.0	37.0	75.1

by those out of work more than forty weeks during the year. As one would expect from these figures, individuals with brief, infrequent unemployment experience contribute only negligibly to overall unemployment. For example, persons out of work less than three months accounted for only 21% of nonemployment among young men who were out of school. While many teenagers experience short periods of unemployment in moving between jobs, these are of little consequence in explaining total weeks of nonemployment.

The statistics in tables 2.5 and 2.6 tell a consistent story. Youth unemployment is properly understood in terms of a fundamental failure of the labor market to meet the needs of some workers. A small portion of the population finds itself chronically unable to locate satisfactory work. They do not have the same ease of transition which characterizes the remainder of the population. Rather, they wait long periods between jobs. Moreover, they experience frequent unemployment because of the frequency with which they leave employment. Whether the source of the problem is a shortage of jobs or that the "hard core" group is unemployable can never be resolved conclusively. Some aspects of the problem are considered in section 2.3.

2.2.3 Racial Differences in Nonemployment Experience

The wide disparity between the unemployment rates of white and nonwhite teenagers has been the subject of considerable academic and public discussion. Research designed to explain racial unemployment differentials has emphasized differences in turnover and minimized the importance of long term joblessness. Writing in 1974, Barrett and Morgenstern stated this view quite clearly: "The high unemployment rates of blacks and young people are attributable almost entirely to their higher turnover—that is, the frequency with which they become unemployed. The major unemployment problem among black Americans is not chronic long-duration unemployment, but frequent job changes and unemployed search. High turnover rates among young people are consistent with a search theoretic model in which frequent flows into unemployment represent a potentially efficient sampling of the job market."[9]

The importance of long-term unemployment, evident in tables 2.5 and 2.6, suggests the need to reexamine explanations of racial differences which rely on turnover and search associated with frequent job changes. Evidence on racial differences in transition probabilities and time to find a job is presented in table 2.7 for male and female teenagers not in school. A

Table 2.7
Differences in unemployment experience for out-of-school teenagers by race,
March–May 1976[a]

Category	Demographic groups			
	Whites		Nonwhites	
	Men 16–19	Women 16–19	Men 16–19	Women 16–19
1. Transition probabilities				
P_{en}	.052	.078	.059	.097
P_{eu}	.042	.020	.129	.067
P_{ue}	.369	.377	.119	.163
P_{un}	.184	.225	.187	.193
P_{nu}	.118	.107	.194	.100
P_{ne}	.240	.153	.102	.048
2. Time to find a job				
(a) Mean duration of unemployment (months)	1.8	1.7	3.3	2.8
(b) Expected months until next job (for the currently unemployed)	3.1	3.7	8.9	10.2
(c) Average months of unemployment to date	3.2	2.7	4.0	3.0
(d) Expected months of nonemployment from beginning of current spell of unemployment until next job	6.3	6.4	12.9	13.2

a. For definitions of the concepts in lines 2–5, see the note in table 2.5. The probabilities are taken from matched CPS files for March–April–May–June 1976. Additional details are contained in the note to table 2.1.

comparison of transition probabilities reveals three major differences between whites and nonwhites. Nonwhite teenagers are three times as likely
to lose or quit their jobs and become unemployed as their white counterparts. Among young men, for example, the probability of leaving employment and entering unemployment is .042 for whites, while the comparable
rate for nonwhites is .129. These differences may reflect a higher propensity of nonwhites to quit jobs, but they are also consistent with the view
that nonwhites are more subject to layoff because of less seniority and
because of discrimination. There are much smaller differences in the probability of employed teenagers leaving the labor force. Indeed, the racial
differences in P_{en} among young men are negligible.

One of the most striking differences in transition patterns is found in the
probabilities of entering employment from unemployment and from outside the labor force. Young white men are three times as likely to find
employment if unemployed than their nonwhite counterparts. Since the
probability of dropping out of the labor force is identical for white and
nonwhite teenage men, nonwhites are much more likely to remain unemployed. Similar patterns are found for young women, where unemployed
whites are more than twice as likely to find work.

The apparent difficulty nonwhite teenagers have in finding work if
unemployed is mirrored in the experience of those classified as outside the
labor force. Using teenage women as an example, the probability of entering the labor force is .36 for whites and .15 for nonwhites. The probability
of successful labor force entry (i.e., entering with a job) given by

$$P_{ns} = \frac{P_{ne}}{P_{ne} + P_{nu}} \tag{5}$$

is two-thirds for whites but only one-third for nonwhites. Not only do
young nonwhites experience more difficulty finding work if unemployed,
they are much more likely to become unemployed upon entering the labor
force. These calculations suggest that racial differences in unemployment
rates are due largely to differences in the probability of entering employment. While differences in layoffs and quittings are important, the dominant explanation is found in the difficulty nonwhites have in locating work.

The implications of job-finding difficulty are examined in line 2 of table
2.7, which presents estimates of time needed to find a job for those
currently unemployed. The differences between whites and nonwhites are
quite striking. On average, unemployed white teenagers could expect to
wait about three (men) or four (women) months before finding work, while
nonwhites faced nine to ten months of further joblessness. Since nonwhites

had already accumulated four months of unemployment, the data reveal that unemployed nonwhite teenagers were in the midst of very long spells without work. These calculations are undoubtedly influenced by the depressed state of the labor market in the spring of 1976. Yet even considerably reducing these estimates to account for the cycle would be unlikely to change the basic conclusion. It appears that nonwhite teenagers have much more difficulty finding work than their white counterparts, and that even when they find it, they are much more likely to be fired, laid off, or quit. As a result they spend extended periods out of work.

2.2.4 Employment Exit and Extensive Unemployment

Many observers regard the brevity of employment spells emphasized in section 2.1 as the root cause of the youth nonemployment problem. The results here call that interpretation into question. For most young people, frequent job change appears to be possible without extensive unemployment. The median length of unemployment spells is probably about three weeks. Half of all job changes occur without any unemployment at all. A person who held five jobs during the year and was unemployed during each change for the median length of time would suffer only twelve weeks of unemployment during the year. Persons with this little unemployment contribute less than one-fourth of all youth unemployment. It is therefore clear that without serious difficulty in job-finding even extreme employment instability could not account for observed patterns of concentrated joblessness.

A similar conclusion is obtained by examining in more detail the experience of young people reporting extensive joblessness. Among persons with over twenty-six weeks of nonemployment, who accounted for 76% of joblessness, the average number of unemployment spells was less than two. In many cases, these spells were separated by periods outside the labor force rather than by jobs. Hence this is an overstatement of the average number of employment spells during the year. Even neglecting this correction the average spell length of the extensively nonemployed appears to last close to five months.[10] Thus, for this group, with whom the real problem lies, the difficulty is prolonged unemployment rather than frequent joblessness.

Previous analyses of unemployment dynamics have emphasized the fact that the average flow into unemployment differs much more among demographic groups than does the average duration of unemployment. This has led them to conclude that the problem of high unemployment groups (e.g., teenagers) is excessive turnover, not difficulty in finding jobs. The results in this section show that this type of analysis can be very misleading. Group averages conceal wide variations. The vast majority of unemployment is experienced by a small minority of the population. Some groups are disproportionately represented in the "hardcore" population. The error is in tracing group differences to general turnover, rather than differences in the incidence of "hardcore" problems.

Nothing in the preceding paragraphs is inconsistent with the common observation that differences in demographic group unemployment rates are due largely to differences in the frequency of spells rather than their duration. The point here is that for the problem population it is very difficult to locate a suitable job. The demographic observation simply addresses the incidence of "problem" people in different subgroups of the population. Once it is recognized that nonemployment is largely a matter of a small minority of all demographic groups with serious job-finding problems, the fallacy of inferring the nature of individual unemployment problem from comparisons of demographic averages becomes clear.

2.3 Cyclical Variations in Employment

The cyclical behavior of youth employment and unemployment can shed light on the nature of the nonemployment problem. If extensive joblessness occurs only because some young people are essentially unemployable, one would expect changes in aggregate demand to have small effects. On the other hand, a finding that changes in aggregate demand had a large impact on young people would imply that at least some unemployment was due to a shortage of attractive opportunities. Of course, a finding that aggregate demand has a potent effect on the youth labor market need not imply the desirability of expansionary macroeconomic policy, which has other perhaps undesirable consequences.

2.3.1 Employment, Unemployment, and Participation

The cyclical sensitivity of unemployment is the reflection of two quite different phenomena. Unemployment can increase either because fewer jobs are available or because more workers decide to seek the available jobs. These two sources of unemployment obviously have quite different welfare implications. While the former is almost certainly indicative of a worsening of labor market performance, the latter may reflect an improvement in conditions. Focusing only on unemployment rates is thus very likely to be misleading. Moreover, the results in section 2.1 suggest that the NILF-unemployed distinction is quite arbitrary. These considerations indicate the importance of examining the cyclical behavior of employment, unemployment, and participation.

These three measures summarize the labor market experience of a given demographic group. They are related by the following identity:

$$\left(\frac{E}{N}\right)_i = \left(\frac{E}{L}\right)_i\left(\frac{L}{N}\right)_i, \tag{6}$$

where E is employment, N is population, L is labor force, and i indexes demographic groups. Taking logs and differentiating yields

$$d\ln\left(\frac{E}{N}\right)_i = d\ln\left(\frac{E}{L}\right)_i + d\ln\left(\frac{L}{N}\right)_i. \tag{7}$$

Thus changes in the employment ratio may be decomposed into changes in employment and participation rates. Since persons in the labor force are either employed or unemployed it is clear that

$$d\ln\left(\frac{E}{N}\right)_i = d\ln(1 - UR)_i + d\ln\left(\frac{L}{N}\right)_i, \tag{8}$$

where UR is the unemployment rate. This decomposition provides the basis for our estimates of the effects of overall economic performance on youth employment.

2.3.2 A Simple Model

The cyclical responsiveness of youth employment is estimated using a quite simple model. For each group we postulate that the unemployment rate and participation rate are functions of aggregate demand, seasonal factors, and time. The time trends are included to reflect the impact of slowly changing social trends and other gradually moving variables omitted from the equation. Seasonal movements are captured with monthly dummies. The basic equations to be estimated are

$$\ln(PR)_{it} = \beta_0 + \sum_{j=0}^{8} \beta_{t-j}\, UPRIME_{t-j} + \sum_{k=1}^{11} \theta_k S_k$$
$$+ \delta_1 T + \delta_2 T67 + v_{it}, \tag{9}$$

$$UR_{it} = \alpha_0 + \sum_{j=0}^{8} \alpha_{t-j}\, UPRIME_{t-j} + \sum_{k=1}^{11} \gamma_k S_k$$
$$+ \phi_1 T + \phi_2 T67 + u_{it}, \tag{10}$$

where PR is the participation rate, $UPRIME$ is the unemployment rate of men 35–44, T is the time trend, $T67$ is a second time trend, which begins in 1967, and S_i are monthly dummies.

The specification of (9) is traditional in analyses of participation.[11] The prime-age male unemployment rate is assumed to measure variation in job opportunities and the ease of job finding. Since workers may respond to changes in the availability of jobs with a delay, lagged unemployment is also included in the equation. While equations of this sort have not been extensively used in studying the cyclical behavior of group unemployment rates, they are justified by essentially the same arguments.

The interpretation of the coefficients of the model is straightforward. For example, the cyclical responsiveness of the participation rate of the ith group is measured by $\gamma_{PR}^i = \sum \beta_{t-j}$. A value of -1.0 implies that a 1 percentage point decrease in $UPRIME$ (e.g., from 0.6 to 0.5) produces a 1% increase in the participation rate of the ith group (e.g., .430 to .434). Equations (9) and (10) have been estimated using both annual and monthly data for the period (1948–77) for various demographic groups. The identity (6) along with the properties of ordinary least squares insures that the relationship between the employment ratio, aggregate demand and time is given by

$$\ln(EN)_{it} = \beta_0 - \alpha_0 + \sum (\beta_{t-j} - \alpha_{t-j}) UPRIME_{t-j}$$

$$+ \sum_{k=1}^{11} (\theta_k - \gamma_k) S_k \tag{11}$$

$$+ (\delta_1 - \phi_1)t + (\delta_2 - \phi_2) T67 + e_i.$$

It follows immediately that the equations presented here can be used to decompose cyclical movements in the employment ratio into unemployment and participation components since

$$\gamma_{EN}^i = \gamma_{PR}^i - \gamma_{UR}^i. \tag{12}$$

In order to insure that this identity is exactly satisfied we have estimated all the equations using ordinary least squares without correcting for serial correlation. The results for individual equations, however, are not sensitive to this choice. The estimated equations are shown in table 2.8.

The principal conclusion that emerges is the tremendous responsiveness of youth employment to aggregate demand. For men 16–19, each one-point decrease in the prime-age male unemployment rate increases the employed proportion of the population by about 4.5%. About two-thirds of the response comes through unemployment, with the remainder due to

Table 2.8
Cyclical behavior of unemployment, participation, and employment by teenage demographic groups (standard errors in parentheses)

Demographic group/ dependent variable	Independent variables				R^2	SEE	DW
	CONS	UPRIME	T (12×10^2)	T67			
1. Men 16–19: total							
Unemployment rate	.02 (.005)	2.77 (.10)	.35 (.02)	−.15 (.06)	.84	.018	.85
Participation rate	−.47 (.01)	−1.87 (.19)	−1.11 (.04)	2.82 (.11)	.95	.035	.73
Employment ratio	−.50 (.01)	−4.64 (.20)	−1.45 (.046)	2.98 (.12)	.95	.037	.72
2. Men 16–19: nonwhite							
Unemployment rate	−.05 (.03)	4.29 (.36)	1.14 (.12)	−.21 (.23)	.69	.051	1.32
Participation rate	−.35 (.03)	−1.99 (.45)	−2.12 (.14)	.84 (.28)	.90	.064	1.13
Employment ratio	−.30 (.04)	−6.29 (.59)	−3.26 (.19)	1.05 (.37)	.87	.085	1.27

Table 2.8 (continued)

Demographic group/ dependent variable	Independent variables				R^2	SEE	DW
	CONS	UPRIME	T (12×10^2)	T67			
3. Women 16–19: total							
Unemployment rate	−.01 (.007)	1.78 (.11)	.52 (.03)	−.36 (.07)	.82	.021	.94
Participation rate	−.83 (.01)	−2.29 (.22)	−.44 (.05)	3.48 (.12)	.93	.039	.69
Employment ratio	−.81 (.01)	−4.07 (.24)	−.96 (.06)	3.84 (.14)	.89	.045	.60
4. Women 16–19: nonwhite							
Employment rate	−.04 (.04)	3.45 (.49)	1.58 (.16)	−.99 (.31)	.58	.070	1.44
Participation rate	−1.11 (.05)	−2.96 (.74)	−.22 (.24)	1.02 (.46)	.75	.105	.82
Employment ratio	−1.07 (.07)	−6.41 (.92)	−1.80 (.29)	2.00 (.58)	.65	.131	.93

a. The coefficient on UPRIME is the sum of the coefficients obtained from a nine-month Almon lag (first degree, far restriction).

increases in participation. For women 16–19, the cyclical responsiveness estimates are comparable, with participation somewhat more responsive, and unemployment somewhat less responsive to aggregate demand. In line with the traditional view of disadvantaged youths as likely to be "last hired" and "first fired," black youth employment is even more cyclically sensitive than the total group. For black men 16–19, each point reduction in the unemployment rate raises the employment ratio by close to 6.3%. A comparable figure obtains for black women.

The substantial cyclical response to changes in aggregate demand suggests that a shortage of job opportunities characterizes the youth labor market. If there were not a dearth of attractive jobs, aggregate demand would not be expected to have a significant impact on youth employment. The very strong response of participation to unemployment confirms the importance of focusing on employment rather than unemployment in assessing labor market conditions. It also supports the argument of section 2.1 that much of the high rate of labor force withdrawal among the unemployed is attributable to discouragement.

It is instructive to consider the cyclical responsiveness of enrolled and nonenrolled young people separately.[12] This is done in table 2.9. The results display dramatic differences in the labor market behavior of enrolled and out-of-school youths. For young men and women enrolled in school

Table 2.9
Cyclical response of teenagers by enrollment status

Enrollment groups	Employment ratio	Participation rate	Employment rate
In school			
Men 16–19	6.97 (1.12)	6.00 (1.05)	.97 (.40)
Women 16–19	6.78 (1.47)	6.39 (1.38)	.39 (.51)
Out of school			
Men 16–19	2.80 (.91)	−.79 (.36)	3.59 (.84)
Women 16–19	3.38 (.85)	1.00 (.72)	2.38 (.45)

Source: These estimates are based on data taken from tables B6 and B7 of the *Employment and Training Report of the President*, 1978. The data are based on the October supplement of the CPS, and cover the period 1954–77. This table is reprinted from Clark and Summers, "Demographic Differences in Cyclical Employment Variation," *Journal of Human Resources*, vol. 16 (Winter 1981).

almost all of the response of employment is due to movements in participation rather than unemployment. The opposite pattern characterizes
youths who are out of school. Increases in employment for this group
come almost entirely at the expense of unemployment. However, employment of out-of-school youths appears to be only about half as sensitive to
demand as that of enrolled young people. The reasons for these disparities
are not clear. One possibility is that youths who are in school tend to await
job offers passively. When offered an attractive job they accept and join the
labor force; otherwise they remain out of the labor force. This would
explain the observed pattern of participation and unemployment dynamics.

2.3.3 Evidence from Gross Flows

The strong response of employment and participation to aggregate demand reflects the large inflows and outflows described in section 2.1. The
surges in employment and participation that accompany increases in aggregate demand may be due either to increased inflows or decreased outflows.
That is, low unemployment may raise employment either by helping
workers get jobs or by helping them hold jobs. In order to examine this
issue we have estimated equations describing the time series movements in
the monthly flow probabilities. In addition to trend, cycle, and seasonal
variables, we also studied the effects of minimum wage legislation and
federal youth employment programs. Since we were unable to isolate a
significant effect of either of these measures on transition probabilities, the
results of estimating the equations in which they were included are not
reported here.

   Table 2.10 summarizes the results of the flow probability equations. The
first set of equations describes the probability of employment entrance. For
men, the rate of entrance is very sensitive to demand. A one-point increase
in the prime-age male unemployment rate reduces the probability of entry
by .014, or about 9%. It is changes in entry rather than exit behavior which
are the prime cause of employment fluctuations among young men. The
probability of job entrance among women is much less affected by cyclical
developments. The reasons for this difference are not clear. One possibility
is that women are the first to be laid off in downturns. A more plausible
explanation is that the entrance rate does not fall as unemployment rises
because more women enter the labor force as their family income falls. The
rate of exit does not appear to exhibit significant cyclical fluctuations.

   The rates of labor force entry and exit also vary cyclically. The rate of
exit falls during recessions largely because the probability of withdrawal is

Table 2.10
Cyclical behavior of transition probabilities 1968–76 (standard errors in parentheses)

Transition probability/ demographic group	Independent variables					
	CONS	UPRIME	T (12×10^2)	$\bar{R}^2$	SEE	ρ
Dependent variable						
1. Probability of employment entrance						
M1619	.093 (.073)	−1.440 (.257)	−.185 (.105)	.937	.019	−.050 (.105)
BM1619	.172 (.032)	−1.420 (.357)	−.264 (.146)	.856	.024	.002 (.105)
W1619	.051 (.011)	−.273 (.110)	.169 (.048)	.930	.010	−.293 (.100)
BW1619	.110 (.023)	−.246 (.254)	−.206 (.104)	.796	.017	.029 (.105)
2. Probability of employment exit						
M1619	.229 (.018)	.214 (.194)	−.377 (.079)	.946	.015	−.105 (.104)
BM1619	.134 (.051)	−.696 (.557)	.216 (.218)	.839	.038	.002 (.104)
W1619	.250 (.017)	.591 (.184)	−.535 (.075)	.940	.015	−.154 (.104)
BW1619	.364 (.059)	−.493 (.642)	−.714 (.262)	.793	.048	−.080 (.104)

Table 2.10 (continued)

Transition probability/ demographic group	Independent variables			$\bar{R}^2$	SEE	ρ
	CONS	UPRIME	T (12×10^2)			
3. Probability of labor force entrance						
M1619	.063 (.024)	−.760 (.266)	.378 (.109)	.961	.020	−.122 (.104)
BM1619	.170 (.039)	−1.148 (.435)	−.115 (.178)	.932	.027	.111 (.104)
W1619	.032 (.013)	−.036 (.142)	.324 (.058)	.959	.012	−.25 (.101)
BW1619	.104 (.030)	.291 (.377)	.064 (1.33)	.385	.023	−.018 (.105)
Dependent variable						
4. Probability of labor force exit						
M1619	.255 (.017)	.578 (.190)	−.541 (.077)	.940	.014	−.041 (.104)
BM1619	.170 (.043)	.498 (.478)	.026 (.195)	.851	.029	.112 (.104)
W1619	.280 (.016)	.627 (.173)	−.592 (.071)	.920	.014	−.158 (.104)
BW1619	.238 (.047)	1.23 (.515)	−.149 (.211)	.753	.036	−.004 (.106)

a. Note: The coefficient on UPRIME is the sum of nine-month Almon lag (first degree, far restriction); each regression was estimated with seasonal dummies, and a correction for first order autocorrelation.

much greater for the unemployed than it is for those who are employed. For the male groups the probability of labor force entrance is strongly cyclical. It is much less cyclical for women because of the added worker behavior noted above.

On balance, the flow probability equations bear out the basic conclusions of this section. They demonstrate that both labor force entry and employment entry become significantly easier during peak periods. This is consistent with the findings about the responsiveness of nonemployment to the state of local labor markets, noted in section 2.3. Taken together with the evidence that most unemployed teenagers have and will experience quite prolonged joblessness, these findings suggest that a shortage of attractive jobs is at least a partial source of the youth unemployment problem.

2.4 Conclusions and Implications

In this section we shall discuss the implications of our results for policies designed to combat youth unemployment. Our argument can be stated in quite bold terms. Expansionary aggregate demand policy is the only proven way of enlarging the employment opportunities for young people. A consistent effort to keep the unemployment rate near its full employment level would do more to help young people find jobs than almost any other conceivable governmental policy. Of course, other considerations might suggest that, on balance, such a policy is not workable. While certain structural policies might have salutary effects, it is highly unlikely that they could succeed except in a full-employment economy. After discussing the positive effects of a tight labor market, we shall turn to an examination of potential structural initiatives.

2.4.1 The Macroeconomy and the Youth Labor Market

As section 2.3 showed, both teenage unemployment and participation respond strongly to labor market conditions. A reduction of one point in the prime-age male unemployment rate raises the proportion of teenagers who are employed by about 4%, which is split about 2 : 1 between a reduction in unemployment and an increase in participation. For black youths the proportion rises about 6.5% split in a similar way. These figures imply that the 1975 recession cost young workers about 800,000 jobs. The growth in the economy during the late 1960s created close to 300,000 jobs for young workers. Evidence from cross-section data underscores the responsiveness of teenage unemployment to changes in demand. Freeman (1982b) and Clark and Summers (1982) have shown that the youth employment ratio is much higher in strong than in weak labor markets.[13]

Expansion of aggregate demand is especially potent in making available opportunities for those who are most disadvantaged. Between 1969, when the aggregate unemployment rate was 3.6%, and 1976, when it was 7.7%, the proportion of 16–19 year olds suffering more than six months of unemployment rose fourfold. For black youths the same figure increased by almost six times. The tremendous impact of demand on the amount of long-term unemployment is particularly important in light of the results of section 2.1. The evidence presented there suggests that while most teenagers experience little difficulty in moving into and out of employment, most unemployment is concentrated among those who face serious difficulties in obtaining jobs. The teenage unemployment problem is not the lack of desire to hold jobs, but the inability to find work. A shortage of jobs appears to be the only explanation for the large responsiveness of employment to changes in demand. If unemployment were simply a matter of instability, there would be little reason to expect it to respond strongly to aggregate demand. We conclude that the existence of a job shortage must be the central reality dominating efforts to evaluate or design structural initiatives to improve the labor market for youths.

This conclusion is buttressed by evidence on job applications for surveys of low-wage employers who have placed "help wanted" ads in newspapers. In November 1978, *Fortune* magazine reported on a survey of want ads in a small city in upstate New York. The investigators tracked down all want ads, but the results for jobs requiring little skill provide insight into the operation of low-wage markets. A focus on low-wage/low-skill markets is critical for the validity of this evidence. The existence of a long queue for good high-paying jobs is not evidence of an overall shortage, since low-paying, dead-end jobs could go unfilled while people searched in the high-wage sector. Yet for jobs requiring no skill or previous experience, the *Fortune* investigators found employers swamped with applications. Many employers offering jobs paying as low as $3 per hour had as many as seventy applicants within twenty-four hours of placing an ad. Interviews with employers revealed that many never placed want ads since they had huge files of applications even for low-paying jobs.

A similar finding was uncovered in a recent study of the hiring policies of one low-wage employer.[14] Analysis of personnel records revealed that vacancies were rarely advertised. When jobs opened, the employer simply called past job applicants. In most cases, previous applicants were still unemployed and eager for work. Other new hirings came from the friends and relatives of current employees.

Further evidence on queues and vacancies has emerged in our continuing analysis of want ads in the Boston area. Focusing on the very worst jobs advertised in the Sunday paper, we have found an average of fifteen to twenty responses within two days of the ads' placement, with some employers receiving more than thirty appliers, over half of whom appeared in person. The available evidence suggests that employers have no difficulty in filling vacancies even for jobs requiring menial tasks that pay close to the minimum wage and have little prospect for improvement. These findings are not definitive, but they do suggest that the long queues characteristic of the high-wage sector may exist in the low-wage sector as well.

The existence of a job shortage is of fundamental importance in assessing the policy implications of the instability view of teenage unemployment. We have noted the allegation that high turnover is the principal culprit in high youth unemployment rates which yields policy prescriptions designed to improve school-to-work transitions and upgrade teenage workers. However, in the face of a job shortage, reduction of turnover will only redistribute the burden of unemployment. Without job vacancies to be filled, or an increase in the number of jobs, reduced instability would simply reduce the frequency and increase the duration of unemployment spells.

Before we turn to an evaluation of potential structural initiatives, it is useful to review the extent to which strong aggregate demand can achieve structural goals. A key objective of almost all structural programs is to aid youths in obtaining the skills and employment experience necessary to succeed in the adult world. These goals are accomplished to a large extent by expansionary macroeconomic policies. Between 1969 and 1976 the rate of job loss rose by about 75%, substantially reducing the ability of young people to accumulate experience. Cyclical decreases in the youth employment rate also cause reductions in on-the-job training. Standard estimates (e.g., those of Mincer) suggest that an extra year's experience raises earnings by about 2 to 3%. Ellwood's results (1982) appear to be consistent with this figure. This figure suggests that the 1975–76 recession reduced by a significant amount the lifetime earnings of the youth cohort. Since each year of youth nonemployment costs about $20,000, the extra nonemployment had a present value cost of about $16 billion. This calculation is a substantial underestimate of the true difference that cyclical conditions can make in human capital formation. It ignores the benefits of both worker upgrading and the likelihood that if labor were in short supply employers would compete, at least in part, by offering training. When these factors are considered, it is clear that expansionary macroeconomic policy can do a great deal to achieve structural goals.

2.4.2 The Role of Structural Policies

The results in section 2.3 bear out Feldstein and Wright's (1976) conclusion that even if the prime-age male unemployment rate were reduced to unprecedented levels, teenage unemployment rates would remain relatively high.[15] This fact has led many to conclude that only structural measures can make an effective dent in the youth unemployment problem. As we have argued elsewhere, this inference is misleading. Youth unemployment rates remain so high when aggregate demand increases in large part because of increases in participation. In Clark and Summers (1979b) we show that if the mature male unemployment rate were driven down to its 1969 level, and participation were not allowed to expand, the teenage unemployment rate would fall to close to 6%. The question remains what, if any, contribution structural measures can make. These policies may be divided into three broad categories: (1) programs to aid workers in searching for jobs through job matching or improved information; (2) job training programs designed to provide workers with necessary skills; (3) job creation programs designed to make available special jobs for youth groups.

A detailed review of the evidence and discussion of the effectiveness of job matching, job training, and job creation programs is beyond the scope of this chapter. Our results, however, suggest the following observations. First, given a shortage of jobs, training and job matching programs offer little prospect for making a significant contribution to the solution of the youth unemployment problem. Aiding any single worker through training or improved transition to work will improve his chances at the expense of others. As long as there is only a fixed number of jobs, total employment cannot be increased by helping all workers augment skills or search more efficiently. Each worker's additional search, for example, detracts from the opportunities open to other workers and so generates a negative externality. Under these circumstances, belief in training and job matching reflects the fallacy of composition. Matching and training programs cannot have the desired effects unless coupled with an expansion in the number of jobs. If such an expansion is forthcoming, and employers experience difficulty in filling vacancies, training and market transition programs could prove useful.

Second, direct job creation through public employment or private sector subsidies appears to offer the most promising structural approach to the youth unemployment problem. Like training programs, the impact of policy can be focused on those groups who account for the bulk of teenage unemployment. Moreover, the policy is directed at the root of the problem: a shortage of jobs. The success of such programs, however, depends on the extent of net job creation and the provision of skills and experience useful to young persons over the longer term. The evidence presented in section 2.3 suggests that governmental efforts to provide seasonal jobs for disadvantaged in-school youths have met with some success. The effect of other governmental programs like the Youth Conservation Corps, the Job Corps, and Public Service Employment remains an open question in need of further research.

2.4.3 Conclusion

This chapter has presented evidence on the characteristics and sources of teenage unemployment. Our results underscore the apparent dynamic character of the youth labor market, but suggest that market dynamics cannot account for the bulk of youth joblessness. The job instability/ turnover view of unemployment is applicable to the majority of teenagers who experience little difficulty in moving into and out of the labor force. Most unemployment, however, is concentrated among those people who are unemployed for extended periods, and who face serious difficulty in obtaining employment. The results suggest that the problem of teenage unemployment arises from a shortage of jobs. The evidence in section 2.4 indicates that aggregate demand has a potent impact on the job prospects and market experience of teenagers.

The authors are grateful to James Buchal, James Poterba, and Daniel Smith for their assistance with the computations.

Notes

1. This view has been expressed in Hall (1970, 1972), Perry (1972), Smith, Vanski, and Holt (1974), Marston (1976), and Feldstein (1973).

2. Feldstein (1973), pp. 11, 16.

3. H. Woltman and I. Schreiner, memorandum, "Possible Effects of Response Variance on the Gross Changes from Month to Month in the Current Population Survey," Bureau of the Census: Washington, D.C.

4. This point is developed in Clark and Summers (1979b).

5. These data are contained in K. Clark and L. Summers (1979c).

6. Ibid.

7. Preliminary statistical analysis suggests that seasonal fluctuations in teenage unemployment have been lower since the inception of various jobs programs in 1965.

8. Layard (1982).

9. Barret and Morgenstern (1974).

10. This figure is also an underestimate because of spells that are not completely contained in a year.

11. See, for example, Bowen and Finegan (1969) and Perry (1973).

12. This section draws on Clark and Summers (1981).

13. R. Freeman, "Economic Determinats of the Geographic and Individual Variation in Labor Market Positions of Young Persons," and Clark and Summers (1978).

14. Schmeisser (1979).

15. Feldstein and Wright (1976).

Reporting Errors and
Labor Market Dynamics

with James M. Poterba

The dynamics of the American labor market have been an important focus of research over the last decade. Early work by Hall (1972), Feldstein (1973), and Marston (1976) suggested that most unemployment was due to normal turnover, not to individuals with special employment problems. A typical conclusion was that of Feldstein (1973), who wrote that "almost everyone who is out of work can find his usual job in a relatively short time" (p. 11). This dynamic view of unemployment has been challenged in the more recent work of Clark and Summers (1979b) and Akerlof and Main (1980). Clark and Summers in particular focus on how analysts can be misled by spurious labor market transitions, writing that "it seems likely that some of the observed flows into and out of the labor force arise from inconsistent reporting of consistent behavior" (p. 28). This paper re-examines the empirical basis of this debate.

Studies of labor market dynamics are of necessity based on survey data. In some cases inferences are drawn from individual responses to retrospective questions. In other cases, presumably more accurate inferences are drawn from panel data in which individuals are interviewed several times. The Bureau of Labor Statistics gross changes data, which have been tabulated since 1948, are a major source of information about individuals' labor market experience. While the data have not been published in recent years due to concerns about accuracy, they have been used in numerous studies of labor market dynamics.[1]

The report of the National Commission on Employment and Unemployment Statistics (1979) recommended that despite the data difficulties, the BLS should resume publication of the gross changes data on an occasional basis. Moreover, the Commission noted that "the importance of

Reprinted by permission of the Econometric Society, with revisions, from *Econometrica* 54:1319–1338, November 1986.

Current Population Survey based gross changes data for enhancing understanding of changes in the labor market requires that very high priority be
given to improvement in the data.... It is possible, of course, that a
solution will not be achieved, but the potential value of the data warrants
an intensive effort" (p. 217).

The flows of individuals between different labor market states are derived from longitudinal data by comparing the responses of individuals on
two different survey dates. On each survey, some individuals are incorrectly classified with respect to labor market status. While these errors may
largely cancel in tabulations of the unemployment rate or other labor
market aggregates, estimated flow rates between labor market states may
be extremely sensitive to them. Individuals who are misclassified in one
month but not in the next are reported as moving from one state to
another even though their behavior has not changed. Some observed
transitions are therefore spurious. This may lead to substantial over-
estimation of the amount of labor market mobility, and impart significant
biases to estimates of the expected duration of both unemployment and
nonparticipation spells. Response errors may also contaminate inferences
about subtler aspects of labor market dynamics, such as differences between demographic groups or the presence of "state dependence" effects.

This paper presents a technique for correcting the classification errors
that plague the Current Population Survey (CPS) gross changes data.
Similar techniques may be applicable to other data sets. We use the CPS
Reinterview Survey to estimate the incidence of errors in the gross changes
data, and then calculate revised labor market flows by adjusting for spurious transitions. Although our findings are not definitive because we make
particular assumptions about the stochastic process generating response
errors, the results suggest that conventional measures may greatly overstate flows into and out of the labor force. As a consequence, standard
estimates of unemployment durations, whether based directly on gross
flows data or on other information such as the average duration of completed or incomplete spells, may display substantial downward biases. The
labor force attachment of some groups, notably women and teenagers, may
also have been significantly underestimated.

This paper is divided into five sections. The first explains our procedure
for estimating the incidence of response errors in the CPS and documents
that the error rates for a single month are in some cases comparable to
transition rates observed from month to month. Section 3.2 presents our
algorithm for adjusting the gross changes data, and contrasts our revised
labor market flows with the unadjusted data. It also examines the precision

of our estimated adjustments. The next section explores the robustness of our findings to some of our method's maintained assumptions. Section 3.4 uses the adjusted flows to analyze several characteristics of the American labor market, focusing on the experience of different demographic groups. The concluding section suggests directions for future work.

3.1 Classification Errors and the Current Population Survey

Our objective is to estimate the true transition rates between the labor market states of employment (E), unemployment (U), and not-in-the-labor force (N). This information is conveniently represented by a transition matrix:

$$P = \begin{bmatrix} P_{EE} & P_{EU} & P_{EN} \\ P_{UE} & P_{UU} & P_{UN} \\ P_{NE} & P_{NU} & P_{NN} \end{bmatrix}, \tag{1}$$

where, for example, P_{EU} is the probability that an individual who is employed in month t is unemployed in month $t + 1$. Data on the transition matrix P may be derived from the monthly CPS since three quarters of the sample in a given month is included again in the next month.[2] The top panel of table 3.1 provides average values of P for the 1977–82 period.

There are strong reasons to believe that these raw data substantially overstate the true amount of turnover in the labor market. Taken literally, they imply that there are over 50 million labor force entrances each year, which seems implausible. Additional evidence is provided by information on CPS error rates that is generated as byproduct of the CPS Reinterview Survey.[3] In the Reinterview Survey, which is used primarily for survey quality control, individuals are contacted about one week after their initial interview and asked once again about their labor market status in the original survey week. Except for errors, the Initial and Reinterview Survey results should coincide. The lower half of table 3.1 presents "transition" rates calculated by comparing the Initial and Reinterview Surveys. It is apparent that these transition rates between different states, which are *all spurious*, are very large relative to observed month to month transition rates. For example, the rate of labor force withdrawal from unemployment is 20.1% in the longitudinal data but appears to be 16.1% in the comparison between the Initial and Reinterview Surveys.

This paper combines error rate information from the Reinterview Survey with observed month to month transition rates to estimate true transition rates. Our first step is to calculate a matrix of response error rates show-

Table 3.1
Actual and spurious transitions in the current population survey[a]

A. Transition probabilities from two consecutive monthly interviews

Initial month labor market status	Subsequent month labor market status		
	Employed	Unemployed	NILF
Employed	.950	.017	.033
Unemployed	.255	.536	.209
NILF	.047	.027	.926

B. Implied transition probabilities from interview and reinterview surveys

Initial interview labor market status	Reinterview labor market status		
	Employed	Unemployed	NILF
Employed	.965	.010	.026
Unemployed	.097	.742	.161
NILF	.038	.023	.940

a. Each entry shows the probability of transiting conditional upon initial labor market status. Panel A is based on the average values of the unpublished gross changes data for all demographic groups for the years 1977–82. Panel B is based on the authors' data set of all Unreconciled Reinterview Surveys conducted between January and June, 1981.

ing the probability that an individual whose *true* labor market status is $i(S_T = i)$ *will* be classified as in state j in the initial CPS interview ($S_1 = j$). We define $q_{ij} = \Pr(S_1 = j/S_T = i)$. The matrix of error rates is

$$
Q = \begin{bmatrix} q_{EE} & q_{EU} & q_{EN} \\ q_{UE} & q_{UU} & q_{UN} \\ q_{NE} & q_{NU} & q_{NN} \end{bmatrix}, \tag{2}
$$

where, for example, q_{EN} is the probability that an individual who is employed will be measured as not-in-the-labor force. There are only six independent probabilities in this matrix, since the elements of each row sum to unity.

The Reinterview Survey includes 5.6% of the CPS respondents in each month. Households which are included in the Reinterview Survey are divided into a Reconciled and an Unreconciled Subsample, accounting for 80 and 20% of the reinterviews, respectively. The allocation of households to subsamples is made prior to the Reinterview Survey. For households in the Reconciled Subsample, the reinterviewer has access to the original survey responses. He conducts a second interview, compares the results with those on the first survey, and then attempts to determine which, if either, of any conflicting responses is correct. The results of this reconciliation are recorded on a third form and tabulated along with the Initial Interview and Reinterview Survey responses. For the 20% of the Reinterview Survey respondents in the Unreconciled Subsample, the reinterviewer is denied access to the Initial Interview data. He conducts a second interview and makes no attempt to compare responses with those on the Initial Interview.

The Bureau of the Census tabulates Reinterview Survey results for some highly aggregated demographic groups. To investigate differences in labor market experience for different demographic groups, we made our own tabulations of error rates from data tapes provided by the Census Bureau. Table 3.2 shows the distribution of recorded labor market status for individuals in the Reconciled and Unreconciled Subsamples of our data set, which contains 25,314 reinterviews conducted between January and June, 1981. Off-diagonal elements correspond to different responses on the two surveys. The table suggests a significant amount of response error in the CPS. More than 5% of the individuals in the Unreconciled Subsample were classified differently on the two surveys.

Table 3.2
Survey response inconsistencies, CPS reinterview survey[a]

Reconciled subsample: initial interview versus reinterview

Initial interview status	Reinterview status		
	Employed	Unemployed	NILF
Employed	57.69	0.17	0.71
Unemployed	0.18	4.02	0.34
NILF	0.90	0.66	35.34

Unreconciled subsample: initial interview versus reinterview

Initial interview status	Reinterview status		
	Employed	Unemployed	NILF
Employed	57.65	0.59	1.53
Unemployed	0.43	3.28	0.71
NILF	1.35	0.82	33.64

a. Each entry represents the percentage of individuals recorded in a particular pair of labor market states. For example, 57.69% of the individuals in the Reconciled Subsample were recorded as employed in both the Interview and the Reinterview Surveys. Calculations are based on the authors' tabulations of Current Population Survey Reinterviews for the period January through June, 1981.

The data in table 3.2 exhibit an important anomaly. The incidence of discrepancies between the Initial and Reinterview Surveys is much greater in the Unreconciled than in the Reconciled Sample. This finding, which has been reported by others using data for different years, may indicate that the procedures specified for reinterviewers are not carried out.[4] Some reinterviewers, when provided with copies of the household's original survey responses for reconciliation purposes, may use them as a guide in completing the Reinterview Survey. This reduces their workload by minimizing the need for reconciliation.

This anomaly complicates the estimation of error rates. We want to use the Reconciled Subsample information in "true labor force status" but at the same time use the Unreconciled Subsample to estimate the actual incidence of error.[5] We therefore proceed as follows. For individuals in the Reconciled Subsample, we estimate the probability of truly being in each labor market state conditional upon reported first and second interview status (S_1 and S_2). These probabilities are

$$w_{ijk} = \Pr(S_T = k | S_1 = i, S_2 = j). \tag{3a}$$

To estimate these probabilities, we assume that when there are inconsistencies between the two survey responses, the reconciliation procedure correctly identifies true labor market status. When the two surveys agree, we follow the BLS reconciliation procedure and assume that they are correct ($S_R = S_1 = S_2$). Our estimator is therefore

$$\hat{w}_{ijk} = \Pr(S_R = k | S_1 = i, S_2 = j). \tag{3b}$$

The twenty-seven probabilities defined by (3b) must satisfy nine adding-up conditions of the form

$$w_{ijE} + w_{ijU} + w_{ijN} = 1 \qquad (i = E, U, N; j = E, U, N). \tag{4}$$

Therefore, only eighteen of the twenty-seven w_{ijk} parameters are independent.

We assume that the Reconciled Subsample contains a partial sample of the cases for which Initial Interview and Reinterview responses are different. Although the Reconciled Subsample provides a misleading estimate of the incidence of response errors, it may nonetheless provide reliable estimates of the fraction of inconsistent cases which should be allocated to each of the two recorded responses.

We use the estimates $\{\hat{w}_{ijk}\}$ to impute a probability distribution of true labor market status for each individual in the Unreconciled Subsample, conditional upon his recorded responses in the Initial Interview and the

Reinterview. The number of individuals in the Unreconciled Subsample with each imputed labor market status is

$\hat{N}_k^U$ = number of individuals in the Unreconciled
      Subsample with imputed labor market status k

$$= \sum_i \sum_j \hat{w}_{ijk} N_{ij}^U.$$

(5)

N_{ij}^U is the number of individuals in the Unreconciled Subsample with Initial Interview status i and Reinterview status j. From these estimates we calculate the probability that an individual observed in a particular labor market state on either the first or second survey is actually in state k. The probability that an individuals' recorded Initial Interview response is y, conditional upon our imputed reconciliation status being x, is

$$\hat{q}'_{xy} = \frac{\sum_j \hat{w}_{yjx} \cdot N_{yj}^U}{\hat{N}_x^U} = \frac{\sum_j \hat{w}_{yix} \cdot N_{yj}^U}{\sum_i \sum_j \hat{w}_{ijx} \cdot N_{ij}^U} = \Pr(S_1 = y | \hat{S}_T = x),$$

(6a)

where $\hat{S}_T$ denotes our imputed labor market status. An identical procedure using the Reinterview Survey (S_2) as the observed response yields

$$\hat{q}''_{xy} = \frac{\sum_i \hat{w}_{jyx} \cdot N_{jy}^U}{\hat{N}_x^U} = \frac{\sum_i \hat{w}_{jyx} \cdot N_{jy}^U}{\sum_i \sum_j w_{ijx} \cdot N_{ij}^U} = \Pr(S_2 = y | \hat{S}_T = x).$$

(6b)

We form the estimated error rates which are used in our subsequent analysis by averaging $\hat{q}'_{xy}$ and $\hat{q}''_{xy}$: $\hat{q}^*_{xy} = (\hat{q}'_{xy} + \hat{q}''_{xy})/2$. Since $\hat{q}'_{xy} \cong \hat{q}''_{xy}$, the last step is of little significance.

Our estimates of classification error probabilities, and their associated standard errors, are shown in table 3.3. Only off-diagonal elements of the Q matrix are shown, since the diagonal terms can be computed from them. The table displays separate error rates for the entire population and seven demographic subgroups. The standard errors are calculated using a "bootstrap" procedure of the type described in Efron (1982).[6] The error rates for the larger population subgroups can be estimated quite precisely, but the estimated error rates for the smaller groups are sometimes subject to substantial uncertainty.

The error rates are highest for unemployed individuals. In the whole survey, over 11% of the unemployed are incorrectly classified as not in the labor force. The fraction of unemployed persons misclassified in this way varies across demographic groups, from less than 7% for men aged 25–59 to over 17% for women aged 16–19. For teenagers of both sexes, the error rate is nearly 14%. At all ages, the error rate is substantially higher for women than for men.

Table 3.3
Estimated response errors in the current population survey[a]

	Sample size	q_{EU}	q_{EN}	q_{UE}	q_{UN}	q_{NE}	q_{NU}
Total	25,314	.0054	.0172	.0378	.1146	.0116	.0064
		(.0007)	(.0018)	(.0070)	(.0109)	(.0013)	(.0009)
Men 16–19	1,220	.0168	.0350	.0644	.1134	.0120	.0143
		(.0085)	(.0119)	(.0300)	(.0358)	(.0072)	(.0075)
Men 20–24	1,399	.0137	.0077	.0550	.0728	.0170	.0378
		(.0054)	(.0039)	(.0302)	(.0280)	(.0151)	(.0196)
Men 25–59	6,812	.0046	.0062	.0316	.0700	.0378	.0332
		(.0013)	(.0016)	(.0136)	(.0207)	(.0134)	(.0127)
Women 16–19	1,281	.0088	.0380	.0222	.1736	.0130	.0114
		(.0062)	(.0118)	(.0182)	(.0454)	(.0060)	(.0055)
Women 20–24	1,538	.0096	.0218	.0234	.1011	.0239	.0105
		(.0051)	(.0067)	(.0254)	(.0391)	(.0102)	(.0065)
Women 25–59	7,711	.0029	.0168	.0380	.1688	.0106	.0062
		(.0011)	(.0025)	(.0164)	(.0254)	(.0022)	(.0020)
Both Sexes, 16–19	2,501	.0126	.0361	.0472	.1393	.0131	.0126
		(.0051)	(.0074)	(.0199)	(.0309)	(.0044)	(.0042)

a. Error rates are calculated from the authors' data set of Reinterview Surveys for the period January through June, 1981. Values in parentheses are standard errors.

Misclassification from unemployment into employment is also important. Almost 4% of the unemployed individuals in the population are incorrectly classified as holding a job; this error rate rises to over 6% for male teenagers. Errors in which employed individuals are classified as not-in-the-labor force are also surprisingly frequent. Nearly 2% of the employed, and 3.5% of employed teenagers, are miscategorized in this way. Most other error rates are small for the total population, although for some demographic groups they are significant. For example, among men aged 25–59 who are out of the labor force, there is a 3.8% probability of misclassification into employment. The demographic variation in error rates highlights the importance of disaggregating the flows before adjusting for classification errors.

These error probabilities, which we use to adjust the gross changes data, may be subject to a number of potential biases. Some of these understate the true error rate. For example, reinterviewers are instructed to try to interview the same person who was interviewed in the original survey. No similar practice is followed in successive months of the regular CPS survey, so it probably has higher response error rates than those reported here. In addition, if the reinterview procedure fails to identify an individual's true labor market status, our estimates of response error will be too small.

There are also biases that work in the opposite direction. The Reinterview Survey may exaggerate the extent of error since a week is allowed to pass between the events being described and the survey week. Reinterviews are also conducted by different interviewers than the initial interview, while two consecutive CPS monthly interviews are typically conducted by the same interviewer. Finally, the Reinterview Survey is also more frequently conducted by phone than the regular CPS, and this may affect response errors.

3.2 Adjusting the Gross Changes Data

This section describes our procedure for using the estimated error rates to adjust the reported gross changes. Let F_{ij} denote the measured flow from labor market state i to state j, while F_{ij}^* is the true flow. The notation $\hat{F}_{ij}$ will refer to our estimates of the true flows. We can use the $\{q_{ij}\}$ to relate the true and measured flows. For example, consider the measured flow from employment to unemployment. There are nine different combinations of actual labor market transitions and response errors which can lead an individual CPS respondent to be classified as making an $E \to U$ transition. By summing the total number of individuals in each of these nine categories, we obtain an expression for the total measured flow:

$$F_{EU} = q_{EE}q_{EU}F_{EE}^* + q_{EE}q_{UU}F_{EU}^* + q_{EE}q_{NU}F_{EN}^*$$
$$+ q_{UE}q_{EU}F_{UE}^* + q_{UE}q_{UU}F_{UU}^* + q_{UE}q_{NU}F_{UN}^* \tag{7}$$
$$+ q_{NE}q_{EU}F_{NE}^* + q_{NE}q_{UU}F_{NU}^* + q_{NE}q_{NU}F_{NN}^*.$$

Regardless of his true labor market status, each individual has *some* chance of being recorded as making an $E \to U$ transition. Of course, for some individuals this probability is trivial. The number of individuals who in fact make $U \to E$ transitions but are twice misclassified, first into employment (when they are unemployed) and then into unemployment (when they are employed), is likely to be quite small. The main contribution to the sum in (7) will come from the terms involving diagonal elements of the Q matrix.

Equation (7) may be written more generally as

$$F_{kl} = \sum_i \sum_j q_{ik}q_{jl}F_{ij}^*. \tag{8}$$

We define F to be the 3×3 matrix of observed flows:

$$F = \begin{bmatrix} F_{EE} & F_{EU} & F_{EN} \\ F_{UE} & F_{UU} & F_{UN} \\ F_{NE} & F_{NU} & F_{NN} \end{bmatrix}. \tag{9}$$

The system of equations in (8) can be compactly written in matrix form as

$$F = Q'F^*Q, \tag{10}$$

where Q is the matrix of classification error probabilities $\{q_{ij}\}$ and F^* is the matrix of true flows. Equation (10) expresses the observed flows as a function of the unobserved true flows and the classification error probabilities. It can be solved for the true flows:

$$F^* = (Q^{-1})'FQ^{-1}. \tag{11}$$

Using our estimates $\{\hat{q}_{ij}\}$ to form $\hat{Q}$, we estimate the true flows as

$$\hat{F} = (\hat{Q}^{-1})'F\hat{Q}^{-1}. \tag{12}$$

Both aggregate gross flows and those for each demographic group can be modified to yield a set of "response-error corrected" gross flows. We also calculate standard errors for the adjusted flows, again using a bootstrap procedure.[7]

An illustration of our adjustment procedure using the total flows, aggregating over all demographic groups, is shown in table 3.4. The table's first panel reports the annual average unadjusted flows for the period January 1977 to December 1982. The table's next panel, labeled "Adjusted Flows, Without Raking," reports the adjusted gross flows calculated using equation (12). Some flows, particularly those involving transitions into and out of the labor force, change dramatically. There is a clear reduction in the number of individuals who are off the diagonal of the flow matrix. While 12.60 million transitions are recorded in the actual gross flow data, our adjusted matrix shows only 5.20 million transitions. This decline in the off-diagonal flows implies a reduction in the escape probabilities from each labor market state. A more complete discussion of the implications for labor market dynamics is provided in section 3.4.

The differences between the adjusted and the unadjusted flows are large relative to the standard errors of the adjusted flows. For the $U \to N$ flow, for example, the estimated change is nine times its standard error. Equally significant changes take place in the $N \to E$ and $E \to N$ flows.

The procedure described above does not impose any restrictions on the number of individuals in each labor market state before and after the flow adjustment. Nor does it constrain the estimated flow data to be consistent

Table 3.4
Total labor market gross flows with and without adjustment[a]

	Final state		
Initial state	Employed	Unemployed	NILF
Unadjusted flows			
Employed	91,865	1,652	3,157
Unemployed	1,857	3,899	1,521
NILF	2,805	1,610	55,541
Adjusted flows, without raking			
Employed	96,040	1,143	748
	(761)	(88)	(211)
Unemployed	1,395	5,391	723
	(89)	(147)	(89)
NILF	347	836	57,282
	(213)	(88)	(410)
Adjusted flows, raked			
Employed	94,361	1,134	668
	(686)	(81)	(204)
Unemployed	1,413	5,517	666
	(80)	(104)	(90)
NILF	388	945	58,283
	(228)	(94)	(435)

a. Unadjusted flows (denominated in thousands of persons) are annual averages for 1977–82, drawn from unpublished BLS tabulations. Adjusted flows are calculated using the procedures outlined in the text. Standard errors for the adjusted flows are reported in parentheses.

with observed changes in labor market stocks. The adjustment procedure substantially lowers the number of individuals classified as NILF and raises the number of unemployed. In the unadjusted data, there are 59.96 million individuals out of the labor force and 7.27 million unemployed. In the adjusted data, however, the number of individuals who are not in the labor force declines to 58.46 million, while the number of unemployed rises to 7.53 million.

To modify our adjusted flows to yield the same marginal totals as those implied by labor market stock data, we use the method of iterative proportional fitting, or "raking." This procedure, due to Deming and Stephan (1940), adjusts the cell proportions of a contingency table to agree with a pre-specified set of marginal totals by minimizing a weighted sum of squared deviations between the initial and "raked" proportions. The adjusted, raked flows, $\tilde{F}_{ij}$, minimize

$$S = \sum_i \sum_j (\tilde{F}_{ij} - \hat{F}_{ij})^2/\hat{F}_{ij} \qquad \text{subject to} \quad \sum_j \tilde{F}_{ji} = \sum_j \tilde{F}_{ij} = M_i, \qquad (13)$$

where M_i designates the required marginal total. We rake the adjusted flows, using an iterative procedure suggested by Deming and Stephan (1940), to conform with the marginal totals implied by the average labor market stocks for 1977–82 as reported in the January issues of *Employment and Earnings*.

Our raked, adjusted flows are reported in the third panel of table 3.4. The raking adjustments lead to substantial changes in some of the flows. For example, the estimated $E \to E$ flow declines by over 1.5 million persons, while the $N \to N$ flow rises by 1 million. The marginal labor market stocks are also affected. The aggregate unemployment rate changes from 7.1% to 7.3%, and the labor force participation rate declines from 64.3% to 63.5%. The transition probabilities between labor market states are, however, virtually unaffected by the raking procedure. The largest change in a transition probability is that for p_{UU}, which rises from .717 to .725.[8]

3.3 Robustness

The standard errors associated with the estimates suggest that they are quite reliable given the assumptions of our adjustment method. It remains to be seen whether our estimates are robust with respect to changes in these assumptions. We focus on our primary maintained assumption, the serial independence of response error probabilities for each individual. It seems plausible that persons who make an error in month t are more likely than others to make errors in month $t + 1$, either because individuals differ in their error-proneness or because individuals in ambiguous circumstances are likely to make similar mistakes in successive months. Either of these possibilities can be modeled by allowing for heterogeneity in individual error probabilities.

We examine the robustness of our procedures by relaxing our earlier assumption that all individuals have identical error rates. While these experiments provide some evidence on the sensitivity of our results, they are restricted in focusing on only one specification of serial dependence. Other stochastic models for response errors might generate different results.

We postulate two classes of survey respondents who differ in their rates of survey response error. Individuals in the first class, who account for $100\alpha\%$ of the population, have error rates $q_{ij}^{(1)} = \lambda_1 q_{ij}$, $i \neq j$, where q_{ij}, where q_{ij} is the full-sample error rate. For the second class, $q_{ij}^{(2)} = \lambda_2 q_{ij}$, $i \neq j$. To preserve population error rates, we require $\alpha\lambda_1 + (1 - \alpha)\lambda_2 = 1$.

This heterogeneity assumption will clearly generate serial correlation in the errors. It also requires modifying (12), the adjustment formula. Define Q_1 as the error matrix with term $q_{ij}^{(1)}$ off the diagonal and $q_{ii}^{(1)} = 1 - \sum_{j \neq i} q_{ij}^{(1)}$ on the diagonal, and define Q_2 similarly. With heterogeneity, the observed flow matrix is related to the true flow matrix F^* by

$$F = \alpha Q_1' F^* Q_1 + (1 - \alpha) Q_2' F^* Q_2. \tag{14}$$

This matrix equation may be rewritten using the vec operator, which stacks the columns of a matrix one upon each other. Since vec $(ABC) = (C' \otimes A)$ vec (B),

$$\text{vec}(F) = [\alpha(Q_1' \otimes Q_1') + (1 - \alpha)(Q_2' \otimes Q_2')] \text{ vec}(F^*), \tag{15}$$

so that

$$\text{vec }(F^*) = [\alpha(Q_1' \otimes Q_1') + (1 - \alpha)(Q_2' \otimes Q_2')]^{-1} \text{ vec}(F). \tag{16}$$

We calculated these adjusted flows for various specifications of α, λ_1, and λ_2, and found that allowing for heterogeneity of this type had relatively little impact on our results. For example, assuming that $\alpha = .5$, $\lambda_1 = 2$, and $\lambda_2 = 0$, the probability that an individual makes an error in period t, conditional upon an error at $t - 1$, is 3.4 times as great as the probability of an error at t conditional on a correct response at $t - 1$. The comparable value is 1.7 in a homogeneous population. In spite of this substantial change in the serial correlation pattern of the errors, the adjusted flows are changed relatively little from the homogeneous case. The most affected values move only 16% of the distance toward their unadjusted values. Even in the more extreme case in which one class of respondents is error free and the other has an error rate five times the population average, which makes the error rate conditional on a lagged error 8.2 times the error rate conditional on a correct lagged response, the average adjustment is .72 times the change in the homogeneous (no serial correlation) case.[9]

Our procedures do not treat the problem of attrition bias in the gross flows data or the problems that arise because individuals move from one demographic category to another as they age. Raking the data into conformity with the observed labor market stocks is a crude way of treating these problems, which can lead to systematic biases in the flows data. The work of Abowd and Zellner (1985a,b) and Stasny and Feinberg (1985), which focuses on the missing data problem, and Fuller and Chua (1983, 1985), which treats the population flow problem, suggests that these issues are of some consequence.

While we regard the findings of our heterogeneity analysis as suggestive, they are not definitive. We consider only one form of serial correlation, and in particular, we have not allowed for differential persistence of different types of classification errors. Further research on the stochastic process that describes response errors must await longitudinal data matching both interviews and reinterviews in several consecutive months; these data are not currently available.

3.4 Results

This section analyzes the results of applying our adjustment procedure to the gross changes data for seven disaggregated demographic groups: men 16–19, men 20–24, men 25–59, women 16–19, women 20–24, women 25–59, and teenagers of both sexes. In each case the estimates of $\{q_{ij}\}$ presented in table 3.3 are used to adjust the annual average gross changes data for the period 1977–82. Because most questions of labor market dynamics hinge on the transition probabilities derived from the gross changes data, table 3.5 presents the transition probabilities corresponding to each group. These probabilities are estimated as

$$\hat{p}_{ij} = \Pr(\text{status at } t + 1 = j | \text{status at } t = i) = F_{ij} \bigg/ \sum_k F_{ik}. \qquad (17)$$

Probabilities from both the unadjusted and the raked adjusted flows are shown, along with the estimated standard errors for the adjusted probabilities. Table 3.5 shows that for smaller demographic groups, the standard

Table 3.5
Labor market transition probabilities from adjusted and unadjusted flows[a]

Unadjusted				Adjusted and raked		

Total

	E	U	N		E	U	N
E	.950	.017	.033	E	.981	.012	.007
					(.002)	(.001)	(.002)
U	.255	.536	.209	U	.186	.726	.088
					(.010)	(.013)	(.012)
N	.047	.027	.926	N	.007	.016	.978
					(.004)	(.002)	(.004)

Men 16–19

	E	U	N		E	U	N
E	.845	.049	.106	E	.901	.031	.068
					(.016)	(.009)	(.014)
U	.263	.454	.283	U	.183	.608	.209
					(.039)	(.049)	(.036)
N	.127	.088	.785	N	.071	.071	.857
					(.017)	(.010)	(.021)

Men 20–24

	E	U	N		E	U	N
E	.934	.035	.031	E	.963	.016	.021
					(.015)[b]	(.007)	(.006)
U	.290	.581	.129	U	.172	.814	.013
					(.051)	(.065)	(.054)
N	.109	.073	.817	N	.072	.023	.905
					(.032)	(.039)	(.069)

Men 25–59[c]

	E	U	N		E	U	N
E	.979	.014	.007	E	.993	.010	−.003
					(.008)	(.002)	(.003)
U	.347	.537	.116	U	.261	.725	.014
					(.042)	(.001)	(.043)
N	.081	.057	.862	N	−.048	.007	1.041
					(.031)	(.020)	(.041)

Women 16–19

	E	U	N		E	U	N
E	.848	.038	.114	E	.897	.033	.070
					(.015)	(.007)	(.015)
U	.247	.423	.330	U	.219	.559	.222
					(.028)	(.042)	(.041)
N	.100	.078	.822	N	.050	.060	.890
					(.013)	(.008)	(.017)

Table 3.5 (continued)

Unadjusted				Ajusted and raked		

Women 20–24

	E	U	N		E	U	N
E	.927	.049	.023	E	.969	.014	.016
					(.018)[b]	(.006)	(.009)
U	.256	.505	.238	U	.185	.662	.154
					(.048)	(.065)	(.004)
N	.083	.065	.852	N	.016	.053	.931
					(.019)	(.009)	(.023)

Women 25–59

	E	U	N		E	U	N
E	.951	.012	.037	E	.979	.009	.011
					(.003)	(.001)	(.003)
U	.225	.519	.256	U	.178	.733	.089
					(.017)	(.036)	(.030)
N	.050	.025	.925	N	.014	.011	.975
					(.005)	(.003)	(.005)

Both sexes 16–19

	E	U	N		E	U	N
E	.846	.043	.110	E	.899	.032	.069
					(.010)	(.006)	(.008)
U	.255	.440	.305	U	.200	.584	.216
					(.023)	(.030)	(.027)
N	.112	.082	.805	N	.059	.065	.875
					(.009)	(.006)	(.011)

a. Unadjusted probabilities are calculated from Gross Changes data for 1977–82. Adjusted flows are described in text; standard errors are in parentheses.
b. Some of the unraked flows constructed using the synthetic data sets in our "bootstrap" procedure yielded negative flows. This prevented us from using the raking algorithm. Standard errors are based on the standard errors for the unraked flows.
c. For men 25–59, the adjusted flows yielded some negative values. We were therefore unable to rake the flows to conformity with labor market stocks. Unraked flows were used to calculate these probabilities and their standard errors.

errors of our adjustments are in some cases nontrivial relative to the differences between the raw and adjusted probabilities.

The disaggregated probabilities reveal a difficulty with our adjustment procedure: the adjusted flows are not constrained to be positive. For men 25–29, our adjustments make the $E \rightarrow N$ and $N \rightarrow E$ flows negative, although the standard errors of the adjusted flows are large. In the $E \rightarrow N$ case, the standard error is as large as the adjusted flow; the $N \rightarrow E$ standard error is two-thirds the size of the adjusted flow. In both cases, the 95% confidence interval for the adjusted flow includes positive values. Our excessive adjustments for some groups may be due to serial correlation of reporting errors, although allowing for heterogeneity as in the last section still generates negative flows. The source and treatment of the negative flow problem should be addressed in future work. The finding, however, demonstrates the importance of demographic disaggregation in manipulating the gross flows data. Analyses which use either aggregate flows or distinguish only men and women, such as Abowd and Zellner (1985a,b) and Fuller and Chua (1985), fail to discover this problem.

The transition probabilities can be used to calculate several summary statistics for labor market activity. These include the expected duration of a completed spell in each labor market state, the probability of an unemployment spell ending in employment, and the probability of labor force withdrawal within a given month. Expected durations of completed spells are calculated as the reciprocal of the exit probability from each state. The probability of an unemployment spell ending in employment entry is $p_{UE}/(p_{UE} + p_{UN})$. The probability of labor force withdrawal is $(p_{UN}\Pi_U + p_{EN}\Pi_E)/(\Pi_U + \Pi_E)$, where Π_E and Π_U denote, respectively, the fraction of the population employed and unemployed.

Marston (1976) presents a complete analysis of the transition matrix differences between demographic groups. Two central conclusions of his analysis are the importance of transitions into and out of the labor force, and the great extent of turnover in the labor market. We focus on the extent to which these conclusions are modified by our adjusted data, and then comment on the implications of our findings for analyses which explore labor market dynamics without making explicit reference to the gross changes data.

Table 3.6 presents estimates of the monthly probability of labor market withdrawal for different demographic groups, estimated from our unadjusted and adjusted data. The unadjusted data imply that over 40% of the labor force can be expected to withdraw within a year. The unadjusted data

Table 3.6
Probabilities of labor force withdrawal and successful unemployment escape[a]

Demographic group	Probability of labor force withdrawal			Probability of successful escape from unemployment		
	Unadjusted flows	Raked adjusted flows	Percentage change	Unadjusted flows	Raked adjusted flows	Percentage change
Total	.044	.013	−71.4	.550	.680	23.6
Men 16–19	.138	.094	−31.8	.481	.467	−2.9
Men 20–24	.042	.016	−62.4	.692	.928	34.1
Men 25–59	.011	—	—	.749	—	—
Women 16–19	.151	.098	−35.0	.428	.497	16.1
Women 20–24	.069	.031	−54.3	.518	.546	5.4
Women 25–59	.049	.016	−67.6	.467	.667	42.7
Both Sexes, 16–19	.146	.096	−34.4	.455	.481	5.7

a. The probability of labor force withdrawal is $(p_{EN}\Pi_E + p_{UN}\Pi_U)/(\Pi_E + \Pi_U)$, while the probability of successful unemployment escape is $p_{UE}/(p_{UE} + p_{UN})$. The calculations are based on probabilities in table 3.5. For the men 25–59 group, the negative probabilities prevented calculations.

also show that among those leaving employment, labor force withdrawal is almost twice as common as unemployment.[10] Perhaps most significant, the unadjusted data imply that almost half (45%) of unemployment spells end in labor force withdrawal. Table 3.6 reports values of one minus this probability, the chance that conditional upon escaping from unemployment the individual finds a job. For women aged 25–59, for example, 46% of unemployment spells end in successful job-finding.

The Reinterview Survey suggests that spurious reporting of labor force withdrawal is the most common form of reporting error. It is therefore not surprising that the adjusted data present a very different view of the importance of labor force withdrawal. The overall withdrawal rate for the entire population is only about one-third as great as that suggested by the unadjusted data. In contrast to the adjusted data, job leaving to unemployment is twice as common as job leaving followed by labor force withdrawal. The adjusted data also imply that about two-thirds of the unemployed end their spell of unemployment by finding a job.

The difference between the unadjusted and adjusted probabilities varies across demographic groups. For men 20–24, for example, there is a 62% reduction in withdrawal probabilities. Male teenagers, who exhibit somewhat higher mobility, experience only a 30% reduction as a result of flow adjustment. The probability of a successful escape from unemployment rises for nearly all demographic groups, with the most pronounced changes for the least mobile groups.

A second striking feature of the unadjusted data is the very high rate of implied labor force turnover. Table 3.7 illustrates this by presenting estimates of unemployment durations. For the entire population, the unadjusted data suggest that the mean duration of unemployment is only about 2.2 months. For women the estimated durations are shorter and for teenagers they are far shorter, 1.8 months. The adjusted data tell a rather different story. For the entire population the estimated duration of a completed unemployment spell is 3.6 months, almost two-thirds greater. For women, the expected spell duration rises from 2.0 to 3.1 months, while for men the change is even more pronounced, 2.4 to 4.5 months.[11] Our adjustments accentuate the differences between teenagers and the remainder of the population, because they revise upwards the teenagers' durations of unemployment by only small amounts.

Response error adjustments have their most dramatic effects on those groups whose labor market behavior is least dynamic. If error rates are relatively constant across demographic groups, then eliminating errors will have the greater proportional effect on groups whose members make the

Table 3.7
Expected unemployment durations[a]

| Demographic group | Expected unemployment duration (months) calculated from | | |
	Unadjusted flows	Raked adjusted flows	Percentage change
Total	2.15	3.65	69.6
Men 16–19	1.83	2.56	39.7
Men 20–24	2.38	5.39	126.3
Men 25–59	2.16	3.63	68.4
Women 16–19	1.73	2.27	31.1
Women 20–24	2.02	2.96	46.3
Women 25–59	2.08	3.75	80.3
Both Sexes, 16–19	1.79	2.40	34.7

a. Expected unemployment durations are $1/(1 - P_{UU})$. Calculations are based on probabilities reported in table 3.5. For men 25–59, unraked adjusted flows are used as in table 3.5.

fewest transitions. The point is exemplified by considering the male 25–59 group. Here the estimated duration of unemployment rises from 2.2 months to 3.6 months. Unfortunately, these results must be discounted because some of the adjusted flow probabilities are negative.

Correction for reporting errors which lead to overestimates of close to 70% in the escape rate from unemployment is likely to increase reasonable estimates of any unemployment duration measure. Even estimates such as those of Clark and Summers (1979b) may underestimate the true extent of concentration in unemployment. Some support for our suggestion that unemployment spells are longer than usually shown in the gross changes data derives from non-CPS sources of labor market information, usually retrospective surveys of individual experience, which often find longer spell lengths for all labor market states than those reported by the CPS.[12] While interpretation of these facts is complicated by the varying definitions of unemployment used on non-CPS surveys, they tend to corroborate our findings.

Our results suggest that the unadjusted gross changes data may lead to misleading inferences about the character of the labor market. We suspect that similar problems plague efforts to use the gross changes data to study cyclical phenomena. In particular, conventional analyses may understate the cyclicality of labor market flows because a relatively constant number of spurious flows are added in all periods to the cyclically variable true flows.

Our results also cast doubt on conventional analyses of unemployment, which do not make explicit use of the gross changes data. One common method for analyzing unemployment durations, pioneered by Kaitz (1970) and Salant (1977), involves inferring the distribution of completed spell lengths from published information on the distribution of interrupted spell lengths. A simple procedure of this type is to estimate the mean duration of completed spell lengths by dividing the number of unemployed persons by an estimate of the flow rate into unemployment, based for example on the number of persons unemployed less than 5 weeks.[13] For 1981 this procedure yields a mean duration of completed unemployment spells of 2.4 months, very close to the estimate produced by the unadjusted gross changes data.

The reason this procedure goes wrong should be clear. Errors in classification lead a large number of persons to be spuriously classified as unemployed, artificially inflating the stock of short term unemployed. Likewise, many of the longer term unemployed are spuriously not measured as unemployed. While these two biases do not have a large effect on the measured stock of unemployed persons because they offset, both biases reduce the mean reported duration of unemployment.

Related difficulties plague studies of the transition out of unemployment that use the techniques of survival analysis, such as Lancaster (1979) and Flinn and Heckman (1982). Some transitions out of unemployment are spurious, and some continuing spells of unemployment are recorded as ending. Estimated hazard functions correspond not to the probability of escaping unemployment, but to the probability of being *measured* as leaving unemployment. The latter may be the outcome of either a classification error or a genuine labor market transition, complicating the structural interpretation of hazard models.[14]

3.5 Conclusions

This paper develops a procedure for adjusting the Current Population Survey gross changes data for reporting errors. Although our findings are not definitive because our procedure makes particular assumptions about the stochastic process generating response errors, the corrected data suggest that the labor market may be much less dynamic than has frequently been suggested. Conventional measures may understate the duration of unemployment by as much as 80% and overstate the extent of movement into and out of the labor force by several hundred percent. The use of our adjusted data also throws demographic differences in patterns of labor market dynamics into sharp relief.

This research could usefully be extended in several directions. Alternative procedures for estimating CPS error rates could be devised to relax the assumption that the reconciliation process correctly estimates individuals' true labor force status. Error probabilities could also be estimated imposing the constraint that the marginal labor market stocks estimated in the CPS are unbiased estimates of the true stocks. Alternative procedures to adjust the actual gross changes data could also be developed.

Our findings suggest that measurement errors distort estimates of basic statistics characterizing the labor market. Statistical techniques for analyzing labor market data that take account of pervasive measurement errors need to be developed. Because of the discrete nature of data on labor market status, and its longitudinal character, standard techniques for the treatment of errors in variables are not applicable. In work now underway (Poterba and Summers, 1982), we are developing a multinomial logit procedure for analyzing labor market transitions which are reported with error.

We are indebted to Bruce Meyer for outstanding research assistance and many helpful discussions, to Irv Shreiner and Paul Flaim for data assistance, and to Wayne Fuller, Francis Horvath, two anonymous referees, and Angus Deaton for helpful suggestions. A preliminary version of this paper was presented at the BLS/Census Conference on Gross Changes Data, July 1984. After completing most of the research reported here, we learned of related work by Fuller and Chua (1983, 1985) and Abowd and Zellner (1985a,b). We thank the NBER and NSF for financial support. This research is part of the NBER Program in Labor Studies.

Notes

1. Clark and Summers (1979b), and Smith (1973), among others, have used unpublished gross flows data to examine labor market dynamics.

2. For a discussion of the gross changes data, see Smith and Vanski (1979b).

3. The CPS Reinterview Survey is described in some detail in Census Technical Report No. 19 (1969), Woltman and Schreiner (1979), and Graham (1979).

4. Discussion of the bias induced by the reconciliation procedure may be found in Schreiner (1980).

5. Abowd and Zellner (1985a,b) present an adjustment procedure for the gross changes data that relies only on the Reconciled Subsample data, while Fuller and Chua (1983, 1985) rely only on the Unreconciled Subsample.

6. The empirical frequency distributions from both the Reconciled and Unreconciled subsamples, which form the basis for our estimates of the w_{ijk} and the N_{ij}^u, are used in calculating bootstrap standard errors. We generate 1,000 synthetic data sets by drawing randomly from these empirical frequency distributions. For each

sample we then carry through the calculations of the q_{ij}^*. Our reported standard errors are the standard deviations of the 1,000 synthetic estimates of q_{ij}^*. We also calculated confidence bands using the .025 and .975 percentile values of the synthetic estimates, but these proved very close to our standard deviation calculations.

7. The standard errors for the adjusted flows were computed by calculating synthetic adjusted flows corresponding to each of the 1,000 synthetic sets of response errors probabilities. The reported standard errors are the standard deviations of these 1,000 draws. Similar calculations are used to compute the standard errors for the transition probabilities.

8. Our raking procedure minimizes (by design) the importance of margin adjustments. Previous attempts to treat both the adjustment and response error problems simultaneously, such as Abowd and Zellner (1985a,b), suggest that margin error corrections may be less important than response error corrections for analyzing labor market dynamics. Abowd and Zellner (1985a) show that although margin corrections can substantially alter the *size* of labor market flows, their effect on the associated transition probabilities is generally much smaller than the response error correction. Their findings are not conclusive, however, because Abowd and Zellner rely on a particular stochastic structure for the missing data process. Alternative approaches to either the margin-error or missing-data problems might lead to larger changes; future research should consider these questions.

9. The adjusted flows taking account of heterogeneity were EE, 95965, EU, 1189, EN, 776, UE, 1439, UU, 5218, UN, 850, NE, 377, NU, 962, and NN, 57126. With the type I persons five times as error-prone as the population average, the flows were EE, 95762, EU, 1318, EN, 852, UE, 1564, UU, 4764, UN, 1180, NE, 456, NU, 1288, and NN, 56721. These should be compared with the flows in the second panel of table 3.4. Although two of the flows moved 61% and 54% of the distance back toward their unadjusted values, some of the other flows were hardly changed at all. Some sense of the changes in transition rates affecting unemployment durations can be obtained from the following. In the unadjusted data, p^{UU} is .536. In the adjusted data with no serial correlation correction, this probability is .726. In the two serial correlation cases presented here, it is .695 and .635, respectively.

10. This calculation is based on the ratio of $P_{EN}/(P_{EN} + P_{EU})$.

11. The results for both male and female aggregates are based on adjusted transition probabilities not reported in table 3.5.

12. Clark and Summers (1979b) discuss some of this evidence.

13. This technique is used by Darby, Haltiwanger, and Plant (1985).

14. Further difficulties affect procedures that rely upon individuals reporting unemployment durations since these data are extremely unreliable. In Poterba and Summers (1984) we demonstrate that only about a quarter of the population gives consistent responses in successive months to questions about the duration of unemployment. A related discussion of survival analysis in the presence of measurement error may be found in Stansny (1983).

II Cyclical Unemployment

4 Demographic Differences in Cyclical Employment Variation

with Kim B. Clark

The cyclical behavior of employment and unemployment is a dominant feature of labor markets. Cyclical fluctuations in economic activity affect the labor market experience of all demographic groups. While the unemployment rates of different demographic groups move together, the levels about which they fluctuate and the amplitude of cyclical fluctuations differ greatly. These differences suggest that understanding the cyclical character of labor markets requires explicit examination of the experience of individual groups.[1] Moreover, an assessment of the welfare implications of alternative policies requires consideration of the incidence of costs and benefits.

The cyclical sensitivity of unemployment is a reflection of two quite different phenomena. Unemployment can increase either because fewer jobs are available or because more workers decide to seek the available jobs. These two sources of unemployment have different welfare implications. While the former is almost certainly indicative of a worsening labor market performance, the latter may reflect an improvement in conditions. Focus only on unemployment rates is thus very likely to be misleading.[2] Recent experience illustrates the point. During 1977 the unemployment rate fell by about one percentage point. If participation had remained constant, the large gains in employment during that year would have caused more than a two-point decline in the unemployment rate. Similarly, a constant participation rate over the last two years would have led to an unemployment rate below 5% today.

The ambiguous character of fluctuations in unemployment suggests that analysis of cyclical behavior will be improved by simultaneous examination

An earlier version of this paper appeared as NBER Working Paper No. 514. It is reprinted by permission from *Journal of Human Resources* 16:61–79, winter 1981. Copyright © 1981 by the Board of Regents of the University of Wisconsin System.

of movements in employment and participation. In this paper we analyze the demographic patterns of cyclical swings in the labor market by decomposing movements in employment into changes in unemployment and participation. The paper focuses on the interrelations among participation, employment, and unemployment, with particular emphasis on the participation rate as a prime determinant of the labor market experience of various demographic groups.

The first section briefly reviews the evidence indicating the importance of participation fluctuations. The empirical model is described and several variants are discussed. The second section of the paper discusses the empirical results for various groups. Differences in labor market experience by age, sex, race, and enrollment in school are considered. The results confirm the importance of the participation rate in affecting the cyclical behavior of both employment and unemployment. A key finding is that young workers bear a disproportionate share of cyclical fluctuations. For example, teenagers, who comprise only 9% of the population, account for more than a quarter of employment fluctuations. The third section of the paper analyzes in greater detail the impact of aggregate demand policy on high-unemployment demographic groups. It is sometimes suggested that these groups have structural problems upon which expansionary policy has a small impact. We show that this conclusion results from ignoring movements in the participation rate. These groups have high unemployment rates in times of very strong macroeconomic performance only because of the surge in participation that accompanies increased employment opportunities. Without participation fluctuations, expansionary aggregate demand could reduce the unemployment rate of almost every demographic group to a very low level. The fourth and final section of the paper summarizes our conclusions and discusses some of their implications.

4.1 Labor Force Participation and the Cyclical Behavior of Labor Markets

The rate of labor force participation is a fundamental measure of labor market activity. As a measure of the supply of labor, participation has been widely studied using aggregate time-series and cross-section data. Mincer's well-known studies (1963, 1966) and the massive study of Bowen and Finegan (1969) demonstrated the importance of participation fluctuations in understanding employment fluctuations, especially among women. It is now widely recognized that structural changes in the labor market (e.g., the minimum wage) must be understood in terms of their impact on participation and employment, as well as unemployment. These insights have generally not been applied to the analysis of cyclical behavior. While many recent studies have examined fluctuations in participation (e.g., Wachter, 1972, 1977; Perry, 1977) and demographic unemployment rates (e.g., Feldstein, 1973; Feldstein and Wright, 1976), relatively little effort has been directed at linking participation and unemployment dynamics together to explain employment fluctuations.

The connections among participation, unemployment, and employment can be seen in the following identity:

$$(E/N)_i = (E/L)_i (L/N)_i, \tag{1}$$

where E is employment, N is population, L is labor force, and i indexes demographic groups. The employment ratio (proportion of the population employed) is the product of the participation rate and the employment rate (one minus the unemployment rate). Fluctuations in the fraction of the population employed thus can be decomposed into the change in the rate of unemployment and the growth of participation. Expressing (1) in logs and differentiating yields the basic decomposition:

$$d\ln(E/N)_i = d\ln(E/L)_i + d\ln(L/N)_i. \tag{2}$$

Since persons in the labor force are either employed or unemployed, it is clear that

$$d\ln(E/N)_i = d\ln(1 - UR)_i + d\ln(L/N)_i, \tag{3}$$

where UR is the unemployment rate.[3]

The results of this decomposition for 1972–77, presented in table 4.1, clearly indicate the importance of fluctuations in participation during the past few years, especially for women. These results underscore the need to examine the interrelations among employment, unemployment, and participation in analyzing cyclical fluctuations in labor markets. Below our method of doing this is outlined.

4.1.1 The Empirical Model

For each demographic group, we postulate that unemployment and participation rates are functions of aggregate demand and time. The time trends are included to reflect the impact of slowly changing social factors and other gradually moving variables omitted from the equation. The basic equations to be estimated are

Table 4.1
Decomposition of changes in the employment ratio (numbers are in percent)

Year	Change in log of employment rate (1)	Change in log of participation rate (2)	Change in log of employment rate (3)
Total population			
1972–73	1.48	0.69	0.78
1973–74	−0.02	0.78	−0.80
1974–75	−3.14	−0.04	−3.10
1975–76	1.43	0.53	0.85
1976–77	2.06	1.34	0.72
Women (16 and over)			
1972–73	2.60	1.91	0.69
1973–74	1.26	2.06	−0.81
1974–75	−1.33	1.48	−2.81
1975–76	2.86	2.11	0.75
1976–77	3.36	3.15	0.22

Source: Bureau of Labor Statistics, *Employment and Earnings.*

$$\ln(PR)_{it} = \beta_0 + \sum_{k=0}^{7} \delta_k UP_{t-k} + \beta_2 T + \beta_3 T67 + v_{it}, \tag{4}$$

$$\ln(1 - UR)_{it} = \alpha_0 + \sum_{k=0}^{7} \lambda_k UP_{t-k} + \alpha_2 T + \alpha_3 T67 + u_{it}, \tag{5}$$

where UP is the unemployment rate of men between the ages of 35 and 44, T is the time trend, $T67$ is a second time trend, which begins in 1967, and i indexes demographic groups.

Equations like (4) are traditional in analyses of labor force participation. They have provided the basis for estimates of "hidden unemployment" (Tella, 1965; Dernberg and Strand, 1966) and estimates of the full-employment potential labor force (Perry 1977). The unemployment rate of middle-aged (ages 35–44) males is used as a measure of aggregate demand. It is expected to influence the level of participation since the costs of search are affected by job availability. Moreover, apart from any changes in the real wage, the quality of available jobs varies over the cycle. In order to avoid simultaneity problems, we use this variable rather than a demographically adjusted unemployment rate as a measure of cyclical conditions. The results using Perry's weighted unemployment rate are very similar to those presented here.[4] We include lagged unemployment rates to take account of recognition and action lags in the response to fluctuations. The estimates of the total impact of unemployment are extremely insensitive to the form of the lag structure. The broken time trend beginning in 1967 ($T67$) is intended to allow for recent changes in secular trends. While the choice of $T67$ is somewhat arbitrary, the results reported below are very insensitive to its omission or to its replacement with trends beginning earlier or later. Estimation of (4) and (5) with a quadratic term in time has no significant effect on the results.

Equations like (5) have not been extensively used in studying group unemployment rates. Feldstein (1973) and Feldstein and Wright (1976) have estimated similar relations in order to study the potential of aggregate demand to reduce demographic unemployment rates. Equation (5) can be justified in much the same way as the participation equation. Aggregate demand will have different effects on the unemployment rates of different groups, because of employers' rules in laying off workers and because of quit patterns. Certain groups are more prone to be laid off, others are more prone to leave jobs, and so their unemployment experience is likely to respond quite differently to aggregate demand.

The equations to be estimated are not designed to provide the best or most detailed explanation of the participation (unemployment) rate of each group. Our purpose is to estimate a common model for each group that captures the response of participation (unemployment) to cyclical fluctuations in aggregate demand. Thus, some potential explanatory variables, such as real wages and inflation, have been excluded precisely because of their cyclical variation. That is, our equation is intended as a reduced form for the individual cyclical effects. Other variables have been omitted because they are essentially orthogonal to the variables included. We have, in work available on request, reestimated the equations reported here including variables reflecting demographic factors, inflationary expectations, and household wealth and liquidity. While these variables are sometimes significant, their inclusion has little impact on the estimated cyclical effects.

The interpretation of the coefficients in equations (4) and (5) is quite straightforward. For example, the cyclical responsiveness of the participation rate of the ith group may be measured by

$$\gamma_{PR}^i = - \sum_{k=0}^{7} \delta_k. \tag{6}$$

A value of $\gamma_{PR}^i = 1.0$ indicates that a one percentage point decrease in the unemployment rate of mature men (i.e., UP declines from .06 to .05) leads to a 1% increase in the participation rate of the ith group (i.e., .430 to .434).

Equations (4) and (5) have been estimated using quarterly data for the period 1950–76 for various demographic groups. The identity (1) ensures that the relationship between the employment ratio and aggregate demand and time is given by

$$\ln(EN)_{it} = \beta_0 + \alpha_0 + \sum_{k=0}^{7} (\delta_k + \lambda_k) UP_{t-k} + (\beta_2 + \alpha_2) T$$
$$+ (\beta_3 + \alpha_2) T67 + e_{it}.$$
(7)

It follows immediately that the equations presented here can be used to decompose the cyclical movements of the employment ratio into its unemployment and participation components since

$$\gamma_{EN}^i = \gamma_{PR}^i + \gamma_{(1-UR)}^i.$$
(8)

We have estimated equations (4) and (5) using a maximum likelihood technique to correct for serial correlation. The change in the employment ratio arising from movements in the unemployment rate and the rate of participation is calculated using the identity (8).[5] Its approximate standard error is found by assuming that there is no covariance between γ_{PR}^i and γ_{UR}^i. The regression equations for various age-sex groups are reported in the appendix. In the next section the estimates of cyclical responsiveness are analyzed.

4.2 Demographic Demand Sensitivities

Table 4.2 presents estimates of the elasticity of cyclical response of employment, unemployment, and participation for several demographic groups.[6] In parentheses beneath the estimates are the estimated standard errors. As noted above, the numbers in column (1), which give the cyclical responsiveness of employment, are the sum of the estimates of the responsiveness of participation and unemployment (i.e., the employment rate) found in columns (2) and (3).

A clear implication of the results for men is that teenagers are particularly sensitive to cyclical developments. The estimates imply that a decline in the prime-age-male unemployment rate from 6 to 5% will produce a 4.5% increase in the proportion of male teenagers employed. Over 35% of this change comes from movements in participation. Among adult males 25–64, participation is not very cyclical, with an elasticity close to zero. The employment rate, however, has an elasticity close to unity, so that on

Table 4.2
Cyclical response of participation, unemployment, and employment by demographic groups[a]

Demographic group	Employment ratio (1)	Participation rate (2)	Employment rate (3)
Men			
16–19	4.52 (.68)	1.91 (.45)	2.61 (.51)
20–24	1.85 (.66)	−.41 (.30)	2.26 (.59)
25–34	1.30 (.28)	.04 (.09)	1.26 (.26)
35–44	1.06 (.19)	.005 (.05)	1.05 (.18)
45–54	1.01 (.19)	.002 (.07)	1.01 (.18)
55–64	1.07 (.27)	−.04 (.24)	1.11 (.12)
65+	2.70 (.71)	1.68 (.71)	1.02 (.08)
Total men[b]	1.70	.38	1.32
Women			
16–19	4.41 (.68)	2.53 (.62)	1.88 (.29)
20–24	2.22 (.68)	.71 (.65)	1.51 (.19)
25–34	2.44 (.49)	1.31 (.46)	1.13 (.18)
35–44	1.50 (.30)	.55 (.26)	.95 (.14)
45–54	.96 (.57)	.13 (.56)	.83 (.13)
55–64	−.06 (.59)	−.79 (.58)	.73 (.09)
65+	−.91 (1.25)	−1.50 (1.25)	.59 (.10)
Total women[b]	1.39	.36	1.03
Total population [b]	1.54	.37	1.17

Source: see appendix for basic regressions; estimates are based on quarterly data over the period 1950–76.
a. Cyclical response is defined as the negative of the sum of the coefficients on the lagged values of UP.
b. Elasticities for total men, women, and total population are population-weighted averages of the age-specific estimates.

average a one-point reduction in unemployment of mature men is associated with a 1% increase in the employment of this group. Among elderly men over 65, the employment rate elasticity is 1.02, close to that for other adult groups. However, for this group participation is almost as responsive as that of teenagers. The net effect is an employment ratio elasticity of 2.70, suggesting that older men are among the prime beneficiaries of an expanding economy. This no doubt reflects the tendency of firms to induce early retirements in times of business-cycle slack.

The results for women reveal substantial cyclical sensitivity among the younger age groups. As in the case of men, female teenagers are very sensitive to cyclical developments. We estimate that a one-point decline in the prime-age-male unemployment rate will lead to a 2.5% increase in the participation rate of very young women. Combined with a large drop in unemployment, the employment ratio of this group is consequently increased by more than 4% for each percentage-point change in the prime-age-male unemployment rate. Large gains in employment also are estimated for women ages 20–24 and 25–34. In each case the elasticity of employment exceeds two, with much of the gain coming in increased participation. Women 16–34 thus display a greater degree of cyclical sensitivity than their male counterparts.

Women 35–64 are less responsive to cyclical changes than are younger women, but on average the employment ratio elasticity is still greater than that estimated for men. The negative coefficients on participation for older women sharply reduce the estimated sensitivity of the group employment ratio to changes in unemployment, even to the point of producing a negative relationship. For example, the participation coefficient for women over 65 is -1.5, a value that swamps the unemployment effect, leading to an estimate of $-.91$ for employment. It should be noted, however, that these estimates are not statistically significant.

4.2.1 Demographic Contribution to Cyclical Variation

The estimates in table 4.2 give evidence of wide variations in cyclical sensitivity across demographic groups. The relative importance of the various age groups in accounting for cyclical movements in aggregate employment is examined in table 4.3. In columns (2) and (3) we have used the population share s_i together with estimated values of γ_{EN}^i to create a measure of each group's contribution to the change in the overall employment ratio. If $\sum s_i \gamma_{EN}^i$ is the predicted change in the overall employment ratio, the contribution of the ith group is

Table 4.3
Population shares and the shares of demographic groups in short-run variations in the employment ratio[a]

Demographic group	Population share (s_i)	Weighted elasticity ($s_i\gamma_{EN}^i$)	Employment ratio share ($s_i\gamma_{EN}^i / \sum_i s_i\gamma_{EN}^i$)
Men	.474	.806	.524
16–19	.045	.203	.132
20–24	.045	.083	.054
25–34	.093	.120	.078
35–44	.089	.094	.061
45–54	.081	.082	.053
55–64	.063	.067	.044
65+	.058	.157	.102
Women	.526	.731	.476
16–19	.047	.207	.135
20–24	.055	.122	.079
25–34	.100	.244	.159
35–44	.096	.144	.094
45–54	.087	.084	.055
55–64	.068	−.004	−.003
65+	.073	−.066	−.042
Teenagers	.092	.410	.267
Women 20–34	.155	.366	.238
Adult men 26–64	.326	.363	.236
Total	1.000	1.537	1.000

a. γ_{EN}^i are taken from table 4.2, column (1); the population shares are means for the sample period.

$$\theta_i = (s_i\gamma_{EN}^i)/(\sum s_i\gamma_{EN}^i). \tag{9}$$

The values of s_i, $s_i\gamma_{EN}^i$, and θ_i are presented in columns (1), (2), and (3), respectively.

The aggregate results, presented at the bottom of the table, show that a 1% decline in the prime-age-male unemployment rate leads to a 1.5% increase in employment. A key result of the calculations is that young workers account for the larger part of the cyclical variations in employment. While teenagers comprise less than a tenth of the population, they account for more than a fourth of cyclical fluctuations. Teenagers and young women 20–34 represent only 25% of the adult population, yet they experience close to 50% of the cyclical variation in employment. Prime age males 25–64 are a large fraction of the population (32.6%), but account for less cyclical employment variation than teenagers who represent only 9% of the population.

Table 4.4
Cyclical response of participation, unemployment, and employment by race[a]

Demographic group	Employment ratio (1)	Participation rate (2)	Employment rate (3)
Nonwhites			
Women			
16–19	6.97	3.48	3.49
	(1.79)	(1.66)	(.66)
20+	1.37	−.10	1.47
	(.29)	(.20)	(.21)
Men			
16–19	6.18	2.03	4.15
	(1.12)	(.76)	(.82)
20+	2.51	.14	2.37
	(.41)	(.16)	(.38)
Whites			
Women			
16–19	4.25	2.78	1.47
	(.81)	(.71)	(.38)
20+	1.17	.45	.72
	(.35)	(.29)	(.19)
Men			
16–19	4.44	2.38	2.06
	(.73)	(.53)	(.50)
20+	.87	−.10	.97
	(.21)	(.04)	(.21)

a. Based on regressions as described in the text. The data are quarterly and cover the period 1954–76.

Table 4.5
Cyclical response of teenagers by enrollment status

Enrollment group	Employment ratio	Participation rate	Employment rate
In school			
Men 16–19	6.97	6.00	.97
	(1.12)	(1.05)	(.40)
Women 16–19	6.78	6.39	.39
	(1.47)	(1.38)	(.51)
Out of school			
Men 16–19	2.80	−.79	3.59
	(.91)	(.36)	(.84)
Women 16–19	3.38	1.00	2.38
	(.85)	(.72)	(.45)

Source: These estimates are based on data taken from tables B6 and B7 of the *Employment and Training Report of the President*, 1978. The data are based on the October supplement of the Current Population Survey and cover the period 1954–77.

The analysis presented in tables 4.2 and 4.3 demonstrates the importance of examining changes in participation in connection with related movements in employment and unemployment. The results suggest that teenagers and young women are particularly sensitive to short-run movements in aggregate economic activity. These patterns are consistent with a significant discouraged-worker effect. However, with negative coefficients among older women, and virtually no responsiveness among prime age men, the aggregate participation rate displays relatively little cyclical sensitivity. While aggregate movements in employment reflect primarily movements in unemployment, substantial variations in the composition of the labor force do occur over the business cycle.

4.2.2 Race and Enrollment Status

Variations in cyclical employment experience may be expected to depend on factors other than age and sex. Two such factors, race and school enrollment, are examined in tables 4.4 and 4.5, where the decompositions discussed above are presented for white and nonwhite workers, and separately for enrolled and nonenrolled young people. The results suggest that these factors make a considerable difference. The employment experience of nonwhites is much more responsive to cyclical conditions than is the experience of whites. A 1% reduction in the mature male unemployment rate raises the proportion of nonwhite youth who are employed by about 7%, compared to a little over 4% for white youths. The employment of older nonwhites is not as responsive to cyclical conditions, but still exhibits substantially more sensitivity than employment among the white population. For nonwhite men over 20, the employment ratio rises by 2.5% for each one-point decline in the prime-age-male unemployment rate. This is almost three times as large as the response for white men.

The results in table 4.5 display dramatic differences in the labor market behavior of enrolled and out-of-school youth. For young men and women enrolled in school, almost all of the response of employment is due to movements in participation rather than unemployment. The opposite pattern characterizes youth who are out of school. Increases in employment for this group come almost entirely at the expense of unemployment. However, employment for out-of-school youth appears to be only about half as sensitive to demand as that of enrolled young people.

The reasons for the disparity are not clear. One possible explanation is that youth who are in school tend to passively await job offers. When offered an attractive job, they accept and join the labor force. Otherwise, they remain out of the labor force. This would explain the observed pattern of participation and unemployment dynamics.

4.3 The Role of Aggregate Demand

The results in section 4.2 indicate that aggregate demand as measured by the prime-age-male unemployment rate has a significant effect on the unemployment and participation rates of most demographic groups. The effect is especially pronounced in those groups that traditionally have the highest unemployment and lowest participation rates. For example, black teenagers, whose unemployment rate averaged over 40% during 1976, benefit most from increased aggregate demand. Their employment ratio rises by over 6% for each one-point decline in the prime-age-male unemployment rate. Yet, many observers judge that the problems of high-unemployment demographic groups, such as black teenagers, are largely the result of structural factors and are quite insensitive to aggregate demand. Perhaps the most widely cited statement of this view is found in Feldstein (1973). In this section we analyze the extent to which aggregate demand can reduce the unemployment of disadvantaged demographic groups.

Pessimism with respect to the efficacy of aggregate demand policy is buttressed by the observation that the unemployment rate of certain disadvantaged groups has remained high even during periods when the overall rate was reduced to quite low levels. In 1969, for example, the unemployment rate for male teenagers was 11.4%, while the unemployment rate of black teenagers was over 23%. The analysis in this paper makes it clear that this may not reflect the impotence of aggregate demand. It may be that the participation rate of high-unemployment groups expands rapidly during periods of economic expansion, causing the group unemployment rate to remain at a fairly high level. On this view, the apparent sluggishness in unemployment arises because the hidden unemployment, which is not measured during times when jobs are unavailable, simply becomes measurable. In order to examine the role of aggregate demand, we have used the equations described in the preceding section to estimate the unemployment rate which would have arisen in 1976 if the unemployment rate of men 35–44 had been driven to its 1969 level (1.3%).

The results, presented in table 4.6, confirm the widespread view that unemployment rates would remain high, even in an expanding economy. For example, the estimates indicate that male teenagers would have had an unemployment rate of 11.5% at the end of 1976 even if the prime-age-male unemployment rate had been driven well below 2%. Likewise, black male teenagers would have had an unemployment rate of over 23%. Similar patterns hold for young women. It is significant that the predicted 1976 rates for male teenagers (both black and white) are virtually identical to the rates that actually prevailed in 1969. This result suggests that the empirical model provides a relatively consistent characterization of the cyclical experience of these groups.

In order to examine the extent to which the resilience of high unemployment rates reflects surges in participation, we have recalculated the unemployment rates under the assumption that participation rates remain constant as aggregate demand expands. Unemployment rates calculated on this basis are shown in column (3) of table 4.6. They indicate that with constant participation, increased aggregate demand could reduce unemployment rates of most demographic groups to very low levels.[7] For example, increased employment would lead to a male teenage unemployment rate of 5.6%, comparable to the average unemployment rate of the entire population over the postwar period. The unemployment rate of young women would be driven down to similarly low levels. However, the unemployment rate of black teenagers would still remain at levels approaching 17% for young men and 16% for young women. While clearly indicative of an important social problem, these calculations indicate that considering par-

Table 4.6
Simulated unemployment rates for 1976, 4th quarter, assuming
1969 levels of aggregate demand[a]

Demographic group	Actual unemployment rate 1976:4 (1)	Estimated unemployment rates with 1969 conditions	
		Full participation response (2)	No participation response (3)
Men			
16–19	19.5	11.5	5.6
20–24	12.8	5.9	7.1
25–34	6.6	2.7	2.6
35–44	4.3	1.1	1.0
45–54	4.5	1.4	1.4
55–64	4.1	.7	.8
65+	4.7	1.6	−3.6
Women			
16–19	18.6	12.8	5.1
20–24	12.4	7.8	5.6
25–34	8.6	5.1	1.1
35–44	6.2	3.3	1.6
45–54	5.2	2.7	2.3
55–64	5.0	2.8	5.2
65+	4.7	2.9	7.5
Black men			
16–19	35.9	23.2	16.9
20+	11.3	4.0	4.5
Black women			
16–19	37.1	26.4	15.7
20+	11.3	6.8	6.5

a. The estimated unemployment rates were calculated as follows: Column (2): Actual unemployment rate in $1976:4 - \gamma^i_{(1-UR)}\nabla$, where $\nabla \Rightarrow$ change in the prime-age-male unemployment rate had 1969 conditions prevailed in the previous two years. Column (3): Same as column (2), except that γ^i_{EN} was substituted for $\gamma^i_{(1-UR)}$.

ticipation increases significantly the apparent power of cyclical expansion in reducing unemployment.

It is somewhat difficult to interpret the results. Were participation to remain constant, it is clear that aggregate demand could eliminate serious unemployment problems for most demographic groups. Participation, however, does not in fact remain constant. This would seem, if anything, to strengthen the case for expansionary policy, since the large surge in participation that inevitably accompanies cyclical expansion must indicate a chronic shortage of jobs, or at least that many persons are outside of the labor force because they expect little gain from further employment search. Encouraging the reentrance of these individuals would seem to be an additional benefit of expansionary policy. It is clearly fallacious to argue that the potential entry of the hidden unemployed renders aggregate demand policy relatively impotent in easing the labor market problems of specific demographic groups.

These findings have important implications for recent legislation designed to move the economy toward full employment. The Humphrey-Hawkins bill provides for mandatory unemployment targets both in the aggregate and for demographic groups. Our analysis indicates that unemployment targets are misguided. Since unemployment-rate movements can reflect either desirable or undesirable changes, it is hardly sensible to design policy with a specific unemployment rate in mind. Rather, a much better means of serving the goals of full employment would be to phrase targets explicitly in terms of employment. Such a measure would avoid all of the ambiguities inherent in a CPS interpretation of the unemployment/nonparticipation distinction, as well as providing a sounder foundation for policy. A potential difficulty with this approach is that changes in labor supply patterns would alter the appropriate employment targets. These changes are typically gradual so that allowing for trends in the employment targets may be feasible.

4.4 Conclusions

The central conclusion of this paper is that understanding the cyclical dynamics of the labor market requires joint focus on unemployment and labor force participation. Both contribute substantially to observed variation in employment. Since their relative contributions differ substantially across demographic groups, both must be considered in making demographic comparisons. Our results suggest that young people bear a very disproportionate share of cyclical employment fluctuations. In large part, this is due to the cyclical movements in their participation. It has frequently been observed that high unemployment rates for some groups persist even in cyclical expansions. We show that the resilience of high unemployment is due to increases in participation rather than continued lack of employment opportunities. This finding suggests that the potential contribution of macroeconomic policy to alleviating the employment problems of specific demographic groups can be quite large.

Appendix

This appendix presents estimates of the basic empirical model for the 14 demographic groups. The equations were estimated with an eight-quarter lag on *UP*, but only the sum of the lag coefficients is presented. The data are available monthly in *Employment and Earnings*, published by the Bureau of Labor Statistics.

Table 4.7
Cyclical response of unemployment of demographic groups
(standard errors in parentheses)[a]

	Constant	UP	T $(\times 10^2)$	$T67$ $(\times 10^2)$	$\bar{R}^2$	SEE	ρ
Men							
16–19	−.034 (.022)	2.617 (.507)	−.074 (.026)	.005 (.068)	.904	.012	.767
20–24	−.009 (.025)	2.258 (.585)	−.003 (.030)	−.091 (.073)	.883	.010	.831
25–34	.001 (.011)	1.267 (.256)	.001 (.001)	.040 (.030)	.892	.005	.791
35–44	.002 (.008)	1.053 (.181)	−.001 (.009)	−.006 (.020)	.893	.004	.806
45–54	−.005 (.007)	1.007 (.018)	.007 (.009)	−.010 (.020)	.873	.004	.754
55–64	−.006 (.005)	1.111 (.123)	.003 (.006)	−.013 (.016)	.900	.004	.692
65+	−.007 (.003)	1.021 (.084)	−.002 (.004)	−.002 (.010)	.811	.005	.433
Women							
16–19	−.031 (.012)	1.876 (.289)	−.129 (.015)	.080 (.038)	.900	.012	.620
20–24	−.010 (.008)	1.515 (.200)	−.045 (.010)	−.029 (.024)	.905	.007	.620
25–34	−.016 (.008)	1.126 (.184)	−.018 (.009)	−.022 (.023)	.867	.005	.706
35–44	−.010 (.006)	.954 (.146)	−.015 (.007)	.001 (.018)	.815	.005	.652
45–54	−.013 (.005)	.826 (.128)	.002 (.006)	.025 (.016)	.811	.004	.655
55–64	−.018 (.004)	.734 (.091)	.015 (.005)	−.046 (.011)	.756	.005	.460
65+	−.009 (.004)	.588 (.098)	−.007 (.005)	−.025 (.013)	.586	.006	.330

a. The coefficient under UP is the negative sum of the coefficients from an eight-quarter, first degree polynomial distributed lag on UP. The dependent variable is $\ln(1 - UR)$, where UR_i is the unemployment rate of the ith group.

Table 4.8
Cyclical response of participation of demographic groups
(standard errors in parentheses)[a]

	Constant	UP	T ($\times 10^2$)	$T67$ ($\times 10^2$)	$\bar{R}^2$	SEE	ρ
Men							
16–19	−.401	1.905	−.271	.661	.898	.017	.621
	(.019)	(.445)	(.024)	(.061)			
20–24	−.132	−.408	−.064	.053	.756	.011	.642
	(.013)	(.297)	(.016)	(.041)			
25–34	−.031	.042	.009	.069	.860	.003	.747
	(.004)	(.097)	(.005)	(.015)			
35–44	−.021	.005	−.008	−.042	.901	.002	.496
	(.002)	(.051)	(.003)	(.007)			
45–54	−.037	.002	−.011	−.097	.961	.003	.584
	(.003)	(.074)	(.004)	(.010)			
55–64	−.132	−.039	−.029	−.319	.987	.005	.873
	(.012)	(.240)	(.019)	(.047)			
65+	−.696	1.678	−.821	.201	.994	.017	.830
	(.034)	(.020)	(.051)	(.126)			
Women							
16–19	−.802	2.530	−.106	.853	.985	.015	.821
	(.026)	(.620)	(.033)	(.084)			
20–24	−.793	.709	.187	.522	.985	.015	.821
	(.029)	(.658)	(.041)	(.106)			
25–34	−1.051	1.313	.205	.794	.991	.015	.718
	(.020)	(.460)	(.027)	(.066)			
35–44	−.917	.547	.255	.272	.990	.011	.545
	(.011)	(.252)	(.013)	(.034)			
45–54	−.953	.129	.489	−.407	.990	.011	.920
	(.033)	(.558)	(.058)	(.144)			
55–64	−1.333	−.793	.706	−.878	.986	.018	.742
	(.026)	(.583)	(.035)	(.087)			
65+	−2.386	−1.496	.099	−.686	.767	.041	.708
	(.054)	(1.248)	(.072)	(.130)			

a. The coefficient under UP is the negative of the sum of the coefficients from an eight-quarter, first degree polynomial distributed lag on UP.

This work was supported by ASPER of the U.S. Department of Labor. We are indebted to Jerry Jacobs and James Poterba for their assistance with the computations.

Notes

1. Feldstein (1973) has demonstrated the importance of demographic distinctions in analyzing unemployment. Other analyses, notably Mincer (1963, 1966) and Bowen and Finegan (1969), have shown the extent of differences in participation behavior across demographic groups.

2. There are additional reasons for treating the unemployment data with caution. Clark and Summers (1979b) have argued that an important part of transitions into and out of unemployment arises from inconsistent reporting of relatively consistent behavior. They cite evidence on rotation group bias, the effects on reporting of slight changes in the survey, and reinterview error rates showing that a sizable fraction of the flows between unemployment and not-in-the-labor-force is an artifact of the monthly survey.

3. Note that as long as $UR < .1$, it differs negligibly from $\ln(1 - UR)$. Hence (3) can be interpreted as showing that the percentage change in employment is equal to the percentage change in the participation rate minus the change in the unemployment rate.

4. For example, the employment elasticity for women 25–34 using Perry's weighted unemployment rate in an annual version of the model was 2.03, compared to 2.44 in the quarterly version with correction for autocorrelation.

5. None of the conclusions is significantly altered when the employment ratio equation is estimated directly. Of course, the identity (8) is no longer satisfied.

6. In interpreting all the results in this section, it may be useful to note that a movement of one point in the prime-age-male unemployment rate corresponds to a change of 1.25 points in the overall rate.

7. These predictions may depend on the functional form of the estimating equation. Feldstein and Wright (1976) found little difference in the response to changes in unemployment between periods of high and low unemployment.

5

Labor Force Participation: Timing and Persistence

with Kim B. Clark

5.1

Much of the development of applied economic theory within the past 25 years has emphasized the importance of viewing economic decisions in a life cycle context. Consumption decisions are today frequently viewed as being determined by wealth or permanent income. The human capital revolution has brought life cycle considerations to the forefront of modern labor economics. While the life cycle dynamics of labor force participation decisions have important implications for macroeconomic theory and policy, they have received relatively little empirical attention. With the notable exceptions of Lucas and Rapping (1969) and Hall (1980), none of the large body of work on cyclical fluctuations in employment has explicitly relied on a dynamic model of labor supply.[1]

This paper uses several types of data to examine two elements of participation dynamics. The first is the aspect of "timing" that is implicit in the work of Lucas and Rapping, and in Mincer's (1966) early discussion of hidden unemployment. The timing argument, which is presented most explicitly in Ghez and Becker (1975), holds that leisure is easily substitutable across periods. Hence relatively small transitory movements in the perceived real wage or real rate of return can have large effects on the path of labor supply as individuals time their participation to coincide with periods of high transitory wages. On the other hand, permanent changes, because they do not affect the timing decision, are expected to have a much smaller effect on participation.

It is this view of labor supply that underlies new classical macroeconomic models. The dependence is made explicit in Lucas (1975), who

---

Reprinted by permission, with revisions, from *Review of Economic Studies*, 49:825−844, 1982. Copyright © 1982 The Society for Economic Analysis Limited.

claims that "what we do know indicates that leisure in one period is an excellent substitute for leisure in other nearby periods." The ability of classical macroeconomic models to explain fluctuations in employment depends on the presence of strong intertemporal substitution effects. Unless leisure is very substitutable across periods, large observed cyclical variations in employment could not possibly be caused by the response of labor supply to the relatively small fluctuations that are found in real wages and real interest rates.

It is by now clear that models in which only timing elements are present cannot fully account for cyclical fluctuations. The restrictions imposed by rationality imply that the expectational errors that generate business cycles are serially uncorrelated. The serial correlation that is characteristic of business cycles can only be explained in terms of mechanisms that cause shocks to be propagated over several periods. While Lucas (1975), Blinder and Fischer (1981), and Sargent (1980) have considered alternative explanations of persistence in the demand for labor, little attention has been devoted to the question of persistence in labor supply. To a substantial extent, a demonstration of substantial persistence in labor supply decisions undercuts the plausibility of models based on a high elasticity of labor supply with respect to transitory wage movements since it is difficult to see why a long-run decision should be strongly responsive to transitory developments.

The second element of labor force dynamics that we consider is embodied in the "persistence" hypothesis. In this view, past work experience is a key determinant of current employment status. Because of high separation costs and costs of finding new employment, those who are employed tend to remain employed. Persistence of employment might also be rationalized on human capital grounds. Those who are employed longer tend to accumulate more human capital, which raises the return to work in the future relative to leisure. Those out of the labor force may also develop household-specific capital or commitments (i.e., children), which reduce the return to working relative to remaining outside the labor force. There is also some reason to believe that the taste for work may be affected by work experience. Such habit formation effects have been well documented in demand analysis.[2]

This aspect of labor force dynamics appears to be quite important in microeconometric studies of employment patterns. Freeman (1976) presents extensive evidence indicating that the probability of separation from employment declines with the duration of employment. This result is obtained separately for voluntary separation (quits) in Freeman (1977) and for involuntary separations (layoffs) in Medoff (1979). Of course it is possible that this pattern results from individual heterogeneity. Those with high withdrawal possibilities are less likely to be observed as employed than those with low probabilities. Heterogeneity has been considered by Heckman (1978) and Yatchew (1977) as an explanation of persistence in labor force participation; both conclude that at least for married women, true state dependence exists. Chamberlain (1978) has devised a methodology for estimating the size of the persistence effect. He finds that, after controlling for individual differences, prior experience raises the odds of participation by a factor of seven. Other researchers have found evidence that persons with employment experience are more likely to be reemployed quickly when unemployed. Persistence effects of this magnitude imply that any measure that affects employment will have important long-run effects.

The differing macroeconomic implications of models in which timing or persistence effects predominate are highlighted by the following example. In an economy that is initially in equilibrium, the government unexpectedly undertakes expansionary policy.[3] Irrespective of whether timing or persistence predominates, the initial impact of the change is an increase in employment and labor force participation. However, timing and persistence effects are opposite in the longer run. An extreme version of the timing hypothesis would hold that individuals desire to spend a fixed proportion of their lives in the labor force, which they schedule to coincide with periods of maximum opportunity. If this is the case, labor supply after the shock will be less than it would have been had the shock never occurred, as individuals "schedule" themselves out of the labor force.

Such scheduling effects have been used to counter arguments that the fluctuations in participation that accompany changes in the unemployment rate imply a significant discouraged worker effect.[4] What appears to be discouragement is actually the effect of individuals timing their participation to coincide with periods of maximum opportunity. When timing predominates, output gains from expansionary policy are illusionary. They will be cancelled by a reduction in subsequent output as workers time their withdrawal from the labor force. Thus, models with strong intertemporal substitution effects imply that a transitory increase in the real wage will reduce subsequent labor supply. Moreover, a permanent upgrading of opportunities in a timing world imply a much smaller increase in participation than observed in the short run because scheduling effects would no longer occur.

Persistence effects, however, yield a long-run increase in labor supply. Short-run increases in employment will tend to persist as workers remain in the labor force because of habit formation, adjustment costs, or human capital accumulation. Hence, concurrent changes, on this view, understate the total increment to output from expansionary policy. The effects of persistence described here potentially complement the process of worker upgrading discussed in Okun (1973) and Thurow (1976).[5]

The relative empirical importance of timing and persistence effects in labor supply is an issue with important implications for macroeconomic theory and policy. Both effects essentially deny the "natural rate" hypothesis as a medium-run proposition. They imply that policy can have an extended impact on the rate of employment without repeatedly fooling economic agents, because in both views labor supply is conditioned by past employment experience.[6] It is this link that translates short-run policy effects into longer-run impacts. As is clear from the preceding discussion, timing and persistence effects have exactly the opposite implications for the long-run direction of expansionary policy. This paper is directed at determining their relative importance in economic fluctuations.

The next section of the paper examines a natural experiment that potentially can shed light on the question at hand. During World War II, the level of female employment and participation rose precipitously. We examine the aftermath of the conflict to see whether the war had a positive or negative impact on subsequent female participation. The third section of the paper lays the groundwork for the econometric analysis, by outlining a simple model of life cycle labor supply that is capable of embodying both timing and persistence effects. The model developed in this section can be examined using several types of data. Section 5.4 of the paper uses the model to examine the relative importance of timing and persistence effects in accounting for the time-series behavior of the aggregate labor force participation rate. The fifth section of the paper examines the timing and persistence effects using cross-section data. Essentially, the analysis relies on the observation that differences in unemployment over time are dominated by transitory movements, whereas geographic differences are for the most part permanent. The sixth section of the paper summarizes the empirical results and discusses their implications.

5.2 The Impact of World War II

Before developing a formal model of life cycle labor supply, it is instructive to examine the one natural experiment that history has provided. The Second World War period and its aftermath offer an ideal testing ground for timing and persistence effects. From 1940 to 1944 real output in the

United States increased 46.4% while the unemployment rate fell from 14.6 to 1.2% and averaged 1.3% for 1943–45. The expansion in real output occurred at a time when large numbers of men were drawn into the Armed Forces, increasing the job prospects and potential earnings of women. After 1945, unemployment rose slightly but remained below 4.0% through 1948. In the recession of 1949, the unemployment rate rose 2.1 points to 5.9%. The decade of the 1940s provides a good example of a large spurt in aggregate demand followed by a return to normal growth.

In perhaps the first statement of the timing hypothesis Milton Friedman underscored the instructive quality of the World War II period:

... the reaction to a higher wage rate expected to be temporary and then to revert to a lower level will tend to be very different than the reaction to a higher wage rate expected to be permanent. The temporarily higher wage rate would seem more likely to bring forth an increased quantity of labour from a fixed population than a permanently higher one, since there would be strong temptation to take advantage of the opportunity while it lasts and to buy leisure later.

An interesting case in point is the experience of the United States during World War II, when both the fraction of the population in the labour force and the average number of hours worked per week were substantially higher than during the pre-war period.[7]

Friedman provides no explicit empirical analysis of changes in participation over the period, yet it is implicit in his discussion that World War II marked a period of transitory wage gains that ought to be followed by an increased purchase of leisure in later years. This effect should have been accentuated by the large buildup of wealth that took place during the war. In contrast, if persistence effects were dominant, market attachment would have increased with increased work experience, and World War II would have had a long-run positive impact on observed participation.

The issue of long-run versus transitory effects seems particularly important for the female labor force, and particularly for married women. Since almost all able males are always in the labor force, there is little variation in male participation and thus little to be learned about the impact of transitory movements in job opportunities and wages. Females participate much less than men, and their behavior appears to be much more sensitive to labor market conditions. Moreover, because of the large increase in the Armed Forces and the consequent increase in job opportunities, women were particularly affected by the expansion of demand during World War II.

The impact of World War II on the participation of adult women is documented in table 5.1.[8] From 1890 to 1940, the participation rate of

Table 5.1
Participation of adult women by marital status and age 1890–1950

Age, marital status	1890	1900	1920	1930	1940	1944	1947	1950
(1) Adult women								
25–64	13.9	16.0	19.6	21.8	25.7	32.5	28.8	31.1
(2) Married women	4.6	5.6	9.0	11.7	15.6	23.9	20.0	23.0
Marital status by age								
(3) Women 25–44	15.1	17.5	21.7	24.6	30.5	36.1	31.2	33.3
Married	—	—	9.0	13.9	16.1	28.8	—	24.3
Single	—	—	—	75.4	76.8	82.0	—	77.7
(4) Women 45–64	12.1	13.6	16.5	18.5	20.2	27.1	25.3	28.8
Married	—	—	6.2	7.3	9.0	21.4	—	19.1
Single	—	—	—	47.5	56.6	59.1	—	64.8

Source: Line 1 is a weighted average of participation rates for women 25–44 and 45–64 taken from census data in *Historical Statistics of the United States (1975)*, part 1, series D38-D39, p. 132. Populations weights were taken from the same source. The values for 1944 and 1947 are based on CPS data and have been *reduced* to make them comparable to the Census definitions. We assumed that the growth rate of participation in the CPS data 1944–50 was accurate; we thus extrapolated the growth rates back from the 1950 census value. The CPS values are 36.1 for 1944 and 32.0 for 1947.

Line 2 is series D60 from p. 133 of *Historical Statistics*. The data are for women 15 and over from 1890–1930, and 14 and over, 1940–50. Married refers to all married women whether husband is present or not. As in line 1, the data for 1944 and 1947 were adjusted to accord with Census definitions. The CPS values were 25.6 for 1944 and 21.4 for 1947.

The data in lines 3 and 4 were taken from Census publications as follows:

1920 U.S. Census, 1920, vol. 4, p. 694, table 5—data refer to married women with no distinction based on absence or presence of spouse. The entry for women 45–64 is the rate of participation of women 45 and over.

1930 U.S. Census, 1930, vol. 5, General Report on Occupation, chapter 5, table 5, p. 274—data refer to all married women.

1940 U.S. Census, 1940, *Employment and Family Characteristics of Women*—Special Report, table 1, p. 9, and table 2, p. 10. Data refer to married women, spouse present.

1950 U.S. Census, 1950, Special Report P-E, No. 1-A, *Employment and Personal Characteristics*, table 10, p. 1A-101. Data refer to married women, spouse present. Data for 1950 suggest that the category married-spouse present dominates the married-total group. Total married participation rates were 25.8 for women 25–44, and 20.4 for women 45–64.

adult women 25–64 increased from 13.9 to 25.7%, a compounded annual rate of increase of 1.2% per year. In striking contrast, between 1940 and 1944, the participation rate rose 23.5% (25.7 to 32.5) or 6.0% per year. Among married women, participation increased 2.5% per year from 1890 to 1940 (4.6 to 15.6), but a remarkable 11.3% from 1940 to 1944 (15.6 to 23.9). The marked increase in participation of married women was not confined to a specific age group. After rising very slowly in the twenty-year period before 1940, for example, participation by married women ages 45–64 more than doubled in the early years of the war.

The data in table 5.1 suggest that the war had a major impact on the market behavior of adult women, particularly those who were married.[9] The data also suggest that the increase in participation was not short-lived. Table 5.2 presents projected values of labor force participation, based on trends estimated over the periods 1890–1930 and 1890–1940, for married women and adult women 25–64. Comparison of actual and predicted values confirms the long-term effects of the war. For adult women 25–64, the trend fitted through 1940 predicts the 1940 participation rate, but the actual rate remains above the trend throughout the subsequent decade. The results for married women are even more striking; the actual rate averages 24.7% above the trend for the three time periods noted.[10]

The failure of the participation rate to fall below the trend after the transitory developments of the war had passed seems to be evidence that persistence effects dominated the effects of timing. It is important to note that both effects seem to have been present. The fact that we observe a decline in participation after 1945 suggests that a significant number of

Table 5.2
Predicted trends in participation 1940–50

	Adult women 25–64			Married women		
	Actual	Predicted 1890–1940 trend	Predicted 1890–1930 trend	Actual	Predicted 1890–1940 trend	Predicted 1890–1930 trend
1930	21.8	22.3	21.9	11.7	11.8	11.5
1940	25.7	25.4	24.4	15.6	15.1	14.6
1944	32.5	26.3	25.5	23.9	16.7	16.0
1947	28.8	27.3	26.4	20.0	17.9	17.2
1950	31.1	28.2	27.3	23.0	19.3	18.4

Source: table 5.1.

women responded to the extraordinary opportunities of that period, and then scheduled themselves out of the labor force in subsequent years. Yet there is little support for a strong version of the timing hypothesis, which would have predicted a fall of labor supply below trend after the war. It seems evident that strong persistence effects were at work. Indeed, the labor force participation rate of women, especially married women, appears to have been permanently increased by World War II.

Two alternative explanations of the apparent positive long-run effect of the war experience deserve further comment. First, it is frequently argued that the war brought changes in social attitudes toward women in the workplace. However, these changes were caused in large part by the increase in the number of women working during the war. Changes in attitudes should be viewed as factors through which the effect of employment experience on long-run increases in participation is mediated. That work experience during the war affected attitudes is evident in a 1944 survey conducted by the United Auto Workers. Half of the women surveyed, who had never worked in a factory before the war, professed a desire to continue in a factory after the war. Over 85% desired to remain employed in some capacity.[11] The view that the increased participation of women was due to a general change in attitudes rather than the conditioning effect of wartime experience is also belied by a comparison of cohort participation rates. The participation rate of women 20–24, who were not directly affected by the war actually fell between 1940 and 1950. If the change in attitudes were general, it would have been expected to rise along with other participation rates.

A second explanation of the long-run increase in female participation following the war relies on the argument that reduced discrimination and increased productivity led to a rise in the permanent relative wage of women following World War II, and thus to an increase in participation. Insofar as this reflected human capital accumulation during the war, it is consistent with persistence effects. However, there is not much evidence that the male-female wage differential fell between the immediate pre- and postwar periods.[12]

The results presented in this section, while quite suggestive, are based on relatively fragmentary data. While there is an indication in the data that persistence effects dominated timing effects, this conclusion deserves much more careful scrutiny. In the next section we develop the model that underlies the more sophisticated econometric analysis of the timing and persistence effects presented in subsequent sections.

5.3 The Model

This section outlines the model that provides the basis for the empirical work in this study. The model follows closely that of Lucas–Rapping (1969). However, it does differ in several respects, notably, the treatment of expectations and our focus on participation rather than aggregate labor supply. Because much of the focus of this study is on how past behavior as well as expected future developments influence participation, it is necessary to employ a three-period framework, rather than the more common two-period formulation.

Individuals are assumed to maximize an intertemporal utility function of the form

$$U = U(c_{t-1}, l_{t-1}, c_t, l_t, c_{t+1}, l_{t+1}),$$ (1)

where c represents consumption and l represents leisure, measured as a proportion of total time endowment. The period $t - 1$ is assumed to represent the entire past, and the period $t + 1$ embodies the whole future. It is assumed that the individual at time t takes consumption and labor supply decisions in period $t - 1$ as given.

Individuals maximize the utility function (1), taking as predetermined previous employment experience, and the level of assets A_t, which may be positive or negative. The solution to the maximization problem will depend on their expectations of future nominal wages, w_{t+1}, future prices p_{t+1}, and the interest rate r_t. The budget constraint holds that lifetime consumption cannot exceed lifetime earnings.

Since the focus of this analysis is on the participation decision, the first-order conditions for the maximization of (1) are of little concern. It suffices to observe that an interior maximum with positive participation will occur if the market wage w_t exceeds the reservation wage w_t^*. The reservation wage, w_t^*, is the minimum wage at which an individual will supply a positive amount of labor, that is, join the labor force.

For the moment we assume, following Lucas and Rapping, that the labor market is in equilibrium, though this assumption will be relaxed subsequently. If the labor market is in equilibrium, the prevailing market wage is potentially available to any possible participants. The reservation wage will depend on tastes, past employment, future opportunities, and assets. This may be written as

$$w_t^* = f\left((1 - l_{t-1}), p_t, \frac{w_{t+1}^e}{(1 + r)}, \frac{p_{t+1}^e}{(1 + r)}, A_t\right).$$ (2)

Notice that we assume here that economic agents know the true price level at each point in time and so rule out misperceptions of the types stressed in some recent macroeconomic models.

The central question of this paper can be posed in terms of the signs of the derivatives of w_t^* with respect to the arguments in (2). The standard assumption that leisure is a normal good yields the unambiguous conclusion that $f_4 > 0$; that is, an increase in wealth, *ceteris paribus*, raises the reservation wage. The signs of the effects of the other variables in (2) depend on the form of the utility function (1).

Consider first the sign of f_1, the impact of previous employment experience on current labor supply. With assets held constant, previous employment will affect the reservation wage only insofar as it affects the marginal rate of substitution between current leisure and consumption. The types of arguments usually put forward in discussions of intertemporal substitution suggest that $\delta w_t^*/\delta(1 - l_{t-1})$ is negative. Increases in previous work effort raise the marginal disutility of current labor. Formulations adopting this assumption explicitly have been used by Sargent (1980) and Kydland and Prescott (1981). The effect, however, is theoretically ambiguous. In the presence of adjustment costs, habit formation effects, or accumulation of "leisure capital" the sign can easily be positive.

The effects of changes in the other arguments of (2) can be analysed in a similar fashion. Both expected future wages and prices have uncertain effects. Increases in future wages have a negative income effect on current labor supply. The substitution effect depends on the sign of $U_{l_t l_{t+1}}$. If it is positive, the substitution effect is positive and leisure today and in the future are complements. In the case of an additively separable utility function $\delta w_t^*/\delta w_{t+1}^e$ is unambiguously negative.[13] This illustrates that past experience and future opportunities do not have symmetric effects, since past employment experience has no effect in this case. The difference arises essentially because of the income effects of future wage changes. Increases in expected future prices have a positive income effect on labor supply, and an ambiguous substitution effect depending on $U_{l_t c_{t+1}}$.

So far the theory has been developed for a single individual. People will in general differ in both their tastes and market opportunities as well as in their previous experience and asset accumulation. As a result there will exist a joint distribution of market and reservation wages. The aggregate participation rate L^s is then given by

$$L^s = \iint_{w > w^*} g(w,w^*)\, dw\, dw^*. \tag{3}$$

It is readily apparent that $\delta L^s/\delta w > 0$: an increase in wages available to all workers will unambiguously raise the participation rate. The so-called "added worker" effect cannot exist in this model. Essentially, this is because at zero labor supply, increases in the wage do not change income. Income effects could be brought in if labor supply was modeled as the result of joint maximization by individuals within a family. They may also arise from changes in noncontemporaneous wages.

It follows from (3) that the participation rate is a function of the wage level, and the determinants of the shadow wage. Recognizing that the labor supply relation is homogeneous of degree zero in wage and the prices leads to the labor supply function,

$$L^s = f\left((1 - l_{t-1}), \frac{w_t}{p_t}, \frac{w_{t+1}^e}{p_t(1 + r)}, \frac{p_{t+1}^e}{p_t(1 + r)}, \frac{A_t}{p_t}\right), \tag{4}$$

where L^s is the function of the population in the labor force. For convenience we assume a logarithmic functional form. Equation (5) may then be rewritten as

$$\ln L^s = \beta_0 + \beta_1 \ln(1 - l_{t-1}) + \beta_2 \ln\left(\frac{w_t}{p_t}\right) + \beta_3 \ln\left(\frac{w_{t+1}^e}{p_t(1 + r)}\right)$$
$$+ \beta_4 \ln\left(\frac{p_{t+1}^e}{p_t(1 + r)}\right) + \beta_5 \ln\frac{A_t}{p_t}. \tag{5}$$

Equation (5) differs from the Lucas-Rapping formulation in that the term $(1 - l_{t-1})$ is included, reflecting the assumed dependence of the demand for leisure on leisure enjoyed during the preceding period. While such a dependence would seem to be a clear property of the Lucas-Rapping model, it is lost in the translation into their estimating equation. The term $(1 - l_{t-1})$ does appear in their equation, but only as a result of a Koyck transformation. While they expect and obtain a positive impact of previous labor supply, it is clear from the above discussion that the effect is actually ambiguous. A strong form of the timing hypothesis would predict a negative effect of lagged labor supply (apart from its role as a distributed lag generator).

At this point, it is useful to consider the expected signs of $\beta_1, \ldots, \beta_5$. The signs depend on the relative importance of persistence and timing elements in fluctuations in labor supply. A key parameter is β_1, the elasticity of current labor supply with respect to past employment experience. Sufficiently large intertemporal substitution effffects would insure that $\beta_1 < 0$ so that increases in experience reduce subsequent participation. On the other hand, persistence effects imply $\beta_1 > 0$ so that increases in employment experience raise the participation rate. The coefficient of β_2 is expected to be positive, as increases in contemporaneous real wages raise the attractiveness of seeking work. The sign of β_3 depends on the relative size of timing and persistence effects. If timing elements predominate, β_3 will be negative as increases in expected wages cause labor supply to decline because of intertemporal substitution effects. In the context of a model like that of Lucas and Rapping, one would expect that $\beta_2 + \beta_3 \simeq 0$, since the long-run wage elasticity of labor supply is expected to be small. If adjustment costs or capital accumulation effects cause labor supply decisions to have a permanent character, the sign of β_3 will be positive. The sign of β_4 is ambiguous while β_5 is expected to be negative.

Equation (5) as it stands is a labor supply curve. If the labor market were always in equilibrium, it could be estimated directly using the employment ratio (proportion of the population who are employed) as the dependent variable. If, however, the labor market does not always clear, the level of employment cannot be taken as measure of desired labor supply. However, a measure of supply is provided by the labor force participation rate, the proportion of the population looking for work or working. This variable is the measure of labor supply used in this study. However, estimates using employment as the dependent variable are also discussed.

It is important to be clear about the issues involved in choosing between the employment and participation rate as dependent variables in equation (5). Lucas and Rapping take the position that an equation like (5) characterizes the level of employment, not the participation rate. On their hypothesis, workers who choose not to work because of a transitory decline in wages show up as unemployed and so are counted as labor force participants. Thus their argument implies that studying the labor force participation rate would obscure the important intertemporal substitution effects of wage changes. Although estimates of equation (5) using employment are presented below, we regard the Lucas-Rapping interpretation of the unemployment rate as problematic for several reasons. First, it provides no explanation for the fluctuations in the participation rate, which account for a sizable part of observed employment fluctuations. Second, unemployment is defined as inability to find work at prevailing wages. Individuals who are intertemporally substituting out of employment presumably know the prevailing wage, and do not desire work. They should therefore not report themselves as unemployed. Finally, our previous analysis, Clark and Summers (1979b), of individual unemployment experience suggests that the assumption of continuous labor market equilibrium is very problematic.

Once the possibility that the labor market may not clear is recognized, it is necessary to modify equation (5). When involuntary unemployment exists, the assumption that all who want them can get jobs at the prevailing wage is no longer appropriate. Individual decisions regarding labor supply will be affected by the knowledge that search costs are higher when unemployment is higher. Since the mean duration of a completed spell of employment in the United States is only about 20 months (Clark and Summers 1979b), relatively small changes in the duration of pre-employment search can have a large impact on the return to seeking employment. By increasing the duration of search as well as by reducing the pool of good jobs, and increasing the risk of layoff, unemployment discourages labor supply. We thus include the unemployment rate as an additional explanatory variable in some of our empirical work. In the next two sections we estimate alternative forms of (5) using both aggregate time-series and cross-section data for different demographic groups.

5.4 Time-Series Evidence

This section describes the estimation of (5) using time-series data. Before the model can be estimated, it is necessary to develop operational measures of the variables. Both the proxy for previous employment experience and the measurement of expectations of inflation and the real wage require discussion. In equation (5) previous experience is represented simply by $(1 - l_{t-1})$. This term is supposed to represent the entire past experience of a population group. Using simply the previous year's employment experience would be inappropriate since the logic of both the timing and persistence effects suggests current labor supply is conditioned by a longer history. We therefore follow the work of Houthakker and Taylor (1970) in developing a measure of the "stock" of past employment. We assume that the labor supply of a cohort depends on a set of variables Z (such as those contained in (5)) and on its past employment experience. Past employment experience is assumed to be represented by

$$E_t^* = \sum_{i=1}^{\infty} \lambda^{i-1} E_{t-1} = \frac{E_{t-1}}{1 - \lambda L}, \tag{6}$$

where L is the lag operator. Since participation is a function of this stock and the set of variables Z it is clear that

$$PR_t = Z_t \beta + \beta_1 E_t^*, \tag{7}$$

where PR_t is the participation rate. Using (6) the model can be expressed in terms of observables as

$$PR_t = Z_t \beta - Z_{t-1} \lambda \beta + \lambda PR_{t-1} + \beta_1 E_{t-1}. \tag{8}$$

Alternatively, as discussed in the previous section, the employment ratio could be taken as the dependent variable. Using equations (5) and (8), and appropriate measures for participation, employment, and Z, the most general specification of our estimating equation can be written

$$PR_t = \beta_0 + \beta_1 E_{t-1} + \beta_2 W_t + \beta_3 \, {}_tW_f^e + \beta_4 \, {}_tP_f^e + \beta_5 t + \beta_6 UM_t$$

$$+ \lambda PR_{t-1} - \lambda [\beta_2 W_{t-1} + \beta_3 \, {}_{t-1}W_f^e + \beta_4 \, {}_{t-1}P_f^e \tag{9}$$

$$+ \beta_5 (t-1) + \beta_6 UM_{t-1}] + v_t,$$

where t indicates times, W_t is the contemporaneous real wage, ${}_tW_f^e$ and ${}_tP_f^e$ are expected future discounted wages and prices, E_{t-1} is the ratio of employment to population in the previous period, UM_t is a measure of the unemployment rate, and v_t is an error term in M.[14] The time trend has been included to reflect the possible influence of slowly changing determinants not captured by other included variables. In this formulation, the coefficient β_1 measures the persistence of labor supply, while λ reflects the lag in formation of the habit stock. The long-run impact of an increase in employment experience is $\beta_1/(1 - \lambda)$. This may be interpreted in two different ways. It represents the increase in the participation rate at time t, if employment in all previous periods were raised by one unit. It also can be interpreted as the sum over all future periods of the increases in participation arising from a one-shot increase in employment.

Equation (6) gives us a way of measuring the employment stock and deriving the estimating equation in (9); the second issue that must be considered is the development of measures of expected wages and prices. Most standard econometric procedures seem inappropriate because theory suggests that labor supply should depend on the expected discounted value of wages and prices over a long horizon. Our procedure for modeling expectations begins with an estimate of a set of vector autoregressions relating wages, prices, and real output.[15] These vector autoregressions are then simulated using data for each year in the sample to generate forecasts of wages and prices for the succeeding 5 years. These variables, ${}_tw_{t+1}^e$, are then adjusted to an after-tax basis and discounted back to year t, using year t's municipal bond rate.[16] They are then averaged to form proxies for $w_{t+1}^e/p_t(1 + r)$ and $p_{t+1}^e/p_t(1 + r)$, which in their logarithmic form we have labeled ${}_tW_f^e$ and ${}_tP_f^e$, respectively.

This procedure is somewhat arbitrary in its choice of horizon and in the specification of the vector autoregressions. However, it seems to be the only computationally feasible way of handling the modeling of expectations that are more than one period ahead. Rational expectations techniques of the sort developed by McCallum (1976) are not applicable in the current example because of the quasi-differencing involved in moving to equation (8).

The data used in the actual estimation cover the period 1951–81. We have chosen to use annual data because timing and persistence effects are likely to be badly confounded with seasonal fluctuations in higher frequency data. Our measures of the participation rate and employment ratio are age-adjusted rates calculated as fixed weight averages of age-specific rates. This age-adjusted participation rate is used to avoid biases introduced by the changing age structure of the population.

In the results reported below, we have omitted assets from the estimating equation. Like others before us (e.g., Lucas and Rapping, 1969), we found assets to have no significant relationship to participation. This conclusion is based on an assets measure that includes the real value of household financial holdings, excluding equity. A variety of other assets measures that included equity, housing, and social security wealth were tried with little change in the results.

Several econometric issues arise in the estimation of equation (9). First, the equation is highly nonlinear in the parameters, necessitating nonlinear estimation. Second, the error term v_t is likely to be serially correlated. Even if the error term in equation (7) relating participation to Z and E^* were not serially correlated, the transformation of E^* involved in deriving the estimating equation would induce moving average error. Serial correlation in the error term is particularly serious in this case because both lagged participation and employment are included in the regression equation. Since there is no reason to suppose that the error in (8) follows a simple autoregressive scheme, the usual corrections (e.g., Cochrane-Orcutt) are not appropriate. We have chosen to estimate the equation using two-stage nonlinear least squares, treating both lagged participation and employment as endogenous. The instrument list includes a time trend, a squared trend, real federal government spending, the rate of money growth, and the real per capita stock of nonresidential capital , along with the included exogenous variables. In addition, to allow for simultaneity, the contemporaneous wage is treated as endogenous.

A third econometric difficulty is collinearity, which frequently precludes disentangling estimates of λ, which determines the mean lag of the "past employment" effect, and β_1, the impact effect of changes in employment experience. Frequently, the estimated values of λ lie outside the range $0 \leq \lambda \leq 1$, and so the equations are not meaningful. Therefore, in many of the equations reported below, the value of λ is constrained to the *a priori* plausible value of 0.9. None of the qualitative conclusions were affected by the imposition of this constraint. In particular, all of the conclusions regarding the effects of transitory wage changes are wholly unaffected by the choice of λ.

Table 5.3 presents estimates of several variants of equation (9) using the log of the participation rate as the dependent variable. The results do not suggest that timing effects have an important role to play in explaining cyclical fluctuations. The estimated elasticity of labor supply with respect to a transitory wage change is always small and sometimes negative. Nor is there any clear evidence of a negative relationship between expected future wages and labor supply, as predicted by models that emphasize timing effects. No clear conclusions emerge about the effects of changes in the price of future consumption. It is noteworthy that the increases in the unemployment rate of mature men do appear to reduce the participation rate, as theory predicts.

The data provide weak support for the importance of persistence in explaining fluctuations in labor supply. It is not possible to interpret the estimated effect of employment experience in equations (3)–(5) of table 5.3 because the estimated value of λ lies outside its permissible range. In equation (8), where a time trend is not included, the estimated effect of the "employment stock" variable is both substantively and statistically significant. However, when a time trend is included as in equation (6) and (7), the "employment stock" coefficient remains positive but becomes insignificant. Estimates using the employment-population ratio as a dependent variable are reported in table 5.4. The results are qualitatively similar to those obtained using the participation rate as a dependent variable. Here the evidence of persistence effects is very weak. Even when the time trend is omitted as in equation (6) of the table, the employment stock variable is statistically insignificant. Not surprisingly, the cyclical indicator, UM_t, enters the employment equations in a highly significant way.

The time-series evidence presented here suggests that transitory variations in the perceived real wage have little effect on the rate of labor force participation. We find no indication in the data of the strong intertemporal substitution effects that are the basis of classical macro models. These findings on the effect of transitory wage changes are consistent with the positive impact of lagged employment found in table 5.3. While the quality

Table 5.3
Timing and persistence effects in time-series participation equations[a]

Equation	CONS	W	W*	P*	UM_t	TIME	E_{t-1}	λ	SEE	D.W.
1	4.975 (0.320)	-0.084 (0.100)	0.009 (0.039)	—	—	—	—	—	0.005	1.48
2	6.620 (0.815)	-0.052 (0.099)	-0.157 (0.122)	0.186 (0.125)	—	—	—	—	0.005	1.72
3	3.814 (0.060)	-0.186 (0.056)	-0.012 (0.041)	—	—	0.007 (0.001)	0.470 (0.234)	-0.501 (0.246)	0.009	1.125
4	3.777 (0.089)	-0.199 (0.060)	-0.030 (0.054)	—	-0.001 (0.003)	0.008 (0.002)	0.326 (0.293)	-0.352 (0.308)	0.008	0.920
5	4.232 (0.052)	0.219 (0.426)	-0.090 (0.454)	0.135 (0.459)	—	—	0.128 (0.444)	-0.127 (0.437)	0.016	0.377
6	0.297 (0.428)	-0.321 (0.179)	0.066 (0.058)	—	—	0.009 (0.005)	0.019 (0.110)	0.9[b]	0.006	1.898
7	0.301 (0.399)	-0.287 (0.181)	0.027 (0.062)	—	-0.002 (0.002)	0.009 (0.004)	0.018 (0.102)	0.9[b]	0.006	1.974
8	-0.584 (0.518)	-0.028 (0.162)	-0.194 (0.466)	0.310 (0.520)	—	—	0.243 (0.123)	0.9[b]	0.006	1.820

a. Numbers in parentheses are standard errors.
b. The parameter was set equal to the value indicated.

Table 5.4
Timing and persistence effects in time-series employment equations[a]

Equation	CONS	W	W^*	P^*	UM_t	TIME	E_{t-1}	λ	SEE	D.W.
1	4.183 (0.041)	0.020 (0.114)	0.158 (0.101)	—	—	—	—	—	0.013	1.94
2	4.197 (0.090)	−0.184 (0.259)	0.434 (0.319)	−0.235 (0.319)	—	—	—	—	0.013	1.91
3	0.128 (2.167)	−0.215 (0.636)	−3.043 (1.966)	3.056 (2.010)	−0.028 (0.010)	0.042 (0.014)	−0.003 (0.497)	0.888 (0.084)	0.021	1.545
4	3.662 (0.387)	0.540 (0.613)	−0.808 (0.922)	0.950 (0.980)	—	0.005 (0.006)	0.261 (0.897)	−0.258 (0.955)	0.018	1.512
5	3.967 (0.021)	−0.051 (0.058)	0.034 (0.057)	−0.169 (0.118)	—	—	−4.121 (2.351)	4.154 (2.346)	0.012	1.801
6	−0.490 (0.994)	−0.564 (0.358)	0.508 (0.457)	−0.166 (0.552)	—	—	0.220 (0.239)	0.9[b]	0.016	2.022
7	0.265 (1.013)	−0.591 (0.422)	0.298 (0.138)	—	—	0.008 (0.011)	0.026 (0.259)	0.9[b]	0.015	2.033
8	1.260 (0.326)	−0.305 (0.096)	−0.009 (0.053)	—	−0.015 (0.001)	0.009 (0.002)	0.05 (0.085)	0.9[b]	0.006	1.490

a. Numbers in parentheses are standard errors.
b. The parameter has been set equal to indicated value.

of the evidence on lagged employment precludes strong conclusions, the results suggest that work may be habit-forming. Clearly, if experience in employment persists so that the decision to work is a relatively long-term commitment, it is not surprising that transitory wage changes have no discernible effect on labor supply.

These results conflict quite sharply with those of Hall (1980), who finds that the data support the intertemporal substitution hypothesis. Part of the conflict may lie in Hall's inclusion of fluctuations in hours per worker. The most serious problem, however, is Hall's measurement of the "intertemporal substitution parameter." He assumes that labor supply decisions are driven only by the price of future consumption in terms of today's labor. It is difficult to see what utility function would have this property in which the current price of consumption and futrue price of leisure are irrelevant. Our findings are consistent with the generally negative results obtained by Altonji (1982) and Mankiw, Rotemberg, and Summers (1985) regarding the intertemporal substitution hypothesis.

5.5 Cross-Section Evidence

The comparison of the relationships between labor market variables that are observed in time-series and cross-section data can shed light on the importance of timing and persistence effects. In particular, this section shows that recognizing the distinction between transitory and permanent effects embodied in the two hypotheses provides a framework for reconciling the large differences between cross-sectional and time-series estimates of the relationship between unemployment and participation rates. The conflict between these two types of evidence emerged in the early 1960s when several studies found large discouraged worker effects using decennial census data on local participation and unemployment rates, while other studies found very small effects using time-series data (Long, 1958; Barth, 1968; Bowen and Finnegan, 1969).

Attempts to reconcile the divergent results have generally focused on possible biases in the cross-section evidence. In his often cited review of the evidence Mincer (1966) conjectured that cross-section estimates were biased by omission of migration, seasonal differences across SMSAs in census timing, and common errors in the rate of participation and unemployment that give rise to a spurious association. Mincer also noted but did not pursue the permanence of state unemployment differentials. Bowen and Finnegan (1969) have examined each of these possibilities and suggest that none can satisfactorily explain the difference between the two sets of estimates.[17] More recent attempts to resolve the anomaly (e.g. Fleisher and Rhodes, 1976) have also been unpersuasive.[18]

These results suggest that cross-section and time-series estimates cannot be reconciled by pointing to biases in the cross-section data. A potentially more fruitful approach is to recognize the fundamental differences between intertemporal and interspatial variations in unemployment. At any point in time in any labor market the rate of unemployment is composed of both a permanent and a transitory component. In cross-section data, most variation in unemployment is presumably due to variation in the permanent component across regions. This is in contrast to the aggregate time-series data where variation in the transitory component is likely to be dominant. Cast in these terms, the cross-section data provide estimates of the long run or permanent effect of unemployment, while transitory effects are captured with time-series data.

At this point, it is important to be clear about the interpretation of the measured unemployment rate. In this section, we adopt the "traditional" interpretation, which holds that the labor market does not clear and that the unemployment rate affects the attractiveness of seeking work. It is then meaningful to speak of the effect of changes in differences in unemployment rates on labor force participation rates. We prefer the traditional interpretation of the unemployment rate to that of Lucas and Rapping for several reasons. Most important, the substantial permanent component in the differences between local unemployment rates suggests that they are not consequences of transitory wage movement. In addition, the evidence that participation and unemployment rates are negatively correlated is difficult to account for in the classical view. Indeed, in its strong form, it lacks an explanation for fluctuations in the participation rate. Other results described below also incline us toward the "traditional" interpretation of unemployment fluctuations.

In order to reconcile the time-series and cross-section estimates, it is necessary to examine the relationship between transitory and permanent effects, and to establish the conditions under which the permanent effect dominates. This is precisely the issue discussed in section 5.3, which distinguishes the timing and persistence effects. There we found that persistence effects imply that employment in previous periods raises current participation. Short-run effects persist. If persistence effects predominate, the response of labor supply to permanent changes in demand should exceed the response to transitory changes. This prediction, which is borne out by the data, is not consistent with strong forms of the timing hypothesis, which imply that the response to transitory fluctuations should exceed the response to permanent changes.

It thus would seem that the predominance of persistence effects receives substantial support in the comparison of cross-section and time-series evidence. Similar support emerges from a comparison of transitory and permanent effects using cross-section data. Use of cross-section data provides a strong test of the relative importance of timing and persistence effects since the two views of labor force dynamics have sharply different implications for the appropriate demand variable in cross-sectional equations. The timing view holds that the important determinant of participation is the deviation of demand from its normal level. When it is above its normal level, workers schedule themselves into the labor force, leaving when it falls below normal. The persistence view, on the other hand, implies that the normal level of demand is the appropriate variable since workers make labor supply decisions on a long-term basis.

The model embodied in this discussion can easily be made explicit. It is assumed that the level of demand may be represented by ER, the proportion of those desiring work who have it $(1 -$ the unemployment rate). We postulate that participation in region i, PR_i, depends on the permanent level of demand, ER_i^p, and the level of transitory demand, ER_i^t, defined as $(ER_i - ER_i^p)$. A simple characterization of the participation equation is given by

$$PR_i = f(ER_i^p, ER_i^t, Z_i), \tag{10}$$

where Z_i is a vector of variables other than demand conditions that influence the participation rate.

As the discussion in the preceding paragraph makes clear, the persistence view predicts that $f_{ER_i^p}$ will be large while $f_{ER_i^t}$ is not important; the timing hypothesis has the opposite implication. The distinction between the two hypotheses may be drawn more sharply by considering their implications for a change in the normal rate of employment holding constant the current rate. It is apparent from equation (10) that

$$\frac{\partial PR_i}{\partial ER_i^p} = f_{ER_i^p} - f_{ER_i^t}. \tag{11}$$

The preceding discussion implies that this expression should be positive if persistence dominates and negative under the timing hypothesis. Intuitively, with current opportunities held constant, a decline in future opportunities will increase labor supplied by a worker who can easily substitute leisure across periods. On the other hand, it will make current employment less attractive to a worker for whom leisure is complementary across periods.

These implications of the timing and persistence hypotheses are clearly subject to empirical verification. To test the conditions laid out above we have estimated a basic labor supply model using the data from the 1970 U.S. Census on participation and selected determinants by state. Time-series data (1966–74) on unemployment by state were taken from the *Manpower Report of the President*. These series are based on a combination of data on unemployment insurance, payrolls, and, for some states, the monthly CPS. In addition to variables measuring the permanent and transitory effects of unemployment we have included measures of the permanent or expected real wage as well as structural and demographic variables that affect participation through the shadow wage. As a first approximation we assume that variation in nominal wages across states reflects primarily variation in the permanent component of real wages, so that the level of prices is excluded from the model.[19] For women the basic equation is

$$\ln PR_{ij} = \alpha_1 + \alpha_2 \ln(WM)_i + \alpha_3 \ln(WW)_i + \alpha_4 EDW_i + \alpha_5 RW_i$$
$$+ \alpha_6 RBW_i + \alpha_7 URB_i + \alpha_8 MIGR_i + \alpha_9 C6_i + \alpha_{10} \ln(ER)_i^p \quad (12)$$
$$+ \alpha_{11} \ln(ER)_i^t + v_{ij},$$

where the variables are defined as follows:

PR_{ij} = participation rate of the jth demographic group in the ith state,
WM = median earnings of men 18 and over,
WW = median earnings of females 18 and over,
EDW = median years of schooling—females 18 and over,
RW = proportion of females in the population 16 and over,
RBW = proportion of nonwhite females in the population 16 and over,
URB = proportion of the population residing in Census urban areas,
$MIGR$ = total net migration 1960–70 as a proportion of 1970 population,
$C6$ = proportion of families with a child less than six living at home,
ER = state aggregate employment rate,
$\ln(ER)^p$ = average of $\ln(ER)$ for 1966–74,
$\ln(ER)^t$ = $[\ln(ER)-\ln(ER)^p]$.

Letting EDM_i indicate median years of schooling of males 18 and over, and RBM the proportion of nonwhite males in the population, the basic equation for the male group is

$$\ln PR_{ij} \approx \beta_1 + \beta_2 \ln(WM)_i + \beta_3 EDM_i + \beta_4 RBM_i + \beta_5 URB_i$$
$$+ \beta_6 MIGR_i + \beta_7 \ln(ER)_i^p + \beta_8 \ln(ER)_i^t + u_{ij}. \tag{13}$$

The expected effects of the structural and demographic variables included in equations (12) and (13) have been dealt with at length in a variety of places and will receive only brief mention here. Education and degree of urbanization are expected to have a positive effect on participation through their effects on labor force attachment and the cost of transportation. Migration is expected to raise participation in the receiving areas and lower participation in states with net outflow. The proportion of black men (women) in the population is included to control for well-known differences in participation behavior between blacks and whites. The variable is expected to have a positive sign in the female equation, and a negative sign in the equation for males. The proportion of women in the population is included as a measure of potential competition among women; the expected sign is negative. The proportion of women with a child under six is expected to raise the shadow wage and thus to reduce participation. The expected sign of own-wage variables (ln WW_i in (12) and ln WM_i in (13)) is positive. Male earnings have been included in the female equation to allow for the effects of joint decision-making in the family and are expected to reduce female participation. Female earnings on the other hand are specified to have no effect on male participation.

The differing implications of the timing and persistence views are captured in the coefficients of $\ln(ER)_i^p$ and $\ln (ER)_i^t$. Using the female equation, under the timing hypothesis α_{11} is expected to be positive and to dominate α_{10}, so that $\alpha_{10} - \alpha_{11} < 0$. The persistence hypothesis, on the other hand, implies that permanent effects are dominant so that $\alpha_{10} - \alpha_{11} > 0$. In addition to the basic equations (12) and (13) we also have estimated a specification that allows no role for transitory effects so that $\alpha_{11} = \beta_8 = 0$.

Estimates of the basic model for both men and women are presented in table 5.5. The principal coefficients of interest, α_{10} and α_{11} (β_7 and β_8 for men), are presented in rows 9 and 10; for convenience we have computed the sum of the coefficients in row 11. The results provide clear support for the importance of persistence effects. The long-run effects of unemployment clearly dominate the transitory effects in virtually all demographic groups. The difference between the permanent and transitory components is less than zero in only three cases, and in no case is the negative coefficient significant. We find the strongest evidence of the persistence effects among women for whom the timing phenomenon was expected to be particularly relevant. In each of the female age groups, except women over 65, the transitory employment rate is totally insignificant, often entering with a negative sign. In contrast, the permanent effects are large and significant. For women 45–64, for example, the permanent effect (α_{10}) is 2.46, which implies that a decline in the permanent rate of unemployment from 0.06 to 0.05 would raise the participation rate by 2.46%. The transitory effect for this group, on the other hand, is -3.15, clearly reflecting the dominance of the permanent employment rate that enters negatively in the deviation. The total effect of the permanent rate is thus 5.61. Similar positive effects are found for younger women as for women 45–64. Only among women over 65 does the timing hypothesis find any support and here the estimates are not particularly precise. The sum of the permanent and transitory effects is -0.10, which may be marginally important in determining the participation behavior of women over the age of 65. A somewhat stronger finding for men over 65 leads to the paradoxical conclusion that the timing view, a construct based on life cycle considerations, finds its support only among those nearing the end of their adult lives.

The results in rows 10 and 11 of table 5.5 clearly suggest that changes in the expected rate of unemployment strongly influence the participation decisions of most demographic groups. This conclusion is buttressed in row 12 of table 5.5, which presents estimates of the effect of unemployment assuming no transitory effects (i.e., $\alpha_{11} = 0$). Among most demographic groups the expected rate of employment enters significantly with a relatively large positive coefficient. Differences in the size of the employment effect within and across demographic groups are consistent with the theoretical role of unemployment laid out in section 5.3. We find that unemployment is more important in those groups where employment durations are short. Thus within the male and female categories teenagers are more sensitive to variations in unemployment than are older persons. Similarly, within age groups, women tend to be more responsive than men. It should be noted, however, that the coefficients for the older adult men are far from trivial. We estimate that a 1 point decline in the long-term unemployment rate (0.06 to 0.05) leads to a 0.6% increase in the participation of men 25–44, and a 1.3% increase in the rate of participation of men 45–64.

The evidence on the relative importance of timing and persistence in the cross-section data relies on the use of the unemployment rate to capture market opportunities. We have already discussed some of our reasons for preferring this kind of interpretation in section 5.3. But there are two additional issues that need to be addressed. In the first place, classical

Table 5.5
Estimates of the basic cross-section model for men and women (standard errors in parentheses)

	Male					Female				
	16–19	20–24	25–44	45–64	65 +	16–19	20–24	25–44	45–64	65 +
1. Male earnings (WM)	0.19 (0.13)	−0.03 (0.07)	0.06 (0.01)	0.17 (0.04)	0.31 (0.21)	0.42 (0.24)	−0.07 (0.11)	−0.39 (0.11)	−0.17 (0.16)	0.04 (0.24)
2. Female earnings (WW)	—	—	—	—	—	0.34 (0.20)	0.40 (0.09)	0.41 (0.09)	0.53 (0.13)	0.55 (0.20)
3. Education (EDM, EDW)	0.05 (0.04)	−0.0007 (0.02)	0.004 (0.005)	0.03 (0.01)	0.17 (0.07)	0.06 (0.08)	−0.01 (0.04)	0.03 (0.04)	0.06 (0.05)	0.21 (0.08)
4. Proportion female (RW)	—	—	—	—	—	2.28 (3.02)	1.65 (1.41)	−0.04 (1.38)	4.13 (1.99)	0.52 (2.93)
5. Proportion black (RBW, RBM)	−0.44 (0.28)	0.02 (0.14)	−0.05 (0.03)	−0.16 (0.08)	0.53 (0.44)	−1.59 (0.52)	−0.30 (0.24)	0.41 (0.24)	−0.41 (0.34)	0.37 (0.50)
6. Urbanization (URB)	−0.0009 (0.001)	−0.0003 (0.0007)	−0.0004 (0.0001)	−0.0003 (0.0004)	−0.004 (0.002)	−0.0002 (0.002)	0.00003 (0.0009)	−0.0004 (0.0009)	−0.001 (0.001)	−0.005 (0.002)
7. Children under 6 (C6)	—	—	—	—	—	0.008 (0.01)	0.004 (0.005)	0.004 (0.005)	0.01 (0.007)	0.02 (0.01)
8. Net migration (MIGR)	0.32 (0.11)	0.21 (0.06)	0.02 (0.01)	−0.05 (0.03)	−0.27 (0.18)	−0.08 (0.19)	0.006 (0.09)	0.23 (0.09)	−0.007 (0.12)	−0.33 (0.18)

Table 5.5 (continued)

	Male					Female				
	16–19	20–24	25–44	45–64	65+	16–19	20–24	25–44	45–64	65+
9. Permanent employment rate (ER^p)	2.56 (1.09)	−0.38 (0.56)	0.63 (0.12)	1.33 (0.30)	3.29 (1.72)	5.97 (1.78)	2.96 (0.83)	2.46 (0.82)	2.31 (1.18)	2.17 (1.73)
10. Transitory employment rate (ER^t)	−3.26 (2.11)	−0.42 (1.08)	−0.05 (0.23)	0.12 (0.58)	4.62 (3.33)	0.85 (3.37)	−0.07 (1.57)	−3.15 (1.55)	−0.29 (2.22)	2.27 (3.27)
11. Full permanent effect (line 9–line 10)	5.82 (2.33)	0.04 (1.19)	0.68 (0.25)	1.21 (0.65)	−1.32 (3.68)	5.12 (3.82)	3.03 (1.78)	5.61 (1.75)	2.60 (2.52)	−0.10 (3.71)
12. Permanent employment rate (ER^p)[a]	2.64 (1.11)	0.37 (0.55)	0.63 (0.12)	1.33 (0.30)	3.18 (1.74)	5.97 (1.76)	2.96 (0.82)	2.45 (0.85)	2.31 (1.16)	2.17 (1.72)
R^2	0.52	0.26	0.65	0.74	0.33	0.71	0.67	0.76	0.60	0.60
SEE	0.09	0.04	0.009	0.02	0.14	0.12	0.06	0.06	0.08	0.12

a. Line 12 reports the coefficient of ER^p when ER^t is excluded from the equation.

models would call for the use of permanent and transitory real wages rather than unemployment rates as explanatory variables. The results of including real wages in time-series regressions have been discussed in the preceding section. We have made an attempt to gauge their effect in the cross-section analysis by calculating real wages by state. We used the BLS Standard of Living Estimates for 35 cities to construct state price indices; wages were based on data for manufacturing by state. Both permanent and transitory wage variations had only minor effects on state participation and employment rates. Therefore the unemployment rate has been used as a proxy for the attractiveness of entering and remaining in the labor force. The role of wages and prices in explaining cross-section differences in participation remains an important area for future research.

A second problem concerns the effect of omitted variables. Although we have included a number of structural characteristics of each state in the equation, there is always the possibility that omitted common third factors account for the observed correlations between unemployment and participation rates. We explored this issue by using other variables such as the employment-population ratio in place of the unemployment rate. This had little effect on the qualitative conclusions.

The analysis in this section has shown the predominance of the expected or natural level of demand in explaining participation differences across states. Except for those over 65, there is no evidence for the notion that transitory changes in opportunities play a significant role in decisions about participating in the labor force. These results suggest that a rise in expected opportunities, holding current opportunities constant, will call forth an increase in participation, a response consistent with the implications of persistence in labor supply. The notion that individuals schedule their labor supply according to variations in current opportunities finds little support in these data.

5.6 Conclusions

The results in this paper suggest the importance of persistence in labor market decisions. A variety of types of evidence suggest that previous employment experience has an important effect on subsequent labor supply. This implies that labor supply decisions are not very responsive to transitory changes in employment opportunities. While no one of the tests presented in this paper can be regarded as decisive, in conjunction they suggest that persistence elements are more important than timing elements in explaining fluctuations in either the number of persons employed or the number participating in the labor force. Our results leave open the possibility that timing elements are important in explaining cyclical fluctuations in average hours worked and in work effort.

Acceptance of these conclusions has important implications for both macroeconomic theory and policy. These results cast doubt on the medium-run relevance of the natural rate hypothesis. Because policy affects the level of employment in the short run, it has a long-run effect on the position of the labor supply schedule. Workers drawn into the labor force by cyclical upturns tend to remain even after the boom has ended. The converse is true for shocks which reduce employment. At this point, the quantitative importance of these effects is uncertain, although our interpretation of the evidence reported here suggests that they are quite important.

This paper has only begun to touch on the implications of alternative life cycle labor supply models for macroeconomic questions. Both the empirical and theoretical work described in this paper could usefully be extended in several directions. It would be valuable to develop tests that can distinguish different aspects of persistence. In particular, the model developed here completely ignores the accumulation of human capital. The explicit inclusion of human capital in the model would provide a more satisfactory basis for rationalizing the observed persistence in labor supply, and would also suggest relationships between employment experience and subsequent wage levels. It would be valuable to extend the empirical work reported here by attempting direction estimation of utility function parameters using recently developed rational expectations techniques. Unsuccessful estimates of a relatively simple utility function that takes no account of persistence effects are presented in Mankiw, Rotemberg, and Summers (1985). While these extensions would be valuable, it is unlikely that they would call into question the main conclusion reached here that a proper theory of labor supply must come to grips with the persistence of participation.

We are grateful for discussions with G. Chamberlain, A. Dammann, R. Freeman, R. Hall, J. Medoff, and C. Sims. Daniel Smith, James Poterba, and George Fenn assisted with the computations. This research was supported by ASPER of the U.S. Department of Labor. An earlier verison of this paper appeared as an ASPER Working Paper in January 1979.

Notes

1. At the conference where this paper was presented we became aware of the important paper by Altonji (1982). His work provides a comprehensive set of econometric tests of what this paper calls the timing hypothesis.

2. The most extensive empirical work is reported in Houthakker and Taylor (1970). Theoretical analysis is surveyed by Pollak (1978).

3. In a Keynesian framework, this may be interpreted as temporarily increasing aggregate demand, and increasing employment opportunities. In the context of a classical model, it can be thought of as an unexpected increase in the money stock, leading to a transitory increase in the perceived real wage. In either case the expansionary policy is taken to be temporary in its direct effect.

4. For a recent statement of this argument, see Wachter (1977).

5. It is tempting but inaccurate to regard persistence effects as arguments in support of expansionary policy. If the economy is initially at an optimal Walrasian equilibrium, locking additional workers into employment is not an efficiency gain. Of course this conclusion does not hold if the "natural rate" of unemployment is inefficiently high, as Phelps (1972) suggests it likely to be the case. If, as has been suggested, work is habit-forming, no clear basis exists for welfare judgments.

6. Such hysteresis effects in which the equilibrium level of employment is affected by the transition path have been discussed by Phelps (1972), but have, to our knowledge, received no empirical attention.

7. Milton Friedman, *Price Theory: A Provisional Text*, 1962, p. 200.

8. Ideally one ought to look at the participation of women of different ages rather than different cohorts. Thus, for example, the appropriate way to examine the impact of the war on 50-year-old women is to look at 46-year-olds in 1940 and 56-year-olds in 1950. Available data, however, precludes such an analysis.

9. This result was also obtained using employment instead of labor force participation as a measure of labor supply. It should be noted that the participation rates for married women have not been adjusted for differences in fertility. As others have noted, adjusting for fertility would accentuate the divergence between actual rates and extrapolation of 1930–40 trends (see Bowen and Finnegan, 1969, pp. 200–201). Fertility in 1940 was exceptionally low, while 1950 was part of the postwar baby boom. It may be that a fertility correction is inappropriate since fertility is jointly determined with labor supply.

10. It might be argued that the purportedly permanent shifts in participation induced by the World War II experience actually reflect the very weak economy of 1940. In order to test this possibility, trends were estimated in 1930. This leads to even greater discrepancies between predicted and actual participation, both during and after the war. As a further check, we estimated trends using data for the whole 1890–1980 period. The results were qualitatively similar, although the estimated effects of the war on subsequent participation were significantly reduced. Of course, this procedure may be inappropriate because the war presumably affected postwar data.

11. *Monthly Labor Review* (May 1944).

12. Both in aggregate and within occupations, there was virtually no change in the ratio of male and female hourly and/or yearly earnings between 1939 and 1950. The data must be interpreted cautiously because of a plethora of selection effects.

13. Strictly speaking, all that is required is that (1) can be represented as $V_1(c_{t-1}, l_{t-1}) + V_2(c_t, l_t c_{t+1}, l_{t+1})$.

14. In the empirical work below, we use the unemployment rate for 35–44-year-old men. This avoids problems of demographic adjustment.

15. The estimates were performed using annual data for the period 1949–81. Two lags on each variable were included. Wages are measured using an index of compensation in the private business sector. Prices are measured using the consumption price deflator, and output is measured as real GNP.

16. The tax rate is the sum of the average marginal tax rate imposed on labor income, federal income taxes, state and local taxes, and Social Security taxes. The municipal bond rate is then used as a crude proxy for the other tax interest rate.

17. In the empirical work reported below, we control for migration so this difficulty does not arise. In results that are not reported, measures of demand other than the unemployment rate were used with very little effect on the results. The problem of seasonality in the census sampling is not dealt with.

18. Fleisher and Rhodes argue that the unemployment rate is properly treated as endogenous in participation equations. However, the instrumental variables they employ, such as the growth rate of employment, are probably at least as likely as unemployment to be correlated with the error term in the participation equation.

19. In the results reported below, earnings are used as a wage proxy. This creates an obvious upward bias in the estimate of wage effects on labor supply.

6

Intertemporal Substitution in Macroeconomics

with N. Gregory Mankiw and Julio J. Rotemberg

6.1 Introduction

Modern neoclassical theories of the business cycle are founded upon the assumption that fluctuations in consumption and employment are the consequence of dynamic optimizing behavior by economic agents who face no quantity constraints. In this paper we present and estimate an explicit operational model of an optimizing household. Our examination of postwar aggregate data provides no support for these theories.

As in many recent studies of consumption and asset returns, we posit that observed fluctuations can be modeled as the outcome of optimizing decisions of a representative individual. The individual has a utility function that is additively separable through time and faces an economic environment where future opportunities are uncertain. Our approach avoids the intractable problem of finding a closed-form solution for the representative individual's choices. Instead, we use the restrictions on the data implied by the first-order conditions for an optimum. The estimation of these first-order conditions makes it possible to recover the structural parameters of the underlying utility function.

The three first-order conditions we consider represent three margins on which the representative individual is optimizing. He can trade off present and future consumption at a stochastic real interest rate measured in terms of the consumption good. He can trade off present leisure and future leisure at a stochastic real interest rate measured in terms of leisure. And he can trade off present consumption and present leisure at the real wage. Thus, the approach here has the potential to recover parameters describing both consumption and labor supply decisions.

Reprinted by permission of John Wiley & Sons, Inc., with revisions, from *Quarterly Journal of Economics*, 225–251, February 1985. Copyright © 1985 by the President and Fellows of Harvard College.

The estimation technique we use is the nonlinear instrumental variables procedure Hansen and Singleton (1982) suggest. It not only produces consistent estimates of the relevant parameters, but also allows us to test overidentifying restrictions implied by the theory. Throughout the study we experiment with different measures of consumption, different lists of instruments, and different frequency data. We also try various functional forms for the underlying utility function. In particular, we allow the utility function to be nonseparable in consumption and leisure. Such experimentation assures that our conclusions are somewhat robust to changes in the various auxiliary assumptions necessary for implementation of the model.

We find that aggregate data are not readily characterized as ex post realizations from a stochastic dynamic optimization. In particular, the orthogonality conditions implied by theory are frequently rejected. More important, the parameter estimates are usually highly implausible. The estimated utility function is often not concave, which implies that the representative individual is not at a maximum of utility, but at a saddle-point or at a minimum. In addition, when the utility function is concave, the estimates imply that either consumption or leisure is an inferior good. We conclude that observed economic fluctuations do not easily admit of a neoclassical interpretation.

Section 6.2 discusses the previous work on intertemporal substitution. Section 6.3 develops the model, while section 6.4 discusses the data. Section 6.5 explains the estimation procedure, and section 6.6 presents the results. Section 6.7 considers the implications of the model's failure for equilibrium theories of the business cycle, and suggests directions for future research.

6.2 Motivation

The major difference between modern neoclassical and traditional Keynesian macroeconomic theories is that the former regard observed levels of employment, consumption, and output as realizations from dynamic optimizing decisions by both households and firms, while the latter regard them as reflecting constraints on households and firms. This distinction is clearest in the case of labor supply decisions. In classical macroeconomic models, observed levels of labor supply represent the optimizing choices of households given their perceptions of the macroeconomic environment. In Keynesian macro models, employment is frequently regarded as "demand determined," and fluctuations in employment do not necessarily correspond to any change in desired labor supply.

The goal of the present paper is to examine the extent to which data on consumption and labor supply for the United States over the postwar period are consistent with the hypothesis on continuous dynamic optimization. At the outset it is crucial to understand the limitations of this empirical inquiry or any investigation of this kind. It is impossible to test the general proposition about continuous optimization discussed above. Only particular simple versions of the dynamic optimization problem can be considered. Any rejections of the models estimated can be interpreted as a failure of the underlying theory or of the particular parameterization of it that is tested. Of course, to the extent that a theory fails when simply expressed, its utility as an organization framework for understanding economic events is called into question.

Explanations of business cycles based on continuous dynamic optimization differ in many respects. However, they share the notion that the elasticity of labor supply with respect to changes in the relative return from working currently and in the near future is likely to be high. This would seem to be a necessary implication of any such theory, since cyclical fluctuations in employment are large and the long-run labor supply elasticity observed in cross sections is typically small. A central thrust of this paper is to examine empirically the differential response of labor supply to permanent and transitory shocks to real wages.

Recent research on consumption by Grossman and Shiller (1980), Hansen and Singleton (1982), Hall (1978, 1981), and Mankiw (1981) shows how it is possible to estimate directly the parameters of the intertemporal utility function characterizing the behavior of the representative individual. Hansen and Singleton (1982) and Mankiw (1981) show how to test the overidentifying restrictions that are implied by the hypothesis of continuous optimization of a stable additively separable utility function. The major virtue of the approach pioneered by these authors is that it permits the direct estimation of utility function parameters without requiring explicit solutions of the consumers' dynamic optimization problem. Unfortunately, both Hansen and Singleton and Mankiw report rejections of their estimated models.

This paper uses techniques similar to those developed in connection with consumption to estimate the parameters of an intertemporal utility function characterizing the labor supply behavior of the representative consumer. This permits judgments about the magnitude of the key intertemporal elasticities. In addition, we can directly test the hypothesis of dynamic optimization using the implied overidentifying restrictions on the data. Another motivation for this research is the rejection of the overidentifying restrictions in the models Hansen and Singleton (1982) and

Mankiw (1981) estimate. These models all maintain the assumption that the marginal utility of consumption depends only on the level of consumption. It is natural to entertain the hypothesis that the utility function is not separable so that the marginal utility of consumption depends on the level of leisure. The intertemporal utility functions we estimate allow this possibility.

Papers like those of Lucas and Rapping (1969), Altonji (1982), and Hall (1980) attempt to estimate the structural labor supply functions that result from the dynamic optimization of a representative individual. These studies face three difficulties. First, the closed-form solution of this optimization problem is unknown when the environment is stochastic. Second, identification is problematic. Since the labor supply schedule is likely to shift through time, it is inappropriate to regard the real wage as an exogenous variable. The problem is that satisfactory instruments are almost impossible to find. Labor supply shocks are likely to affect most macroeconomic policy variables.

The third difficulty involves the measurement of expectations. The theory holds that labor supply should be a function of the distribution of the entire path of future real wages and interest rates, not just of the first moments of those variables in the succeeding period. Satisfactory proxies for these expectations are almost impossible to develop.

Altonji (1982) also estimated, for a utility function that is separable in consumption and leisure, the first-order condition that equates the real wage and the marginal rate of substitution of consumption for leisure. This is analogous to some of the procedures used in this paper.

In recent papers MaCurdy (1981a,b) examines intertemporal substitution effects at the microeconometric level. It might at first seem that micro data provide a much firmer basis for estimating intertemporal substitution effects than do aggregate data. However, the use of micro data involves serious problems.

At the micro level even when wages and changes in wages are treated as endogenous, variables like schooling and age are used as instruments for the wage. The validity of these variables as instruments is doubtful, since they are likely to be correlated with the individual's taste for working.

6.3 Theory

This section describes the model. Its estimation requires a number of auxiliary assumptions about the behavior of consumers. These assumptions pertain to issues such as the information set available to consumers and the functional form of their utility functions. Tests of the model are also tests of these auxiliary assumptions, so they require careful attention. We make a major effort to explore alternative sets of auxiliary assumptions to increase the robustness of our conclusion regarding the economic issues of major interest.

We examine a basic premise of many classical macroeconomic models that observed movements in per capita consumption and leisure correspond to the behavior of a rational individual who derives pleasure from these two goods and whose utility function is stationary and additively separable over time.[1] That is,

$$V_t = E_t \sum_{\tau=t}^{\infty} \rho^{\tau-t} U(C_\tau, L_\tau). \tag{1}$$

Here, V_t is expected utility at t, E_t is the expectations operator conditional on information available at t, ρ is a constant discount factor, C_τ is consumption of goods at τ, L_τ is leisure at τ, and U is a function that is increasing and concave in its two arguments.

Given a specification of the budget constraint, and of the conditional distributions of all future wages, prices, and rates of return on all assets, it would in principle be possible to use (1) to find consumers' choices of consumption and leisure at time t. In practice, it is almost impossible to conceive of all this information being available to the econometrician. Even if it were available, analytical solutions of (1) do not exist even for very simply functional forms. Therefore, following earlier work on consumption by Mankiw (1981), Hansen and Singleton (1981), and Hall (1982), we attempt to estimate directly the form of U in (1) without specifying a model capable of predicting the chosen levels of C_t and L_t. We exploit the restrictions on the data imposed by the first-order conditions necessary for the maximization of (1) subject to a budget constraint.

We assume that the representative individual has access to some financial assets that can be both bought and sold. In addition, he has access to spot markets in which labor and consumption are freely traded. As long as the optimal path lies in the interior of the budget set, we can use simple perturbation arguments to establish certain characteristics of this optimal path. At any point along an optimal path, the representative individual cannot make himself better off by forgoing one unit of consumption or leisure at time t and using the proceeds to purchase any other good at any other point in time. In particular, when the representative individual is following his optimal path of consumption and leisure, these three first-order conditions must hold:

(S): $\dfrac{W_t \, \partial U / \partial C_t}{P_t \, \partial U / \partial L_t} - 1 = 0;$

(EC): $E_t \, \rho \, \dfrac{\partial U / \partial C_{t+1}}{\partial U / \partial C_t} \, \dfrac{P_t (1 + r_t)}{P_{t+1}} - 1 = 0;$

(EL): $E_t \, \rho \, \dfrac{\partial U / \partial L_{t+1}}{\partial U / \partial L_t} \, \dfrac{W_t (1 + r_t)}{W_{t+1}} - 1 = 0.$

Here, P_t is the nominal price of a unit of C_t, W_t is the wage the individual receives when he forgoes one unit of L_t, and r_t is the nominal return from holding a security between t and $t + 1.$[2]

The static first-order condition (S) says that the individual cannot make himself better off by forgoing one unit of consumption (thereby decreasing his utility by $\partial U / \partial C_t$) and spending the proceeds (P_t) on P_t / W_t units of leisure, each of which he values at $\partial U / \partial L_t$. The reverse transaction is also unable to increase his utility. Note that the model considered here, in which tastes are constant, implies that equation (S) holds exactly. Since we assume at time t that the consumer knows the real wage $(W/P)_t$, he chooses consumption and leisure to equate the real wage and the marginal rate of substitution.

The Euler equation for consumption (EC) states that along an optimal path the representative individual cannot alter his expected utility by giving up one unit of consumption in period t, investing its cost in any available security, and consuming the proceeds in period $t + 1$. The utility cost of giving up a unit of consumption in period t is given by $\partial U / \partial C_t$. The expected utility gain is given by

$$E_t \, \rho \, \frac{\partial U}{\partial C_{t+1}} \, \frac{P_t}{P_{t+1}} (1 + r_t).$$

Equating the cost and gain from this perturbation yields the first-order condition (EC). It is important to be clear about the generality of this result. The condition (EC) will hold even if labor supply cannot be freely chosen, and trading is not possible in many assets, as long as some asset exists that is either held in positive amounts or for which borrowing is possible.

Finally, the Euler equation for leisure (EL) asserts that along an optimal path the representative individual cannot improve his welfare by working one hour more at t (thereby losing $\partial U / \partial L_t$ of utility) and using his earnings W_t to purchase a security whose proceeds will be used to buy back $W_t (1 + r_t) / W_{t+1}$ of leisure at $t + 1$ in all states of nature. Such an investment would increase expected utility by $E_t \rho[\partial U/\partial L_{t+1}] W_t(1 + r_t)/W_{t+1}$. Therefore, (EL) ensures that this expression is equal to $\partial U/\partial L_t$.

If the static first-order condition (S) held exactly, one of (EC) and (EL) would be redundant. We can see this by replacing $\partial U/\partial C_t$ and $\partial U/\partial C_{t+1}$ in (EC) using (S). This procedure produces (EL). However, since (S) is unlikely to hold exactly in the data, we use the information in all three of these first-order conditions to estimate the parameters of the utility function (1).

In order to estimate the instantaneous utility function U, it is necessary to specify a functional form. The most general utility function we use is

$$U(C_t, L_t) = \frac{1}{1 - \gamma} \left[\frac{C_t^{1-\alpha} - 1}{1 - \alpha} + d \frac{L_t^{1-\beta} - 1}{1 - \beta} \right]^{1-\gamma}. \tag{2}$$

This utility function, which is similar to MaCurdy's [1981], has, as special cases, an additively separable utility function in consumption and leisure, $(\gamma = 0)$;[3] a CES form for the ordinal utility function characterizing single-period decision making $(\alpha = \beta)$;[4] and a logarithmic utility function $(\alpha = 1, \beta = 1, \gamma = 0)$. This functional form also provides for the possibility of differential degrees of intertemporal substitution in consumption and leisure. This is easiest to see when $\gamma = 0$, so that $1/\alpha$ represents the elasticity of intertemporal substitution in consumption and $1/\beta$ represents the corresponding elasticity for leisure.[5]

Previous work on intertemporal substitution in consumption estimates the condition (EC) maintaining the hypothesis that $\gamma = 0$. Even if this supposition is correct, this is not an efficient estimation procedure, since it neglects the information contained in (S).

Below, we describe how to test statistically the orthogonality restrictions implied by the hypothesis of dynamic optimization. Here, we describe how the parameter estimates can be used to examine the issues of economic interest. This may provide a more satisfactory way of testing the relevance of the model than is provided by statistical tests of over-identifying restrictions. The model is at best an approximation to reality. Therefore, with enough data the point hypotheses corresponding to the overidentifying restrictions will be rejected at any given critical value.

We assess the estimates in two ways: by checking that they obey the restriction on utility functions implied by economic theory, and by examining the implied values of short-run and long-run elasticities. Theory requires that the function U be concave; otherwise, the first-order conditions correspond to a local minimum or saddle-point rather than a local maximum. We check this by verifying that the matrix of second derivatives of U is negative definite at all points in our sample.

In informal discussion of the importance of intertemporal substitution, it is often pointed out that the responses of consumption and leisure to temporary changes in prices and wages must be different from the response to permanent changes in these magnitudes. However, the actual responses are impossible to compute without first solving the stochastic control problem whose objective is (1). Instead, we compute some simple measures of responses of consumption and leisure. We derive all measures under the assumption that individuals face a deterministic environment.

The "short-run" elasticities illustrate the changes in consumption and leisure at t in response to temporary changes in W_t, P_t, and r_t. We derive these elasticities under the assumption that the effects of these changes on consumption and leisure after t can be neglected. These effects are all mediated through the change in total wealth at $t + 1$ that results from the changes in W_t, P_t, and r_t. Insofar as this change in wealth must be very small compared with the wealth of the individual at $t + 1$ if he still has long to live, this approximation is valid. The "short-run" elasticities can be computed by totally differentiating (EC) and (EL):

$$
\begin{bmatrix}
C_t \dfrac{\partial^2 U}{\partial C_t^2} & L_t \dfrac{\partial^2 U}{\partial C_t \partial L_t} & \dfrac{dC_t}{C_t} \\[2ex]
C_t \dfrac{\partial^2 U}{\partial C_t \partial L_t} & L_t \dfrac{\partial^2 U}{\partial L_t^2} & \dfrac{dL_t}{L_t}
\end{bmatrix}
$$

$$
= \begin{bmatrix}
\dfrac{\rho P_t(1+r_t)}{P_{t+1}} \dfrac{\partial U}{\partial C_{t+1}} & 0 & \dfrac{\rho P_t(1+r_t)}{P_{t+1}} \dfrac{\partial U}{\partial C_{t+1}} & \dfrac{dP_t}{P_t} \\[3ex]
0 & \dfrac{\rho W_t(1+r_t)}{W_{t+1}} \dfrac{\partial U}{\partial C_{t+1}} & \dfrac{\rho W_t(1+r_t)}{W_{t+1}} \dfrac{\partial U}{\partial C_{t+1}} & \dfrac{dW_t}{W_t} \quad \dfrac{dr_t}{1+r_t}
\end{bmatrix}.
$$

$$(3)$$

One simple measure of the "long-run" or average response of consumption and leisure when the real wage changes permanently is obtained from assuming that the individual has no nonlabor income, that both the real interest rate in terms of leisure and the one in terms of consumption $[P_t(1 + r_t)]/P_{t+1}$ and $[W_t(1 + r_t)]/W_{t+1}$ are equal to $1/\rho$. Then, the individual plans to maintain a constant level of consumption and of leisure. His plan is consistent with a static budget constraint that makes his expenditure on consumption equal to his labor income:

$$C_t - (W_t/P_t)(N - L_t) = 0, \tag{4}$$

where N is the endowment of leisure. Totally differentiating (4) and (S), one obtains the following long-run elasticities:

$$
\begin{bmatrix}
C_t & \dfrac{W}{P}L_t \\[2ex]
\dfrac{C_t\,\partial^2 U/\partial C_t^2}{\partial U/\partial L_t} - \dfrac{C_t\,\partial^2 U/\partial C_t\,\partial L_t}{(\partial U/\partial L_t)^2} & \dfrac{L_t\,\partial^2 U/\partial C_t\,\partial L_t}{\partial U/\partial L_t} - \dfrac{L_t\,\partial U/\partial C_t\,\partial^2 U/\partial L_t^2}{(\partial U/\partial L_t)^2}
\end{bmatrix}
\begin{bmatrix}
\dfrac{dC_t}{C_t} \\[2ex]
\dfrac{dL_t}{L_t}
\end{bmatrix}
$$
$$
(5)
$$
$$
=
\begin{bmatrix}
(N - L_t)\dfrac{W_t}{P_t} \\[2ex]
\dfrac{P_t}{W_t}
\end{bmatrix}
\dfrac{d(W_t/P_t)}{(W_t/P_t)}.
$$

6.4 Data

Estimation of the parameters of (2) requires several choices about the data to be used. These choices are of pivotal importance because the estimation results depend on their validity as well as on the basic theoretical notions being examined.

The first-order conditions (S), (EC), and (EL) characterize optimization for a single individual with a given utility function. Their application to aggregate data is more problematic. Rubinstein (1974) presents results showing that if all individuals have identical, separable utility functions, and if all risky assets including human capital are freely traded, the model we consider here can be rigorously justified as applied to aggregate data. To state these conditions is to recognize their falsity. They imply that the consumption of all individuals should be perfectly correlated. Hall and Mishkin (1982) present data indicating that, at least using one measure of consumption, there is only negligible correlation between the consumption of different individuals.[6] It is standard in studying consumption to model per capita consumption as if it were chosen by a representative consumer. We follow the standard convention of using consumption and labor input per member of the adult population. As Summers (1982) points out, the rationale for this procedure is unclear. If it is appropriate to give individuals under 16 zero weight, presumably because they consume little, might it not also be appropriate to weight individuals of different ages according to their consumption or labor supply in constructing per capita variables? This approach is taken in Summers (1982), where it has a significant impact on the results. It is not pursued here because of the difficulty in finding a population index that is appropriate for both consumption and leisure.

The main problem with measuring consumption is that the available data pertain to consumer expenditure, which, as Mankiw (1982) points out, has a durable component. The pen with which this sentence is written was classified as nondurable consumption nine months ago. We use as our measure of consumption alternatively real expenditures on nondurables and nondurables and services as reported in the National Income and Product Accounts. The NIPA price deflators are used to measure prices.[7]

The measurement of leisure also poses problems. Somewhat arbitrarily we specify that the representative individual has a time endowment of $7 \times 16 = 112$ hours a week. We compute leisure by subtracting per capita total hours worked by the civilian labor force from this time endowment. In principle, it would be possible to estimate econometrically the size of the time endowment. In practice, this parameter is difficult to estimate, so we constrain it a priori. The specification we adopt here based on total hours worked is open to the serious criticism that it does not distinguish between changes in the number of persons working and in average hours per worker. The former poses serious problems for the model, since the first-order conditions (S) and (EL) need not hold for individuals whose labor supply is at the corner solution of zero hours worked.

The measurement of the price of leisure, the wage, also involves a choice between less than fully satisfactory alternatives. The series we use refers to average total compensation of employees in the nonfarm business sector. We calculate after-tax wages by using a time series of marginal tax rates on labor income, measured as the sum of federal income taxes,[8] Social Security taxes, and state income taxes. The problems with this measure of wages include its partial coverage and its failure to include some forms of compensation, such as the accrual of Social Security and private pension benefits. Perhaps more seriously, the extent to which market wages reflect the marginal return from working has been questioned. Hall (1980) argues that certain features of the economy's cyclical behavior can be explained by assuming that wages do not reflect true compensation for working on a period-by-period basis, even though the economy always attains the Walrasian equilibrium level of employment.

The final data decision is the choice of an asset return r. We experiment with estimates of both the before- and after-tax Treasury Bill interest rate. As a crude approximation, we assume a 30% tax rate on interest income. Since the results are fairly similar, only the after-tax results are reported. The Treasury Bill rate is appropriate for recent years when savings instruments paying near market rates of return were widely available. Its appropriateness is less clear during the bulk of the sample period when interest rate ceilings constrained the rates obtainable by most individuals. The extent to which installment credit rates match with the Treasury Bill rate is not clear. Summers (1982) finds very similar results in a study of fluctuations in consumption that uses both time deposit and Treasury Bill yields. The time deposit rate is not used here because data are not available over a long enough period.

A final issue is the appropriate period of observation. As is now well-known, the use of discrete time data can lead to biases if the data are generated by a continuous time process. In particular, time averages of a random walk will not have serially uncorrelated increments. There is the additional problem that the link between consumption and consumption expenditure is likely to be better at lower than at higher frequencies. Because of the latter problem we reject the common view that models of this type should be estimated with data for as short a period as possible. In addition, the assumption of additive separability is more realistic for large period lengths. We use two different procedures. The first, which we employ with apology but without excuse, is to use seasonally adjusted quarterly data. There is a risk that the averaging involved in seasonal adjustment disturbs the results. The second procedure involves using only data from the fourth quarter of each year. The interval between observations reduces time aggregation problems. In addition, the gap between observations may reduce the problems that come from the use of expenditure to proxy consumption. Finally, the use of data from only one quarter may reduce seasonality problems.

An appendix containing the data we used is available from the authors upon request. We use three lists of instruments for every specification we estimate. List A includes a constant, the rates of inflation between $t - 2$ and $t - 1$ and between $t - 5$ and $t - 1$, the nominal rate of return between $t - 1$ and t, and the holding period yield between $t - 5$ and $t - 1$. List B includes a constant and the levels of consumption, the interest rate, leisure, prices, and wages at $t - 1$ and $t - 2$. Instead, List C includes the values of these variables at t and $t - 1$. Therefore, list C allows us to check whether the estimates worsen when current variables are included as instruments.

6.5 Estimation Method

We estimate the parameters α, β, d, and γ of the function U given by (2). This is done by fitting the implied first-order conditions (S), (EC), and (EL) to U.S. data. Hansen and Singleton (1982) suggest that the theoretically correct method for estimating Euler equations like (EC) and (EL) is a nonlinear instrumental variables procedure. The rationale for this procedure can be stated as follows: the equations (EC) and (EL) state that the expectation at t of a function of variables at t and $(t + 1)$ is zero. Hence they can be written as $E_t h(X_{t+1}, \theta) = 0$, where h is a vector function, X_{t+1} includes variables at t and $t + 1$, and θ is a vector of parameters. This implies that the expectation of the product of any variable in the information set at t with the actual values of $h(X_{t+1}, \theta)$ must be zero. This suggests as a natural estimator for θ the value of θ that minimizes an appropriately weighted sum of the squares of the product of instruments at t with $h(X_{t+1}, \theta)$. Hansen (1982) derived the weights that produce the smallest asymptotic standard errors for θ even when the hs are heteroskedastic conditional on the instruments. For simplicity, we assume instead that the hs are conditionally homoskedastic. This allows estimation by three-stage least squares.[9]

Hansen (1982) also provides a statistic J, which, under the null hypothesis, is asymptotically distributed as χ^2 with degrees of freedom equal to $(qm - r)$, where q is the number of equations, m the number of instruments, and r the number of estimated parameters. This provides a very simple test of the overidentifying restrictions. These restrictions simply require that the addition of extra instruments should not increase the value of J very much. This is so because, according to the model, at the true θ, the expectation of the cross product of any new instrument and h is zero.

The main problem with using any variable in the information set at t as an instrument is that this procedure is appropriate only when the sole reason for h to differ from zero is that, at $t + 1$, agents discover new information about prices and incomes. If this were indeed the only source of uncertainty in the economy, then the static condition (S) would hold exactly; there is no reason for the marginal rate of substitution of consumption for leisure to be different from the real wage. However, it is inevitable that any empirical estimate of (S) will not fit perfectly. Any of the natural explanations of this residual seems to invalidate the use as instruments of all the variables known at t. One explanation is that tastes are random and that, for instance, d follows a stochastic process. This is the view taken in Altonji (1982) when he estimates a version of (S). However, if d were stochastic, our methods would not allow us to estimate (EL) and (EC). Other explanations include the presence of errors of measurement of the variables, errors of specification, the presence of nominal contracts, and the absence of full information by the agents at t about variables that occur at t. These last two explanations for the residual in (S) appear to be consistent with assuming that all three first-order conditions hold in expectation with respect to a weaker conditioning set than the one Hansen and Singleton (1981) suggest.

In particular, suppose that workers sign contracts at $t - 1$ for t specifying the nominal wage and the amount they will work. Then, the static first-order condition becomes

$$E_{t-1} \frac{\partial U}{\partial L_t} E_{t-1} \frac{\partial U}{\partial C_t} \frac{W_t}{P_t}.$$

When the utility function is separable in consumption and leisure, $E_{t-1}(\partial U/\partial L_t)$ becomes known as $t - 1$, and this condition reduces to (S) with an error term uncorrelated with information available at $t - 1$. Likewise, in a model like that of Lucas (1973) the first-order conditions would hold when the conditioning set is the set of economy wide variables known by agents at t. However, the aggregation over agents who signed contracts at different dates or over agents who have different private information might present serious difficulties. In any event, these considerations suggest that an appropriate estimator of α, β, d, and γ can be obtained by estimating the system of equations (S), (EL), and (EC) by nonlinear three-stage least squares where the instruments are variables whose realizations occur before t. In fact, we compare the results of using current and lagged instruments with those of using only lagged instruments.

The estimation of the systems might be thought to present a problem, since the residuals are not independent. Indeed, letting u_t^s, u_{t+1}^{EC}, and u_{t+1}^{EL} denote the residuals of (S), (EC), and (EL) as these equations are written in section 6.3, we see it is easy to verify that

$$(1 + u_{t+1}^{EC})(1 + u_t^s) = (1 + u_{t+1}^s)(1 + u_{t+1}^{EL}).$$

This does not, however, make one equation redundant from the point of view of estimation because the products of instruments and residuals in one equation are not linear combinations of the products of instruments and residuals of the other equations.[10]

6.6 Results

We begin by estimating the three first-order conditions separately, since each of these equations requires a different set of assumptions regarding which markets clear. We then estimate the entire system of equations. These system estimates require that the individual does not face a quantity constraint in any market. Because the estimated parameters using only fourth quarter data are essentially identical to those using quarterly data, we report only the latter.

Table 6.1
Estimates of Euler equation for consumption (EC) separable case[a]

	(1)	(2)	(3)	(4)	(5)	(6)
Consumption measure	*ND*	*ND*	*ND*	*ND + S*	*ND + S*	*ND + S*
Instrument list	A	B	C	A	B	C
α	0.234	0.174	0.512	0.330	0.092	0.333
	(0.219)	(0.199)	(0.193)	(0.237)	(0.209)	(0.182)
ρ^{-1}	0.997	0.997	0.996	0.996	0.997	0.996
	(0.001)	(0.001)	(0.001)	(0.001)	(0.001)	(0.001)
Concave?	Yes	Yes	Yes	Yes	Yes	Yes
J	25.48	43.06	35.43	24.8	47.41	44.78
Critical J* at 1%	11.34	21.66	21.66	11.34	21.66	21.66

a. Standard errors are in parentheses.

The first Euler equation (EC) requires that the expectation of the product of the marginal rate of substitution between consumption in t and consumption in $t + 1$ with the real interest rate equals unity. This condition holds so long as the individual is not constrained either in the goods market or in the capital market. In particular, (EC) does not embody any assumption regarding the determination of the level of employment.

Table 6.1 contains the estimates of (EC) imposing additive separability between consumption and leisure ($\gamma = 0$) as is done implicitly in earlier work. The estimates of α are positive, as is necessary for concavity. They vary between 0.09 and 0.51, and center at about 0.3. Other studies estimate this Euler equation in the additively separable case and generally report higher estimates of α. Hansen and Singleton (1982) find α to be about 0.8; Summers (1982) about 3; Mankiw (1981) about 4; and Hall (1981) about 15. *In all cases*, the overidentifying restrictions are clearly rejected, indicating that the orthogonality conditions upon which these estimates are premised do not hold. This is the same rejection Hansen and Singleton (1982) and Mankiw (1981) report. (We do not reject the overidentifying restrictions with only fourth quarter data.) Beyond the variations in the measure of consumption and the instrument list shown in the table, we also experimented with the use of pretax returns, with little impact on the results.

Table 6.2 contains the estimates of (EC) that allow nonseparability between consumption and leisure. The standard errors of the parameter estimates are extremely high. In particular, we cannot reject the null hypothesis of additive separability between consumption and leisure ($\gamma = 0$).

Table 6.2
Estimates of Euler equation for consumption (EC) nonseparable case[a]

	(1)	(2)	(3)	(4)	(5)	(6)
Consumption measure	ND	ND	ND	ND + S	ND + S	ND + S
Instrument list	A	B	C	A	B	C
α	1.118	0.257	0.375	-0.204	0.147	0.799
	(118.13)	(1.568)	(1.302)	(15.94)	(4.112)	(0.393)
β	-45.827	151.9	150.99	-71.39	134.5	-41.858
	(12,839.8)	(472.3)	(612.97)	(872.6)	(248.95)	(800.2)
γ	-4.730	0.098	0.086	-0.537	0.1780	0.034
	(1,299.3)	(1.592)	(1.329)	(21.8)	(3.757)	(0.549)
d	1.383	280.8	280.0	301.2	264.3	284.2
	(332.3)	(3,480.0)	(3,364.8)	(23,595.)	(2,840)	(4,454.)
ρ^{-1}	0.999	0.997	0.997	1.001	0.996	0.993
	(0.048)	(0.001)	(0.001)	(0.015)	(0.002)	(0.002)
Concave?	No	Yes	Yes	No	Yes	No
J		29.23	24.63		33.51	27.50
Critical J^* at 1%		16.81	16.81		16.81	16.81

a. Standard errors are in parentheses.

Table 6.3
Estimates of Euler equation for leisure (EL) separable case[a]

	(1)	(2)	(3)
Instrument list	A	B	C
β	-0.739	-0.996	0.121
	(0.959)	(0.474)	(0.480)
ρ^{-1}	0.994	0.994	0.994
	(0.001)	(0.001)	(0.001)
Concave?	No	No	Yes
J	8.47	15.75	21.7
Critical J^* at 1%	11.35	21.66	21.66

a. Standard errors are in parentheses.

Alternative values of α, β, and γ have very similar implications for the short-run and long-run behavioral elasticities. For example, if d is close to zero, it will be impossible to separately identify α and γ. Furthermore, we continue to reject the overidentifying restrictions. Thus, the rejection of the model Hansen and Singleton (1982) and Mankiw (1981) report cannot be attributed to their maintained hypothesis of separability between consumption and leisure.

The second Euler equation (EL) specifies that the product of the marginal rate of substitution of leisure in t and leisure in $t + 1$ and the real interest rate in terms of leisure has an expectation of 1. This condition is premised upon the absence of quantity constraints both in the capital market and in the labor market.

Table 6.3 presents the estimates of (EL) in the additively separable case. The estimates of β often have the wrong sign (negative) and are thus inconsistent with concavity. Note that when the concavity restriction is violated, the estimated parameters imply a utility function whose maximum is given by a corner solution, or which does not exist. In principle, concavity of the utility function should be imposed as it is impossible to observe interior solutions for consumption or leisure if the utility function were truly convex. In practice, imposing this restriction is difficult. Therefore, it is hard to interpret in a very meaningful way the standard errors or the parameters in the case where the concavity restrictions are rejected. Nonetheless, the data indicate no clear relation between the quantity of leisure and the relative price of present versus future leisure. This result casts serious doubt on the premise of most classical macroeconomic models that observed labor supply represents unconstrained choices given perceived opportunities. Note especially that the results are not very sensitive

Table 6.4
Estimates of Euler equation for leisure (EL) nonseparable case[a]

	(1)	(2)	(3)	(4)	(5)	(6)
Consumption measure	ND	ND	ND	ND + S	ND + S	ND + S
Instrument list	A	B	C	A	B	C
α	2.286	−0.227	1.6332	1.696	1.970	2.947
	(5.490)	(39.4)	(35.9)	(2.975)	(2.434)	(64.315)
β	8.753	−1.032	0.1837	13.083	7.23	0.481
	(22.78)	(4.504)	(52.0)	(19.374)	(11.49)	(2344.9)
γ	−18.42	−0.318	−0.466	−21.457	−18.8	−9.678
	(217.3)	(9.155)	(30.4)	(143.31)	(110.1)	(1754.)
d	0.528	1.132	0.510	1.355	0.478	0.021
	(7.763)	(344.3)	(118.7)	(13.5)	(3.305)	(121.9)
ρ^{-1}	0.995	0.995	0.994	1.0002	0.996	0.994
	(0.001)	(0.0001)	(0.0009)	(0.008)	(0.002)	(0.002)
Concave?	No	No	No	No	No	Barely[b]
J	8.26	21.63			5.76	25.47
Critical J^* at 1%	16.81	16.81	16.81	16.81	16.81	16.81

a. Standard errors are in parentheses.
b. The determinant of the matrix of second partials of U is negative, but very close to zero, making inversion of the matrix, and thus computation of elasticities, impossible.

to the choice of instrument list. In particular, the use of lagged instruments to capture the possibility of imperfect information has little effect on the results.

Table 6.4 presents the estimates of (EL) that allow nonseparability. The standard errors are huge, and thus do not reject separability. The estimated utility function is almost never concave. Hence, the failure reported above for the separable case cannot be attributed to the then maintained hypothesis of separability.

The third condition (S), which equates the marginal rate of substitution between consumption and leisure to the real wage, is the crucial test of labor-market clearing. Unlike either of the other first-order conditions, this static relation does not rely upon the assumed absence of liquidity constraints. It relies only upon the ability of the individual to trade off consumption and leisure within a single period. Since consumers are generally not constrained in the goods market, this equation should hold so long as observed employment lies on the labor supply curve.

Table 6.5 presents the estimates obtained from the estimation of (S). In almost every case, the estimate of α is positive, and the estimate of β is negative. We find these signs for different instrument lists, for different measures of consumption, for different frequency data, and for different estimation periods. Although not displayed, these signs also emerge when (S) is estimated in first differences. Altonji (1982) also reports estimates of α and β with these signs.

This result provides powerful evidence against the hypothesis that observed labor supply behavior can be described as resulting from continuous maximization of a stable additively separable intertemporal utility function. The estimated utility function is extremely implausible, as can be illustrated easily. Holding the real wage constant, consider an increase in nonlabor income. If α and β have opposite signs, then either consumption or leisure must fall. That is, since consumption and leisure move in opposite directions for any given real wage, one must be inferior if the movements represent voluntary maximizing behavior. These results probably emerge because over the business cycle consumption and leisure move in opposite directions. At the same time, we simply do not observe at the aggregate level the procyclical movements in the real wage that would rationalize this behavior.

We next estimated the three first-order conditions jointly as a system. These estimates also generally rejected the overidentifying restrictions. In the separable case the estimates for β continued to be negative.

Table 6.6 presents the system estimates for the nonseparable case. The

Table 6.5
Estimates of static condition (S)[a]

	(1)	(2)	(3)	(4)	(5)	(6)
Consumption measure	ND	ND	ND	ND + S	ND + S	ND + S
Instrument list	A	B	C	A	B	C
α	1.873	2.377	4.636	3.694	3.639	2.789
	(0.118)	(0.053)	(0.040)	(0.035)	(0.032)	(0.032)
β	0.018	−1.107	−8.042	−5.426	−16.231	−0.212
	(1.417)	(1.097)	(5.306)	(10.038)	(9.324)	(4.235)
J	63.98	118.05	118.97	87.91	118.25	121.86
Critical J^* at 1%	9.21	20.09	20.09	9.21	20.09	20.09

a. Standard errors are in parentheses.

Table 6.6
System estimates: nonseparable case[a]

	(1)	(2)	(3)	(4)	(5)	(6)
Consumption measure	ND	ND	ND	$ND + S$	$ND + S$	$ND + S$
Instrument list	A	B	C	A	B	C
α	1.407	1.680	1.713	0.789	0.889	0.928
	(0.030)	(0.033)	(0.035)	(0.017)	(0.014)	(0.018)
β	−4.937	−0.340	0.158	−3.637	−1.718	−0.688
	(0.549)	(0.414)	(0.493)	(0.464)	(0.281)	(0.324)
γ	−6.452	0.050	0.321	−2.720	−2.716	0.080
	(1.791)	(0.035)	(1.178)	(0.967)	(0.602)	(0.176)
d	0.843	146.406	16.540	8.297	−0.640	114.612
	(0.448)	(71.198)	(68.970)	(4.112)	(0.776)	(310.028)
ρ^{-1}	0.997	0.994	0.993	0.999	0.997	0.993
	(0.001)	(0.0005)	(0.001)	(0.001)	(0.001)	(0.0005)
Concave?	No	Yes	Yes	No	No	Yes
J	21.308	41.91	47.23	31.45	99.07	128.24
Critical J^* at 1%	21.67	46.96	46.96	21.67	46.96	46.96

a. Standard errors are in parentheses.

estimated utility function is concave for only half of the estimates. In most of the concave cases, α and β have opposite signs, implying that either consumption or leisure is an inferior good.

We next experimented, imposing the constraint $\alpha = \beta$. When γ was allowed to vary, the estimates were usually not concave. Only when we also imposed separability ($\gamma = 0$) did we obtain consistently concave parameters. In this latter case we obtained for all three instrument lists estimates of α near 1.5 for nondurables and near 1.0 for nondurables and services.

Various elasticities are presented in table 6.7 for those nonseparable estimates that imply a concave utility function.[11] Since the estimates of the utility function parameters vary greatly, the estimated elasticities also vary greatly. The long-run elasticity of consumption with respect to the wage is approximately 0.6, and the long-run elasticity of leisure with respect to the wage is 0.26, implying a backward-bending long-run labor supply curve.

Probably the most important elasticity for evaluating the intertemporal substitution hypothesis is the short-run elasticity of leisure with respect to the current wage. This elasticity varies from -0.0027 to -0.99 across estimates. This implies a short-run labor supply elasticity between 0.01 and 17, since leisure is roughly four times labor supply. Note that the elasticity of leisure with respect to changes in the interest rate is in all cases but one essentially identical to the elasticity with respect to the wage. The short-run elasticity of consumption with respect to changes in price varies from -0.6 to -3.4. It is not surprising, given the poor performance of the model that these short-run elasticities are not well pinned down.

6.7 Conclusions

The empirical results reported in this paper are consistently disappointing. The overidentifying restrictions implied by the model of dynamic optimization in the absence of quantity constraints are rejected by virtually all of the estimates using quarterly data. The estimated utility function parameters always imply implausible behavior. We can conclude that the data strongly reject specifications of the type used in this paper. In this final section we examine a number of alternative explanations for the results obtained.

A first possibility is that our poor results are a consequence of problems of measurement and estimation. As emphasized in the initial discussion of the data, our measures of consumption and leisure are all open to question, as is our proxy for real returns. Probably more serious is the use of seasonally adjusted data. Seasonal fluctuations, which account for most of

Table 6.7
Elasticities implied by the estimates

Table/column of estimates	6.2/2	6.2/3	6.2/5	6.6/2	6.6/3	6.6/6
Short-run elasticities						
C with respect to P	−3.1	−2.4	−3.4	−0.61	−0.60	−1.1
C with respect to W	0.0055	0.0047	0.0061	−0.64	0.55	1.8
C with respect to 1 + r	−3.1	−2.3	−3.4	−0.045	−0.045	−0.72
L with respect to P	0.0015	0.00086	0.0038	0.0005	−0.18	0.21
L with respect to W	−0.0027	−0.0028	−0.0035	−0.36	−0.25	−0.99
L with respect to 1 + r	−0.0013	−0.0020	−0.00030	−0.36	−0.22	−0.99
Long-run elasticities						
C with respect to W/P					0.54	0.61
L with respect to W/P					0.26	0.26

the variance in leisure, should be explained by dynamic optimization rather than averaged out as in our data. Utility presumably depends on actual consumption not on consumption as adjusted by $X - 11$. Time aggregation issues are possibly serious as well.

A second, more likely, possibility is that the auxiliary assumptions we maintain to make the problem tractable are false. Aggregation in models of this type is very problematic. It is also possible that our assumption of additive separability across time is the root of the problem. Over some intervals, this assumption is unwarranted. People who have worked hard want to rest. Mealtimes are not staggered through the day by accident. How serious these types of effects are at the macro level remains an open question. Clark and Summers (1982) examine several types of evidence bearing on the effects of previous employment experience on subsequent experience, and conclude that habit formation and persistence effects predominate over intertemporal substitution effects. This suggests that while nonseparability may help to explain the failure of our results, the sign of the key cross derivatives may well be the opposite of that usually assumed in intertemporal substitution theories.

A third general class of explanation for the results we obtained involves changing tastes. Just as the identification of traditional demand curves depends on the predominance of technological shocks relative to taste shocks, identification in models of the type estimated here depends on the maintained hypothesis of constant tastes. This is clearly a fiction. In every arena where taste shocks are easy to disentangle, fashion being an obvious example, they are pervasive. Even if the tastes of individuals were stable over time, the tastes of individuals of different ages differ, and the age distribution represented by the representative consumer has changed through time. An important topic for future research is the estimation of models that allow for changing tastes, either through random shocks, or endogenously on the basis of experience. The latter possibility relates closely to the problem of nonseparability in the utility function.

A final possible reason for the failure of the model is that individuals are constrained in the labor or capital market. The apparently large effects of sharp nominal contractions that have been observed in repeated historic episodes support the view that wages are rigid. Analyses of the macro character of unemployment, such as Clark and Summers (1979b) and Akerlof and Main (1981), find that it is extremely concentrated among relatively few individuals whose employment is strongly procyclical. This suggests a role for disequilibrium in certain labor market segments in explaining cyclical fluctuations.

In sum, the results of this investigation are discouraging. We find little evidence in favor of any of the models estimated here. In particular, we conclude that taking account of leisure does not rationalize the failure of previous models of consumption based on intertemporal decision-making.

We are grateful to David Runkle for his research assistance and to Henry Farber, Robert Shiller, and two anonymous referees for helpful comments. We have all, in one form or another, benefited from the largesse of the National Science Foundation.

Notes

1. The models of Prescott and Mehra (1980), Long and Plosser (1983), and King and Plosser (1984), for example, exhibit this feature. Some models, such as those of Kydland and Prescott (1982), rely on the absence of additive separability to generate intertemporal substitution effects. We return to this possibility in the final section of the paper.

2. If more than one security is available, (EC) and (EL) should hold for all securities that can be freely bought and sold.

3. This restricted utility function ($\tau = 0$) is the one considered by Altonji (1981) and Blinder (1974) among others.

4. In fact we consider a slight variation of (4) when we impose $\alpha = \beta$. This variation has been used by Auerbach and Kotlikoff (1981) and Lipton and Sachs (1981) is given by

$$[C_t^{1-\alpha} + dL_t^{1-\alpha}]^{(1-\alpha/1-\alpha)}.$$

This utility function has the advantage that α and γ are readily interpretable. $1/\alpha$ is the elasticity of substitution of consumption for leisure, while $1/\tau$ is the intertemporal elasticity of substitution of the composite good:

$$[C_t^{1-\alpha} + dL_t^{1-\alpha}](1/1 - \alpha).$$

5. This elasticity is simply the percentage change in the ratio of consumption (or leisure) at $t + 1$ to consumption (or leisure) at t over the percentage change in the real interest rate $P_t(1 + r_t)/P_{t+1}$ (or $W_t(1 + r_t)/W_{t+1}$). Elasticities like these have been studied by Hall (1981) and Hansen and Singleton (1982).

6. Grossman and Shiller present another aggregation theorem. However, their theorem cannot be used to justify rigorously the estimation of a representative consumer's utility function as is done here. Their results are only local and so do not apply over the discrete intervals that generate the data, unless the utility function has a special form, different from the one assumed here. Furthermore, their theorem assumes interior solutions for each agent, which is unrealistic for leisure.

7. Both measures of consumption with which we experiment in this study can proxy only part of total consumption, since the expenditure and the services from

durable goods are completely excluded. Implicitly, each of our alternative specifications imposes the assumption that the excluded forms of consumption enter the utility function in additively separable ways. This standard assumption is obviously problematic. Consider freezers and food, or cars and gasoline. An alternative defense of using a subset of consumption as a proxy for aggregate consumption is to rely on Hicks or Leontief aggregation. There is, however, no empirical support for the view that either the relative price of different types of consumption is fixed or that different goods are consumed in fixed proportions.

8. The data on average federal marginal tax rates came from Seater (1980).

9. We also reestimated some of our equations allowing for conditional heteroskedasticity without affecting our results.

10. The inclusion of the third equation is analogous to the inclusion as instruments of nonlinear transformations of the instruments. Such an inclusion would also leave the asymptotic properties of our estimators intact.

11. These elasticities are computed using data corresponding to the first quarter of 1980. A problem arises from the fact that all three equations have a residual in this period. This residual is ignored in our calculations that use the actual values for C, L, P, W, and r on both sides of (3) and (5). Alternatively, we could have changed some of these variables to make (S), (EC), and (EL) hold exactly and then computed the elasticities.

III   Structural Unemployment

7

Unemployment Insurance and Labor Market Transitions

with Kim B. Clark

An unemployment rate above 4% was once regarded as synonymous with slack in the economy. That view is no longer widely held. Indeed, some observers today believe that rates of unemployment below 6% place unsustainable inflationary pressure on the economy. This change in viewpoint has been the result of both labor market developments and new perspectives on the causes of unemployment. The apparent upward trend in unemployment has been a source of major concern to policymakers and the focus of research by a number of economists. Central to many explanations of the rising natural rate of unemployment is the role of government transfer programs.

The impact of transfers on measured unemployment includes both real effects on the intensity of search and the willingness to accept offers, and a pure reporting effect. Where program participation depends on registration for possible employment, the measured rate of unemployment could be higher simply because some individuals change the way they report otherwise unchanged behavior. A full evaluation of the impact of transfers on conventional measures of labor market tightness requires an assessment of both real and reporting effects. Although most analyses of transfer programs focus on changes in incentives to find jobs, these programs' effect on the reporting of constant behavior may also be quite significant.

This study reports preliminary estimates of an econometric simulation model capable of a comprehensive evaluation of the effects of unemployment insurance (UI) on measured and actual employment, unemployment, and nonparticipation. The data are longitudinal, comprising information from 75,000 households sampled in the Current Population Survey (CPS) of March and April 1978. A computer program was developed to impute UI benefits conditional on becoming unemployed for each individual in the sample. The program uses information on each state's benefit formula and eligibility rules, as well as information on federal and state tax codes to calculate a hypothetical replacement rate for each individual in the March sample.

The simulation model is constructed from multinomial logit equations characterizing individuals' labor force transitions. These equations express an individual's probability of transiting between labor force states as a function of his characteristics and of variables reflecting UI benefits (such as the replacement rate and the potential duration of benefits). This technique makes it possible to estimate the impact of UI on both the length of unemployment spells and their frequency. The former depends on UI effects on the probability of exit from employment, while the latter depends on UI effects on the probability of transition into unemployment. The model also can be used to examine the effect of UI reforms on both the level of employment and rate of nonparticipation.

The methodology and data used here have several advantages over previous studies of the effects of UI. Most important, they permit a comprehensive evaluation of the effects of the program. Previous studies have typically focused on the effects of UI on just one labor force transition. Our study provides the first estimate of UI effects on the rate of job loss, labor force exit, and labor force entrance into unemployment. The common data and methods in this study make it possible to combine the estimates of UI effects on individual transition probabilities to yield an estimate of overall impact.

Second, this evaluation of UI makes use of data from the CPS. As has been well documented, measures of unemployment derived from different surveys diverge widely.[1] The use of CPS data means that the results obtained here can be used as a basis for evaluating the effects of UI on unemployment as it is officially measured. The focus here on the reporting effects of UI as well as its behavioral effects also improves the realism of our estimates of the impact of UI on measured unemployment. Recognizing reporting as well as behavioral effects is crucial when using CPS data, as almost half of all unemployment spells culminate in labor force withdrawal.

A third advantage of the approach used here is that it takes account of the effect of UI on the composition of the unemployed and employed populations. Previous studies have been flawed by the failure to take account of the fact that UI will affect the mix of persons becoming unemployed. If, for example, UI induces many short-term layoffs, it may reduce the average duration of unemployment even while increasing spell lengths for each individual. The transition probability approach taken here avoids this difficulty, because explicit account is taken of the effect of UI on the flow into unemployment.

Many previous efforts to evaluate the effects of UI have failed to take account of the taxes that are necessary to finance the system. This study also attempts an examination of the effects of the payroll taxes used to finance UI on levels of employment and unemployment.

It should be clear at the outset that estimating the impact of social insurance programs on the measured unemployment rate is in no way equivalent to examining their desirability. One important goal of social insurance is to make it possible for persons for whom work is likely to be very burdensome (the aged or disabled) to subsist without holding jobs. An important function of UI is facilitating the mobility between jobs that is necessary to accommodate changing product demands. This does mean encouraging persons to become unemployed. Moreover, the reporting effects of social insurance programs have little welfare significance. If UI encourages workers who would otherwise withdraw from the labor force to engage in normal search activity and report themselves as unemployed, there is no real social cost.

However, an evaluation of the impact of social insurance programs on the level of unemployment is crucial to interpreting labor market conditions. If UI has induced a large increase in the measured unemployment rate, then current high rates of unemployment are not a warrant for public policies to promote employment. If the increases in unemployment cannot be linked to UI or other social programs, the case for policies to combat the increase may be strengthened.

7.1 A Theoretical Framework

The relationship between UI and unemployment has been extensively studied.[2] Most previous studies have focused on the relationship between unemployment duration and UI. This is only a small part of the story. There may also be important linkages between UI and the rate of flow into unemployment. Martin Feldstein has argued that UI encourages temporary layoffs and irregular work scheduling.[3] Daniel Hamermesh has suggested that UI may actually increase the labor force participation of some workers.[4] He points out that labor force entrance is more attractive if part of the compensation for employment includes the chance to take advantage of unemployment insurance. UI may also encourage quits in states where job leavers are eligible for benefits.[5]

In order to model these various effects it is necessary to use a framework that takes account of labor market dynamics. The approach taken here builds on the work of Hall, Perry, and Marston, which treats transitions between labor market states as a Markov process.[6] Specifically we assume that each individual's behavior can be characterized by a matrix of transition probabilities given by

$$\mathbf{p}^i = \begin{bmatrix} p^i_{ee} & p^i_{eu} & p^i_{en} \\ p^i_{ue} & p^i_{uu} & p^i_{un} \\ p^i_{ne} & p^i_{nu} & p^i_{nn} \end{bmatrix}, \tag{1}$$

where, for example, p^i_{en} represents the probability that the ith worker would be not in the labor force (NILF) in month $t + 1$, conditional on being employed in month t. Since a worker must always be in one of the three labor force states, the rows of p sum to one.

From the transition probability matrix $\mathbf{p}^i$ it is possible to calculate the proportion of the time individual i spends in each of the three labor force states. Let π^i_j be the fraction of time that individual i spends in state j. We solve for the π^i_j by finding the root of the linear equation system

$$\mathbf{p}^i \pi^i = \pi^i, \tag{2}$$

for which $\pi^i_u + \pi^i_e + \pi^i_n = 1$.[7] The unemployment rate, the fraction of the labor force which is unemployed, is given by $\pi_u/(\pi_u + \pi_e)$. The steady-state distribution of the population across labor market states can be found by averaging individual probabilities. That is,

$$\Pi_j = \frac{1}{N} \sum_{i=1}^{N} \pi^i_j, \tag{3}$$

where N is the size of the population. The aggregate unemployment rate is given by $\Pi_u/(\Pi_u + \Pi_e)$.

In table 7.1 we provide the 1974 averages of the individual transition probability matrices for various demographic groups. The striking feature of the table is the importance of flows into and out of the labor force. It is instructive to consider the group with the greatest labor force attachment and contact with the UI system, prime-age males. Even though the participation rate in the group averages 92%, over one-third of employment entrances came from outside the labor force, and 28% of employment spells ended in labor force withdrawal. This suggests the potential importance of UI effects on reported participation as well as on employment.[8]

Table 7.1
Labor market transition probabilities, by age and sex, 1974 annual average

	Men			Women			
Probability	16–19	20–24	25–59	16–19	20–24	25–59	Total
Unemployment to employment	0.284	0.287	0.309	0.250	0.255	0.172	0.254
Unemployment to nonparticipation	0.286	0.133	0.105	0.318	0.159	0.272	0.208
Employment to unemployment	0.045	0.032	0.011	0.033	0.026	0.012	0.020
Employment to nonparticipation	0.102	0.033	0.004	0.133	0.047	0.042	0.033
Nonparticipation to employment	0.144	0.180	0.071	0.093	0.071	0.050	0.050
Nonparticipation to unemployment	0.085	0.079	0.032	0.067	0.034	0.013	0.020

Source: Unpublished tabulations by the Bureau of Labor Statistics adjusted by the Urban Institute as described in Jean E. Vanski, "Recession and the Employment of Demographic Groups: Adjustments to Gross Change Data," in Charles C. Holt and others, *Labor Markets, Inflation, and Manpower Policies*, final report to the U.S. Manpower Administration (Washington, D.C.: Urban Institute, 1975), pp. C-1–C-14.

The approach taken in this paper is to use multinomial logit analysis to estimate the impact of individual characteristics and UI on individual transition probability matrices p^i. These estimates are then combined using equations (2) and (3) to generate estimates of UI impacts on the unemployment and participation rates. This "transition probability" approach has the virtue of being closely linked to theories of labor market choice that emphasize the role of transition decisions. The use of Markov transition matrices involves the assumption that individuals' transition decisions do not depend on how long they have been in a state. This assumption of no state dependence has been examined in earlier work with mixed results. Econometric identification of state dependence is difficult because any heterogeneity among individuals in their transition probabilities will lead to apparent state dependence. The assumption here is necessitated by the absence of data on how long individuals have occupied their initial states.

7.1.1 UI and the Unemployed

The duration of unemployment spells has been the focus of most research on UI and the unemployed. In terms of the framework developed here, this is equivalent to studying the relationship between UI and the transition probabilities p_{ue}^i and p_{un}^i. The duration of completed spells of unemployment is related to the transition probabilities p_{ue}^i and p_{un}^i by the identity

$$D_u^i = \frac{1}{p_{ue}^i + p_{un}^i}. \tag{4}$$

In thinking about the impact of UI on the duration of unemployment, it is crucial to distinguish between individuals who are searching for work and those on layoff from jobs to which they are permanently attached.

We begin by analyzing the decision problem faced by workers who are eligible for UI but not attached to permanent jobs. Dale Mortensen's excellent theoretical study of the decision problem faced by these workers brings out the crucial effects.[9] He finds that the impact of an increase in the UI benefit level on the probability of reemployment is likely to be positive but is theoretically ambiguous. Increases in UI benefits will tend to increase the length of spells by reducing the opportunity cost of both leisure and job search. The consequent rise in the reservation wage tends to prolong unemployment. However, it is possible that for some workers this effect will be offset by another. Since jobs are not permanent, workers will recognize that the sooner they take a job, the sooner they will again be eligible for UI. This effect is likely to be particularly important for persons near exhaustion of benefits.

Mortensen's analysis does not treat the question of UI's impact on the probability of labor force withdrawal. Increases in UI are likely to reduce labor force withdrawal through both real and reporting effects. By raising the rewards of working, increases in UI reduce the incentive to withdraw from the labor force. In most states, eligibility for UI requires a worker to be available and actively looking for work. When enforced, this will cause some workers to search for work rather than withdraw from the labor force. However, this requirement is usually very poorly enforced. Disqualifications from UI are quite rare, affecting fewer than 0.1% of claimants. Nonetheless, knowledge of the requirement is likely to lead at least some persons to profess to be looking for work even if they are not in fact seriously seeking a job. This effect may also occur because workers regard mandatory registration with the state employment service as a form of job search.

It is important to be clear about the relationship between this analysis and statements about the impact of UI on the average duration of unemployment. The question examined here is the impact of an increase in UI on a given worker's probability of reemployment. The average duration of unemployment will be affected by changes in this probability, as well as by changes in the composition of the unemployed. Even if UI reduced the probability of exiting unemployment for any given individual, the average length of unemployment spells might also be reduced if persons with high reemployment probabilities were encouraged to become unemployed. This problem would seem to be a serious drawback of previous studies that have relied on comparisons of averages of unemployment durations.

Similar considerations suggest that increases in the potential remaining duration are likely to reduce the probability of unemployment exit by delaying returns to employment. An additional complication is posed by those who are waiting to receive benefits. This group (mostly quitters) will also be sensitive to increases in benefits, even though benefits are not received contemporaneously.

7.1.2 UI and Exit from Layoff Unemployment

The importance of distinguishing between the behavior of workers who are attached to permanent jobs and those not attached has been recognized since the influential work of Feldstein.[10] In an ex-post sense, the duration of layoff spells is determined by the employer rather than the employee. In an ex-ante sense, of course, this is not the case. Explicit, or more likely implicit, contracts will determine the length and frequency of spells of temporary layoff unemployment. These contracts will depend on both workers' tastes and the availability of UI. The nature of these interactions is discussed in more detail below. However, in the presence of imperfect experience rating, increases in UI at the margin will lead to longer and more frequent layoffs.

A second consideration suggests a positive relationship between benefit levels and the length of spells of layoff unemployment. A large fraction, perhaps as great as 50%, of those in the temporary layoff category do not in fact return to their original employer. For this group, the considerations discussed above for ordinary job losers should be relevant. It does not appear on theoretical grounds that there should be important effects of UI on labor force withdrawal from layoff unemployment.

7.1.3 UI and the Flow into Unemployment

Previous research on demographic, cyclical, and regional differences in unemployment rates has all found that most variations can be attributed to

differences in the rate of flow into unemployment rather than the duration
of unemployment spells. This suggests the importance of examining the
relation between UI and the rate of entrance into unemployment. While
most of the research in this area has examined the relationship between UI
and temporary layoff unemployment, it is also likely that there are important effects of UI on permanent separations.

7.1.4 UI and Employment Exit

In order to examine the relationship between UI and permanent separations, it is necessary to provide a model for determining the duration of
employment. We use the framework developed by Robert Hall to attack
this problem.[11] The optimal separation rate is determined by the interaction of workers' tastes and employers' cost functions.

In general it is reasonable to suppose that employers have some optimal
turnover rate. If jobs are too short, costs of staffing and training become
prohibitive. If they are too long, the ability to adjust to changing product
market conditions is likely to be impaired. This suggests that the employers' isoprofit curves between wages and separation rates look like that
depicted by *EE* in figure 7.1. Workers also are likely to prefer intermediate
durations. If jobs are too short, they will have to incur excessive search
costs. If they are too long, they lose flexibility.

The set of tangencies of indifference and isoprofit curves trace out an

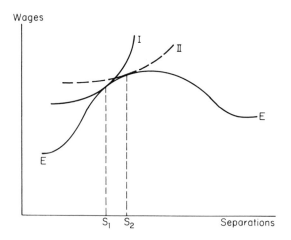

Figure 7.1
Equilibrium wages and separations without experience rating.

expansion path in wage separation space. The condition that the supply and demand for labor be equated determines the level of wages and separations. In general, it is clear from the configuration of these curves that the optimal, or equilibrium, separation rate can involve either a positive or negative rate of substitution between wages and separations.

Consider first the impact of introducing a non-experience-rated UI system. Employers' isoprofit curves are unaffected. However, since UI reduces the costs of changing jobs, it is reasonable to suppose that the shape of workers' indifference curves changes from I to II as shown in figure 7.1. At any given level of wages and the separation rate, the introduction of UI reduces the rate of substitution between wages and separations. Graphically, the associated slope of the indifference curve at each point declines. This means that the introduction of UI leads to a new equilibrium with a higher separation rate (S_2). The magnitude of the impact of UI on the equilibrium level of rates and separations depends on the shape of the indifference curves. The figure would seem to suggest that UI represents a Pareto improvement. This is a consequence of deferring consideration of the taxes necessary to finance the program.

The basic result, that UI raises the equilibrium separation rate, should not be surprising. Since it subsidizes job search, it makes separation less costly for workers. This directly encourages quits. Employer-initiated separations are also encouraged. Since workers will demand less compensation for a high risk of layoff, employers will find it profitable to shift to production methods involving a higher risk of separation.

The UI system considered so far was not experience rated. That is, an employer's contribution to the system was assumed to be independent of his own separation experience. Consider now the extreme opposite case of perfectly experience-rated UI. In this case, depicted in figure 7.2, the employers' isoprofit curve is shifted (from EE to $E'E'$) in a fashion parallel to the change in workers' indifference curves. Hence the separation rate at the point of tangency (between indifference curve III and isoprofit curve $E'E'$) is unaffected. A fully experience-rated system of UI will have no impact on the separation rate.

This result can be seen intuitively. Efficiency considerations dictate an optimal rate of substitution between wages and separation rates. The announcement by the government that the employer must make transfers to the employee in the case of separation will have income effects, but will not affect the optimal contract.

The extent of experience rating in the UI system is examined below. At this point, it is useful to point out that if wages are taxed, a fully

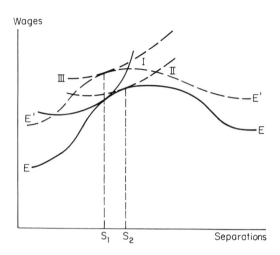

Figure 7.2
Equilibrium wages and separations with experience rating

experience-rated system requires that the employer pay the full UI costs of separations, and that the government receive the revenue it would have received if the UI benefits had been paid out as wages. If UI benefits are not taxes, and if the firm is not charged for the government's forgone revenue on those benefits, there will be an inducement toward separations. Thus, even if the UI system is perfectly experience rated internally, there is still a distortion because of forgone tax revenue on benefits.

This analysis suggests that UI is likely to increase the separation rate. This conclusion is not affected by taking account of additional complexities. In many states, separations labeled as quits leave the worker ineligible for UI. This will tend to reduce the effect considered here and give a strong inducement for quits to be labeled as job loss. If implicit contracts can be enforced, even separations induced by the employee will be labeled as layoffs. If one assumes that implicit contracts are not enforceable, and that employers are indifferent to their reputations, then only quit decisions will be affected by the level of UI benefits.

A final issue is the state occupied by persons exiting from employment. The prediction is an unambiguous increase in the probability of transiting from employment to unemployment. The effects of an increase in UI on the rate of transition from employment to NILF is ambiguous since workers who would otherwise enter this state are likely to become unemployed instead in order to collect benefits.

This analysis suggests that the effect of UI on the permanent separation rate is theoretically unambiguous. However, UI may have an ambiguous effect on the division of separations between quits and job loss.

7.1.5 UI and Permanently Attached Workers

The relationship between UI and temporary layoff unemployment has been extensively studied. Martin Feldstein has presented a theoretical analysis demonstrating that the introduction of an imperfectly experience-rated UI system encourages this form of unemployment.[12] The nature of long-term contract arrangements has been discussed in detail by Robert Hall.[13] He shows that optimal contracts involve employing workers wherever their marginal product exceeds their marginal valuation of time out of work. Since UI raises the marginal valuation by workers of time out of work, it increases the number of states of the world where workers are laid off. This effect will occur unless firms are perfectly experience rated, in which case the UI system will have no impact on layoff unemployment.

7.1.6 UI and Labor Force Entrance

As Daniel Hamermesh has pointed out, the entitlement effect of UI is likely to increase labor force entrance. This effect is similar to the proemployment effects for the unemployed described above. The ability to collect UI after a spell of work raises the effective wage and so is likely to encourage labor force entrance. This entry may be through either the unemployment or NILF states. Some workers outside the labor force may be immediately eligible for benefits if they reenter the unemployment state. For this group, who have been recently employed, the impact of UI is likely to be particularly pronounced.

In table 7.2, the conclusions of this section are summarized. The theo-

Table 7.2
Effect of unemployment insurance on labor market transition probabilities

Initial labor market state	Final labor market state		
	Employment	Unemployment	Nonparticipation
Employment	−	+ +	−
Unemployment	−	+ +	− −
Nonparticipation	?	+ +	−

retical analysis leads to predictions regarding the effects of UI on all the transition probabilities except for the movement between nonparticipation and employment. Note that the effect of UI on total unemployment is almost certain to be positive, because the transition rate into unemployment from each of the alternative states is increased.

7.1.7 Financing the UI System

The UI system is financed partially out of a payroll tax levied at a variable rate on the first $6,000 of income on a given job. This tax, which reduces after-tax wages, will tend to discourage transitions into employment and to encourage labor force withdrawal. It will tend to offset the entitlement effect of UI discussed above. In considering UI reform, it may be reasonable to assume that the taxes and benefits are changed simultaneously. Alternatively, it may be appropriate to consider the case where marginal UI funds come from other expenditure programs so that the tax system is unaffected. Both cases are considered in the empirical work below.

7.2 Imputing UI Benefits

A complete analysis of UI and labor market flows imposes formidable information requirements. We require an estimate not only of the level and potential duration of benefits received by the unemployed, but also of what the system would provide other individuals if they were to join the jobless ranks. Furthermore, theory suggests that the variables affecting economic decisions are the after-tax replacement ratios; thus we require an estimate of the applicable marginal tax rate. In order to derive these data, we have designed a computer program embodying federal tax rules and each state's UI laws and tax codes. The UISIM program determines UI eligibility, calculates basic and dependent benefits (where available), establishes the maximum allowable duration of benefits, and estimates federal and state marginal tax rates.

The program has been designed to use information from the annual work experience survey conducted in March 1978 as a supplement to the regular Current Population Survey. Federal extended benefits and supplemental assistance were not in force at that time, so that variation in UI parameters depended only on differences in state laws. Since information on income and work experience in the CPS is not as detailed as the law requires, a number of assumptions underlie our calculations.[14]

Table 7.3
Parameters of the unemployment insurance system in a typical state, and common variations

Parameter	Typical state rule	Common variations
Weekly benefit amount	$\frac{1}{26}$ of high-quarter wages (minimum $20, maximum $110)	50% of average weekly wage
Eligibility	Able/available for work Base-period earnings more than 125% of high-quarter wages and at least $800 Quit disqualification	Earnings test supplemented by a weeks-of-employment requirement Quitters qualified after waiting period
Maximum potential duration of benefits	Given weekly benefit amount, choose longest duration possible that is at least 10 weeks and no more than 26 weeks; weekly benefit amount times duration is less than or equal to one-third of base earnings	Maximum of 39 weeks Secondary limit based on weeks of employment

Source: U.S. Department of Labor, Employment and Training Administration, Unemployment Insurance Service, *Comparison of State Unemployment Insurance Laws* (Government Printing Office, 1978).

7.2.1 The UI System: Rules and Definitions

An individual's participation in the UI system—the level and duration of benefits—is conditioned by previous work experience. The specific rules for eligibility, benefit amounts, and duration are determined by each state. Though no two states are identical, a number of common elements are present. In order to highlight the basic structure of the system, table 7.3 presents key rules for a hypothetical "typical" state.

Within limits, the weekly benefit amount in our typical state is defined as 1/26 of the individual's wages in the high quarter of the base period (that is, four quarters prior to the quarter in which the claim is filed); the minimum and maximum benefit limits are $20 and $110, respectively.[15] To be eligible for benefits, a claimant must be available for and actively seeking work, and must not have left the last job voluntarily without "good cause."[16] In addition, base-period earnings must be at least $800 and must exceed 125% of high-quarter wages. Once determined, benefits are fixed for a period (fifty-two weeks) called the benefit year.[17] Within that period, all eligible claimants receive benefits for at least ten weeks; the maximum number of weeks for receipt of benefits is twenty-six. Actual potential duration is chosen so that total potential benefits are less than or equal to one-third of base-period earnings.

While variations on this theme are legion, the basic structure—including eligibility for and level of benefits linked to past work experience and minima and maxima for benefits and duration—is found in each state. Most of the interstate variations reflect either different numerical formulas (for example, 1/23 versus 1/26) or different reference values (for example, average weekly instead of high-quarter wages). Actual formulas can be quite complex. In twelve states, for example, the fraction of high-quarter wages received in weekly benefits depends on previous work experience and earnings. There are two variations, however, of a more fundamental nature. Twelve states provide additional benefits to claimants with dependents (usually ranging from $3 to $5 per dependent per week), and sixteen states allow quitters to receive benefits after a waiting period, varying from five to fourteen weeks, has elapsed. Although these provisions are found in a minority of states, they are potentially applicable to a significant fraction of the unemployed. In March 1978, for example, states with dependents' benefits accounted for 32% of all the unemployed; for quitters' benefits, the figure was 24%.

7.2.2 The UISIM Program

Our model of the UI system incorporates the rules for eligibility and the determination of benefits and taxes for each state. The program is designed to use information available in the CPS work experience survey conducted in March 1978. Information on family income, marital status, and dependents is used to calculate federal and state marginal tax rates, including Social Security taxes.[18] Data on weeks worked and wage and salary income from the previous year provide the basis for determining eligibility and the level of benefits. For those out of the labor force in March 1978 who had no work experience in 1977, we imputed an average weekly wage (described below). The output of the program consists of a weekly benefit, maximum potential duration, the quit disqualification period (where applicable), the marginal tax rate, and weeks of employment needed to qualify for benefits (NILF only).

The federal tax module in the program is based on previous work conducted at the National Bureau of Economic Research. We modified the NBER's TAXSIM program to work with CPS data and to interact with a new state tax module especially developed for UISIM. State income taxes have not received as detailed attention in the public finance literature or the empirical work on UI as have federal taxes. While state marginal tax rates are much lower than the federal taxes, they are not insignificant. In several states, marginal rates as high as 10% are not uncommon. Moreover, variation across states and across income classes within states may be important. In light of these considerations, it seems inappropriate both to ignore state taxes and to apply an average for each state. UISIM thus includes a module with an income tax algorithm for each state. Both the federal and state tax modules incorporate provisions in force as of March 1978.

Given an individual's basic earnings and employment information, the bulk of the program is a relatively straightforward and mechanical application of tax laws and state UI rules. There are three parts of UISIM, however, that required a good measure of approximation. First, in order to derive marginal tax rates we had to determine whether an individual would itemize deductions and how large the deductions would be. Information from the CPS by itself provides no guidance. Our approach to the problem involved two steps. We first used tax return information from the NBER TAXSIM file to calculate the frequency of itemization and average deductions for itemizers by income class and filing status.[19] The second step was to calculate two marginal tax rates, one assuming the standard deduction and the other assuming average itemized deductions as estimated from the sample of returns in TAXSIM. We then computed a weighted average with weights based on the frequency of itemization.

The second major area of uncertainty in the design of the simulator was the calculation of potential duration and the problem of the benefit year. At the time an initial claim is filed, weekly benefits and maximum duration are determined and fixed for the benefit year. If the individual files another claim (that is, begins a second spell of unemployment) within the benefit year, benefits available for the second spell are equal to the initial entitlement minus benefits already paid in the benefit year. For individuals with no unemployment in 1977 (the previous year) this presents no problem, since the current spell of unemployment (captured in March) can be taken as the first spell of the benefit year. For those with previous unemployment, however, the calculation is more complex. The easiest way to illustrate our approach is to consider the case of an individual who had just become unemployed at the time of the survey (March) and who had one ten-week spell of unemployment in the previous year.

In calculating maximum continuous duration of benefits in the current spell, there are three possibilities.[20] If last year's spell of unemployment began before March, the current spell marks the beginning of a new benefit year and the individual receives the maximum duration consistent with previous work experience; let this amount be MAX. If last year's spell began after March (actually after the week of the March survey), one of two conditions holds. Assume that the survey occurs in week number 10, and define the critical week (CW) to be $CW = MAX - U_{t-1} + 10$, where U_{t-1} is weeks of unemployment last year (ten in our example).[21] If last year's spell began after the critical week, say in week number 38, the individual is still in the first benefit year, and will exhaust benefits before the beginning of the second benefit year is reached; maximum potential duration is thus $MAX - U_{t-1}$ (note that we assume in this example that the current spell has just begun). If U_{t-1} began after March but before CW, the individual will reach the end of the first benefit year without exhausting benefits, and will be allowed to begin a new benefit year with a new MAX (call it $MAX2$) and weekly benefit. $MAX2$ will be conditional on whatever work experience has been accumulated during the base period (which now includes some part of the old benefit year). If the individual meets eligibility requirements for the second benefit year, maximum potential duration (continuous) for the current spell would be $MAX - U_{t-1} + MAX2$.[22]

Unfortunately, the annual work experience survey does not tell us when spells of unemployment occur. Thus, in order to derive an expected maximum potential duration, we compute a weighted average of the three possibilities. The weights are determined under an assumption that the probability of becoming unemployed is distributed uniformly across weeks. For the individual in our example, the calculation is as follows:

$$DUR = w_1(MAX) + w_2(MAX - U_{t-1}) + w_3(MAX - U_{t-1} + MAX2),$$

where

$$w_1 = \frac{10}{52},$$

$$w_2 = \frac{CW - 10}{52},$$

$$w_3 = 1 - w_1 - w_2.$$

The third major issue in the design of the simulator was the whole problem of people out of the labor force at the time of the survey. The CPS provides sufficient information to determine current eligibility status and, where applicable, to calculate marginal tax rates, weekly benefits, and potential duration. Thus some in the NILF group have enough work experience and previous earnings to qualify for benefits immediately. Others would be eligible for benefits only after some minimum period of work experience. For individuals currently ineligible, we calculated taxes and UI benefits assuming that weeks employed just satisfied minimum requirements. The applicable weekly wages were either taken from the previous year where available or imputed using an earnings function. The earnings function was estimated using data on the employed population from the May 1978 CPS; estimated earnings were corrected for selectivity bias using Mills's ratio.[23]

7.2.3 Simulation Results

The use of CPS information necessarily entails significant assumptions in the design of the simulator. It is clear that some error is possible because work experience data is not as detailed as the law requires and some tax information has to be estimated. Furthermore, the raw CPS data, particularly reported annual income, may not be accurate. With respect to the parameters of the UI system, however, substantial effort has been made to ensure their accuracy. We have made extensive use of internal Department of Labor documents made available to us by the Employment and Training Administration. We have also directly verified provisions for a large number of the states and in a few instances have engaged in extensive discussions with state officials to determine the appropriate specifications.

The results of the simulation suggest that the program provides a plausible description of the UI system. Table 7.4 presents estimates of the distribution of marginal tax rates, after-tax replacement ratios, and potential durations for the employed and the unemployed. If we look first at tax rates for the employed, the results appear to be consistent, both internally and with estimates generated by existing tax simulation models. The exclusion of wage income above $50,000 and the underreporting of other incomes appear to have only moderate effects on the overall distribution of rates. The fact that the bulk of the unemployed are found in the bottom tax bracket reflects the marginal income position of many of these individuals, as well as the use of the previous year's income, which may understate potential earnings.

The evidence on net replacement ratios accords with previous estimates. We find that 61% of the unemployed receive no benefits, while those who do have an average replacement ratio of 66.6%. This compares with 55% reported in Feldstein.[24] It should be noted that the calculations for the unemployed assume that all leavers are ineligible for benefits. The calculations for the employed predict what they would receive if they were to lose their jobs. We find that 19% are ineligible for benefits, while about

Table 7.4
Estimated marginal tax rates, replacement ratios, and potential durations of
employed and unemployed (percent except where otherwise indicated)

Parameter	Employed	Unemployed
Marginal tax rate		
0	1.0	1.6
0–20	17.0	53.3
20–30	31.7	26.7
30–40	33.6	14.3
40–50	12.3	3.3
Over 50	4.3	0.7
Replacement ratio		
0	19.2	60.7
0–25	1.1	1.5
25–40	7.2	2.8
40–60	25.2	10.8
60–80	39.9	18.4
Over 80	7.4	5.8
Potential duration (weeks)		
0	19.2	61.1
0–5	0.1	2.9
5–10	0.4	5.9
10–15	1.6	8.5
15–20	2.0	8.0
Over 20	76.7	13.4

40% of the unemployed would receive benefits replacing 60 to 80% of the after-tax wage.

It is instructive to compare the employed and unemployed groups after adjusting for eligibility. If we look only at those receiving or potentially receiving benefits, we find that close to 15% of the unemployed recipients have replacement ratios above 0.8; the comparable figure for the employed is 0.9. The other categories are quite close together, with a greater fraction of the employed in the lower ranges. These calculations are suggestive of the disincentive effects of UI.

The distribution of durations for the unemployed and employed appear quite reasonable. After correcting for eligibility, we find that more than 34% of the unemployed have a potential duration that exceeds twenty weeks, while 7.5% are within five weeks of exhausting remaining benefits. The remainder of the eligible unemployed are quite evenly distributed between five and twenty weeks. Among the employed the distribution is skewed toward eligibility for long durations. Clearly work of the employed group has accumulated sufficient wage credits and work experience to qualify for weeks close to the maximum (usually twenty weeks).

As a further check on the consistency of the program, we compared predicted benefits with those actually paid out in March 1978.[25] Estimates of weekly benefits are quite close to the actual values, while the program overestimates total weeks compensated by about 9%.

	Actual ($)	Predicted ($)
Average weekly benefits	85.45	83.51
Total weeks compensated (millions)	11.124	12.08

One explanation of the difference is the tendency for only some job leavers to receive benefits, a fact that we have not reflected in the predicted values. Both the internal checks on consistency and the actual-predicted comparisons suggest that UISIM provides plausible, relatively accurate values of the principal variables of interest.

7.3 Empirical Analysis

Our analysis of UI and labor market transitions is based on the flows between labor market states captured in the March and April 1978 Current Population Surveys. The CPS focuses principally on labor market activity, but also provides a good deal of information about other personal and family characteristics, generally obtained from one (presumably knowledgeable) member of the household. In addition to the regular or basic questionnaire, the Census Bureau administers short supplementary questionnaires on a variety of topics. Data on usual weekly earnings, for example, are obtained in May, while school attendance is dealt with in October. The supplement to the March CPS referred to earlier covers employment and earnings experience in the previous year and is the most extensive of the supplementary interviews.

The structure of the CPS allows us to follow individuals through four months of labor market activity. A given household in the survey is interviewed in four consecutive months, then is dropped from the survey for eight months before returning for a final four months of interviews. By watching individuals and households in successive months, flows between labor market states can be estimated.

The probability framework relating UI to transitions assumes that alternative states of the labor market are clearly defined, and that changes in status reflect meaningful changes in behavior. It is well known, however, that the definitions of unemployment and nonparticipation in the CPS are somewhat ambiguous. Observed movements into and out of these states may occur because otherwise unchanged behavior is reported in a different way. While the results should thus be interpreted with caution, it is our view that the estimated transition probabilities convey useful information. Clearly, reporting problems are likely to be less important in flows involving employment. Moreover, the available information on reasons for unemployment can be used to enhance the reliability of results. The layoff category, for example, is likely to be somewhat less affected by arbitrary distinctions.

7.3.1 Variable Definition and Empirical Specification

The theoretical analysis has treated UI as an exogenous aspect of the choice set facing individuals and firms. Yet the earlier discussion makes clear that both the level and duration of benefits depend on previous work experience and earnings. These factors are likely to have an independent effect on transitions. In order to isolate the effects of UI, it is necessary to control for the level of wages and weeks worked. Transition decisions are also influenced by differences in opportunities and constraints related to demographic characteristics, marital status, education, and local labor market conditions. Table 7.5 presents definitions and mean values of the variables in the CPS that we use to control for these factors.

Two specifications are used to estimate the impact of UI on transitions between labor market states. The first and simplest is the linear probability model given by

$$p_{hk}^i = a_0 + b_1 \, UIBEN_i + \sum_{j=2}^{n} b_j x_j^i, \tag{5}$$

where p_{hk}^i is the probability of transition from h to k, and x_j^i represents the jth characteristic for the ith individual. In estimation, p_{hk}^i takes on the value one if a transition occurred from month t (March) to month $t + 1$ (April), and zero otherwise. The assumption of linearity in equation (5) has significant limitations. First, the data come in the form of observations on individuals' labor force states in succeeding months. Since the dependent variable is essentially trichotomous (movement into one of three states), there is no natural scale, and standard regression techniques are inappropriate. A linear specification also fails to enforce the constraint that the probabilities lie between zero and one.

Because of these limitations, the linear probability model is used only to illustrate the effect of alternative specifications. Inferences about the effects of UI on specific transitions and analysis of the overall impact of UI on unemployment and labor force participation will make use of estimates based on the cumulative logistic probability function. In this framework, the logarithm of the odds of a transition occurring (rather than the probability) is a linear function of the characteristics of the individual. Although in the present case there are three possible states, and three transition probabilities for a given base period, the logistic form and the adding-up constraint imply that coefficients for only two of the transitions need be estimated; the third equation can be derived from the other two.

In order to illustrate the approach more formally, consider the case of the transitions out of unemployment. The model is given by[26]

$$\ln(p_{ue}^i / p_{uu}^i) = \alpha_{ue} + \beta_{ue} UIBEN_i + \sum_{j=2}^{n} \gamma_j x_j^i, \tag{6}$$

$$\ln(p_{un}^i / p_{uu}^i) = \alpha_{un} + \beta_{un} UIBEN_i + \sum_{j=2}^{n} \delta_j x_j^i, \tag{7}$$

where the x_j^i are defined as before, and the βs measure the effect of UI on the odds of a transition relative to remaining unemployed. Similar models can be written for transitions out of employment and into the labor force.

Table 7.5
Basic current population survey variables, by labor market state

Variable (mean)	Labor market state[a]		
	Employment	Unemployment	Non-participation
UIBEN (replacement ratio: ratio of benefits to after-tax wage)	0.494	0.249	0.484
AWW (average weekly wage)	198.56	111.96	68.05
WKSWKD (weeks worked in 1977)	44.75	21.35	5.08
Age	38.05	29.76	48.3
Marital status by sex			
MARRYM (1 = male, married; 0 = other)	0.43	0.23	0.17
MARRYW (1 = female, married; 0 = other)	0.24	0.18	0.47
SINGLEM (1 = male, single; 0 = other)	0.16	0.33	0.12
SINGLEF (1 = female, single; 0 = other)	0.17	0.26	0.24
SCHOOL (years of schooling)	12.5	11.5	11.0
SMSA (1 = living in SMSA; 0 = otherwise)	0.58	0.57	0.56
CCITY (1 = living in central city; 0 = otherwise)	0.23	0.27	0.24
UMARCH (state unemployment rate in March 1978)	6.43	6.79	6.49
HSGRAD (1 = high school grad; 0 = otherwise)	0.78	0.61	0.55
WKSND (weeks needed to qualify for benefits)	—	—	9.1
RACE (1 = nonwhite; 0 = otherwise)	0.10	0.23	0.11

a. Numbers in survey sample: employed, 42,593; unemployed, 3,057; nonparticipant, 24,173.

Estimates of the coefficients in these model are obtained by maximizing the likelihood function.[27] The coefficients can be used to derive an estimate of the derivative of a given probability with respect to *UIBEN*. The formula for p_{ue}, for example, is

$$\frac{\partial p_{ue}}{\partial UIBEN} = \hat{\beta}_{ue}(1 - p_{ue}) p_{ue},$$
(8)

where $\hat{\beta}_{ue}$ is the estimated coefficient on *UIBEN*.

Throughout the analysis, the effect of UI on the transition probabilities is captured by the replacement ratio. Theory provides little guidance about the form this variable ought to take. Our use of a linear specification reflects the fact that the more complicated nonlinear expression failed to dominate the simple approach. We examined several alternative UI variables, including category dummies, a quadratic term, and linear splines. The results were uniform and consistent; none of the variants produced significant value added when compared to the linear form.

In addition to its linearity, *UIBEN* also stands alone in capturing the effects of UI. We found that maximum potential duration provided little additional insight or explanatory power. Moreover, since duration is likely to interact with *UIBEN*, its presence in the equation significantly complicates attempts to use parameter estimates to assess the impact of changes in replacement rates. We did find, however, that other aspects of the UI system, notably adjustments for weeks of employment needed for eligibility, were important. These will be noted and reported below.

The expected impact of UI on the transitions has been extensively discussed. Other variables are expected to have a significant influence on movements in the labor market. Wide variations across demographic groups in the propensity to leave and enter the labor force or employment are well known. For a given demographic mix, conditions in the local labor market as measured by the state unemployment rate influence available opportunities. We expect individuals in states with higher rates of unemployment to have greater difficulty in finding work and to be at a greater risk of job loss. It is possible that job finding and labor force entrance will be affected by residential location. *SMSA* and *CCITY* are included to capture the possibility of mismatches between the location of jobs and workers.

The demographic variables and other personal characteristics are included to control for differences in preferences and individual opportunity. As noted above, the generosity of UI is likely to be related to personal factors, which are correlated with transition decisions. Two of the most important of these variables are weeks worked last year (*WKSWKD*) and average weekly wage (*AWW*). The *WKSWKD* variable is designed to capture two effects. First, it is likely to be highly correlated with job tenure and thus will capture some of the effects of seniority on the possibility of layoff and recall. Second, it should reflect both attachment to the labor force and personal stability. If these are important aspects of individual heterogeneity, *WKSWKD* may help to isolate the effects of UI that do not depend on individual quality. The wage variable plays a similar role.

7.3.2 Transitions from Unemployment

Table 7.6 presents the coefficients estimated from a multinomial logit model of transitions from unemployment. Estimates are presented by destination state (such as employed, NILF) for the total unemployed population, and for each of three unemployment groups: those on layoff, quitters, and other job losers (including reentrants). In the layoff and loser regressions, *UIBEN* is entered as calculated by UISIM. In the quit regression, however, an adjustment was made to reflect the possibility of outright disqualification and the effect of the waiting period where applicable. Where quitters are disqualified, we set *UIBEN* to zero. For potentially eligible quitters, an adjusted *UIBEN* is given by

$$UIBEN_i^* = UIBEN_i \left(\frac{k - q_i}{k} \right), \tag{9}$$

where q is the number of weeks a quitter must wait until benefits will be received, and k is the expected remaining duration of the unemployment spell. The parameter k is given by

$$k = \frac{1}{p_{ue} + p_{un}}. \tag{10}$$

Average values of p_{ue} and p_{un} for the entire quit sample were used to calculate average k. Variation in *UIBEN** thus reflects variation in *UIBEN* and q.

Looking just at the results for the three categories of unemployment, the effect of UI is generally inconsistent with expectations, although the large standard errors preclude clear conclusions. We do find negative effects among those on layoff, where the impact of UI on withdrawal from the labor force is quite strong. Among the other groups, however, the co-efficients are positive, though relatively imprecise. When the evidence is

Table 7.6
Multinomial logit estimates of transitions from unemployment, by reason for unemployment[a]

	Independent variable								
Transition	Constant	UIBEN	SMSA	CCITY	RACE	AWW	WKSWKD	UMARCH	SCHOOL
Unemployment to employment									
Layoff	-0.541 (0.756)	-0.700 (0.436)	-0.120 (0.190)	-0.054 (0.273)	-0.585 (0.328)	-0.002 (0.001)	0.027 (0.008)	0.195 (0.072)	-0.014 (0.059)
Quit	-2.150 (0.938)	0.185 (0.719)	-0.204 (0.190)	0.471 (0.264)	-0.452 (0.356)	0.001 (0.001)	0.013 (0.004)	-0.102 (0.067)	0.115 (0.067)
Loser	0.898 (0.369)	0.269 (0.135)	0.112 (0.096)	-0.581 (0.129)	-0.469 (0.121)	-0.0004 (0.0003)	0.007 (0.003)	-0.111 (0.030)	-0.064 (0.028)
Total	0.469 (0.325) 0.092	0.162 (0.180) 0.032	-0.036 (0.102) -0.007	-0.254 (0.124) -0.050	-0.560 (0.123) -0.110	-0.0001 (0.0003) -0.00001	0.012 (0.003) 0.002	-0.076 (0.028) -0.015	-0.055 (0.025) -0.011
Unemployment to not in labor force									
Layoff	-2.331 (1.345)	-1.878 (0.778)	-0.129 (0.247)	-0.663 (0.406)	-1.187 (0.624)	-0.003 (0.001)	0.012 (0.015)	0.200 (0.085)	-0.072 (0.091)
Quit	-2.518 (0.987)	1.557 (0.766)	0.658 (0.317)	-0.173 (0.348)	0.440 (0.345)	0.002 (0.001)	-0.010 (0.005)	-0.022 (0.041)	0.107 (0.081)
Loser	-0.417 (0.100)	0.132 (0.217)	-0.153 (0.101)	0.127 (0.126)	0.055 (0.117)	-0.002 (0.0004)	-0.012 (0.004)	0.006 (0.016)	0.023 (0.008)
Total	-1.273 (0.386) -0.027	0.116 (0.230) 0.019	-0.067 (0.118) -0.011	-0.213 (0.131) 0.035	0.067 (0.117) 0.011	-0.002 (0.0006) -0.0003	-0.020 (0.004) -0.003	0.028 (0.031) 0.004	0.057 (0.029) 0.009

a. The numbers in parentheses are standard errors; the value given below the standard error for the total results is the derivative of the probability with respect to the variable. All equations include age-sex dummies and controls for marital status and high school graduation.

pooled by estimating the model for the total sample, we find very weak and insignificant effects. In addition to the logit coefficients, we report the derivatives of the probability for the total sample. It can be seen that the estimated effects are not only statistically weak, but substantively small. In the case of entering employment, for example, the derivative (0.032) implies that changing the replacement rate by 0.10 would change the probability of finding a job by 0.003. This compares with an average job-finding probability of 0.31.

In light of the strong theoretical arguments and previous empirical evidence on duration and transitions, the relatively weak effects of UI are surprising. Furthermore, the positive effects for losers and quitters remain a puzzle. A possible explanation of the findings for job losers and of the general imprecision of UI estimates in table 7.6 is individual heterogeneity. If unmeasured quality differences are positively correlated with eligibility for UI (and the level of benefits), as well as the likelihood of finding work, then the coefficient of UI would be biased upward.

A possible correction for this heterogeneity problem is to introduce the duration of the current spell of unemployment as a control variable. The argument is simply that current duration indicates the degree of success in finding work and is thus an indicator of individual quality. While this procedure apparently does reduce the upward bias, the general character of the results is unaffected. The signs remain unchanged, while the size of the coefficients declines slightly.

The heterogeneity argument does not explain the positive effect of UI on labor force withdrawal by quitters. It would seem that more able individuals would find work more easily whether the previous separation were initiated voluntarily or not. A somewhat more plausible explanation is the absence of any controls for other income, especially the income of the spouse. Since marginal tax rates are based on family income, secondary earners may have both high replacement rates and high family income. Without controls for other income, strong income effects could lead to individuals with high replacement rates leaving the labor force. Once again, however, it is not clear why this effect should apply only to quitters. And indeed adding other income variables has only negligible effects. The impact of UI on labor force exit by quitters remains paradoxical.

7.3.3 Transitions from Employment

In contrast to rather weak results on the unemployed, the evidence on the impact of UI on employment decisions is quite strong. Two sets of estimates are presented. We first use the linear probability model to study the impact of UI on unemployment transitions, with particular emphasis on subsamples defined by the reason for becoming unemployed. For comparison, linear probability estimates for the total sample are provided. Linear probability models are used because the computational cost of multinomial logit with many destination states is prohibitive. In the second set, we estimate the transitions from employment using the multinomial logit framework and present coefficient estimates and the associated derivatives. The linear probability estimates in table 7.7 reveal a significant positive effect on the flow into unemployment. The bulk of this effect occurs in the layoff group, where the *UIBEN* coefficient is well over half the size of the average transition probability from employment to layoff unemployment. These results are consistent with the evidence presented by Feldstein. While the layoff group dominates in the UI effect, we also find a statistically significant positive impact on quit behavior. The flow of other job losers, however, appears to be unaffected by rates of replacement.

The theory suggests that the flow out of employment will depend on the extent of experience rating of firms. The UI tax system allows only partial experience rating over a limited range of tax rates and previous unemployment behavior. Maximum and minimum tax rates are built into all the state tax laws. These have the effect of setting the marginal cost of a layoff to the firm (net of separation costs) to zero. The experience-rating hypothesis was tested using data on fraction of covered weeks at the minimum and maximum in each state. Using various combinations of minima and maxima, we found experience rating to have no effect on the flow out of employment. The conclusion applied to transitions into all of the different states of unemployment and NILF.

We argued earlier that UI may raise the gain to labor force attachment and thus reduce the probability of leaving the labor force from employment. The evidence in table 7.7 indicates overwhelming support for this hypothesis. It appears that higher UI benefits discourage labor force withdrawal. While the direction of the effect is consistent with the theory, the magnitude of the impact in the linear probability model is implausible. The logic of the connection between UI and labor force withdrawal requires an offsetting flow into unemployment. This is because the decision to remain employed is based on the attractiveness of becoming unemployed at some point in the future. If the negative effect of UI on p_{en} were due to the attractiveness of unemployment, we would expect to see a flow into unemployment of comparable magnitude.

Much of the disparity in the estimates disappears in the logit framework.

Table 7.7
Linear and multinomial logit estimates of the probability of leaving employment[a]

	Independent variable									Summary statistic	
Transition	Constant	UIBEN	SMSA	CCITY	RACE	AVW/1,000	WKSWKD/100	UMARCH/100	SCHOOL/100	R^2	Standard error
Linear probability models											
Employment to unemployment											
Layoff	0.013 (0.002)	0.005 (0.001)	−0.001 (0.001)	0.001 (0.001)	0.0001 (0.0010)	−0.001 (0.002)	−0.023 (0.002)	0.069 (0.018)	−0.050 (0.013)	0.004	0.003
Loser	0.029 (0.003)	0.0001 (0.0016)	−0.001 (0.001)	0.0001 (0.001)	0.004 (0.001)	−0.005 (0.003)	−0.046 (0.003)	0.031 (0.026)	−0.025 (0.020)	0.013	0.006
Quit	0.007 (0.002)	0.002 (0.001)	0.0000 (0.0003)	0.0010 (0.0006)	−0.002 (0.0007)	−0.002 (0.002)	−0.009 (0.002)	−0.009 (0.010)	−0.015 (0.011)	0.003	0.002
Total	0.049 (0.004)	0.008 (0.002)	−0.002 (0.001)	0.002 (0.001)	0.002 (0.002)	−0.008 (0.004)	−0.077 (0.005)	0.090 (0.035)	−0.091 (0.026)	0.016	0.011
Employment to not in labor force											
Total	0.148 (0.006)	−0.042 (0.003)	0.0003 (0.002)	0.0000 (0.002)	−0.0001 (0.003)	−0.038 (0.006)	−0.200 (0.007)	0.046 (0.053)	−0.002 (0.040)	0.062	0.027

Table 7.7 (continued)

| Independent variable | | | | | | | | | | Summary statistic | |
Transition	Constant	UIBEN	SMSA	CCITY	RACE	AWW/ 1,000	WKSWKD/ 100	UMARCH/ 100	SCHOOL/ 100	R^2	Standard error
Multinomial logit models											
Employment to unemployment											
Total	−1.804	0.791	−0.142	0.119	0.088	−2.552	−5.133	9.048	−9.442	—	—
	(0.354)	(0.238)	(0.116)	(0.135)	(0.149)	(0.561)	(0.403)	(3.108)	(2.517)		
	−0.020	0.009	−0.002	0.001	0.001	−0.028	−0.057	0.100	−0.104		
Employment to not in labor force											
Total	−2.171	0.694	−0.002	0.114	0.025	−3.491	−3.570	4.878	2.221	—	—
	(0.276)	(0.158)	(0.085)	(0.098)	(0.112)	(0.446)	(0.271)	(2.358)	(1.896)		
	−0.045	0.014	−0.0000	0.002	0.001	−0.072	−0.074	0.101	−0.046		

a. The numbers in parentheses are standard errors; the value given below the standard error for the multinomial logit totals is the derivative of the probability with respect to the variable. Each regression includes age-sex dummies and controls for marital status and high school graduation.

There we find that the derivative of UI in the p_{eu} equation is 0.009, while the estimated effect in the p_{en} equation is -0.014. Although the p_{en} effect is still somewhat larger (in absolute value), the difference between them is not statistically significant.[28] It appears that imposition of linearity distorts the evidence on labor force withdrawal. When a more appropriate functional form is applied, estimates are obtained that are reasonably consistent with the notion of offsetting flows. Overall, the evidence points to UI as a major factor in decisions to leave employment.

7.3.4 Transitions into the Labor Force

Estimates of the effect of UI on movements into the labor force are examined in table 7.8. Both linear probability results and results from the logit specification are presented. The results are based on an estimate of what benefits would be available if one were eligible and became unemployed.[29] We have also calculated the number of weeks of employment needed to qualify for benefits and estimated its impact.

It is evident in both sets of results that UI encourages the flow into unemployment through the benefit structure. In row 2, however, we find that eligibility rules and attachment tests appear to cut the other way. The results indicate a negative effect of WKSND, while UIBEN is positive and statistically significant. The sign of WKSND seems reasonable. We would expect that individuals with a requirement of a week or two would appear in the unemployment category sooner and more readily than those where weeks needed were sizable. This is particularly true in light of the fact that an important part of the NILF group (10%) has accumulated sufficient weeks and earnings to qualify for benefits. While a large number of those individuals are likely to have quit their most recent job, it is quite likely that some significant number are essentially eligible for benefits immediately.

The contrast with the flow into employment is symmetric; higher benefits are associated with reduced movements into employment, while weeks needed has a positive association. It is likely that the signs of these effects are more than coincidence. One explanation for the negative effect of benefits on p_{ne} is that those with very attractive replacement ratios choose to enter unemployment. Likewise, the WKSND variable reveals the eligibility effect—people choosing to enter employment over remaining out of the labor force or becoming unemployed tend to require more weeks worked in order to qualify for benefits.

In order to simplify later analysis of UI and rates of employment and unemployment, we have dropped WKSND from the logit specification.

The evidence in rows 5−8 is consistent with our previous remarks: UI has a positive effect on the flow into unemployment, and tends to reduce the flow into employment. As in the case of movements out of employment, we find that decisions regarding labor force entry are apparently inter-related, although the orders of magnitude of the derivatives suggest that unmeasured differences in individuals may be affecting the results.

In summary, the evidence in tables 7.6−7.8 points to a significant and consistent impact of UI on the flow into unemployment out of employ-ment, a strong effect on the transition from employment to nonparticipa-tion, generally mixed results for the unemployed, and some indication of influence on flows into the labor force.

7.4 Estimating the Impact of UI on the Unemployment Rate

This section uses estimates of the multinomial logit model to assess the impact of UI on the measured rate of unemployment, the employment ratio, and the nonparticipation rate. At the outset it is important to realize that the estimates here can be regarded only as an approximation to a fully dynamic stochastic simulation.

The approach we have adopted makes use of the steady-state relation-ship between transition probabilities and the fraction of the population in the three labor market categories. If we let $\mathbf{P}$ indicate the 3×3 matrix of probabilities, and use $\mathbf{\Pi}$ to represent the 3×1 vector of proportions, then we know that in steady state $\mathbf{P\Pi} = \mathbf{\Pi}$. The $\mathbf{P}$ matrix is not of full rank, but we can use the fact that the elements of $\mathbf{\Pi}$ sum to one, together with the steady-state identity, to solve for $\mathbf{\Pi}$ as a function of $\mathbf{P}$.

The first step in estimating the impact of UI is to obtain an estimate of $\mathbf{\Pi}$ using actual values of the independent variables including *UIBEN*. A $\mathbf{P}$ matrix is estimated for each individual using the logit coefficients in tables 7.6−7.8 (total sample estimates) and the individual's characteristics. We then solve for the $\mathbf{\Pi}$ vector associated with each individual (that is, the fraction of time the individual could expect to spend in each state) and cumulate across individuals to get the aggregate proportions.

In order to gauge the impact of UI, two situations are examined. In the first, we reduce potential UI benefits by 10%, while potential UI benefits are eliminated completely in the second. In both cases, a new $\mathbf{P}$ matrix and a new $\mathbf{\Pi}$ are calculated for each individual, and new aggregate steady-state proportions are derived. These can be compared to the original steady-state estimates to see the change induced by UI.

Table 7.8
Transitions into the labor force[a]

Transition	Constant	UIBEN	WKSND/100	AWW/1,000	WKSWKD/100	UIMARCH	SCHOOL/100	HSGRAD	RACE	MARRYW	SINGLEM	R^2	Standard error
Linear probability models													
Not in labor force to unemployment													
1. Without eligibility variable	0.009 (0.008)	0.007 (0.004)	—	0.057 (0.020)	0.076 (0.009)	0.003 (0.001)	−0.060 (0.060)	−0.002 (0.004)	0.022 (0.004)	−0.017 (0.004)	0.009 (0.005)	0.029	0.024
2. With eligibility variable	0.010 (0.008)	0.015 (0.006)	−0.040 (0.021)	0.051 (0.020)	0.065 (0.011)	0.003 (0.001)	−0.060 (0.060)	−0.002 (0.004)	0.022 (0.004)	−0.017 (0.004)	0.009 (0.005)	0.029	0.024
Not in labor force to employment													
3. Without eligibility variable	0.088 (0.012)	−0.017 (0.006)	—	−0.199 (0.029)	0.406 (0.013)	−0.003 (0.001)	0.002 (0.001)	0.004 (0.005)	−0.0005 (0.0050)	−0.005 (0.005)	0.001 (0.007)	0.070	0.050
4. With eligibility variable	0.085 (0.012)	−0.030 (0.008)	0.064 (0.031)	−0.188 (0.029)	0.424 (0.015)	−0.003 (0.001)	0.002 (0.001)	0.004 (0.005)	−0.001 (0.005)	−0.006 (0.005)	0.002 (0.007)	0.070	0.050

Table 7.8 (continued)
Transitions into the labor force[a]

	Independent variable											Summary statistic	
Transition	Constant	UIBEN	WKSND/100	AWW/1,000	WKSWKD/100	UIMARCH	SCHOOL/100	HSGRAD	RACE	MARRYW	SINGLEM	R^2	Standard error
Multinomial logit models													
Not in labor force to unemployment													
5. Estimated coefficient	−4.055 (0.335)	0.148 (0.174)	—	0.959 (0.449)	3.124 (0.284)	0.100 (0.028)	−3.649 (−2.377)	−0.148 (0.147)	0.616 (0.121)	−0.930 (0.144)	0.368 (0.195)	—	—
6. Effect on probability	−0.095	0.004	—	0.022	0.073	0.002	−0.086	−0.003	0.014	−0.022	0.009	—	—
Not in labor force to employment													
7. Estimated coefficient	−2.582 (0.237)	−0.336 (0.114)	—	−0.143 (0.049)	4.560 (0.169)	−0.048 (0.021)	4.400 (1.787)	0.027 (0.105)	0.068 (0.110)	−0.185 (0.107)	0.069 (0.133)	—	—
8. Effect on probability	−0.127	−0.017	—	−0.071	0.225	−0.002	0.217	0.001	0.003	−0.009	0.003	—	—

a. The numbers in parentheses are standard errors. Each regression includes age-sex dummies and controls for location (SMSA, central city). Rows 6 and 8 contain the derivatives associated with the logit coefficients.

Table 7.9
Impact of changes in unemployment insurance on employment and unemployment
with no change in wages (percent)

Simulated UI situation	Labor force state		
	Employment ratio	Unemployment rate	Nonparticipation ratio
Actual rates, 1978	59.4	6.0	36.8
UI down 10%	−0.02	−0.08	0.08
No UI	−0.62	−0.65	1.11

Table 7.9 presents estimates of the impact of changes in UI on the employment ratio, the unemployment rate, and the rate of nonparticipation. The first line presents average values of these indicators as measured by the CPS during 1978. The unemployment rate averaged 6.0% in that year, while a little over 59% of the population was employed. The estimated effect of UI is examined in the next two lines. First, the change in UI is applied to the whole sample, and the difference between the steady-state proportions with and without the change is reported. The first entry in the employment column, for example, indicates that reducing UI by 10% would lower the steady-state fraction of the population employed by 0.02 percentage point. Unemployment would be reduced by 0.08 point, and nonparticipation would increase by a similar amount.

When UI benefits are eliminated, however, these magnitudes are much larger. In the case of unemployment, for example, we estimate that elimination of UI would lower the unemployment rate by more than half of a percentage point. With the overall rate on the order of 6 percentage points, the effect is sizable. Coupled with a decline in the employment ratio of 0.62 point, the unemployment effect leads to a significant increase in the rate of nonparticipation. Indeed, the dominant effect of UI in these data appears to be its impact on movements into and out of the labor force. As the coefficient estimates suggested, it is likely that transitions into and out of employment play a significant role in the overall effect.

The estimates in table 7.9 are derived under assumptions about changes in UI, but no changes in other variables are introduced. Many of the independent variables would be unaffected, but it is likely that wages, in particular, would be affected by changes in UI. Table 7.10 presents estimates of the UI impact on labor market states allowing for the effect of taxes on wages. We assume that the burden of the UI tax falls entirely on labor, so that reductions in the tax are fully reflected in an increase in the

Table 7.10
Impact of changes in unemployment insurance on employment and unemployment with wages adjusted for tax changes (percent)

Simulated UI situation	Labor force state		
	Employment ratio	Unemployment rate	Nonparticipation ratio
Actual rates, 1978	59.4	6.0	36.8
UI down 10%	0.00	−0.08	−0.06
No UI	−0.59	−0.65	1.09

wage. The tax rate used was 0.86%. It was calculated by dividing total UI receipts by total wage and salary income for 1978. The rate is small both because the UI tax applies to only a portion of total earnings and because the rate is not large to begin with.

The basic algorithm used to identify the effect of UI is the same, with the only change being an adjustment in the wage in addition to changes in UI. It is clear from the table that the tax adjustment has little impact on the estimated UI effect. In the results for elimination of UI, for example, comparison with table 7.9 shows that employment would fall somewhat less and nonparticipation would rise somewhat less if wages were adjusted for tax changes. But the differences are trivial. At least with the estimated coefficients and tax rates used here, failure to address the tax issue has a negligible effect on inferences about the UI effect.

Overall, the results suggest that UI has a sizable impact on the rates of unemployment and labor force participation. Taken literally, the estimates indicate that the growth of UI over the last decade may have played an important role in the upward trend in participation. However, the estimates also imply that UI raises employment, a result that probably reflects the relative size of the UI effect in the p_{en} and p_{eu} equations. Since these estimates may reflect errors of measurement, or nonlinearities in the UI variable, further analysis seems in order.

In spite of the preliminary nature of the evidence, the analysis does underscore the importance of studying the effect of UI on other labor market groups besides the unemployed. Much empirical work in this area has concentrated on the behavior of the unemployed, but the impact of UI is clearly much broader. It appears that transitions into and out of the labor market, particularly in and out of employment, play a central role in the overall effect of UI.

7.5 Conclusions

The results in this paper are all based on microeconometric evidence. The information used is basically a comparison of the behavior of persons receiving high UI benefits with those receiving lower benefits. This approach assumes that the effect of a general change in UI would simply be the sum of the individual effects. Previous experience suggests that extrapolating micro relationships to the macro sphere is perilous. Here we list some of the biases in our procedure.

First, the estimates reported here may underestimate the impact of UI on some of the transition probabilities. Consider, for example, the relation between UI and temporary layoffs. Employers can tailor their layoff policy to the UI situation of their typical worker but not to each individual worker. Hence increases in the general level of UI will tend to cause greater increases in layoffs than would be implied by comparisons of individuals receiving more or less generous benefits. A similar point applies with respect to permanent separations.

Second, the calculation described here depends on the assumption that the transition probabilities are determined independently. While this is reasonable in considering cross-sectional variation among workers, it may not be tenable in assessing policies with large impacts. Consider, for example, a measure that sharply reduced the flow from unemployment to employment. This would raise employers' hiring costs, and so would be likely to reduce the optimal separation rate. A similar point applies to the relation between the flows from nonparticipation to unemployment and from unemployment to employment.

Third, changes in UI may have important macro effects. The role of UI as an automatic stabilizer has been discussed frequently. The program's impact on the extent of wage rigidity may be as important. By making unemployment more palatable, UI is likely to reduce the downward pressure it places on wages. This will tend to reinforce the stickiness of wages, which according to many theories is the cause of unemployment. The cross-sectional analysis presented here has no way of taking account of these effects.

Fourth, there are strong reasons to believe that the effects of UI depend on the overall unemployment rate. The rate of unemployment was 6.0% in 1978. The results might be very different at business cycle troughs and peaks. One would expect that the effect of UI is most pronounced when labor is in excess demand, and least pronounced when jobs are being rationed. These propositions could in principle be tested by replicating this study with data sets drawn at different parts of the business cycle.

Beyond the difficulties inherent in the microeconometric approach taken here, there are a variety of ways in which the results can be refined. The preliminary results regarded here consider only small variations in theoretical form. Only crude account is taken of the potential duration of UI benefits. A crucial problem is errors in variables. The UI variables used here necessarily involve some imputation error. Perhaps more important, there is evidence that the dependent variables suffer from significant measurement error. It appears that the rate of flow between labor force states may be exaggerated by as much as a factor of two or three. In future work we hope to address these issues. It is also hoped that it will be possible to explore a broader menu of alternative reforms.

Several conclusions emerge from our research at this stage. UI has large effects on the decisions to seek and leave employment. The possibility of becoming eligible for benefits attracts many workers into the labor force. The program also encourages persons leaving employment to enter unemployment rather than leave the labor force. To some extent this may be a reporting rather than a behavioral effect. Taken together, these results imply that UI has a substantial positive effect on labor force participation. Our econometric estimates suggest that eliminating the program would reduce the labor force participation rate by about 1%. This drop-off would come from a decline of about half a percent in the employment ratio, and about two-thirds of a percent in the employment rate.

Our results suggest that a focusing on unemployment effects of UI, as has been done in most previous research, may be very misleading. Our estimates imply that the program simultaneously increases both employment and unemployment. Future research should concentrate on the direct employment impact of the UI program.

These results must be used cautiously in interpreting labor market developments. The effects of the UI program probably increased somewhat during the 1970s as benefits and coverage levels were raised. Of equal importance, rising marginal tax rates, due primarily to increasing Social Security payroll taxes, raised replacement rates. The results suggest that these developments may have contributed to the increase in the national unemployment rate and participation rate that were observed during the decade. Since the increase in the level of the average replacement rate was probably less than 20%, it is doubtful that the effects studied here can account for a large part of the movements that have taken place. It may be that other social insurance programs have contributed to the remaining increase. This question is left for future research.

We are indebted to Tom Chesterman and Daniel Smith for valuable research assistance. This research was supported by the Office of the Assistant Secretary for Policy, Evaluation, and Research of the U.S. Department of Labor.

Notes

1. For example, see Freeman and Medoff (1982).

2. An excellent survey of this large literature is Gustman (1980).

3. Feldstein (1978).

4. Hamermesh (1979).

5. The quantitative importance of this effect has been questioned in Marston (1979).

6. Prominent contributions include Hall (1970), Perry (1972), and Marston (1976).

7. Note that any one equation of system (2) is linearly dependent on the others. Hence, a unique root satisfying

$$\pi_i^i + \pi_e^i + \pi_n^i = 1$$

exists. This theorem, which is proved in any textbook in Markov processes, assumes that all the P_{jk}^i are positive. The vector $\mathbf{\Pi}$ can be calculated as the eigenvector corresponding to the unit eigenvalue of the matrix $\mathbf{P}$. The vector $\mathbf{\Pi}$ is the ergodic steady state corresponding to the matrix $\mathbf{P}$.

8. A much more extensive discussion of the significance of observed labor force transitions may be found in Clark and Summers (1979c, 1982).

9. Mortensen (1977).

10. Feldstein (1975).

11. Hall (1979).

12. Feldstein (1976).

13. Hall (1980).

14. The work experience survey provides no information on the pattern of earnings (high quarter, low quarter, etc.) throughout the year, or on the timing of spells of unemployment. Furthermore, earnings above $50,000 are not reported, and nonwage and salary income tend to be underreported.

15. In this example, the benefit year is specifically individually determined. In a few states the benefit year is fixed for all individuals by statute, but administrative rulings have the effect of making it specific to the individual.

16. The definition of "good cause" varies greatly by state; while usually restricted to action by the employer, a number of states makes exceptions for "compelling personal reasons."

17. Three states and the District of Columbia employ a "bracket step down" in determining eligibility. If a claimant does not meet the basic test, a second, less restrictive, test is applied; passing the second test brings a lower benefit. The number of such brackets ranges from three to five: U.S. Department of Labor (1978), pp. 3–28.

18. The program for calculating tax rates uses a modified version of the federal and state tax simulation models developed at the National Bureau of Economic Research.

19. For a description of TAXSIM see Feldstein and Frisch (1977). The data are based on 1976 returns and were updated to reflect 1978 income levels.

20. The "continuous" aspect of this calculation deserves emphasis. Note that we ignore the possibility that an individual could exhaust benefits, wait for a short period until the beginning of a new benefit year, and resume receipt of benefits if qualified. Our calculation stops at the point of exhaustion unless a new benefit year is reached.

21. Since the individual is assumed to have just become unemployed at the time of the survey, there is no need to adjust for weeks of benefits already received in the current spell. The adjustment incorporated in the program is as follows: if U_t is weeks in the current spell, $CW = MAX - U_{t-1} + 10$. Our calculation assumes that all weeks of unemployment in the previous year were accumulated in one spell. This formula assumes no overlap between benefit years. The true formula is weeks to exhaust $+ MAX2$. We have no information on the point at which the spell of unemployment began and therefore have ignored the overlap problem. The effect is to overstate somewhat potential duration.

22. The possibility of overlapping benefit years may reward some individuals who have experienced some unemployment in the previous year. Consider the case of two individuals, each laid off at the same time. Assume that one has no previous unemployment experience, while the other was unemployed for four weeks nine months ago. Given sufficient earnings and weeks of unemployment, the first individual will begin a benefit year and have a maximum potential duration of twenty-six weeks. The second individual, however, will reach the end of the first benefit year in twelve weeks, and, subject to eligibility tests, will receive an additional twenty-six weeks in the second benefit year. Thus the individual with unemployment experience has a potential duration of thirty-eight weeks, while the first individual has twenty-six.

23. The sample used to estimate the earnings function was composed of employed individuals who participated in both the March and May 1978 CPS. The specification included controls for years of schooling, race age, region, weeks worked in the previous year, location (SMSA, central city), sex, marital status, and Mills's

ratio. The dependent variable was the log of usual weekly earnings. Mills's ratio was estimated using a probit model of employment status. For Mills's ratio, see Heckman (1976). The results are available on request.

24. Feldstein (1978).

25. U.S. Department of Labor (March 1978), table 3c.

26. In the general case, a given probability for the ith individual can be written as

$$p_j^i = \frac{\exp(x_i \beta_j)}{1 + \sum_{j=1} \exp(x_i \beta_j)},$$

where j indexes choices, and the xs are characteristics. The likelihood function can be formed as a product of the appropriate probabilities, and maximized with conventional nonlinear techniques.

27. Such models have been developed and used in several places. See McFadden (1974) for a discussion and review of the statistical literature.

28. Inspection of the data set for left-out variables that may lie at the foot of the unrealistic p_{en} coefficient suggests one possibility. Because of technological differences and differences in required skill and ability, an individual's occupation and industry may be an important determinant of labor force exit. In order to test this possibility, we estimated a new set of regressions with broad industry and occupation dummies. In doing this we run the risk of "overcontrolling" possible effects of *UIBEN* that may work through occupational choice or the decision of where to work. The results are instructive. We find that the industry and occupation dummies reduce the coefficient of *UIBEN* on p_{en} from 0.042 to 0.027. All of the impact occurs through the occupational variables, suggesting that the omitted variables of interest have to do with skills and training, rather than conditions of demand or risk shifting through contracts. This view is supported in the layoff regression. There we find that the industry and occupation dummies have virtually no effect on any of the previous coefficients.

29. Where wage data were not available, we imputed a wage based on an earnings function (see note 23).

8

Hysteresis and the European Unemployment Problem

with Olivier J. Blanchard

After 20 years of negligible unemployment, most of Western Europe has suffered since the early '70s a protracted period of high and rising unemployment. In the United Kingdom unemployment peaked at 3.3% over the 1945–70 period, but has risen almost continuously since 1970, and now stands at over 12%. For the Common Market nations as a whole, the unemployment rate more than doubled between 1970 and 1980 and has again doubled since then. Few forecasts call for a significant decline in unemployment over the next several years, and none call for its return to levels close to those that prevailed in the 1950s and 1960s.

These events are not easily accounted for by conventional classical or Keynesian macroeconomic theories. Rigidities associated with fixed length contracts or the costs of adjusting prices or quantities are unlikely to be large enough to account for rising unemployment over periods of a decade or more. And intertemporal substitution in labor supply is surely not an important aspect of such a protracted downturn. The sustained upturn in European unemployment challenges the premise of most macroeconomic theories that there exists some "natural" or "nonaccelerating inflation" rate of unemployment toward which the economy tends to gravitate and at which the level of inflation remains constant. The European experience compels consideration of alternative theories of "hysteresis" that contemplate the possibility that increases in unemployment have a direct impact on the "natural" rate of unemployment.

This paper explores theoretically and empirically the idea of macroeconomic hysteresis—the substantial persistence of unemployment and the protracted effects of shocks on unemployment. Our particular motivation is the current European situation. We seek explanations for the pattern of high and rising unemployment that has prevailed in Europe for the past decade and for the very different performance of the labor market in the United States and Europe, and reach some tentative conclusions about the extent to which European unemployment problems can be solved by expansionary demand policies. The central hypothesis we put forward is that hysteresis resulting from *membership considerations* plays an important role in explaining the current European depression in particular and persistent high unemployment in general. The essential point is that there is a fundamental asymmetry in the wage setting process between insiders who are employed and outsiders who want jobs. Outsiders are disenfranchised and wages are set with a view to insuring the jobs of insiders. Shocks that lead to reduced employment change the number of insiders and thereby change the subsequent equilibrium wage rate, giving rise to hysteresis. Membership considerations can therefore explain the general tendency of the equilibrium unemployment rate to follow the actual unemployment rate. A number of types of empirical evidence consistent with our hypothesis are adduced. The paper is organized as follows:

Section 8.1 documents the dimensions of the current European depression. It documents, by looking at the movements in unemployment in the United States and United Kingdom over the past century, that high unemployment is in fact often quite persistent. It reviews standard explanations of the current European situation and finds them lacking. It then considers a number of mechanisms through which high persistence of unemployment could be generated.

Section 8.2 explores what we find the most promising of the possible mechanisms for generating hysteresis. It presents a formal model illustrating how temporary shocks can have a permanent effect on the level of employment in contexts where wages are set by employers who bargain with insiders. Persistence results in this setting because shocks change employment and membership in the group of insiders, thus influencing its subsequent bargaining strategy. We then discuss the role of unions and whether such effects can arise in nonunion settings.

Section 8.3 examines the behavior of postwar Europe in light of our theory of hysteresis. It presents direct evidence on the role of unions on the behavior of wages and employment and on the composition of unemployment. We find the European experience quite consistent with our model. Europe appears to have high hysteresis, much more so than the United States. High unemployment in Europe and low unemployment in the United States are well explained both by different sequences of shocks, especially in the 1980s, and by different propagation mechanisms, with Europe exhibiting more persistence than the United States.

Section 8.4 returns to an issue that is of fundamental importance for policy. Granting that Europe has more hysteresis than the United States, is it really due to unions or is hysteresis itself endogenous, being triggered by bad times? In an attempt to answer this question, the section compares Europe now to Europe earlier when unemployment was low, and compares the current European depression to the U.S. Great Depression. This last comparison is especially important, given the ability of the United States to decrease unemployment drastically in 1939 and 1940, mostly through aggregate demand.

The conclusion summarizes our beliefs and doubts, and draws the implications of our analysis for policy.

8.1 The Record of Persistent Unemployment

We start this section by documenting the dimensions of the current European depression. We then demonstrate that persistently high unemployment like that experienced in Europe at present is not historically unusual. Data for the past century suggest a surprisingly high degree of persistence in unemployment in both the United States and the United Kingdom. We argue that such persistence is not easily explained by standard natural rate theories and conclude that theories that allow for hysteresis, by which we mean a very high dependence of current unemployment on past unemployment,[1] are required to explain such persistence.

8.1.1 The European Depression

Table 8.1 presents some information on the evolution of unemployment in three major European countries as well as the United States over the past 25 years. While European unemployment rates in the 1960s were substantially lower than those in the United States, unemployment rates in Europe today are substantially greater than current U.S. unemployment rates. The unemployment rate in the United States has fluctuated considerably, rising from 4.8 to 8.3% in the 1973–75 recession, then declining to 5.8% in 1979, then rising to 9.7% in 1982 before declining to around 7.0% today. In contrast, unemployment in Europe has risen seemingly inexorably since 1973. In France, the unemployment rate has increased in every single year since 1973, while it has declined only twice in Germany and the United Kingdom. The differences between the European countries

Table 8.1
European and U.S. unemployment 1961−86 (percent)

	United States	United Kingdom	France	West Germany
1961−70	4.7	1.9	.9	.8
1971−75	6.1	2.8	2.6	1.8
1976−80	6.7	5.2	5.3	3.7
1980	7.1	6.0	6.4	3.4
1981	7.6	9.2	7.7	4.8
1982	9.7	10.6	8.7	6.9
1983	9.6	11.6	8.8	8.4
1984	7.5	11.8	9.9	8.4
1985	7.3	12.0	10.7	8.4
1986[a]	7.2	11.7	10.9	8.0

Source: *Annual Economic Review*, Commission of the European Communities, 1986.
a. Forecast.

and the United States are most pronounced after 1980. While the U.S. unemployment rate is at roughly its 1980 level, the unemployment rate has approximately doubled in the three European countries. The rapid decline in U.S. unemployment after 1982 contrasts sharply with the continuing increase in unemployment in Europe. The last line of the table gives forecasts of unemployment by the European Commission for 1986: they show little expected change. Longer run forecasts are very similar: baseline projections by the European Commission put unemployment for the EEC as a whole at 10.4% in 1990, compared to 10.8% in 1985.

Differences in unemployment rates actually understate the differences in the performance of American and European labor markets over the past decade. Europe has suffered the concomitants of high unemployment—reduced labor force participation and involuntary reductions in hours—to a much greater extent than has the United States. Between 1975 and 1983, the labor force participation rate of men in the United States remained constant, while the corresponding rate in OECD Europe declined by 6%. Average annual hours worked declined by 2.7% in the United States between 1975 and 1982 compared with declines of 7.5% in France and 8.1% in England. Perhaps the most striking contrast of the labor market performances of Europe and the United States is the observation that between 1975 and 1985 employment increased by 25%, or about 25 million jobs, in the United States while declining in absolute terms in Europe.

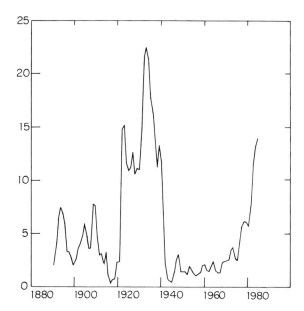

Figure 8.1
Unemployment rate in the United Kingdom.

8.1.2 Unemployment Rates in the United Kingdom and the United States over the Last 100 Years

European unemployment has steadily increased and, pending an un-expected change in policy, is expected to remain at this new higher level for the foreseeable future. How unusual is such high and persistent un-employment? To answer this question, we now examine the behavior of unemployment over the last 100 years in both the United Kingdom and the United States.

Figures 8.1 and 8.2 plot unemployment for each of the two countries, for the period 1890–1985 for the United Kingdom, and 1892–1985 for the United States.[2]

Estimation of an AR(1) process for the whole sample for each country gives

U.K.: $u = .93u(-1) + e;$ $\sigma_\infty = 2.1\%,$
         (.04)

U.S.: $u = .90u(-1) + e;$ $\sigma_\infty = 2.0\%.$
         (.04)

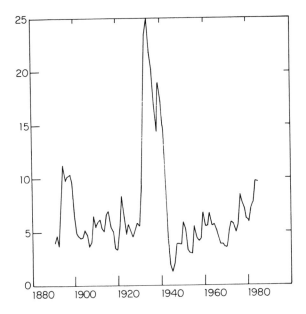

Figure 8.2
Unemployment rate in the United States.

In both cases, the degree of first order serial correlation is high. Unemployment is indeed surprisingly persistent. It exhibits at best a weak
tendency to return to its mean.

Examination of the two figures—as well as statistical work—suggests
that the evolution of the unemployment rate over the past 100 years is not
well captured, however, by any simple linear autoregressive representation.
The degree of persistence as captured by the degree of first order serial
correlation reported above arises in large part from relatively infrequent
changes in the level around which unemployment fluctuates. In the United
Kingdom, when unemployment goes up from 1920 to 1940, it shows little
tendency during that period to return to its pre-1920 level; it then returns
to a low level during World War II, to stay there until the 1960s. The
current episode, both past and forecast, is a second instance in which
unemployment, after having sharply increased, stabilizes at a new, high
level. The United States experienced a sustained increase in unemployment
from 1929 to 1939, only to see unemployment drop sharply during and
after the war to a new, much lower, level. When the degree of persistence
in unemployment is estimated separately for periods of high and low

average unemployment, there is some weak evidence of greater persistence within periods of high average unemployment.

The time series studied in isolation give little indication as to the cause of the changes in the mean level, which account for much of the persistence in unemployment. They could be exogenous or instead be triggered by unemployment itself, with a few years of high unemployment triggering an increase in the mean level of unemployment, a few years of low unemployment triggering in turn a decrease in that level. In the absence of a tight specification of how this triggering occurs, we do not believe that the data can easily distinguish between these two possibilities and we shall not attempt to do so at this stage.

Our finding that unemployment exhibits a very high degree of persistence over the past century parallels the findings of Nelson and Plosser (1982), Campbell and Mankiw (1987), and others that a variety of economic variables follow random walks or other nonstationary processes. In many cases such findings can be easily rationalized by recognizing that the level of technology is likely to be nonstationary and that other variables, like the level of output, depend on productivity. But the failure of unemployment to display more of a mean reverting tendency is troubling. It is unlikely that nonstationarity in productivity can account for the persistence of unemployment since the secular increase in productivity has not been associated with any trend or upward drift in unemployment.

8.1.3 Diagnosing Unemployment Problems

What sort of theories can account for persistent high unemployment in general and the current European experience in particular? We highlight the general difficulties one encounters in explaining persistent unemployment by focusing on the problem of explaining the current European situation. The central puzzle it poses is its persistence. While it is easy to point to substantial, adverse supply and demand shocks over the last 15 years, we argue that our standard theories do not easily explain how they have had such enduring effects on the level of unemployment.[3]

Aggregate Demand
There is little question that Europe has been affected by large adverse demand shocks, especially since 1980 (see, for example, Dornbusch et al., 1983). In the 1980s, Europe has to a large extent matched tight U.S. monetary policy while at the same time engaging in a major and prolonged fiscal contraction (see Blanchard and Summers, 1984, for the United King-

dom, Germany, and France; see Buiter, 1985, for a more detailed study of the U.K. fiscal policy).

But to the extent that aggregate demand shocks do not affect the equilibrium or natural rate of unemployment, one would expect sustained high unemployment to be associated with rapid declines in the rate of inflation. More generally, standard models of the effects of aggregate demand shocks would not predict that previous estimates of the relationship between inflation and unemployment would break down. There is substantial evidence, however, that this relation has broken down and that there has been a much smaller decline in inflation than would have been predicted by past relationships. Below we examine the relation between wage inflation and unemployment in detail. But the basic point that previous relations have broken down is evidenced in table 8.2, which gives the rates of inflation and unemployment in 1984 and 1985 for the United Kingdom, France, and Germany. Despite the high rates of unemployment, there is no sign of disinflation, with the United Kingdom and Germany experiencing a small increase in inflation and France a small decrease. Econometric estimates of the rate of unemployment consistent with stable inflation show rapid increases over the past decade. Layard et al. (1984), using crude time trends in a Phillips curve relation, find the unemployment rate consistent with steady inflation to have risen from 2.4 in 1967−70 to 9.2 in 1981−83 in Britain, from 1.3 to 6.2 in Germany, and from 2.2 to 6.9 in France. Coe and Gagliardi (1985), also within the framework of the Phillips curve but using instead of a time trend a battery of potential determinants of equilibrium unemployment as right-hand side variables, obtain roughly similar results. Aggregate demand shocks have clearly played a role in explaining the increase in European unemployment; but they cannot be the whole story given the increase in the rate of unemployment consistent with steady inflation.

Table 8.2
Inflation and unemployment in the United Kingdom, France, and Germany 1984−85 (percent)[a]

	United Kingdom		France		Germany	
	π	μ	π	μ	π	μ
1984	4.4	11.8	7.0	9.9	1.9	8.4
1985	5.5	12.0	5.7	10.7	2.1	8.4

Source: *Annual Economic Review*, Commission of the European Communities, 1986.
a. π − rate of change of GDP deflator. μ = unemployment.

Aggregate Supply

Aggregate supply explanations appear more promising if the goal is to explain an increase in equilibrium unemployment. This is indeed the approach followed by much of the recent research. Sachs (1979, 1983) and Bruno and Sachs (1985) have argued that unemployment in Europe is in large part the result of a combination of adverse supply shocks and real wage rigidity. The argument is that real wages do not adjust to clear the labor market so that adverse supply shocks that reduce the demand for labor at a given real wage create unemployment. This argument has two parts, real wage rigidity and the occurrence of adverse supply shocks. We start by reviewing the evidence on the second.

Table 8.3 presents some information on the behavior of various supply factors with a potential bearing on unemployment in the United Kingdom since 1960.[4]

Table 8.3
Supply factors and U.K. unemployment[a]

Year	Unemployment rate (%)	Replacement rate (%)	Mismatch index (%)	Productivity growth (%)	Change in tax wedge (%)
1960	2.3	42	—	1.9	.0
1965	2.3	48	41	2.8	1.0
1970	3.1	51	38	3.2	1.0
1975	4.7	49	43	2.7	.8
1976	6.0	50	38	1.5	2.8
1977	6.4	51	35	1.7	1.9
1978	6.1	50	35	1.4	−.9
1979	5.6	46	35	2.1	1.3
1980	6.9	45	37	1.5	1.3
1981	10.6	50	41	1.4	2.6
1982	12.8	54	37	1.1	1.0
1983	13.1	54	—	.5	−1.8

a. Standardized unemployment rate; source OECD. Weighted average of replacement rates relevant to families of different sizes, source Layard and Nickell (1985). Index constructed as $\sum |u_i - v_i|$, where u_i and v_i are the proportions of unemployment and vacancies in occupation i, respectively, source Layard, Nickell, and Jackman (1984). Rate of change of total factor productivity growth, derived by assuming labor augmenting technical change; the first four numbers refer to the change in the rate (at annual rate) over the previous five years; source Layard and Nickell (1985). The tax wedge is the sum of the employment tax rate levied on employers and of direct and indirect tax rates levied on employees; the first four numbers refer to the change in the rate (at annual rates) over the previous five years, source Layard and Nickell (1985).

A first candidate is *unemployment benefits*. Unemployment insurance may raise unemployment if it causes workers to search longer or less intensively for jobs, reducing the pressure that unemployment puts on wages. The second column of table 8.3 gives the average replacement ratio, that is, the average ratio of after tax unemployment benefits to earnings for different categories of workers; it shows no clear movement over time. This is not necessarily conclusive evidence against a role for unemployment benefits: one can easily envision mechanisms through which increases in unemployment benefits lead to higher real wages, higher unemployment, but little or no change in the replacement ratio. Indeed, another way of reading the column is that it shows an increase in real unemployment benefits of roughly 30% since 1970. Furthermore, it has been argued that the principal changes in unemployment insurance have occurred through changes in eligibility rules rather than benefit levels. Attempts to estimate the effect of unemployment benefits on unemployment have not been very successful (see Minford, 1982, and Nickell, 1984, for further discussion) and one is led to conclude that the increase in unemployment benefits probably does not account for a large portion of the increase in unemployment.

A second candidate explanation is *structural change*. The argument is that the need for large scale reallocation of labor associated with structural change tends to increase unemployment. Often it is suggested that the energy shocks of the 1970s increased the rate of structural change and so led to higher unemployment. The adjustment to structural changes may be complicated by real wage rigidity. The fourth column of table 8.3 presents the index of "mismatch" developed by Layard, Nickell, and Jackman (1984). The index tries to represent the degree of structural change in the economy by examining the extent to which unemployment and vacancies occur in the same sectors. The results in the table look at occupational mismatch, but results are largely similar when industrial and regional measures are used.[5] There is little evidence of an increase in the rate of structural change since the 1960s when the unemployment rate was consistently low.

Perhaps the most common supply based explanations for persistent high unemployment involve factors that reduce labor productivity and or drive a wedge between the cost of labor to firms and the wage workers receive. The fourth and fifth columns of the table give time series for *total factor productivity growth* and the change in the *tax wedge*.[6] It is clear from the table that there has been a substantial reduction in the rate of total factor productivity growth in the wake of the oil shocks. Over the years the total tax wedge has also risen substantially, by 30% since 1960, by 10% since 1970. While it is still true that the real after-tax wage consistent with full employment has risen fairly steadily, it has increased more slowly than it had in the first half of the postwar period.

The Problem with Aggregate Supply Explanations

We have now documented the presence of adverse supply developments relative to what might have been expected in the early 1970s. But for these shocks to have a long lasting effect on unemployment, there must be long lasting real wage rigidity. If and when labor supply becomes inelastic, supply shocks are then reflected in real wages, not in unemployment. Individual labor supply is surely largely inelastic in the long run. As with aggregate demand explanations, we face the problem of explaining the mechanism that causes shocks to have long lived effects.

Recent models of union behavior (notably McDonald and Solow, 1981) have addressed this problem by showing that if wages are the result of bargaining between unions and firms, the result may be real wage rigidity, with shocks affecting employment only. There is, however, a fundamental difficulty with this line of argument. To take the model developed by McDonald and Solow, if real wages were truly rigid at a rate determined by the interaction of union preferences and firms' production technology, employment would steadily increase and unemployment steadily decrease through time. Annual productivity improvements due to technical change are equivalent to favorable supply shocks. As long as productivity increments and capital accumulation led to the demand curve for labor shifting outward faster than the population grew, unemployment would decline. This appears counterfactual.[7] Even over the last decade, the cumulative impact of productivity growth has almost certainly more than counterbalanced the adverse supply shocks that occurred.

To rescue this line of thought, it must be argued that real wages are rigid along some "norm," which may increase over time. But this has two implications. The first is that the dynamic effects of supply shocks on employment then depend on the way the norm adjusts to actual productivity and this is left unexplained. The second and more important one here is that adverse supply shocks have an effect only as long as the norm has not adjusted to actual productivity. Thus, unless the norm never catches up with actual productivity, adverse supply shocks cannot affect unemployment permanently. It seems implausible that the current persistence of high unemployment can all be attributed to lags in learning about productivity. Both the United Kingdom and the United States have experienced enormous productivity gains without evident reduction in unemployment over the last century. High unemployment therefore cannot be blamed simply on poor productivity performance. It can only be attributed to *surprises* in productivity performance. But then it is hard to see how to explain protracted unemployment from lower productivity growth.

Where does this leave us? We have argued that there is plenty of evidence of adverse shocks, be it lower than expected productivity growth, increases in the price of oil, or in the tax wedge in the 1970s or contractionary aggregate demand policies in the 1980s. But we have also argued that standard theories do not provide us with convincing explanations of how these shocks can have such a sustained effect on unemployment. Put differently, it is difficult to account for the apparent increase in the equilibrium rate of unemployment—or equivalently in the unemployment rate consistent with stable inflation—by pointing to these shocks. Borrowing from the business cycle terminology, it is not difficult to find evidence of negative impulses; the difficulty is in explaining the propagation mechanism. This leads us to look for mechanisms that can explain the propagation of adverse supply or demand shocks over long periods of time. These include the possibility that current unemployment depends directly and strongly on past unemployment.[8] We now consider various channels through which this may happen.

8.1.4 Theories of Hysteresis

Three types of explanation, which loosely speaking might be referred to as the "physical capital," "human capital," and "insider-outsider" stories, can be adduced to explain why shocks that cause unemployment in a single period might have long term effects.

The physical capital story simply holds that reductions in capital stock associated with the reduced employment that accompanies adverse shocks reduce the subsequent demand for labor and so cause protracted unemployment. This argument is frequently made in the current European context, where it is emphasized that, despite the very substantial increase in the unemployment rate that has occurred, capacity utilization is at fairly normal levels. For the EEC as a whole, capacity utilization has shown no trend over the last decade. It currently stands at 81% compared with 76% in 1975, 83% in 1979, and 76% in 1983. It is then argued that the existing capital stock is simply inadequate to employ the current labor force.

We are somewhat skeptical of the argument that capital accumulation effects can account for high unemployment for two reasons. First, as long as there are some possibilities for substitution of labor for capital ex-post, reductions in the capital stock affect the demand for labor just like adverse supply shocks. As noted above, it is unlikely that an anticipated supply shock would have an important effect on the unemployment rate. Second, as we discuss in section 8.4, substantial disinvestment during the 1930s did not preclude the rapid recovery of employment associated with rearmament in a number of other countries. Nor did the very substantial reduction in the size of the civilian capital stock that occurred during the war prevent the attainment of full employment after the war in many countries.[9] The argument that reduced capital accumulation has an important effect on the level of unemployment is difficult to support with historical examples.

A second and perhaps more important mechanism works through "human capital" broadly defined. Persuasive statements of the potentially important effects of unemployment on human capital accumulation and subsequent labor supply may be found in Phelps (1972) and Hargraves-Heap (1980).[10] Some suggestive empirical evidence may be found in Clark and Summers (1982a). Essentially, the human capital argument holds that workers who are unemployed lose the opportunity to maintain and update their skills by working. Particularly for the long term unemployed, the atrophy of skills may combine with disaffection from the labor force associated with the inability to find a job to reduce the effective supply of labor. Early retirement may, for example, be a semiirreversible decision. More generally, if for incentive or human capital reasons employers prefer workers with long horizons, it may be very difficult for middle aged workers to find new jobs. A final point is that in a high unemployment environment, it will be difficult for reliable and able workers to signal their quality by holding jobs and being promoted. The resulting inefficiencies in sorting workers may reduce the overall demand for labor.

Beyond the adverse effects on labor supply generated by high unemployment, the benefits of a high pressure economy are forgone. Clark and Summers (1982a) demonstrate that in the United States at least World War II had a long lasting effect in raising female labor force participation. Despite the Baby Boom, in 1950 the labor force participation of all female cohorts old enough to have worked during the war was significantly greater than would have been predicted on the basis of prewar trends. The causal role of participation during the war is evidenced by the fact that the participation of very young women who could not have worked during the war was actually lower than would have been predicted on the basis of earlier trends. Similarly, research by Ellwood (1981) suggests that teenage unemployment may leave some "permanent scars" on subsequent labor market performance. One channel through which this may occur is family composition. The superior labor market performance of married men with children has been noted many times. The effect of the Great Depression on fertility rates, both in the United States and in Europe, has often been noted.

Gauging the quantitative importance of human capital mechanisms generating hysteresis is very difficult. Some of the arguments—early retirement, for example—suggest that labor force participation should decline rather than that unemployment should increase in the aftermath of adverse shocks. Perhaps a more fundamental problem is that to the extent that there is some irreversibility associated with unemployment shocks, it becomes more difficult to explain why temporary shocks have such large short run effects. If early retirement is forever, why should it be taken in response to a temporary downturn? Overall, while it seems likely that human capital mechanisms can explain some of the protracted response to shocks, it is doubtful that they are sufficient to account completely for the observed degree of persistence.

A third mechanism that can generate persistence and that we regard as the most promising relies on the distinction between "insider" and "outsider" workers, developed in a series of contributions by Lindbeck (see Lindbeck and Snower, 1986b, for example) and used in an important paper by Gregory (1985) to explain the behavior of the Australian economy. To take an extreme case, suppose that all wages are set by bargaining between employed workers—the "insiders"—and firms, with outsiders playing no role in the bargaining process. Insiders are concerned with maintaining their jobs, not insuring the employment of outsiders. This has two implications. First, in the absence of shocks, any level of employment of insiders is self-sustaining; insiders just set the wage so as to remain employed. Second and more important, in the presence of shocks, employment follows a process akin to a random walk; after an adverse shock, for example, which reduces employment, some workers lose their insider status and the new smaller group of insiders sets the wage so as to maintain this new lower level of employment. Employment and unemployment show no tendency to return to their preshock value, but are instead determined by the history of shocks. This example is extreme but nevertheless suggestive. It suggests that, if wage bargaining is a prevalent feature of the labor market, the dynamic interactions between employment and the size of the group of insiders may generate substantial employment and unemployment persistence. This is the argument we explore in detail in the next section.

8.2 A Theory of Unemployment Persistence

This section develops a theory of unemployment persistence based on the distinction between insiders and outsiders. As the example sketched at the end of the previous section makes clear, the key assumption of such a theory is that of the relation between employment status and insider status. We can think of this key assumption as an assumption about *membership rules*, the rules that govern the relation between employment status and membership in the group of insiders. The possibility of persistent fluctuations in employment arises because changes in employment may change the group's membership and thereby alter its objective function.[11]

In the first part of this section, we develop a partial equilibrium model of bargaining between a group of insiders and a representative firm and characterize employment dynamics under alternative membership rules. (We use the term "group" rather than the more natural "union" to avoid prejudging the issue of whether the membership considerations we stress are important only in settings where formal unions are present.) The second part of the section extends the analysis to a general equilibrium setting and shows how both nominal and real shocks can have permanent effects on unemployment. In the remaining part of the section, we consider mainly two issues; the first is that of the endogeneity of membership rules, and the second is that of whether our analysis is indeed relevant only or mostly in explicit union settings.

8.2.1 A Model of Membership Rules and Employment Dynamics

To focus on the dynamic effects of membership rules on the decision of the group of insiders, the "group" for short, we formalize the firm as entirely passive, as presenting a labor demand on which the group chooses its preferred outcome.[12] We start by characterizing employment and wages in a one period model. In a one period model, initial membership is given and membership rules are obviously irrelevant. But it is a useful intermediate step, which will allow us to contrast our later results with traditional ones that treat membership as exogenous. Throughout, we make no attempt at generality and use convenient functional forms and some approximations to retain analytical simplicity.

The One Period Model
The group has initial membership n_0 (in logarithms, as are all variables in what follows, unless otherwise mentioned). It faces a labor demand

function given by

$$n = -cw + e, \tag{1}$$

where n is employment, w is the real wage, and e is a random technological shock, with mean Ee, uniformly distributed in $[Ee - a, Ee + a]$. The coefficient a captures the degree of uncertainty associated with labor demand. The group must decide on a wage w before it knows the realization of e. Given w and the realization of e, the firm then chooses labor according to the labor demand function. If n exceeds n_0, $n - n_0$ outsiders are hired. If n is less than n_0, $n_0 - n$ insiders are laid off. The probability of being laid off is the same for all insiders.

Before specifying the objective function of the group, we can derive, for given w and n_0, *the probability of being employed*. The probability of being employed for an insider is equal to one if $n > n_0$. For $n < n_0$, we approximate the probability (which is not in logarithm) of being employed for an insider by $1 - n_0 + n$. This approximation will be good as long as n is not too much smaller than n_0. Under these assumptions, the probability p of being employed is given by (all derivations are in the appendix)

$$p = \begin{cases} 1 - (1/4a)(n_0 + cw - Ee + a)^2 & \text{for} \quad n_0 + cw \geqslant Ee - a \\ 1 & \text{for} \quad n_0 + cw \leqslant Ee - a. \end{cases} \tag{2}$$

If even under the worst outcome—which is $e = Ee - a$ and thus $n = -cw + Ee - a$—n is larger than n_0, then the probability of employment is clearly equal to one. Otherwise, the probability is an increasing function of expected productivity Ee, and a decreasing function of initial membership n_0 and of the wage w. It is also a decreasing function of the degree of uncertainty a; the larger a, the lower the probability of being employed in bad times, while the probability remains equal to one in good times.

The second step is to derive *the choice of w*. This requires specifying the utility function of the group. The group maximizes the utility function of the representative group member, which we specify as

$$U = p + bw.$$

Utility is linear in the probability of employment and the wage. This specification is not the most natural but it is, however, attractive, for two reasons. The first reason is that, as will be seen below, it implies, together with the specification of probabilities given above, that the group exhibits the stochastic equivalent of inelastic labor supply: an increase in Ee is entirely reflected in an increase in real wages and leaves the probability of employment unchanged. We have argued in the previous section that this is a desirable feature of any model of wage determination given the absence of major trends in unemployment rates over long periods of time.[13] Note, however, that our assumption of stochastically inelastic labor supply is the opposite of that used by McDonald and Solow. Where they postulate a rigid real wage so that the labor supply curve is perfectly elastic, we postulate perfectly inelastic labor supply. The second reason is that it is analytically convenient.

Replacing p by its value from (2) and solving for the optimal wage w gives

$$w^* = (1/c)(-n_0 + Ee + a(2(b/c) - 1)).$$

Replacing in labor demand gives

$$n = n_0 - a(2(b/c) - 1) + (e - Ee).$$

Replacing w^* in equation (2) and rearranging gives the optimal probability:

$$p^* = 1 - a(b/c)^2.$$

Thus the wage depends negatively on initial membership. As by definition $E(e - Ee) = 0$, whether expected employment exceeds membership depends on the sign of $a(2(b/c) - 1)$, thus on whether b/c is less than $1/2$ or not. The lower b, the more importance workers attach to employment protection as opposed to the wage; the higher c, the smaller the wage reduction required to increase expected employment. If b/c is less than $1/2$, workers set a wage low enough to imply expected net hirings of outsiders by the firm. Note, as mentioned above, that the optimal probability of being employed depends neither on the initial membership nor on expected productivity.[14]

Until now, the analysis has been rather conventional: Given the initial membership, insiders choose a wage. This wage and the realization of a disturbance determine employment. But when we go from this one period model to a dynamic one, there may well be a relation between employment this period and next period's membership. This relation will depend on the form of membership rules. We now examine how this affects employment dynamics.

We first define *membership rules*. We can think of various membership rules as being indexed by m. Those workers who have been working in the firm for the last m periods belong to the group, are insiders. Workers who have been laid off for more than m periods lose membership,[15] become outsiders. There are two extreme cases: the first is the case where m is equal to infinity, so that the initial membership never changes. The second is the case where $m = 1$ so that membership always coincides with current employment. The extreme cases highlight the effects of alternative membership rules so we consider them before turning to the more difficult intermediate case.

The Case of a Constant Membership (m = *Infinity*)
Let us denote by $\bar{n}_i$ beginning of period i membership, and by n_i realized employment in period i. In the present case, membership is equal to $\bar{n}_0$ forever. So, each period, if n_i exceeds $\bar{n}_0$, all members work; if n_i is less than $\bar{n}_0$, the probability of being employed is given for each member by (approximately) $1 - \bar{n}_0 + n_i$. We assume that the one period utility function of a worker is given, as above, by $(p_i + bw_i)$ and that the workers' discount factor is equal to θ. Thus the utility of a member as of time zero is given by

$$U_0 = E_0 \sum_{i=0}^{\infty} \theta^i [p_i + bw_i], \qquad \text{where} \quad \theta \text{ is less than one.}$$

Assume for the moment that the shocks affecting labor demand are uncorrelated over time, or more precisely that e_i is iid (independent and identically distributed), uniform on $[-a, +a]$. (We shall return below to the case of serially correlated shocks.) Then by the analysis of the previous section, the probability of being employed in period i, conditional on w_i is given by (using the fact that $Ee_i = 0$):

$$p_i = \begin{cases} 1 & \text{for} \quad \bar{n}_0 + cw_i \geqslant -a \\ 1 - (1/4a)(\bar{n}_0 + cw_i + a)^2 & \text{for} \quad \bar{n}_0 + cw_i \leqslant -a. \end{cases}$$

Given that employment outcomes do not affect future membership, and given the assumption that shocks are white noise, the problem faced by members is the same every period, and thus its solution is the same as that derived above:

$$w_i^* = (1/c)(-\bar{n}_0 + a(2(b/c) - 1)),$$

$$n_i = \bar{n}_0 - a(2(b/c) - 1) + e_i. \tag{3}$$

In response to white noise shocks, employment will also be white noise. Whether employment is on average larger or smaller than membership depends on whether (b/c) is smaller or larger than $1/2$. If the insiders want strong employment protection, they will choose a wage so that, on average, employment exceeds membership and the firm has a cushion of outsiders who are laid off first in case of adverse shocks.

It is easy to see that the result that employment is white noise will continue to hold regardless of the stochastic process followed by e. As shown above, our assumptions insure that labor supply is stochastically inelastic. Changes in the expected value of e affect real wages but do not affect the level of employment. Only the deviation of e from its expected value affects the level of employment. By the properties of rational expectations, the unexpected component of e must be serially uncorrelated.

The Case Where Membership Equals Employment (m = 1)
We now go to the opposite extreme, in which membership comes and goes with employment. In this case membership at time i is simply given by employment at time $i - 1$: $n_i = n_{i-1}$. If the group kept the same decision rule as in equation (3) but applied it to n_i rather than to n_0, equation (3) would become

$$n_i = n_{i-1} - a(2(b/c) - 1) + e_i. \tag{3'}$$

Thus, employment would follow a random walk, with drift. Optimal wage behavior under the assumption that membership equals beginning of period employment is, however, not given by (3'). Unlike the behavior implied by (3') current members should recognize their inability to commit future memberships to wage policies. The subsequent policies of the group will depend on its then current membership. This changes fundamentally the character of the maximization problem. The group membership, when taking wage decisions today, knows that wage decisions will be taken next period by a membership that will in general be different from that of today. This implies in particular that if an insider is laid off, he becomes an outsider and thus considerably decreases his chances of keeping employment with the firm; this presumably leads him to choose a lower wage than in the previous case, where being laid off did not affect his future chances of being hired.[16]

Even with the simplifying assumptions we have made so far, the problem is intractable unless we further simplify by linearizing the group's intertemporal objective function. Let w' be the wage around which the objective function is linearized and let the shocks to labor demand be white noise. The solution to the maximization problem is then

$$w_i^* = (1/c)(-\bar{n}_{i-1} + a(2(b/c)(1/(1 + b\theta w')) - 1)),$$

$$n_i = n_{i-1} - a(2(b/c)(1/(1 + b\theta w')) - 1) + e. \tag{4}$$

The probability of employment for a member is a constant and is given by

$$p_i^* = 1 - a[(b/c)(1/(1 + b\theta w'))]^2.$$

Thus, under this membership rule, employment follows a random walk with drift. For a given labor force, there is unemployment hysteresis. Uncorrelated shocks to labor demand affect current employment, and through employment, membership and future expected employment. The drift is positive if (b/c) is less than $(1 + b\theta w')/2$, if workers care sufficiently about the probability of employment as compared to the wage. In such a case, although they do not care about the unemployed, they will set the wage each period so as to have the firm hire on average new employees. For a given membership, the wage is always set lower than in the $m = $ infinity case and thus the probability of employment is set higher; this is because being laid off implies a loss of membership and imposes a much larger cost than before.

This analysis can again easily be extended to the case where labor demand shocks are serially correlated. The results remain the same; employment continues to follow a random walk. This is a consequence of our maintained assumption that expected changes in labor demand have no effect on the level of employment.

The Intermediate Case (m between 1 and Infinity)
The intermediate case where workers remain insiders for some time after losing their jobs and where newly hired workers eventually but not immediately become insiders raises an additional conceptual problem. There will no longer be unanimity among insiders. Those who have already experienced some unemployment, or those who have been working in the firm for a short period of time, for example, will favor more cautious wage setting policies than those who have not. A theory of behavior in the face of conflict between members is beyond our grasp.[17] A plausible conjecture is that allowing for values of m between 1 and ∞ leads to wage setting policies that are less cautious than in the $m = \infty$ case but more cautious than in the $m = 1$ case.

More important, rules corresponding to m between one and infinity are likely to generate unemployment behavior such as that shown in figures 8.1 and 8.2, namely, infrequent but sustained changes in the level of unemployment. Short sequences of unexpected shocks of the same sign have little effect on membership and thus on mean employment. In the case of adverse shocks, insiders are not laid off long enough to lose insider status; in the case of favorable shocks, outsiders do not stay long enough to acquire membership. But long—and infrequent—sequences of shocks of the same sign have large effects on membership and may lead to large effects on the mean level of employment. The length of the shock necessary to cause a permanent change in employment depends on the membership rules. In general there is no reason why these rules have to be symmetric. The length of time after which an unemployed worker becomes an outsider need not equal the length of time until a new worker becomes an insider. Hence favorable and unfavorable shocks may persist to differing extents.

The results of this section have been derived under very specific assumptions, from fixed membership rules to the assumption that the firm was passive and that outsiders played no role, direct or indirect, in the negotiation process. We must return to these assumptions. Before we do so, however, we first show how the model of this section can be used to generate permanent effects on aggregate employment of both nominal and real shocks.

8.2.2 Persistent Effects of Nominal and Real Disturbances on Unemployment

We now assume that there are many firms in the economy, each dealing with its own group of insider workers. We further assume that wages are set in nominal terms, so that nominal disturbances can affect employment. We then characterize the effects of nominal and real disturbances on employment and real wages.

The Derived Demand for Labor Facing Each Group

The economy is composed of many firms indexed by j, each selling a product that is an imperfect substitute for all others, but being otherwise identical. The demand facing firm j is given by

$$y_j = -k(p_j - p) + (m - p), \qquad k > 1.$$

All variables are in logarithms and all constants are ignored for notational simplicity. The variables y_j and p_j denote the output and the nominal price charged by firm j, respectively; m and p denote nominal money and the price level. Demand for the firm's output depends on the relative price as well as on aggregate real money balances. The restriction on k is needed to obtain an interior maximum for profit maximization.

Each firm operates under constant returns to scale; the relation between output and employment is given by $y_j = n_j$. If w_j is the wage that firm j pays its workers, constant returns and constant elasticity of the demand for goods imply that prices are given by $p_j = w_j - e$, where e is a random technological shock, which is assumed common to all firms.[18]

Each firm j faces a group of insiders with the same objective function as above, which chooses a nominal wage and lets the firm determine employment. Given the relation between p_j and w_j, we can think of each group j as choosing w_j subject to the demand function:

$$n_j = k(w_j - e - p) + (m - p). \tag{5}$$

The Choice of the Wage and Employment

We now characterize the decisions of each group j at time zero (and for the moment we do not introduce the time index explicitly). We assume each group to operate under the membership rule $m = 1$, so that at time zero, membership in group j is given by $n_j(-1)$. The group now chooses a nominal rather than a real wage, based on its expectation of the price level, Ep, nominal money, Em, and the expected value of the technological shock, Ee, which all enter the derived demand for labor. As we have shown earlier, given such a demand function and its objective function, it chooses a wage so that the expected level of employment is equal to its membership plus a constant term. Ignoring again the constant, this implies

$$k(w_j - Ee - Ep) + (Em - Ep) = n_j(-1), \tag{6}$$

which defines implicitly w_j as a function of $n_j(-1)$, Em, Ep, and Ee.

To solve for w_j, we must solve for the value of Ep. We do so under the assumption of rational expectations. As all firms and groups are the same, and are all affected by the same aggregate nominal shock, all groups have the same membership: $n_j(-1) = n(-1)$. Furthermore all nominal prices are the same and equal to the price level, so that the first term in (6) is equal to zero. Thus, from (6)

$$Ep = Em - n(-1) \qquad \text{and} \qquad w_j = Ee + Em - n(-1).$$

The expected price level depends on expected nominal money and negatively on membership. The nominal wage in turn depends positively on expected nominal money and the expected technological shock, and negatively on membership. Replacing w_j and Ep by their values in (5) and aggregating over j gives the equation characterizing the dynamic behavior of aggregate employment,

$$n = n(-1) + (m - Em) + (e - Ee),$$

or, if we reintroduce the time index i,

$$n_i = n_{i-1} + (m_i - Em_i) + (e_i - Ee_i). \tag{7}$$

Shocks, Employment, and Wages
From (7) only unexpected shocks affected employment. In the case of real shocks, this comes as before from the assumption of inelastic labor supply, which imply that each group sets wages so as to leave employment unaffected by anticipated real shocks. In the case of nominal shocks, the result is the same as in other nominal contract models (Fischer, 1977) and the intuition is straightforward. Workers set a nominal wage that, in view of expected aggregate demand, will maintain last period's level of employment. Firms simply mark up over this nominal wage. Unexpectedly low aggregate demand leads to unexpected decreases in output and employment, with no changes in nominal wages (by assumption) and in prices (because of constant returns).[19]

These unexpected nominal and real shocks, unlike other contract models, have, however, permanent effects on employment. This is the result of our assumptions about membership rules. Once employment has decreased, it remains, in the absence of other shocks, permanently at the lower level. A sequence of unexpected contractions in aggregate demand increases equilibrium unemployment permanently. If we assumed that m, the membership rule, was greater than one, we would again obtain the result that while short sequences of adverse shocks had no effect on equilibrium unemployment, a long sequence of such shocks would increase equilibrium unemployment permanently.

While the implications for employment are straightforward, the model implies that there is no simple relation between employment and real wages. Consider in particular the effects of nominal shocks. By our assumption of constant returns to scale and constant elasticity of demand, they leave the markup of prices over wages unaffected. Equivalently, they leave the real wage unaffected. Thus, a sequence of adverse nominal disturbances will decrease employment, with no effect on the real wage. This lack of a simple relation between real wages and employment comes from our assumptions of monopolistic competition and constant returns, not from our assumptions about insiders and outsiders. As our focus is on the dynamic effects of membership rules, we do not explore the relation between real wages and employment further. But it is an important caveat to the line of research that has focused on the role of real wages in "explaining" high European unemployment. In the model constructed here, it is quite possible to have sustained high unemployment without high real wages. It is also possible for expansionary policies to raise employment without altering real wages.

8.2.3 The Endogeneity of Membership Rules

In the rest of this section, we return to the original model and examine various extensions. Here, we focus on the determination of the membership rules.

We have shown that the time series evolution of employment depends critically on the nature of these rules. To the extent that insider status is closely linked with employment, substantial persistence is likely to result. If membership does not change or changes relatively little when employment changes, employment is likely to be much less persistent.

It is clear that at any point in time the currently employed would find it optimal to commit the group to maximizing their interests indefinitely, while ignoring the welfare of those currently laid off. That is, they would like to apply the rule $m = 1$ this period and $m = \infty$ hereafter. But this means that if the currently employed are those who decide about membership, the only time consistent rule is $m = 1$, which is always the best current period rule for the currently employed. The issue is therefore whether the group can precommit itself, or more accurately whether the currently employed can commit the group to take care of their interest in the future whether or not they are still employed by the firm.

Achieving the $m = \infty$ solution is probably not feasible. But it seems plausible that the group will be able to commit itself to at least some extent. The factor limiting the commitment will be the degree of divergence between the original membership and the group of employed workers in some subsequent period. Where the divergence is too great, current employees will wrest control of the group from those controlling it in the interests of some group of past workers. The extent to which groups can commit themselves is probably greatest where demand shocks are small so that level and composition of employment change relatively little from period to period.

This suggests that m will depend on the distribution of the shocks. If shocks have large variance, m may have to be close to one to avoid large differences between membership and the employed. Or m may instead be a function of the realization of the shocks. A sequence of large positive or negative unexpected shocks may lead to the takeover of the group by the then current employees. When a large fraction of original labor force is on layoff, the incentive for the workers still employed to ignore them and thus not take the pay cut required to get them back may be strong. This is much less likely in the face of small shocks. Changes in the values of m associated with major shocks provide another possible explanation for coincidence of persistent and high unemployment.

Our model thus suggests two alternative explanations for the empirical observation that unemployment remains at high levels for long periods of time. First, for a given fixed value of m greater than one but less than infinity, a sequence of adverse shocks will lead to a change in membership and therefore alter the level of employment permanently. Second, in bad times currently employed workers are more likely to take over and disenfranchise the unemployed, thus reducing the value of m and increasing persistence. The two differ in their implications for the process for unemployment at high levels. In the first, after the level change, the process for unemployment will have higher mean but the same degree of persistence around the new mean as it had before. In the second case, unemployment will not only be higher but exhibit more persistence.

8.2.4 Limitations and Extensions of the Model

In developing our analysis, we have made a number of simplifying assumptions regarding functional forms and the structure of bargaining between workers and firms. The question arises of how sensitive our results are to these assumptions. We have also carefully avoided using the term "union" to refer to the group of insiders. But it is clear that "union" would often have sounded more appropriate and the issue arises of whether our analysis is actually relevant in nonunion contexts. We now discuss these issues informally.

Other Bargaining Structures
It is well known that even in a one period model, it is in general inefficient to let the firm choose employment unilaterally given the wage (see, for example, Oswald, 1985). In our multiperiod model, the assumption that the firm chooses employment according to its short run profit maximizing labor demand is even more questionable. Even if bargaining takes the form of the union setting a wage and allowing the firm to control the level of employment, firms will not choose to operate on their short run labor demand curves. Through its employment decision, the firm can affect future membership (unless $m = \infty$). By employing more workers this

period, it can increase membership next period and thus lower the expected cost of labor. This will lead the firm to choose a level of employment higher than that implied by short run profit maximization. We suspect that taking account of this consideration would not substantially alter our analysis of employment dynamics. Rather, it would simply shift each period's labor demand curve outward.

Another important possibility would be for the firm to introduce two tier systems, where newly hired workers get lower wages than those hired previously. Under such systems, insiders should have no reluctance to let firms hire more workers, and employment should increase until new hirees are paid their reservation wage. The general reluctance of unions to accept such arrangements, especially in Europe, suggests that a central issue is that of what happens over time to those hired at lower wages. Unions do not encourage two tier arrangements at least in part because of the fear that second tier workers will come to control the wage setting process. Indeed the rarity of two tier arrangements is strong evidence for the relevance of the membership considerations stressed here. Without some such consideration, it is difficult to see why unions do not always favor such systems as a way of maximizing the rents that they can capture.

Going back to the setting of the wage, if we allow the wage not to be set unilaterally by the insiders but to be determined by bargaining between insiders and the firm, wages will depend both on the utility of insiders and on the value of the firm, the present discounted value of profits. Profit is a decreasing function of the wage. Thus, the larger is the weight of the firm in bargaining, the lower is the wage, and thus the higher the average level of employment. The implications for employment persistence depend on the weight of the firm in bargaining when the wage is far from the reservation level of workers. If the firm is relatively more powerful when the wage is much above the reservation wage, then the wage will tend to decrease when it is high; employment will tend to return to a higher level. Whether or not this happens depends on the structure of bargaining between insiders and the firm.

The specific utility function we have used for insiders is also important for our results. Its main implication, which we have argued is a desirable one, is that the probability of employment chosen by the group is invariant to the size of the group of insiders, or to the level of productivity. If instead an increase in membership given productivity led the group to choose both a lower wage and a lower probability of employment—which we can think of as the stochastic equivalent of elastic labor supply—employment would depend on both the anticipated and unanticipated components of productivity and may show less persistence. Even under the rule $m = 1$, an unanticipated increase in employment would, if the increase in productivity was temporary, lead to the choice of a lower wage and a lower probability of employment in the following period, implying an expected return to the initial level of employment over time. The same effects would also arise if as unemployment became larger and being unemployed became more costly, the group chose a higher probability of employment, leading to an expected increase in employment over time.

Groups or Unions?

Is our analysis still relevant when workers are not formally organized in unions, when, for example, wages are simply set unilaterally by the firm?

The work of Lindbeck and Snower (1986a, b, c) suggests that even in the absence of formal unions current workers have some leverage vis-à-vis firms. And Slichter (1950) provides confirming empirical evidence suggesting that even before unions were economically important, wages tended to be high in industries with relatively inelastic labor demand.

In many nonunion settings, current incumbent workers and prospective workers cannot be regarded symmetrically. The requirement of cooperation among workers and the collective knowledge possessed by incumbent workers make their position very different from that of prospective new workers. This leads us to suspect that the membership considerations we have stressed are at least somewhat applicable even in nonunion contexts. The potential applicability of our analysis to nonunion settings may be argued informally as follows. Imagine a firm facing a collection of insider workers. The firm must choose a wage and an employment level. It cannot credibly threaten to lay off all its workers and replace them, except at very high cost, because of the specialized expertise of its labor force. On the other hand, the firm cannot credibly threaten to replace workers individually with lower wage workers because the remainder of the labor force will not tolerate the hiring of "scabs." Under these conditions, wages and expected employment will be set in some way to divide the surplus resulting from a continued relationship between workers and firms. Workers will in general be able to extract some surplus even when they are unorganized. If firms make an "inadequate" wage offer, they can refuse to work. As long as they have some specific capital, it will be preferable for management to make another higher offer rather than lay the worker off.

If agreements are renegotiated only periodically and firms are permitted to vary employment in the interim, shocks will in general influence the level of employment. Even without a formal model of the bargaining process between workers and firms, it seems reasonable to expect that a reduction in the number of incumbent workers will lead to the setting of a higher wage and a lower level of expected employment. Thus persistence in employment, though not necessarily as much as with unions, may result even in that case. Note that this also may help explain what goes on in the nonunion sector of economies with large unions.

This argument is clearly tentative. But we conclude from it that, while the effects we have described are more likely to be present when there are explicit unions, they may also arise in settings in which insider-outsider considerations are important.

The Presence of a Nonunion Sector

We finally consider how our conclusions must be modified if part of the labor market is neither unionized nor subject to insider-outsider considerations.

The simplest analysis of a setting with a competitive sector would hold that there was no involuntary unemployment. Wages in the nonunion sector would fall to the point where all those workers ejected from the union sector could find employment.[20] There are at least three reasons why, even granting the existence of a competitive sector, this analysis is suspect. First, competitive firms may be reluctant to lower wages because of the fear of being unionized after they have alienated their current labor force. Second, unemployment benefits may be sufficiently high that the market clearing wage in the nonunion sector is below some workers' reservation wage. In one sense their unemployment is voluntary since jobs are available. In another sense the unemployment is involuntary since the unemployed may envy workers with the same skill in the union sector. The general consideration is that when there are wage differentials across jobs, the concept of involuntary unemployment becomes elusive (see Bulow and Summers, 1985, for an elaboration of that theme). Third, unemployment may occur even with a competitive sector if remaining unemployed is in some sense useful—or thought to be useful by workers—in getting a union job. This may occur if substantial search effort or queuing is required or alternatively if accepting a low quality job sends a bad signal to employers. This unemployment is related to that of Harris and Todaro (1970), where workers must migrate to urban areas to have a chance at high wage urban jobs.

There is a more fundamental point regarding the inability of a nonunion sector to prevent unemployment. As Weitzman (1982) persuasively argues, there are strong reasons to believe that most economic activity involves fixed costs and monopolistic competition. Imagine a monopolistically competitive economy with fixed costs of production and constant marginal costs where there is initially no involuntary unemployment. Suppose that an adverse demand shock reduces the demand for goods in this economy but that nominal wages remain constant in all existing firms. Then employment and output will fall as will the profitability of existing firms. Will it pay new firms to enter the market and hire the unemployed at low wages? It may not because, unlike incumbent firms, new firms must cover fixed as well as variable costs. Particularly in settings where labor costs do not represent a large fraction of sales, entry may not be able to insure the employment of the unemployed.[21] These considerations may enhance the power of unions because they reduce the incentive to start up new non-union firms.

8.3 Empirical Evidence on Hysteresis Theories

Having developed a formal theory of hysteresis, we now examine whether the model is consistent with the observed patterns of persistently increasing unemployment in Europe and whether it can illuminate the very different behavior of unemployment in Europe and the United States in the recent past. We start by giving direct, institutional evidence on the strength of unions in Europe. We then estimate wage and employment equations implied by our model, for both Europe and the United States. We finally examine patterns of labor market turnover, in the United Kingdom and the United States.

8.3.1 The Role of Unions in Europe

The Size of the Union Sector
Our model suggests that, even if hysteresis may arise in nonunion contexts, it is probably more likely to arise the stronger and the larger the union sector. Thus, we start by reviewing the role of unions in Europe; we limit, as before, our investigation to the United Kingdom, France, and Germany.[22]

Membership figures indicate a union density of approximately 45% for the United Kingdom, 20% for France, and 38% for Germany. But these figures give very limited information as to the strength of unions. A better indicator is union coverage, that is, of the proportion of workers covered by some form of collective bargaining. For the United Kingdom, coverage is of approximately 70% for manual workers, and of 55% for nonmanual workers. For France and Germany, the proportion of all workers exceeds 80%. But even coverage numbers are misleading. To understand why, one must be given some institutional background.

On the surface, the three countries appear to be very different. In France there are three main national unions. In Germany, there are only industry unions. In the United Kingdom, there is a maze of craft and industry unions. But the structure of bargaining is in fact quite similar and can be described as follows: in all three countries, most of the formal bargaining is done at the industry level. But, in all three countries, wages are determined much more at the company or plant level.

In the United Kingdom, industry bargaining sets rates, which are usually floors that have little effect on actual wages. Until the Employment Act of 1980, there was scope for extension, that is, for provisions to extend the terms of the agreement to the whole sector. These provisions have been eliminated in 1980. In the last 20 years, there has been an increase in the amount of bargaining, both formal and informal, at the plant level, between shop stewards and employers. Given that plant/company bargaining is the really important level of bargaining, it is relevant to look at how many workers are covered by both industry and plant/company level bargaining. In 1978, the number of workers covered by at least a company agreement was 33% for all industries and 47.7% for manufacturing. Given the importance of informal bargaining, these figures understate the importance of unions in setting wages.

In France, the "Conventions collectives," which are usually but not always at the industry level, perform most of the formal bargaining. These agreements are signed between a "representative" union and a "representative" employer and apply even if not all unions sign it (which is frequently the case). Subject to some minor conditions, they can be extended to all firms in the industry, by decision of the Minister of Labor. As in the United Kingdom, however, the importance of industry agreements with respect to wages should not be exaggerated. They usually set floors, which do not appear, either directly or indirectly, to have a large effect on actual wages. As in the United Kingdom, a growing portion of the bargaining takes place at the company level, although often in haphazard fashion. Until 1982, wages were largely determined unilaterally by firms, or in response to complaints of union representatives in the plant, with little bargaining or even consultation; local strikes were, however, a standard instrument used by unions to achieve a better deal. Since 1982, there has been a change in the law (Lois Auroux) that requires annual bargaining at the company level on pay and other matters. The result has been a drastic increase in the number of company level agreements.

In Germany, most of the formal bargaining again takes place at the industry level. Agreements can be extended—to either firms in the same industry or to nonunion workers in firms that sign the agreements—by the state or federal Minister of Labor if (1) half of the employees of the sector are employed by firms that have signed the agreeement and (2) extension is approved by both unions and employers who have signed.[23] But, as in the other two countries, bargaining is increasingly taking place at the company level and there is general agreement that pay is very largely determined at the company level.

To conclude, it is difficult to give an exact estimate of the "union sector" in these countries. To the extent that much bargaining over wages in fact takes place at the company level, union coverage numbers, which are based on both company and industry level bargaining, probably overstate the number of workers for whom the wage is determined as a result of bargaining between unions and employers. Even with this adjustment, the size of the union sector still remains high, much higher than in the United States. Also, if we believe that the more disaggregated the level of bargaining the less likely it is to take into account the interests of the unemployed as a whole, then these countries are good candidates for hysteresis in the union sector.[24]

An alternative approach is to ask the question, Can a firm be nonunion? Can a firm become nonunion? In the United Kingdom, the answer is yes: a firm can be or can become nonunion. There is nothing in the law that prevents it. There are some well known examples of nonunion firms, most often subsidiaries of U.S. companies (Kodak). There are very few examples of firms going nonunion.[25] In France and Germany, extension agreements put some constraints on firms in a given sector. There are nonunion firms in both countries. In France, these are nearly exclusively small firms. In France furthermore, various requirements are imposed on firms with more than 50 employees. In particular, they must allow for the presence of "délégués du personnel" who are union representatives within the firm. All national unions have a right to be represented. Since 1978, firms must also allow for the presence of a "section syndicale d'entreprise," for the presence of the union inside the firm. Together, these facts suggest that it is difficult to be or go nonunion in these countries.

Finally, there is the question of how different the nonunion sector is from the union sector. A study by Kaufman (1984) of the competitive sector in the United Kingdom finds relatively little difference in wage behavior across the two sectors. Together with the arguments given in the previous section, this suggests that the size of the formal union sector may not be a major determinant of the extent of hysteresis. We shall return to this question in the next section.

Membership Rules

Membership rules determining whom the union represents at each point in time play an important role in our analysis. The empirical evidence on actual membership rules is fairly clear: workers have the right to join unions if they want to. Workers who are laid off can remain in the union although they often lose the right to vote; this may happen either because of formal restrictions or because voting takes place inside the plant. But this tells us little about the question of in whose interest the union actually acts. A study of the unemployed and the unions in the United Kingdom (Barker et al., 1984) gives some information. It finds that, while laid off workers are officially encouraged to remain in the union and have their union fees waived, they do not, for the most part, see reasons to stay in the union.[26] This provides support for the idea that the union cares mostly about the currently employed.

8.3.2 Wage and Employment Equations

Theory

We now derive, and then estimate later, the wage and employment equations associated with an expanded version of the model of the previous section. There are two extensions. First, we allow for a dynamic specification of labor demand; the reason for introducing it will be clear below. Second, we specify explicitly an alternative hypothesis to that of hysteresis.

We thus specify labor demand as[27]

$$n = sn_{-1} - (1 - s)b(w - p) + e. \tag{8}$$

Following the analysis of the previous section, we assume that the union acts to set expected employment according to the relation

$$En = (1 - a)n^* + an_{-1}. \tag{9}$$

The case where $a = 1$ corresponds to the case where $m = 1$ in the preceding section and there is hysteresis; the case where $a = 0$ corresponds to the case where the union's policy is independent of history and so there is no hysteresis. Clearly, intermediate outcomes are also possible.[28]

Finally, let the wage that satsifies (8) and (9) be denoted by w^*. We assume the actual wage to be given by

$$w = w^* + u,$$

where the disturbance term u is assumed to be white, uncorrelated with w^* and reflects factors outside the model. Combining this assumption with equations (8) and (9) yields a wage and an employment equation:

$$w = Ep + (1/b(1 - s))[-(1 - a)n^* + (s - a)n_{-1} + Ee] + u, \qquad (10)$$

$$n = (1 - a)n^* + an_{-1} + [e - Ee + (1 - s)b(p - Ep - u)]. \qquad (11)$$

The wage equation holds that the wage of the union is a decreasing function of n^*. When the union is larger, it is more cautious in setting wages. The impact of n_{-1} is ambiguous. A larger value of n_{-1} raises the size of the group in whose interest the union is maximizing but it also increases labor demand.

The employment equation on the other hand implies that employment follows a first order process. The degree of persistence depends only on a, not at all on s. Unexpected movements in employment are due to price and productivity surprises, and deviations of wages from target. Equation (11) can be estimated by OLS (ordinary least squares). This is, however, not the case for equation (10): expected productivity is likely to be correlated with past productivity and thus with past employment. Therefore we now derive the reduced form wage equation. To do so requires an assumption about the process followed by e: we assume that e follows a random walk.[29] Lagging (8) and substituting it in (11) yields

$$w - w_{-1} = k + (Ep - p_{-1}) + (1/b(1 - s))[(1 + s - a)n_{-1} - sn_{-2}] + u, \qquad (12)$$

where $k \equiv -(1/b(1 - s))(1 - a)n^*$.

This equation can be estimated by OLS. It gives the rate of wage inflation as a function of expected price inflation, and employment lagged once and twice. It is worth examining further.

Consider first the case where there are no costs of adjustment in labor demand. In this case the relation gives a relation between expected real wage growth and lagged employment only. If $a = 1$, then expected wage growth does not depend on employment but if $a < 1$, it does: after an unexpected decline in productivity, which leads to lower employment, the remaining workers accept a cut in real wages only to the extent that they care about the workers who have been laid off.

Table 8.4A
Wage equations 1953–84[a]

Country	π_{t-1}	$\log E_t$	$\log E_{t-1}$	$\log E_{t-2}$	Time × 100	θ	D.W.	R^2
Germany								
(1)	.6[b]	—	.92	.80		.07	1.99	.54
			(4.0)	(−4.2)		(.3)		
(2)	.6[b]	—	.71	−.57	−.12	.04	2.03	.59
			(2.4)	(−2.2)	(1.5)	(.2)		
(3)	.6[b]	1.12	−.89			−.10	2.00	.74
		(9.6)	(−8.9)			(−.5)		
(4)	.6[b]	(.96)	−.74		−.07	−.13	2.01	.76
		(6.2)	(−5.1)		(−1.5)	(−.7)		
United Kingdom								
(5)	.75[b]	—	.67	−.76	—	.25	2.01	.23
			(2.6)	(−2.5)		(1.5)		
(6)	.75[b]	—	.86	−.84	.19	.09	1.97	.31
			(3.2)	(−2.8)	(1.9)	(.5)		
(7)	.75[b]	.13	−.08	—	—	.21	1.83	.07
		(.4)	(−.2)			(1.0)		
(8)	.75[b]	.34	−.19	—	.20	.16	1.84	.15
		(1.0)	(−.5)		(1.5)	(.7)		
France								
(9)	.8[b]	—	.58	−.39	—	—	2.03	.12
			(1.5)	(−.9)				
(10)	.8[b]	—	.61	−.42	.00	−.05	1.92	.13
			(1.2)	(−.7)	(.0)	(−.2)		
(11)	.8[b]	.97	−.74	—	—	—	2.04	.29
		(2.9)	(−2.1)					
(12)	.8[b]	1.28	−1.16	—	.12	—	2.09	.33
		(3.1)	(−2.1)		(1.2)			
United States								
(13)	.7[b]	—	−.07	.00		.54	2.03	.26
			(−.8)	(.0)		(2.2)		
(14)	.7[b]	—	−.07	.00	.00	.54	2.02	.26
			(−.8)	(.0)	(.0)	(2.2)		
(15)	.7[b]	.24	−.25	—	—	.48	1.98	.49
		(4.6)	(−4.8)			(2.5)		
(16)	.7[b]	.28	−.16	—	−.13	.34	1.99	.63
		(5.9)	(−3.3)		(−3.9)	(1.7)		

Source: OECD data bank, extended back to 1950 by D. Grubb. See Grubb (1984).
a. $\dot{w}$, rate of change of average hourly earnings in manufacturing; π, rate of change of the consumer price index; E, manufacturing employment. t-statistics in parentheses. All equations for Europe are run with a first order autocorrelation correction. All equations for the United States are run with a first order moving average correction.
b. Coefficient from a regression of π on $\pi(-1)$ for each country for the sample period.

Table 8.4B
Wage equation residuals 1953−84[a]

Year	Germany	United Kingdom	France	United States
1980	− 1.91	1.7	1.6	− 1.2
1981	− .32	− 4.1	1.4	− .8
1982	− .75	3.9	− .0	− .1
1983	.57	− 2.7	.1	− .9
1984	− .44	1.1	− 1.5	.3
	$\sigma = 1.87$	$\sigma = 3.2$	$\sigma = 3.9$	$\sigma = 1.5$

a. Residuals are from equations (3), (5), (11), and (15) in table 8.4A.

If there are costs of adjustment to employment, then expected real wage growth depends on employment lagged both once and twice. If $a = 0$, then the ratio of employment lagged twice to employment lagged once cannot exceed $1/2$ (in absolute value). But as a increases, the ratio tends to one. If $a = 1$, the ratio equals unity: expected real wage growth depends on the change rather than on the level of employment.

Note that we cannot identify a and s separately from estimation of the wage equation. But a must be positive if we find the ratio described above to be larger than $1/2$. Furthermore, a can be directly obtained from the employment equation.

While we have derived the wage equation (12) from a rather specific theory of union behavior, it can be motivated in other ways. Following the logic of the monopolistic competitive model in the preceding section just as we have followed the logic of the competitive model gives rise to an equation for wage inflation paralleling (12). Much more generally, equation (12) is very close to a standard Phillips curve that allows for a rate of change effect, à la Lipsey. The only real difference is the presence of employment rather than unemployment on the right-hand side. We now turn to estimation of the wage and employment equations.

Results
The results of estimation of the wage equations for the United Kingdom, France, Germany, and the United States, for the period 1953−84, are reported in tables 8.4A and 8.5.

In table 8.4A, four alternative specifications of the wage equation are estimated for each country. Because the appropriate timing is unclear with annual data, we estimate the equations using alternatively contemporaneous and once lagged employment, and once and twice lagged employ-

Table 8.5
Wage change equations 1953–84[a]

Country	π_{t-1}	U_t	U_{t-1}	U_{t-2}	Time × 100	ρ	D.W.	R^2
Germany								
(1)	.6[b]	—	−2.86	2.62	—	.30	1.97	.57
			(−4.3)	(3.8)		(1.6)		
(2)	.6[b]	—	−2.41	2.12	−.08	.27	1.94	.59
			(−3.0)	(2.6)	(−1.1)	(1.4)		
(3)	.6[b]	−2.39	1.68	—	—	.06	1.99	.50
		(−4.0)	(2.6)			(.3)		
(4)	.6[b]	−1.60	.95	—	−.10	.08	2.00	.54
		(−2.1)	(1.2)		(−1.5)	(.4)		
United Kingdom								
(5)	.75[b]	—	−2.31	2.58	—	.04	2.02	.33
			(−3.6)	(3.4)		(.2)		
(6)	.75[b]	—	−2.57	2.46	.14	(−.03)	2.02	.37
			(−4.0)	(3.3)	(1.4)	−.2		
(7)	.75[b]	−.96	.78	—	—	.22	1.83	.12
		(−1.0)	(.7)			(1.0)		
(8)	.75[b]	−1.43	.62	—	.28	.13	1.85	.25
		(−2.0)	(.8)		(2.4)	(.6)		
France								
(9)	.8[b]	—	−1.42	1.35	—	.07	1.93	.03
			(−.7)	(.6)		(.4)		
(10)	.8[b]	—	−3.01	2.10	.25	−.10	1.86	.15
			(−1.3)	(.9)	(2.1)	(−.5)		
(11)	.8[b]	−3.57	3.78	—	—	.13	1.99	.14
		(−1.97)	(1.8)			(.7)		
(12)	.8[b]	−4.97	4.12	—	.33	−.10	1.91	.33
		(−2.9)	(2.2)		(3.0)	(.5)		
United States								
(13)	.7[b]	—	−.07	−.06	—	.40		
			(−.2)	(−.1)		(1.3)		
(14)	.7[b]	—	.11	.07	−.07	.47	2.01	.24
			(.3)	(.2)	(−1.7)	(1.6)		
(15)	.7[b]	−1.02	.47	—	—	.41	1.99	.62
		(−6.0)	(2.9)			(2.2)		
(16)	.7[b]	−1.05	.43	—	.02	.42	1.99	.63
		(−5.8)	(2.4)		(.6)	(2.2)		

Source: OECD and Grubb (1984).
a. See table 8.4A. U, standardized unemployment rate.
b. Coefficient from a regression of π on $\pi(-1)$ for each country for the sample period.

ment.[30] We also estimate each equation with and without a time trend; many researchers have captured the shift of the Phillips curve by a time trend, that is, by an increase over time unrelated to the history of unemployment, and it is interesting to see what happens to our specification when a time trend is allowed. This gives us the four alternative specifications. Finally, we use for expected inflation the forecast of inflation obtained from estimation of an AR(1) process for inflation over the sample period and constrain the coefficient on expected inflation (which is therefore equal to a constant plus a scalar times lagged inflation) to equal unity.

In table 8.5, we perform the same set of estimations, but using unemployment rather than employment as a right-hand side variable. We do this because unemployment is the variable used in standard Phillips curve specifications. Some theories of hysteresis, such as the idea that the long term unemployed exert less pressure on wages than those recently laid off, also suggest that unemployment is more appropriate than employment in the Phillips curve.

Tables 8.6 and 8.7 give the results of estimation of the employment and unemployment processes for each country for the period 1953–84. Here again, while our theory has implications only for employment, we think it is useful to report results for unemployment as well.

The results are fairly clearcut and indicate that there are substantial differences between the European countries and the United States. Starting with the wage equations, one can draw the following conclusions:

(1) Virtually all specifications for Germany, France, and the United Kingdom in tables 8.4A and 8.5 suggest a substantial degree of hysteresis.

Let us denote by R the absolute value of the ratio of the coefficient on lagged employment (unemployment) to the coefficient on contemporaneous employment (unemployment)—or of the coefficient on employment (unemployment) lagged twice to the coefficient on employment lagged once as the case may be. As we have seen, under strict hysteresis ($a = 1$) this ratio should be equal to unity. R is indeed close to unity for nearly all specifications; it is not affected by the inclusion of a time trend, or by the use of employment versus unemployment. There is little difference across countries: R is higher in the UK, sometimes exceeding unity. It is closer on average to .85 for Germany and France.[31]

The time trend itself contributes little. If the increase in unemployment was due to an autonomous increase in the natural rate over time, the coefficient on the time trend should be positive. Only in the United Kingdom when employment is used, and in the United Kingdom and France when unemployment is used, is the time trend positive and either

Table 8.6
Employment processes 1953–84[a]

Country	ρ	θ	$\alpha \times 100$	R^2
Germany				
	.76	1.00	—	.96
	(22.3)	(5.3)	—	
	.86	.78	-1.9×10^{-2}	.97
	(26.7)	(3.9)	(.0)	
United Kingdom				
	1.07	.54	—	.96
	(23.3)	(2.6)	—	
	.95	.41	$-.20$	.94
	(16.3)	(2.0)	(-3.8)	
France				
	.94	.81	—	.94
	(19.5)	(3.0)	—	
	1.08	.48	$-.13$	.94
	(19.5)	(2.5)	(-4.0)	
United States				
	.82	.07	—	.72
	(7.5)	(.3)	—	
	.34	.46	.40	.77
	(1.5)	(1.6)	(2.5)	

a. Results of estimation of

$$\log E = \rho \log E(-1) + \alpha(\text{TIME}) + \varepsilon + \varepsilon\theta(-1).$$

E, manufacturing employment.

Table 8.7
Unemployment processes 1953−84[a]

Country	ρ	θ	$\alpha \times 100$	R^2
Germany				
	.92	.65	—	.91
	(14.8)	(3.4)	—	
	.94	.39	.06	.93
	(17.5)	(1.9)	(5.0)	
United Kingdom				
	1.02	.77	—	.95
	(20.9)	(3.9)	—	
	.81	.82	.09	.96
	(9.9)	(3.9)	(3.5)	
France				
	1.12	−.06	—	.97
	(32.7)	(−.3)	—	
	1.04	−.22	.02	.97
	(18.2)	(−1.1)	(1.4)	
United States				
	.72	.06	—	.58
	(4.5)	(.2)	—	
	.36	.31	.07	.63
	(1.4)	(.9)	(1.9)	

a. Results of estimation of
$U = \rho U(-1) + \alpha(\text{TIME}) + \varepsilon + \theta\varepsilon(-1)$.
U, standardized unemployment.

significant or marginally significant. Even then, its quantitative contribution is small. In the case in which it is largest and most significant (equation (12) for France in table 8.5), it only explains a 1.5% increase in the unemployment rate consistent with a given level of expected real wage growth over the sample period. Further evidence that the apparent increase in the natural rate through time is a consequence of rising unemployment and not autonomous comes from the absence of substantial serial correlation in our estimated Phillips curves. An upward drift in the constant term would manifest itself in the form of serial correlation.

A final piece of evidence is given in table 8.4B, which reports the residuals associated with the best fitting equations from table 8.4A, not including a time trend, for each country, for 1980–84. There is little evidence of significant prediction errors in recent years. This is in sharp contrast to the performance of wage equations, which do not allow lagged employment to enter.

(2) In contrast to the results for Europe, the results for the United States provide evidence of much less hysteresis. There is evidence of a significant effect of either lagged employment or lagged unemployment. But, with the exception of one specification using employment, the value of R for the United States is smaller than for Europe, being in most cases around .5. There is also no evidence in favor of a time trend in the wage equation.

(3) A comparison of the results of estimation in tables 8.4A and 8.5 does not give a clear answer as to whether employment or unemployment belongs in the wage equation. Using R^2 gives a draw, with employment doing better for France, unemployment doing better for the United Kingdom. We have also run regressions including current and lagged values of both unemployment and employment—or equivalently, employment and the labor force. They give the same ambiguous answer, with the labor force being significant in the United Kingdom, but not in France or Germany. We see the United Kingdom results, however, as presenting a problem for our model.

The employment and unemployment equations reported in tables 8.6 and 8.7 confirm to a large extent the conclusions from the wage equations. Both unemployment and employment are more persistent in Europe than in the United States. In particular, the process generating unemployment appears nonstationary in all three European countries, whether or not a time trend is included in the regressions. The U.S. process is, instead, stationary. The data, however, strongly suggest that an ARMA(1, 1), rather than the AR(1) process implied by our theory, is needed to fit the employment and unemployment processes of all four countries. This may reflect a difference between the length of a period in the model and annual frequency of observation used in the estimation.

8.3.3 Patterns of Labor Market Turnover

A central element in our theory of hysteresis is the lack of concern of employed workers for the unemployed. It is the fear of job loss for current workers and not the outstanding labor market pool that restrains wage demands. Indeed the formal model explains why firms hire at all only by assuming that wages that are set low enough to insure the jobs of current workers will sometimes make it profitable for firms to hire new workers. While this is clearly an oversimplification, the point remains that insider-outsider or union models of the type we have considered are really theories of why the unemployed are not hired, not theories of why layoffs take place. This suggests the utility of looking at data on labor market turnover. A finding of high turnover with many workers having short spells of unemployment and then being rehired would tend to cast doubt on the relevance of insider-outsider formulations, while a finding that the rate of flow into and out of employment was relatively low but that the unemployed remained out of work for a very long time would tend to support these theories.

Table 8.8 presents some evidence on the rate of flow into unemployment in the United States and United Kingdom over the past decade. The flow is measured as the number of persons becoming unemployed over a three month period. For the United States, this is estimated as the number of unemployed reporting durations of less than 14 weeks. For Britain it is the number of unemployment registrants over a three month period.

Two conclusions emerge clearly from the table. First, despite the much higher rate of unemployment in the United Kingdom than in the United States, the rate of flow into unemployment is actually lower there. The implication is that the unemployment problem is not one of an excessive rate of job loss but of an insufficient rate of hiring of the unemployed. The second striking feature of the data is that the rate of flow into unemployment in Britain has increased surprisingly little as unemployment has soared. Between 1970 and 1984 when the rate of unemployment in Britain rose more than 300%, the rate of flow into unemployment has risen by only about 75%. This pattern of rising unemployment with only a modest increase in the rate of inflow appears more pronounced in British than American labor markets. In the United States, the inflow rate has accounted for a significant part of the increase in unemployment during recession

Table 8.8
Patterns of inflow to unemployment

Year	United States		Great Britain
	Number unemployed less than 14 weeks as a percent of employment	$\dfrac{14 \times \text{unemployed}}{\text{employment} \times \text{average duration (weeks)}} \times 100$	Quarterly inflow as a percent of employment[a]
1970	4.4	8.4	3.3
1971	4.8	7.8	3.6
1972	4.5	6.9	3.6
1973	4.2	7.2	2.9
1974	4.8	8.5	3.2
1975	6.3	9.2	4.2
1976	5.7	7.4	4.9
1977	5.5	7.5	4.7
1978	5.0	7.6	4.5
1979	5.0	8.0	4.2
1980	5.8	9.0	4.9
1981	6.0	8.4	5.2
1982	7.2	9.6	5.5
1983	6.5	7.4	5.5
1984	5.5	6.2	5.6

a. Average of quarterly values.

Table 8.9
The importance of long term unemployment

	United States		United Kingdom		Germany		France	
	1980	1984	1980	1984	1980	1984	1980	1984
Unemployment rate	7.2	7.5	6.5	12.7	3.4	8.1	6.6	10.0
Average duration of unemployment for adult men currently unemployed	3.6	5.8	12.2	19.4	8.6	12.6	12.6	14.4
Percent contribution to adult male unemployment of those unemployed at least								
6 months	50	72	91	96	85	92	92	93
12 months	15	39	74	87	59	75	75	80
18 months	4	18	57	76	38	58	58	64
24 months	1	8	41	65	23	43	43	56

Source: Based on authors' calculation.

periods. For example, between 1979 and 1982, unemployment increased by 67% and the inflow rate rose by 44%.

The OECD (1985) summarizes the fragmentary information available on labor market turnover for other European nations. The data in general parallel our findings for Britain—suggesting relatively modest increases in the rate of flow into unemployment starting from a very low base. They do suggest, however, that the composition of the newly unemployed has changed over time as the unemployment rate has increased. Layoff rates have increased while quit rates have declined.

Given the magnitude of the increases in European unemployment rates and the relatively small increases in flow rates, it is inevitable that unemployment durations have increased substantially. Table 8.9 presents some information on the increasing importance of long term unemployment in Europe. Along with information on the average duration of unemployment, it presents estimates of the fraction of all unemployment due to persons whose complete spells will exceed various threshold lengths.[32] The table demonstrates that at the same level of unemployment, long term unemployment is much more important in Europe. In 1980, when the American unemployment rate was 7.2%, only an estimated 15% of all unemployment was due to persons out of work for more than a year. The corresponding percentages were 74%, 59%, and 75% in the United Kingdom, Germany, and France even though the unemployment rates were lower. The table also demonstrates that long term unemployment has increased in importance as overall unemployment rates have risen in Europe. Indeed, the increase in duration of unemployment is almost proportional to the increase in unemployment.

Summary

In this section, we have shown that unions play an important role in Europe and that the behavior of European unemployment is consistent with our hypothesis about hysteresis. It is obviously tempting to conclude that unions are at the root of the European problem. But the temptation must be strongly resisted. First, even if unions create hysteresis, they just create a channel for persistence, which implies that both favorable and adverse shocks will have long lasting effects. The sequence of unfavorable shocks at least some of which are the consequence of policy may equally well be said to be the cause of persistent high unemployment. Second, it is as yet unclear whether the cause of hysteresis in Europe is unions or the sequence of adverse shocks that have caused high unemployment. We consider this issue in the next section.

8.4 Is Eurosclerosis Really the Problem?

The previous section has shown that our model of persistent unemployment may explain important aspects of the current European depression and the very different behavior of European and American labor markets. The evidence presented so far leaves open a crucial question, however. Is the presence of hysteresis in European unemployment a consequence of the heavily regulated and unionized character of European labor markets? Alternatively, is hysteresis the result of a sequence of adverse shocks to employment? The case that major structural reforms are needed if full employment in Europe is to be restored depends on an affirmative answer to the first question, while the case for expansionary macroeconomic policies is more compelling if the second question can be given a positive answer.

Resolving whether the source of hysteresis lies ultimately in European institutions or in the sequence of adverse shocks that have buffeted European economies requires comparisons of the current situation with situations where only one of these elements is present. Comparison with the

United States at present cannot resolve the issue because the American economy lacks institutions like those in Europe and has not suffered a sequence of contractionary aggregate demand shocks like those experienced by Europe in the 1980s. But we are able to make two comparisons that can shed some light on the sources of hysteresis. The first is a comparison of the behavior of European labor markets in the recent period with their behavior over the 1953–68 period. Broadly speaking, labor market institutions were similar in the two periods but the patterns of shocks was very different.[33] The second comparison is between the current European depression and the U.S. depression of the 1930s. At the time of the U.S. depression, unions were weak, social programs and labor market regulations were a small factor, and there were few if any important adverse supply shocks. The U.S. depression may also shed light on the role of expansionary policies in alleviating persistent high unemployment. We consider these comparisons in turn.

8.4.1 European Labor Markets before the Current Depression

The previous section has examined the persistence of unemployment and the behavior of wages in Europe over the past 35 years. This long interval contains the current depression period and the period of unparalleled prosperity of the 1950s and 1960s. We examine the extent to which hysteresis is a product of bad times by considering labor market behavior separately over each of the two periods. Table 8.10 presents estimates of the stochastic process followed by unemployment separately for the 1952–68 and 1969–84 periods.[34] The degree of persistence in unemployment in Europe is much higher in the latter period when unemployment was high. Similar but somewhat less dramatic results are obtained using employment rather than unemployment. For the earlier sample period, unemployment appears to be more persistent in the United States than in the United Kingdom or France. These results tend to suggest that hysteresis is a feature of bad times rather than a consequence of the structure of European labor markets.

Table 8.11 presents estimates of wage change equations paralleling those reported in table 8.5, but now for the 1953–67 period. Taken together the results suggest somewhat less hysteresis in the 1953–67 period than is present over the whole sample period, with the difference being pronounced in the United Kingdom, where the ratio R, which was close to one for the full sample, is now close to .5. However, the results for the 1953–67 period, like those for the entire period, suggest a greater degree

Table 8.10
The persistence of unemployment in good and bad times[a]

Country	ρ	θ	SE regression
France			
1952−68	.41	.81	.3
	(1.1)	(1.8)	
1968−84	1.11	−.48	.4
	(5.0)	(1.4)	
Germany			
1952−68	.86	.22	.5
	(12.3)	(.9)	
1968−84	1.07	.51	.8
	(5.1)	(1.4)	
United Kingdom			
1952−68	.01	.97	.5
	(.0)	(2.5)	
1968−84	1.0	.99	.9
	(27.6)	(3.8)	
United States			
1952−68	.75	−.37	1.0
	(1.6)	(−.7)	
1968−84	.59	.50	1.1
	(1.7)	(1.1)	

a. The results represent estimates of an ARMA(1,1) process for the unemployment rate.

of hysteresis in Europe than in the United States. The fact that persistence is present in the early period in Europe to a greater degree than in the United States but that it becomes increasingly important as the unemployment rate increases makes it difficult to draw any firm conclusion about its causes.

On balance, evidence on the changing behavior of European labor markets suggests that bad times as well as unions account for findings of hysteresis. But this evidence is not sufficiently powerful to permit a judgment about their relative importance.

8.4.2 A Tale of Two Depressions

Salient features of many discussions of the current European depression include pessimistic forecasts that unemployment will never return to earlier

Table 8.11
Wage equations 1953–67

Country	π_{t-1}	U_{t-1}	U_{t-2}	Time $\times$ 100	ρ	D.W.	R^2
Germany							
(1)	.6[a]	−6.48	5.86	—	−.14	1.91	.55
		(−3.7)	(3.7)		(−.4)		
(2)	.6[a]	−6.25	4.53	−.60	−.14	2.07	.60
		(−3.6)	(2.2)	(−1.1)	(−.4)		
United Kingdom							
(3)	.75[a]	−2.91	1.89	—	−.00	1.71	.50
		(−3.2)	(2.0)		(.0)		
(4)	.75[a]	−3.49	1.74	.16	−.17	1.71	.57
		(−3.8)	(1.9)	(1.4)	(−.5)		
France							
(5)	.9[a]	−6.11	4.53	—	−.47	2.18	.61
		(−3.8)	(2.8)		(−1.8)		
(6)	.9[a]	−6.25	4.12	−.06	−.50	2.19	.62
		(−3.8)	(2.3)	(−.5)	(−1.9)		
United States							
(7)	.7[a]	−1.23	.37	—	.73	2.05	.66
		(−5.2)	(1.7)				
(8)	.7[b]	−1.25	.57	−.17	−.04	1.90	.86
		(−7.0)	(3.2)	(−4.2)	(−.1)		

a. See tables 8.4A and 8.5.

levels, concern that reduced investment and lower capital stocks have made it impossible to employ the entire labor force, and fears that expansionary policies will lead directly into inflation with little or no favorable impact on output or employment. These pessimistic views are premised on the conviction that structural problems are central to high unemployment in Europe, and that the causes of persistent high unemployment go beyond a sequence of adverse shocks. Yet the American depression of the 1930s was ended by the expansion in aggregate demand associated with rearmament. Unemployment recovered to pre-Depression levels. Recovery was not inhibited by an insufficient capital stock or by the overly rapid adjustment of wages and prices. Are this experience and the current European experience sufficiently comparable to permit the inference that hysteresis arises from a sequence of adverse shocks rather than from structural problems in the labor market? Or do major differences in the character of the American and European depressions render the American experience irrelevant for thinking about current European problems?

We begin by briefly reviewing the record of the American economy over the 1925–45 period. A number of basic economic statistics are presented in table 8.12. The outstanding feature of the period is of course the dramatic upsurge in unemployment that began in 1929. Unemployment rose from levels comparable to those experienced in Europe in the late 1960s and early 1970s to 25% in 1933 and remained above 14% until 1940. As in Europe today employment actually declined over a 10 year period despite a rapidly increasing population. Beginning in late 1939 with the declaration of war in Europe, unemployment began to decline rapidly as rearmament stimulated the economy. The benefits of increased defense spending spilled over widely into the rest of the economy. While there were only 822,000 men in the Army in November 1940 and 2.1 million a year later, nonagricultural employment increased by 16% or 6 million persons between 1939 and 1941. Production of a variety of nondefense goods increased rapidly. Mitchell (1947) reports that between 1939 and 1941 automobile sales rose by 35%, refrigerators by 69%, and washing machines by 63%. Overall industrial production rose 20%.

These rapid improvements in economic performance were unexpected. Indeed in the wake of the 1937 recession many observers had despaired of any eventual return to full employment. Paul Samuelson noted in 1944 that "in the years just prior to 1939 there were noticeable signs of dwindling interest in the problem of unemployment which took the form of ostrich-like attempts to think away the very fact of unemployment by recourse to bad arithmetic and doubtful statistical techniques. And even among econo-

Table 8.12
The American economy 1925−45

Year	U	$\dot{w}$ (all workers)	$\dot{p}$ (CPI)	Index of productivity	Nonresidential capital (1958$)
1925	3.2	.9	4.0	92.6	211.0
1926	1.8	1.5	0.0	95.0	218.7
1927	3.3	3.2	−6.0	95.4	223.9
1928	4.2	.3	−1.0	96.1	229.3
1929	3.2	3.5	−1.0	100.0	236.6
1930	8.9	−0.6	−3.0	97.0	238.8
1931	16.3	−5.0	−8.3	98.5	233.5
1932	24.1	−8.9	−9.0	95.4	222.8
1933	25.2	−5.8	−5.0	93.2	212.2
1934	22.0	12.0	2.6	103.3	203.9
1935	20.3	2.3	2.6	106.7	198.3
1936	17.0	1.9	1.2	111.3	197.0
1937	14.3	5.9	3.7	110.4	198.4
1938	19.1	1.8	−2.4	113.5	194.5
1939	17.2	1.2	−1.2	117.6	192.2
1940	14.6	2.4	1.2	122.2	193.6
1941	9.9	9.7	4.9	124.2	198.3
1942	4.7	26.9	10.5	123.3	193.5
1943	1.9	10.6	6.3	124.6	186.5
1944	1.2	7.8	2.0	134.4	183.0
1945	1.9	9.0	1.9	142.0	185.5

Source: Baily (1983) and *Historical Statistics.*

mists there was increased emphasis on the recovery of production and income to 1929 levels." Such pessimism was pervasive even among those charged with alleviating the situation. Harry Hopkins, a liberal confidant of Roosevelt, wrote in 1937 that "it is reasonable to expect a probable minimum of 4 to 5 million unemployed even in future prosperity periods" (Leuchtenberg, 1963, p. 263). Similar sentiments were echoed by others, including LaGuardia, who concluded that the situation had passed from being an emergency to being the new norm.

Similar pessimism is often expressed in Europe today. The pessimism reflects the view that unlike the U.S. depression's persistent unemployment, persistent unemployment in Europe is caused by structural problems, not merely the residue of adverse shocks. H. Giersch has coined and popularized the word "eurosclerosis" to denote these structural problems. Is there some important difference between the two situations that suggests that rapid expansionary policies would fail in Europe today even where they

Table 8.13
Wage equations and the American Depression[a]

	U_t	U_{t-1}	$\log E_t$	$\log E_{t-1}$	π_{t-1}	R^2	D.W.
(1)	−.06	—	—	—	.22	0.0	1.71
	(.2)				(.8)		
(2)	−1.13	1.26	—	—	.50	.29	2.13
	(2.9)	(3.2)			(2.1)		
(3)	—	—	.67	—	.24	.03	1.75
			(.50)		(.9)		
(4)	—	—	2.71	−2.72	.38	.36	1.99
			(.74)	(3.2)	(1.7)		

a. The dependent variable is the rate of wage inflation. Data are drawn from *Historical Statistics of the United States.*

succeeded so spectacularly in the United States in 1940? There are surprisingly many similarities between the two experiences. The failure of inflation and real wages to recede more rapidly is an often noticed aspect of the current European experience. Indeed, it is this observation that drives conclusions that problems are structural and that the equilibrium rate of unemployment has increased. In the latter half of the Depression, a similar pattern appears in the United States. Between 1936 and 1940 unemployment fluctuated around a very high mean but there was essentially no deceleration in inflation and real wages rose by about 10%, close to the normal rate of productivity growth. Previous to the 1930s periods of steady inflation had had much lower average unemployment rates.

Just as unemployment in Europe is highly persistent today, it appeared highly persistent during the American Depression. The autocorrelation of unemployment was .874 in the United States over the 1919–41 period. To further examine the issue of hysteresis during the Depression, table 8.13 presents some estimated wage equations for the 1920–41 period. The war years are omitted because of the influence of controls. The results dramatically suggest hysteresis paralleling that found in Europe today. When only contemporaneous employment or unemployment is entered into the equation, it is insignificant, but the change in employment or unemployment is strongly associated with changes in the rate of wage inflation.[35] These results are robust to a variety of ways of treating expected inflation. While paralleling our results for present day Europe, these results differ from our results using American data for the postwar period. This may be taken as evidence that hysteresis is a phenomenon associated with bad times rather than with particular labor market institutions.

In considering contemporary European labor markets, we laid considerable stress on the importance of long term unemployment emphasizing that turnover rates were if anything lower in Europe than in the United States. Table 8.14, drawn from Woytinsky (1942), presents some of the limited evidence available on patterns of labor market turnover during the American depression. Again, the results parallel Europe today. There is little evidence of an increase in the flow rate into unemployment, though quits decline and layoffs increase. As in Europe today the duration of unemployment appears to have increased substantially. Woytinsky reports evidence from a 1937 Philadelphia survey that found that 61.7% of unemployed adult men had been out of work for more than a year. More generally, he concludes that the Depression era saw the emergence of a new group of hard core unemployed. Patterns in labor market turnover do not appear to provide a basis for distinguishing European labor markets and American labor markets during the Depression.

Hysteresis appears to be an important feature of the American Depression. Earlier in the paper, we suggested three possible sources of hysteresis. Of these physical capital accumulation appears an unlikely culprit. As table 8.12 demonstrates, the real value of the nonresidential capital stock actually declined between 1929 and 1939. This reduction did not represent an important bar to full employment during or after the war when demand for goods was strong. This makes us somewhat skeptical of claims that insufficient capital is holding up a European recovery. However, it should be noted that Mitchell (1947) claims that capacity utilization rates were very low prior to the 1939 expansion. This is not true in Europe today. There is some evidence of human capital hysteresis in labor force participation. The labor force participation rate of men over 65 dropped from 54 to 42% between the 1930 and 1940 censuses.[36] This is considerably more rapid than its trend rate of decline. Between 1920 and 1930, it fell by only 1%, and it remained essentially constant between 1940 and 1950. It seems unlikely, however, that this could have much effect on unemployment. Indeed to the extent that marginal workers were induced to drop out of the labor force, bad times might have reduced subsequent unemployment.

This leaves our insider-outsider story of wage setting. Beyond documenting the importance of hysteresis, and confirming its implications for wage equations, it is difficult to test the story directly. But the judgment of Leuchtenberg (1963) is perhaps revealing: "By Roosevelt's second term, as it seemed the country might never wholly recover, the burden of the unemployed had become too exhausting a moral and economic weight to

Table 8.14
Labor market turnover and the American Depression

Extent of labor turnover from 1919 to 1929,
(median monthly rates per 100 workers)[a]

Year	Accessions	Separations			
		Total	Quits	Discharges	Layoffs
1919	10.1	7.5	5.8	1.1	0.6
1920	10.1	10.3	8.4	1.1	0.8
1921	2.7	4.4	2.2	0.4	1.8
1922	8.0	5.3	4.2	0.7	0.4
1923	9.0	7.5	6.2	1.0	0.3
1924	3.3	3.8	2.7	0.5	0.6
1925	5.2	4.0	3.1	0.5	0.4
1926	4.6	3.9	2.9	0.5	0.5
1927	3.3	3.3	2.1	0.5	0.7
1928	3.7	3.1	2.2	0.4	0.5
1929	4.4	3.8	2.7	0.5	0.6

Extent of labor turnover from 1930 to 1940, by years
(average monthly rates per 100 workers)[b]

Year	Accessions	Separations			
		Total	Quits	Discharges	Layoffs
Median rates					
1929	4.4	3.8	2.7	0.5	0.6
1930	1.6	2.4	1.1	0.2	1.2
Weighted average rates					
1930	3.1	5.0	1.6	0.4	3.0
1931	3.1	4.1	1.0	0.2	2.9
1932	3.4	4.3	0.7	0.2	3.4
1933	5.4	3.8	0.9	0.2	2.7
1934	4.7	4.1	0.9	0.2	3.0
1935	4.2	3.6	0.9	0.2	2.5
1936	4.3	3.4	1.1	0.2	2.1
1937	3.5	4.4	1.2	0.2	3.0
1938	3.8	4.1	0.6	0.1	3.4
1939	4.1	3.1	0.8	0.1	2.2
1940	4.4	3.35	1.0	0.15	2.2

Source: Woytinsky (1942).
a. Source for top part of table: *Monthly Labor Review* (July 1929), pp. 64–65; (February 1931), p. 105.
b. Source for bottom part of table: *Monthly Labor Review* (1930–1941); for a summary of labor turnover from 1931 to 1939 (September 1940), pp. 696–704.
c. Including miscellaneous separations because of death, retirement on pension, etc., reported separately since January 1940.

carry. Those who drew income from other sources could hardly help but feel that the Depression had been a judgement which divided the saved from the unsaved. Increasingly, the jobless seemed not merely worthless mendicants but a menacing Lumpenproletariat." While Leuchtenberg is referring primarily to public attitudes toward the unemployed, similar private attitudes are the driving foce behind the hysteresis mechanism we have stressed.

The finding of so many parallels between the current European depression and the American depression suggests to us that hysteresis in Europe may be more the result of a long sequence of adverse shocks than the result of structural problems. Perhaps most telling is the observation that the apparent natural rate of unemployment drifted upward following the actual unemployment rate during the American depression just as it has in Europe. Given the absence of structural explanations for this drift, the inference that it resulted from high past unemployment seems compelling. So too, the high apparent European natural rate of unemployment may be the result of hysteresis arising in the aftermath of a sequence of adverse shocks. As we discuss below, this implies that expansionary macroeconomic policies may well work in reducing unemployment in Europe.

8.5 Conclusions

Periods of persistently high unemployment are not uncommon events in broad historical context. Yet standard macroeconomic theories have a difficult time accounting for them. We have argued that they can only be understood in terms of theories of hysteresis that make long run equilibrium depend on history. And we have argued that membership effects may well be important sources of hysteresis. Such effects appear to be an important source of persistence in unemployment in Europe today.

High unemployment is not, however, always persistent. A crucial issue is identifying the circumstances under which persistence is likely to arise. The main issue is that of whether hysteresis is the result of specific labor market structures, of the presence of unions in particular, or whether it is itself the result of adverse shocks, which by increasing unemployment, trigger the insider-outsider dynamics we have discussed in the paper. Our tentative conclusion, from the historical record, is that membership effects become important in bad times and are not crucially dependent on the presence of unions. We have not provided, however, a fully satisfactory theory of membership effects in nonunion settings.

Our theory permits a broad-brush account of the increase in unemployment in Europe over the past 15 years. In the 1970s European economies were hit with surprises in the form of rising oil prices, the productivity slowdown, and rapid increases in tax rates. With wages rigid in the short run each of these types of shocks created unemployment. Because of the membership considerations stressed here, the decrease in employment was validated by higher wage demands. As a result by the end of the 1970s the equilibrium level of unemployment had increased substantially. In the 1980s, the European economies, unlike the U.S. economy, experienced a series of adverse aggregate demand shocks as European monetary policies followed U.S. policies, but fiscal policies turned contractionary. This led to further unemployment, which was then validated by wage demands by those who remained employed. At this point, unemployment will remain high even if there are no more adverse shocks, because of the power of insider workers to set wages.

Our argument is that Europe has experienced a sequence of adverse shocks during the past 15 years each of which had a fairly permanent effect on the level of employment. Current high unemployment can equally be blamed on a propagation mechanism that leads the adverse shocks of the past to have a lasting impact, or on the shocks themselves. Unlike simple Keynesian explanations for the European depression, which stress only aggregate demand, our theory explains increases in the apparent natural rate of unemployment. Unlike some classical explanations for European unemployment that deny any role for demand management policies, our theory explains how aggregate demand can have protracted effects even in the absence of any long lasting nominal rigidities.

This view of the European unemployment problem has a number of fairly direct policy implications. First, "enfranchising" additional workers may tend to increase employment. If worksharing programs cause more workers to be employed and therefore represented in wage setting decisions, they may lead to reduced wage demands and increased employment. Profit sharing plans such as those proposed by Weitzman (1985) may also raise employment by making it possible for employers to reduce the cost of labor by increasing hiring. On the other hand they would increase unions' resistance to hiring new workers and might thereby increase membership problems. An obvious alternative policy is measures to reduce the power of unions and thereby allow outsider workers to have a larger impact on wage bargains. Our findings regarding the U.S. depression, where unions were probably not of great importance, lead us to be somewhat skeptical of the efficacy of such measures. Certainly it does not yet appear that efforts to reduce the power of unions in the United Kingdom have borne macro-economic fruit.

Our model suggests that shocks, positive or negative, are in a sense self-validating. If employment changes, wage setting practices adapt to a new level of employment. This means that positive shocks contrived through demand management policies can reduce unemployment regardless of the source of the shocks that caused it. Even if unemployment initially originated from adverse productivity shocks, expansionary policies, if they succeed in raising the level of employment, will yield permanent benefits. Symmetrically, even if most of the increase in unemployment in the 1980s is due to demand, the large decrease in the price of oil may well decrease it permanently. At the same time the model suggests that only policies or shocks that are in some sense surprises will be efficacious. This means that it may be difficult to increase employment a great deal with expansionary policies. The crucial question becomes the length of time over which expansionary policies can "surprise" wage setters. To whatever extent they can, very long lasting benefits will be derived.

Do the many parallels between the American and European depressions imply that a major expansion in aggregate demand would create the same miracles in Europe as it did in the United States? Unfortunately comparison of the two depressions cannot lead to a very definite answer. While it does dispose of the idea that the apparent increase in the natural rate of unemployment means that demand expansion cannot possibly succeed, and of the idea that real wage growth must be restrained if expansion is to take place, an important problem remains. The likelihood of achieving a surprise for a protracted period through inflationary policies may well have been much greater in the United States after a decade including a major deflation than it is in Europe today after a decade of stagflation. On the other hand, the very political infeasibility of expansion in Europe suggests its possible efficacy. Certainly the protracted high unemployment caused by the deflationary policies of the recent past stands as a testament to the potent effects of macroeconomic policies.

Notes

1. Formally, a dynamic system is said to exhibit hysteresis if it has at least one eigenvalue equal to zero (unity, if specified in discrete time). In such a case, the steady state of the system will depend on the history of the shocks affecting the system. Thus, we should say that unemployment exhibits hysteresis when current unemployment depends on past values with coefficients summing to one. We shall instead use "hysteresis" more loosely to refer to the case where the degree of

dependence on the past is very high, where the sum of coefficients is close but not necessarily equal to one.

2. For the United States we made use of the revised unemployment rates calculated by Romer (1986) for the 1890–1929 period.

3. This part relies heavily on the empirical work presented for individual European countries at the Chelwood Gate Conference on Unemployment, to be published in *Economica*, 1986. The reader is referred to individual country papers for further evidence.

4. We focus on the United Kingdom because detailed data are more easily available. Available data for France and Germany tell a very similar story.

5. The mismatch index by industry goes up, however, in 1981 and 1982—which are the last two years for which it has been computed.

6. Let a be the rate of growth of productivity and θ be the change in the tax wedge. Then the rate of growth of the after tax real wage consistent with a given capital labor ratio is approximately given by $a - \theta$.

7. When a time trend is added to the AR(1) specification of unemployment estimated above, its coefficient is both small and insignificant, for both countries.

8. This is also the direction of research recently followed by Sachs (1985) to explain European unemployment.

9. Unemployment remained high—around 10%—in Italy until about 1960 but other factors are thought to have been at work in that case.

10. Drazen (1979) constructs a related model, based on learning by doing, which also generates hysteresis. Hall (1976) explores the possibility that unemployment has long lasting effects on productivity, and its implications for economic policy.

11. The issue of membership and membership rules is clearly closely related to the issue of union size and union membership in the union literature. See Farber (1986, section 6) for a survey. This literature has not, however, focused on the dynamic implications of membership rules.

12. Formalizing the firm as passive allows us to concentrate on the effects of alternative membership rules on the decisions of the group of insiders. Allowing for wage bargaining between the firm and insiders as well as for some control of employment ex post by insiders introduces additional issues, which we shall discuss later.

13. The assumption of stochastically inelastic labor supply maintained here is not realistic for a single firm. It is best to think of the firm under consideration as a representative firm, facing the same shocks as other firms.

14. Because we use a log linear approximation to define p, p^* as defined can be negative. But the approximation is only acceptable for p close to one, that is, for values of $a(b/c)^2$ not too large.

15. We may also think of asymmetric rules where it takes m_1 periods to acquire membership, and m_2 periods to lose it. We shall briefly return to their likely implications later.

16. There is another effect, which works in the opposite direction. Choosing a high real wage leads to lower expected employment, thus lower membership and higher expected real wages in the future. This effect, however, turns out to be dominated by that emphasized in the text.

17. Farber (1986) reviews the research on union behavior when members have different seniority status, and thus conflicting interests.

18. Thus, we assume implicitly that the technological shock affects costs, but not the relation between output and employment. This is the case, for example, if output is produced with two inputs, labor and a nonlabor input, according to a Leontieff technology, and the technological shock reflects changes in the relative price in the nonlabor input. A change in productivity growth would instead affect both the relation between output and employment, and between prices and wages. Allowing the technological shock to affect the relation between output and employment in the model is straightforward but introduces ambiguities in the effects of supply shocks on employment that are not central to our argument.

19. As in other contracting models, staggering of wage decisions across unions would lead to effects of even more anticipated nominal shocks. See Taylor (1979).

20. There is some evidence that this has actually occurred in Britain. Despite the legal changes that have decreased the legal power of unions in the last decade, the size of the union wage differential appears to have risen sharply in recent years.

21. Consider a simple example. Suppose restaurant wages were rigid, and a big decline in the demand for restaurant meals took place so there were unemployed chefs. Would it pay to open a new restaurant with a low paid chef? Probably not if fixed costs were high. These considerations may have something to do with why in bad times employment growth may be concentrated in small establishments.

22. Given that our paper is written for an American audience, we do not review the role of unions in the United States in any detail. As will be clear from our description of Europe, unions in the United States play a much more limited role than in Europe.

23. Actual extensions are rare but the threat of extension is considered to be very effective in making all firms respect the content of these agreements.

24. In future research, it would be valuable to study Japanese labor market institutions with a view to evaluating the theories of persistent unemployment put forward here. There are a number of similarities between Japanese and European institutions including the importance of company level bargaining. There may, however, be important differences as well, particularly in the attitude of Japanese unions toward outsiders.

25. Two recent cases have been in the news, that of British Petroleum, which has gone nonunion for some of its shipping operations, and that of Rupert Murdoch, who has in effect gone to a more accommodating union.

26. The reason why unions encourage the unemployed to remain in the union appears to be due in part to their desire to increase membership figures, and through these, their role in the national union movement.

27. Allowing labor demand to depend on current and expected real wages, as it should under costs of adjustment, would complicate our task here.

28. Note that a between 0 and 1 does not correspond exactly to m between 1 and ∞. As we have argued before, m between 1 and ∞ leads to a more complex, nonlinear, specification.

29. This is plausible and convenient assumption. Suppose we assumed instead that productivity was the sum of a linear function of observable variables and a stationary or borderline stationary process, say an AR(1) process with coefficient ρ. The wage equation would then differ from that in the text in two ways. The first would be the presence of lagged real wages, with coefficient $\rho - 1$. The second would be the presence of the ρ first differences of the observable variables affecting productivity. We have explored these more general specifications empirically for the United Kingdom and found our simple wage equation not to be misleading.

30. Because our wage data refer to manufacturing wages, we use manufacturing employment as the employment variable in the results reported here. Very similar results were obtained using total employment.

31. All these findings are quite robust. The value of Z is substantively the same if, following the argument of the previous note, the lagged real wage, current and lagged values of the capital-labor ratio, the price of oil, and a proxy for productivity growth (when available) are added to the regressions. The results are also robust to changes in the coefficient on lagged inflation—say, within .2 of the values used in the table.

32. The motivation for calculations of this type is laid out in Clark and Summers (1979b). In performing the calculations, we have assumed that the exit rate from unemployment is not duration dependent. If, more realistically, we allowed for its decline, the estimated concentration of unemployment in long spells would show up even more clearly.

33. Some of the institutional rigidities of European labor markets date, however, from social policies introduced in the 1960s and 1970s.

34. It is clear that with such short samples, and such a drastic increase in unemployment in the second subsample, estimation cannot be very precise.

35. A similar finding is emphasized by Gordon and Wilcox (1979), who also provide evidence that it holds for Europe during the Depression period. Gordon (1983) emphasizes the importance of the rate of change effect in the Phillips curve

during the Depression period in both the United States and the United Kingdom but finds the level effect to be dominant outside of this interval.

36. This dropoff may reflect to some extent the effects of the introduction of Social Security. The program was sufficiently small in 1940 that this is unlikely to be the whole story. Moreover, the timing of its introduction surely had something to do with the fact of the Depression.

9

Why Is the Unemployment Rate So Very High Near Full Employment?

In a well-known paper in one of the inaugural issues of the *Brookings Papers*, Robert Hall posed the question, "Why Is the Unemployment Rate So High at Full Employment?"[1] Hall, writing in the context of the 3.5% unemployment rate that prevailed in 1969, answered his question by explaining that the full-employment rate was so high because of the normal turnover that is inevitable in a dynamic economy where some sectors are expanding and others are contracting and because of the special problems of certain disadvantaged groups. Hall himself was pessimistic about the prospects for maintaining unemployment consistently below 4% through expansionary policies. But he raised the prospect that successful structural policies could do so. While aspirations became attuned to expectations as unemployment rose during the 1970s, the Humphrey-Hawkins Full Employment and Balanced Growth Act of 1978 nonetheless set an unemployment target of 4% for 1983.

Today, four years into an economic recovery, the unemployment rate hovers around 7%. Over the past decade, it has averaged 7.6% and has never fallen below 5.8%. Even most forecasts that call for steady growth over the next five years do not foresee unemployment rates dipping back below 6%. It is helpful to recall that unemployment peaked at 7.2% during the relatively severe recession of 1958. While some of the difference between recent and past levels of unemployment has resulted from cyclical developments, it is clear that a substantial increase in the normal or natural rate of unemployment has taken place. Where Kennedy-Johnson economists set 4% as an interim full-employment target, contemporary policymakers would regard even the temporary achievement of 6% unemployment as a great success.

Reprinted by permission, with revisions, from *Brookings Papers on Economic Activity* 2:339–383, 1986. Copyright © 1986 by the Brookings Institution.

This paper describes and explains the substantial recent increase in normal unemployment. The first part of the paper assesses the relationship between unemployment and other indicators of labor market tightness and describes changes in the composition of the unemployed population. The data reveal that the level of unemployment consistent with any given level of vacancies, capacity utilization, or change in inflation has increased significantly over time. It appears that little of this movement can be traced to measurement difficulties in the Bureau of Labor Statistics' Current Population Survey. Rather, increases in unemployment are a serious problem because they are concentrated among mature men, job losers, and the long-term unemployed. The portrayal of rising unemployment as the consequence of an increase in the share of secondary workers in the labor force that was popular during the 1970s is no longer accurate.

The second and more speculative part of the paper draws on the dramatic variations in state and regional economic performance that have taken place over the past fifteen years in an effort to get at the causes of rising unemployment. It links observed increases in unemployment with structural changes in the economy that have lowered employment in high-wage sectors and increased it in low-wage sectors. The structural changes include both macroeconomic developments that have reduced the demand for the output of high-wage industries and labor market pressures, particularly in unionized sectors, that have pushed up wages in sectors where they were already high. I conclude that reversing the dramatic sectoral shocks of the last few years can make an important contribution to reducing unemployment.

9.1 Increasing Unemployment in the United States

Figure 9.1 depicts the evolution of the total U.S. unemployment rate and the unemployment rate for married men since the Korean War. The fairly steady increase in both rates is interrupted only during the 1960s. While the amplitude of fluctuations in the unemployment rate has increased, it is also clear that the normal level of unemployment has risen. A conspicuous feature of the data is that the rate for married men has increased in tandem with the overall rate.

Table 9.1 presents information on the unemployment rate and the employment ratio (the ratio of employed adults to the total adult population) over the seven business cycles since 1953. Again, a secular increase in unemployment is evident. With the exception of the boom of the 1960s and the early 1970s, each cycle has higher peak, trough, and average

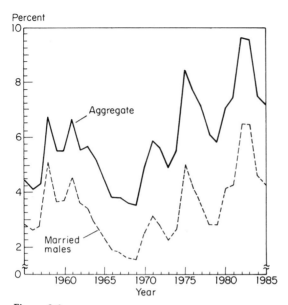

Figure 9.1
Aggregate and married male unemployment rates, 1955–85. Source: U.S. Department of
Labor Statistics, *Handbook of Labor Statistics* (June 1986), table 25.

unemployment rates than the one that preceded it. Indeed, the unemployment rate at the last peak, in July of 1981, was comparable with the rates
reached at most previous cyclical troughs. Unemployment at the next peak
is not knowable. But most forecasts do not call for substantial declines. The
most recent Congressional Budget Office forecast, which assumes fairly
steady growth uninterrupted by recession for the next five years, calls for
unemployment to decline only to 6.0% by 1991.[2]

The secular increase in unemployment contrasts sharply with the behavior of the employment ratio, which has trended upward and is today
close to its historical peak. The rise reflects the rapid increase in the labor
force participation of adult women, from 37.6% in 1960 to 43.3% in 1970,
51.3% in 1980, and 54.7% in 1985. Since 1973, both unemployment and
employment have grown quite rapidly. Total employment increased by
25% between 1973 and 1985.

Unemployment can increase for either cyclical or structural reasons.
Before I turn to an analysis of changes in the structure of the labor market, it is necessary to address the possibility that rising unemployment is
merely a by-product of weakness in aggregate demand in recent years. A
natural way to test that possibility is to examine how the unemployment
rate has moved relative to other measures of cyclical conditions and to

Table 9.1
Increasing unemployment over the business cycle, July 1953–July 1986 (percent)[a]

Cycle (peak to peak)	Peak		Trough		Average	
	Unemployment rate	Employment-population ratio[b]	Unemployment rate	Employment-population ratio[b]	Unemployment rate	Employment-population ratio[b]
Jul. 1953–Jul. 1957	2.5	59.5	5.7	57.3	4.3	58.6
Aug. 1957–Mar. 1960	4.0	58.7	7.2	56.9	5.7	57.5
Apr. 1960–Nov. 1969	5.1	58.0	6.7	57.1	4.7	58.0
Dec. 1969–Oct. 1973	3.4	59.8	5.7	58.4	5.2	58.5
Nov. 1973–Dec. 1979	4.8	59.4	8.4	57.1	6.6	59.0
Jan. 1980–June 1981	6.2	60.9	7.7	59.8	7.1	60.2
Jul. 1981–Jul. 1986	7.1[c]	60.1[c]	10.6	58.2	8.2	60.0

Source: U.S. Department of Labor, Bureau of Labor Statistics, *Employment and Earnings*, various issues.

a. Peak unemployment is the rate at the beginning of the cycle. Trough unemployment is measured at the cyclical trough. The dating of the cycles is based on National Bureau of Economic Research chronology.

b. Employment is total civilian employment as measured from the Current Population Survey. Population is the civilian noninstitutional population over 16 years of age.

c. The cyclical peak has not yet been observed in this expansion.

Table 9.2
Corrected unemployment trends, various periods, 1955−85 (percentage points)[a]

Sample period	Control	Unemployment rate	
		Total	Males, aged 35−44
1955−85	Vacancy rate	0.133	0.079
		(0.009)	(0.011)
1967−85	Vacancy rate	0.167	0.157
		(0.030)	(0.028)
1967−85	Capacity utilization	0.147	0.159
		(0.025)	(0.020)

Source: Author's calculations based on data from BLS, *Employment and Earnings*, various issues.
a. Regressions of the unemployment rate on a constant, several controls, and a time trend. The controls indicated are the contemporaneous index (vacancy rates or capacity utilization) and the first two lags of the series. Vacancy rates are derived from the Conference Board index of help-wanted advertisements with adjustments made as suggested in Katharine Abraham, "What Does the Help-Wanted Index Measure?" (Brookings, 1986). Standard errors are in parentheses.

consider whether the relationship between unemployment and inflation has changed.

Table 9.2 examines the trend in unemployment relative to two cyclical indicators—vacancies and capacity utilization. The results indicate that at any given level of vacancies or of capacity utilization, both overall unemployment and the unemployment of middle-aged men have increased sharply.[3] Over the past two decades total unemployment appears to have increased by between 0.13 and 0.17 percentage points per year after adjustment for changes in cyclical conditions. Similar increases from a much lower base show up in the unemployment rate of mature men. Of the roughly 3.5 percentage point increase in total unemployment between its 1969 low point of 3.5% and the present rate, the equations indicate that between 2.5 and 2.9 percentage points are attributable to structural factors captured by the time trend, with the relatively small remainder being attributable to changes in the capacity utilization and vacancies cyclical indicators.

Estimation of Phillips curves for various periods does not yield sufficiently precise estimates of the natural rate of unemployment to permit definitive statements about its evolution. But the data do suggest that, particularly when the mature male unemployment rate is used, the natural rate has increased. A calculation is instructive. Between 1965 and 1974, the inflation rate as measured using the GNP deflator increased by 6.4 percentage points, while the unemployment rate of men aged 35 to 44 averaged 2.2%. Between 1980 and 1985, the inflation rate declined by 5.7 percentage points while the same unemployment rate averaged 5.5%. If one assumes, in line with the data, that a reduction of 1 percentage point in the inflation rate requires 1.5 percentage point years of extra unemployment, the implied natural rate is 3.2% for the earlier period and 4.0% for the later one, an increase of one-fourth. To the extent that supply shocks were partially responsible for changes in the inflation rate over both periods, the calculation understates the change in the natural rate.

On balance, the evidence suggests that the current high level of unemployment, particularly the rate for mature men, cannot easily be explained as a consequence of a cyclical decline in demand. I therefore turn to an exploration of structural factors that could possibly account for rising unemployment.

9.1.1 Changes in Labor Force Composition

One explanation for increases in the unemployment rate is that the composition of the labor force has changed so that the share of groups with high unemployment rates has increased. In that case, measured unemployment might increase even though the risk of unemployment for any particular individual with given characteristics had not changed. It would also be true that any given level of unemployment would indicate less labor market slack than had once been the case and so presumably should be a cause for less concern.

George Perry put forward an argument of this type in considering the breakdown in the Phillips curve relation during the late 1960s.[4] He suggested that the increasing share of workers from groups whose unemployment was typically relatively high—women and teenagers—had raised the level of measured unemployment corresponding to any given amount of labor market slack. Perry constructed an alternative unemployment series by taking a fixed weighted average of the unemployment rates of different age-sex groups, thus controlling for changes in labor force composition. Since his introduction of this notion, the construction of "Perry weighted" unemployment rates has become standard in the estimation of Phillips curves and in discussions of changes in the natural rate of unemployment.[5]

There is no reason why the logic of adjusting for changes in labor force composition should be applied only to changes in its age-sex composition.

Arguments similar to those originally made by Perry can be applied to other changes in labor force composition as well. Some of the changes work in the opposite direction to Perry's demographic adjustment. More educated workers tend to have lower unemployment rates than do less educated workers, and the labor force has become more educated over the past thirty years. Likewise, mining, construction, and manufacturing tend to have higher average unemployment rates than do services, trade, and finance, and the share of the labor force engaged in the latter pursuits has increased. Thus it is not clear a priori that changes in the composition of the labor force have tended to increase measured unemployment.

Table 9.3 presents estimates of adjustments to the measured unemployment rate for changes in labor composition by age and sex, marital status, schooling, and primary industry. The adjustment for each year is calculated by first creating an adjusted unemployment rate as a fixed weighted average of group-specific unemployment rates using 1965 labor force shares as weights. That is,

$$AUR_t = \sum s_{i65} UR_{it}. \tag{1}$$

The adjusted unemployment rate, AUR, is the unemployment rate that would prevail in a given year if each labor force group had its 1965 share, s_{i65}, of the labor force. The adjustment for changing labor force composition is then the difference between the actual and the adjusted unemployment rate.

While it would be ideal to estimate the adjustment using a single decomposition of the labor force into subgroups, it is not possible to do so with the available data. The table therefore presents four separate adjustments. The age-sex adjustment is based on a decomposition of the labor force into the fourteen categories used by Perry.[6] The marital status adjustment divides the labor force into six categories—men and women who are single, married with spouse present, and widowed, separated, or divorced. The schooling adjustment is based on a division of the labor force into six categories ranging from workers with less than five years of schooling to those completing four or more years of college.[7] Finally, the industry adjustment is based on a decomposition of the experienced labor force into categories corresponding to the one-digit standard industrial classification (SIC) code.[8]

The changing age-sex composition of the labor force can account for relatively little of the increase in unemployment in recent years. The adjustment (relative to 1965) peaked at 0.7 percentage point in the mid-1970s and has declined since then to only 0.3 point in 1985. The

Table 9.3

Changes in labor force composition and the unemployment rate, 1954–85
(percentage points)

Year	Unem- ployment rate	Adjustment[a] Age-sex	Marital status	Schooling	Industry
1954	5.5	−0.3	n.a.	n.a.	0.3
1955	4.4	−0.2	0.3	n.a.	0.2
1956	4.1	−0.2	0.3	n.a.	0.1
1957	4.3	−0.2	−0.1	n.a.	0.1
1958	6.8	−0.2	−0.1	n.a.	0.2
1959	5.5	−0.2	0.0	0.4	0.2
1960	5.5	−0.2	−0.1	n.a.	0.1
1961	6.7	−0.2	0.0	n.a.	0.1
1962	5.5	−0.2	−0.2	0.2	0.1
1963	5.7	−0.1	−0.1	n.a.	0.1
1964	5.2	−0.1	−0.1	0.0	0.0
1965	4.5	0.0	0.0	0.0	0.0
1966	3.8	0.1	−0.1	0.0	−0.1
1967	3.8	0.0	−0.1	−0.1	−0.1
1968	3.6	0.1	−0.1	−0.1	0.0
1969	3.5	0.1	0.0	−0.1	0.0
1970	4.9	0.2	0.0	−0.1	−0.1
1971	5.9	0.3	0.0	−0.3	−0.1
1972	5.6	0.4	0.2	−0.2	0.0
1973	4.9	0.5	0.2	−0.2	0.0
1974	5.6	0.5	0.3	−0.3	−0.1
1975	8.5	0.7	0.4	−0.8	−0.3
1976	7.7	0.7	0.5	−0.7	−0.2
1977	7.1	0.7	0.6	−0.8	−0.1
1978	6.1	0.7	0.6	−0.7	−0.1
1979	5.8	0.6	0.5	−0.8	−0.1
1980	7.1	0.6	0.5	−1.1	−0.2
1981	7.6	0.6	0.7	−1.4	−0.1
1982	9.7	0.6	0.7	−1.8	−0.4
1983	9.6	0.4	0.7	−2.3	−0.3
1984	7.5	0.3	0.6	−2.1	−0.2
1985	7.2	0.3	0.6	−2.1	−0.1

Source: Author's calculations. Actual unemployment rate and data before 1984 used in calculations of adjustments are from BLS, *Handbook of Labor Statistics*, Bulletin 2217 (June 1985). Unemployment rates by demographic group are listed in table 27, pp. 69–73; rates by marital status are in table 50, pp. 115–18; rates by education are in table 62, p. 169; rates by industry are in table 30, p. 77. Weights for demographic civilian labor force status are from table 4, pp. 14–17; weights for marital status are from table 6, pp. 22–23; weights for educational attainment are from table 61, p. 164; weights for industrial composition are from table 30, p. 76. Statistics for 1984 and 1985 are from BLS, *Employment and Earnings*, vol. 33 (January 1986).

a. The adjustment for each year is calculated by creating an adjusted unemployment rate using 1965 labor force shares as weights—see equation (1) in text. The adjustment for changing labor force composition is then the difference between the actual and the adjusted unemployment rate. n.a. = not available.

decline in the adjustment reflects two developments: the decline in the labor force share of teenagers and the declining relative unemployment rate of women. The labor force share of teenagers has fallen from 7.9% in 1965 to 6.8% in 1985, a decline that is assumed here to have no effect on the youth unemployment rate. If, as Michael Wachter has argued, crowding effects cause increases in the youth unemployment rate, the decline in the adjustment in recent years would be significantly greater.[9]

The dramatic change in the composition of the labor force in recent years has been the increase in female labor force participation. If unemployment rates for men and women had maintained the pattern they exhibited in the 1960s, the measured unemployment rate would have increased substantially. But, as I discuss later, the gap between the unemployment rates of men and women has narrowed in recent years, so the effect is not very large.

More important than the age-sex adjustment is the adjustment for the changing marital status of the labor force. It rose to 0.6 percentage point in the mid-1970s but, unlike the age-sex adjustment, has not turned down since. The major marital status change is the drop in the fraction of men in the labor force who are married. In 1965, 18% of the male labor force had never been married, compared with 27% in 1985. Given that unemployment rates were three times as high for single as for married men in 1985, the effect of reductions in the share of the labor force that is married is quite substantial.[10]

Quantitatively, the most important adjustment for changes in the composition of the labor force involves education. Assuming no changes in group-specific unemployment rates, recent increases in education should have reduced the unemployment rate by 2.1 percentage points between 1965 and 1985. That adjustment dwarfs the demographic and marital status corrections.[11] Over the past twenty years the share of the labor force that received some college education nearly doubled, from 22 to 40%, while the share with less than an eighth-grade education fell from 33% to only 7%.

It is arguable that the educational adjustment made here is inappropriate because the differentials in unemployment between different educational groups reflect not the effects of education but rather differences in the innate skills of more and less educated workers. Undoubtedly, the adjustment calculated here is an overestimate of the true effect of increased educational attainment on unemployment for this reason, but the overestimate may not be large. The premise of policies directed at discouraging teenagers from dropping out of high school is that more schooling means less unemployment. And the fact that the relative unemployment rate of college graduates has dropped as their number has swelled casts doubt on the importance of sorting effects of the type noted above.

Finally, the industry adjustment shown in the final column of the table indicates that changes in the industrial mix, particularly the decline in the share of employment in the volatile manufacturing sector, has also worked to reduce unemployment. In some recent years, when manufacturing has been weak because of adverse cyclical conditions, the adjustment has been quantitatively significant, reaching 0.4 percentage point in 1982.

While it is inappropriate to sum the various adjustments in table 9.3 because they are not independent, it seems clear that mix effects cannot account for the recent increase in unemployment. The mix effects that should have led to decreases in unemployment, increases in education, and reductions in manufacturing employment are quantitatively much more important than the demographic mix effects that are emphasized in most discussions of rising unemployment. Taking into account the changing composition of the labor force does not reduce and may even increase the size of the rise in unemployment that must be explained.

9.1.2 Whose Unemployment Has Increased?

Since changes in labor force composition cannot account for increases in employment, it is natural to ask how the increase in unemployment in recent years has been distributed across the population. Table 9.4 presents unemployment rates for various subgroups of the population in 1965, 1974, 1978, and 1985. The years 1965, 1974, and 1978 are contrasted with 1985 because each is a year of moderately low but not cyclically minimal unemployment. The broad conclusions that emerge in the discussion are not sensitive to the choice of years.

The most dramatic relative increases in unemployment have occurred among prime-aged males. While aggregate unemployment increased by 18%, from 6.1% to 7.2%, between 1978 and 1985, the unemployment rate for men aged 35 to 44 increased by 75%, from 2.8% to 4.9%. The increase occurred despite a rise in that cohort's labor force nonparticipation rate from 4.3 to 5.0%. A similar but less pronounced increase in unemployment is observed for men in the other under-65 age groups. It is noteworthy that even going as far back as 1965, the conclusion that unemployment among mature men has risen disproportionately remains valid.

Unemployment rates for women have risen relatively little, despite huge increases in labor force participation rates. For women aged 35 to 44, the

Table 9.4
Unemployment rates for population subgroups, 1965, 1974, 1978, and 1985 (percent)

Category	1965	1974	1978	1985
Total	4.5	5.6	6.1	7.2
Age-sex				
Males, 16−19	14.1	15.6	15.8	19.5
Males, 20−24	6.4	8.8	9.2	11.4
Males, 25−34	2.9	4.0	4.4	6.6
Males, 35−44	2.5	2.6	2.8	4.9
Males, 45−54	2.5	2.4	2.7	4.6
Males, 55−64	3.3	2.6	2.8	4.3
Males, 65 and over	3.5	3.3	4.2	3.1
All males	4.0	4.9	5.3	7.0
Females, 16−19	15.7	16.6	17.1	17.6
Females, 20−24	7.3	9.5	10.1	10.7
Females, 25−34	5.5	6.2	6.7	7.4
Females, 35−44	4.6	4.6	5.0	5.5
Females, 45−54	3.2	3.7	4.0	4.8
Females, 55−64	2.8	3.2	3.2	4.3
Females, 65 and over	2.9	3.6	3.8	3.3
All females	5.5	6.7	7.2	7.4
Marital status				
Single men	10.1	11.8	11.7	12.7
Married men	2.4	2.7	2.8	4.3
Divorced, separated, or widowed men	7.2	6.2	6.6	9.2
Single women	8.2	10.5	10.9	10.7
Married women	4.5	5.3	5.5	5.6
Divorced, separated, or widowed women	5.4	6.3	6.9	8.3
Education[a]				
Less than 5 years	7.1	4.8	7.7	11.3
5 to 8 years	5.6	6.2	8.5	13.0
1 to 3 years of high school	7.4	9.6	12.4	15.9
4 years of high school	4.1	4.8	6.2	8.0
1 to 3 years of college	3.3	4.2	4.6	5.1
4 or more years of college	1.4	2.0	2.5	2.6

Sources: BLS, *Handbook of Labor Statistics* (June 1985). Unemployment rates by age-sex are from table 27, pp. 69−73; by marital status, from table 50, pp. 115−18; and by education, from table 62, p. 169. Data for 1985 are taken from *Employment and Earnings*, vol. 33 (January 1986).
a. Education statistics for 1985 were obtained by telephone from the Bureau of Labor Statistics.

unemployment rate increased only 10%, from 5.0 to 5.5%, during 1978–85. The relative increases in unemployment were somewhat smaller for younger women and somewhat greater for older women. There is a substantial difference between the experience of young men and that of young women. While increases in the unemployment of women aged 16 to 19 and 20 to 24 have been relatively small since 1974, there have been significant increases in the unemployment rate of young men, particularly those aged 16 to 19.

The total unemployment rate is a weighted average of the unemployment rates of different demographic groups with weights depending on their shares of the labor force. A simple way of combining the effects of changing demographic composition and changing group-specific unemployment rates is to ask what contribution different demographic groups make to total unemployment in different years. The contribution of a given group to total unemployment is the product of its labor force share and its unemployment rate. Performing this calculation reveals two significant developments. First, the amount of unemployment attributable to teenagers has declined in recent years. Teenagers contributed 1.2 percentage points to the 4.5% unemployment rate in 1965, 1.5 points to the 5.6% unemployment rate in 1974, 1.5 points to the 6.1% unemployment rate in 1978, but only 1.3 points to the 7.2% unemployment rate in 1985. Second, the bulk of the increase in unemployment in recent years is attributable to men aged 20 and above, whose contribution to total unemployment increased from 1.9 percentage points in 1965 to 2.3 points in 1978 and 3.3 points in 1985.

Data on unemployment rates for different marital status groups reveal that unemployment has increased most dramatically among married and formerly married men. The rate for these groups increased by about 50% between 1978 and 1985. For single men and women and for married women the data reveal only very minor increases in unemployment since 1974. These patterns cast doubt on the arguments that increases in measured unemployment are primarily the result of a rise in the fraction of the population on the margin between working and not working.[12] Surely mature men, especially those who are married, are the group for whom it is least plausible that social changes have made marginal labor force attachment attractive.

Finally, the breakdown of unemployment rates by education in table 9.4 reveals that the extent of the increase in unemployment over the past decade declines steadily with increased education. The unemployment rate of high school drop-outs increased by more than one-fourth between 1978 and 1985, compared with an increase of only 4% for college graduates and 11% for workers with some college education. The unemployment rate for those with only one to five years of schooling rose by almost 50%. The level of unemployment is not, however, monotonically related to education either in the 1970s or at present. People receiving no high school training have significantly lower unemployment rates than do high school drop-outs.[13] That pattern at least raises a question about arguments that unemployment is due to a lack of skills on the part of workers.

9.1.3 What Types of Unemployment Have Increased?

The discussion so far suggests that the increase in measured unemployment is potentially a serious social problem. Further evidence to that effect can be gleaned from data on changes in the composition of unemployment by reason and duration. As table 9.5 suggests, most of the increase in unemployment over the last decade is concentrated among job losers. The unemployment rate attributable to job loss rose from 1.6% in 1967 to 2.4% in 1974, 2.5% in 1978, and 3.6% in 1985. Unemployment attributable to job leavers has not increased at all since 1974, while unemployment among new entrants to the work force has increased modestly. Noticeable increases in unemployment have also taken place among workers reentering the work force. For reasons spelled out in detail in my earlier paper with Kim Clark, I believe that a substantial part of the reentrant category is composed of workers who have recently lost jobs.[14] If even a portion of the increase in reentrant unemployment is added to the job losers category, it appears clear that the bulk of the increase in unemployment in recent years is the result of job loss.

The data also suggest that a large part of the observed increase in unemployment is due to increases in the duration of unemployment. Of the 1.1 percentage point increase in the unemployment rate between 1978 and 1985, 0.5 point, or almost half, is attributable to increases in the number of people reporting themselves as out of work for more than twenty-seven weeks. The incidence of such long-term unemployment has more than doubled since 1965. Only a relatively small part of the observed increase in unemployment is due to an increase in the number of people reporting themselves as unemployed for fewer than five weeks.

Data on unemployment duration are difficult to interpret because of the high incidence of reporting errors. It appears that almost three-quarters of the unemployed population report their duration of unemployment inconsistently from month to month.[15] There is also the complication, empha-

Table 9.5
Unemployment by reason and duration, various years, 1965–85
(percent except where otherwise indicated)

Year	Unem- ployment rate	Reason for unemployment			
		Job losers	Job leavers	Reentrants	New entrants
1967[a]	3.8	1.6	0.5	1.2	0.5
1974	5.6	2.4	0.8	1.6	0.7
1978	6.1	2.5	0.8	1.8	0.9
1985	7.2	3.6	0.8	2.0	0.9

Year	Unem- polyment rate	Duration of unemployment				Mean duration (weeks)[b]	Share of long-term unem- ployment[c]
		0–5 weeks	6–14 weeks	15–26 weeks	27 or more weeks		
1965	4.5	2.2	1.3	0.5	0.5	11.8	42.5
1974	5.6	2.8	1.7	0.6	0.4	9.8	45.2
1978	6.1	2.8	1.9	0.8	0.6	11.9	46.0
1985	7.2	3.0	2.2	0.9	1.1	15.6	54.0[d]

Sources: BLS, *Handbook of Labor Statistics* (June 1985). Unemployment by reason for unemployment is in table 32, pp. 80–81. Unemployment by duration of unemployment is in table 31, pp. 78–79. Statistics for 1985 are from *Employment and Earnings*, vol. 33 (January 1986), table 12, p. 166, and table 14, p. 167.
a. Data on reason for unemployment do not begin until 1967.
b. Mean duration of interrupted spells.
c. Fraction of the year's unemployment due to persons with more than twenty-seven weeks of unemployment as derived from the Work Experience Survey.
d. Because 1985 data are unavailable, data from 1984 are used.

sized by many authors, that almost half of all unemployment spells end in withdrawal from the labor force rather than in employment.[16] Nonetheless, the available information suggests that unemployment is increasingly concentrated among a relatively small group that is unemployed for long stretches of time.

An easy way to see this point is to note that doubling the mean duration of incomplete spells of unemployment (shown in table 9.5) provides an estimate of the mean duration of the completed spell for those currently unemployed.[17] As Clark and I argued in our earlier paper, this concept is far superior to the more commonly studied mean duration of a completed spell for those entering unemployment in assessing the dynamics of unemployment. The expected total duration of unemployment for the unemployed is now thirty-one weeks, compared with twenty-four weeks in 1978, twenty weeks in 1974, and twenty-four weeks in 1965. Taking account in some way of the shortening of reported spells of unemployment that can be attributed to labor force withdrawal would further increase the estimated duration of joblessness for the currently unemployed population.

Additional evidence on the concentration of unemployment among the long-term unemployed is provided by the retrospective Work Experience Survey conducted annually in March as a supplement to the CPS. The March survey, in which respondents are asked about the extent of their unemployment and employment experience in the preceding year, makes it possible to calculate the fraction of total unemployment attributable to people experiencing different amounts of unemployment in the preceding year. In our earlier paper, Clark and I used this data to suggest that a large fraction of unemployment in 1969, 1974, and 1975 was attributable to the relatively small subgroup of the population that experienced more than six months of unemployment in the preceding year.[18] Replicating our calculations for subsequent years suggests that the importance of long-term unemployment has increased significantly. While people out of work for twenty-seven or more weeks accounted for 45.2% of all unemployment reported in the 1974 Work Experience Survey, they accounted for 46.0% of unemployment in 1978 and 54.0% of unemployment in 1984, the most recent year for which data are available.

Increases in normal unemployment over the past twenty years represent a serious problem. The view that the current high level of unemployment is primarily the result of the increased unemployment of secondary workers is simply false. In fact, the increases in unemployment have been relatively greatest for mature men with dependents. And they have resulted primarily from job loss and increases in duration of unemployment.

9.1.4 CPS Unemployment and Other Labor Market Indicators

A number of recent analyses have called attention to the fact that the observed increase in the official unemployment rate has not coincided with substantial increases in other labor market indicators.[19] It could be that some flaw in the CPS measure of unemployment accounts for the observed increase, though such an argument is difficult to evaluate. Unemployment as reflected in the CPS is more a state of mind than an objective reality. The substantial importance of rotation group bias and the sensitivity of the measured unemployment rate to even small changes in the phrasing or the order of the questions asked suggests the subjective nature of measured unemployment.[20] This means that it is difficult to examine whether or not the CPS is correctly measuring unemployment. In an important sense, unemployment is what the CPS says it is.

Nonetheless, it is useful to contrast movements in CPS unemployment rates with movements in other variables that are likely to reflect changes in labor market conditions. Table 9.6 presents estimates of the CPS unemployment rate, the insured unemployment rate, the unemployment rate as inferred from the annual retrospective Work Experience Survey, and the discouraged worker rate.[21] A major mystery is the sharp recent decline in the ratio of insured unemployment to total unemployment. The insured unemployment rate—the number of recipients of unemployment benefits divided by the number of jobs covered by unemployment insurance—was about 15% lower in 1985 than it was in 1978 and 20% lower in 1985 than it was in 1974. It was only one-third greater than it was in 1969. As Gary Burtless explains, one would expect insured unemployment to be below actual unemployment since many of the unemployed are ineligible for benefits.[22] Burtless also suggests that the increasing share of the population covered by unemployment insurance can account for some of the pre-1980 trend decrease in the ratio of insured unemployment to total unemployment. But there is no apparent explanation for the divergence of these two measures in recent years. The mystery is deepened by the observation, noted above, that most of the recent increase in unemployment has been due to increases in the job loser category, the category most eligible for unemployment benefits.

Burtless considers a number of possible explanations for the recent low level of the insured unemployment rate without finding any that are wholly persuasive. It appears that many people who, based on their answers to the CPS questionnaire, appear to be eligible for unemployment insurance are not collecting it, possibly because benefits began to be taxed

Table 9.6
Unemployment and alternative labor market indicators, 1960–85 (percent)

Year	Unemployment rate	Work Experience Survey unemployment rate[a]	Insured unemployment rate	Discouraged worker rate
1960	5.5	6.0	4.8	n.a.
1961	6.7	6.6	5.6	n.a.
1962	5.5	6.2	4.4	n.a.
1963	5.7	5.7	4.3	n.a.
1964	5.2	5.2	3.8	n.a.
1965	4.5	3.9	3.0	n.a.
1966	3.8	3.2	2.3	n.a.
1967	3.8	3.1	2.5	n.a.
1968	3.6	2.9	2.2	0.9
1969	3.5	3.0	2.1	0.7
1970	4.9	4.7	3.4	0.8
1971	5.9	5.6	4.1	0.9
1972	5.6	5.1	3.5	0.9
1973	4.9	4.2	2.7	0.8
1974	5.6	5.3	3.5	0.8
1975	8.5	8.0	6.0	1.2
1976	7.7	7.3	4.6	1.0
1977	7.1	6.4	3.9	1.0
1978	6.1	5.3	3.3	0.8
1979	5.8	5.0	2.9	0.7
1980	7.1	6.8	3.1	0.9
1981	7.6	7.4	3.5	1.0
1982	9.7	9.4	4.6	1.4
1983	9.6	8.4	3.8	1.5
1984	7.5	6.9	2.8	1.1
1985	7.2	n.a.	2.8	1.0

Source: Author's calculations and BLS, *Handbook of Labor Statistics* (June 1985). Data for 1984 and 1985 are from *Employment and Earnings*, vol. 33 (January 1986).
a. Calculated from published tabulations as the ratio of total weeks of unemployment to labor force time. n.a. = not available.

in 1980 or, more plausibly, because administrative changes have increased the logistical difficulties associated with collecting benefits. It is conceivable that receipt of benefits carries more stigma in the Reagan era than it once did. Perhaps the most plausible explanation, in view of the increasing average duration of unemployment, is that many of the unemployed have exhausted their unemployment insurance eligibility during either their current unemployment spell or a previous one. Although it is not clear what the low insured unemployment rate means, at a minimum it exonerates unemployment insurance as a cause of the high level of unemployment. If a smaller share of the labor force is collecting benefits than used to be the case, unemployment insurance can hardly be blamed for increasing unemployment.

The second column of table 9.6 follows George Akerlof and Janet Yellen in reporting the Work Experience Survey unemployment rate, calculated as the ratio of reported unemployment for the preceding year to reported labor force participation, defined as the sum of time spent employed and unemployed.[23] As they note, using data for the 1960–81 period, there has been a tendency for the retrospective unemployment rate to decline relative to the official rate over time. Between 1974 and 1984, the Work Experience Survey unemployment rate increased by 1.6 points; the official rate, 1.9 points.

Akerlof and Yellen estimate that the CPS unemployment rate corresponding to any given Work Experience Survey unemployment rate rose by about 0.8% per year through 1981, a relationship that has held up over the three additional years for which data have since become available.[24] The CPS rate has thus risen by about 12%, or 1 percentage point, relative to the retrospectively reported unemployment rate over the past fifteen years. Akerlof and Yellen find, however, that there has been essentially no trend increase in the ratio of CPS unemployment to retrospective unemployment for either prime-age men or prime-age women over this period. They also report that about one-fourth of the movement in official unemployment relative to Work Experience Survey unemployment can be explained by changes in the composition of the labor force, particularly the influx of women, for whom the ratio of retrospective unemployment to official unemployment is particularly low.

Citing a variety of psychological studies suggesting that the more painful an experience the better people recall it, Akerlof and Yellen attribute the rising differential between the two rates to a decrease in the discomfort associated with unemployment. They buttress their claim by noting that the ratio of retrospective unemployment to official unemployment is

highest for mature men and that it rises in recessions. A natural interpretation of the Work Experience Survey information is that unemployment has become a less painful and salient experience for young workers. It
might be more accurate to say that the unemployment of young workers
has become less salient for their parents, since one member of a household,
typically an adult, provides information on the labor market status of all
household members in the Work Experience Survey, as in the CPS. The
reduction in the salience of unemployment is not surprising given the sharp
increase in the share of young people in school. It seems reasonable to
conclude from the Work Experience Survey data that a 7% unemployment
rate today is associated with less distress than was once the case. But the
data shed little light on the observed increase in unemployment, most of
which has come from adults.

The final column of the table presents the "discouraged worker" rate,
estimated as the number of discouraged workers divided by the total labor
force. Discouraged workers are defined as those who cite inability to find
work as their sole reason for not searching. Many analysts have argued
that they should properly be counted as unemployed. The discouraged
worker rate has moved in parallel with the official unemployment rate over
the past fifteen years. If, as some have argued, an increasing percentage of
unemployment reflects marginal labor force attachment, one might have
expected to see a decline in the ratio of discouraged workers to unemployed persons. The observed increase in discouragement over the past
decade suggests that increases in unemployment do in fact reflect increases
in the difficulty of job finding.

Different labor market indicators capture different aspects of labor
market performance. It does not appear that other labor market indicators
provide a basis for concluding that the observed increase in CPS unemployment reflects measurement error. However, they do suggest that the
nature of unemployment may have changed over the past fifteen years.

9.1.5 The Search Activities of the Unemployed

Oversimplifying slightly, people are counted as unemployed if they report
being available for work in the Current Population Survey week and report
having looked for work in the preceding four weeks. In practice, the first
question regarding availability for work is the principal determinant of
unemployment status. All survey respondents are asked their primary
activity. Five answers are possible for the unemployed: with a job (to which
they expect to return), looking for work, keeping house, in school, and

Table 9.7
Major activity of the unemployed, 1973–84 (percent except where otherwise indicated)

Year	With a job	Looking for work	Keeping house	In school	Other activities[a]	Average number of search methods used
1973	6.8	34.3	27.3	18.0	13.5	1.52
1974	6.5	35.7	25.5	17.7	14.7	1.54
1975	12.1	38.3	23.2	13.2	13.2	1.58
1976	6.1	38.4	23.4	15.4	16.7	1.58
1977	4.8	36.7	25.2	16.3	16.9	1.57
1978	5.4	34.0	26.8	15.9	17.9	1.53
1979	4.7	33.2	25.8	16.6	19.7	1.54
1980	9.4	34.2	21.6	13.0	21.8	1.58
1981	6.3	34.5	21.9	13.9	23.4	1.59
1982	6.8	36.4	20.4	12.8	23.6	1.63
1983	5.1	38.6	20.1	12.4	23.9	1.64
1984	5.0	37.0	21.3	14.2	22.5	1.63

Sources: Average number of search methods used is from BLS, *Handbook of Labor Statistics* (June 1985), table 35, pp. 85–88, and from *Employment and Earnings*, vol. 33 (January 1986). Major activity of the unemployed was computed by the author using data from the Current Population Survey for May of each year. Figures are rounded.
a. Includes those unemployed who are listed as unable to work.

other. The last category includes but is not limited to retired workers. If increasing unemployment reflects an increase in the number of people marginally attached to the labor force, the number reporting their primary activity as looking for work should have declined. The intensity of their search should also have declined.

While data on the primary activity of the unemployed are not published, I was able to construct a time series on primary activity using raw data from the CPS for May of each year from 1973 through 1984. A conspicuous feature of the data reported in table 9.7 is that only a minority of the unemployed report themselves as having a job or report their primary activity as looking for work.[25] The fraction reporting their primary activity as looking for work or as having a job to which they expect to return varies cyclically but shows no trend during 1973–84. The data reveal significant declines in the proportion of the unemployed reporting their primary activity as keeping house or being in school, a finding that is supported by the observation that the average number of search methods used by unemployed persons has gradually increased.

The mystery in table 9.7 is the dramatic increase in the number of people listing "other" as their primary activity. While "other" includes retirement, it is implausible that the large increase in the category could be accounted for by increasing retirement.[26] As shown in table 9.8, which presents an age-sex breakdown on the primary activity of the unemployed for 1974 and 1984, increases in the "other" category are not confined to older workers for whom the retirement explanation is plausible. The fraction of men aged 25 to 34 reporting "other" as their primary activity rose from 21.3% to 35.3% between 1974 and 1984. Perhaps more important, the table reveals large demographic differences in the nature of the changes in primary activity. There appear to be quite substantial declines in the number of men looking for work except for the cohort aged 20 to 24, while the number of women looking for work has increased slightly. More detailed tabulations suggest that the declines in the fraction of those whose primary activity is looking for work are concentrated among job losers and leavers.

Given the ambiguities associated with the "other" category, it is not clear how to interpret these figures. They may well be related to the greater increase in unemployment among men than among women. They may also have something to do with broader social trends regarding the division of family responsibilities between men and women. Another possibility is that single men, who have increased as a share of the male labor force in recent years, feel less pressure to look for work than their married counterparts.

All of the information presented so far on the increase in unemployment suggests that it is a serious problem. Increases in normal unemployment reflect neither measurement problems nor changes in the demographic composition of the labor force. Rather, unemployment has increased in those segments of the population where it is most serious—among married men, job losers, and the long-term unemployed.

9.2 Regional Differences in Unemployment

So far my object has been more to account for the observed increase in unemployment than to explain it. Inevitably, aggregate time series data are not rich enough to distinguish alternative explanations for rising unemployment. In seeking explanations, I turn to information on the different labor market experiences of different parts of the country.[27]

Data by state reflect widely noted patterns in recent regional economic growth. During the past fifteen years, for example, New England has

Table 9.8
Major activity of the unemployed, by age and sex, 1974 and 1984 (percent)

Category	With a job		Looking for work		Keeping house		In school		Other activities	
	1974	1984	1974	1984	1974	1984	1974	1984	1974	1984
Males										
16–19	1.9	2.0	31.8	24.3	0.3	0.4	50.7	56.7	15.4	16.6
20–24	7.6	3.7	48.7	54.2	0.6	0.7	17.6	12.1	25.5	29.4
25–34	13.6	7.7	60.5	52.3	0.8	1.1	3.9	3.7	21.3	35.3
35–44	11.0	9.8	60.6	54.4	0.0	1.8	0.0	1.6	28.4	32.4
45–54	11.2	9.7	66.4	50.0	0.0	1.4	1.6	0.4	20.8	38.6
55–64	13.6	11.3	55.7	47.2	1.1	0.9	0.0	0.0	29.6	40.6
65 and over	0.0	2.6	41.2	25.6	8.8	2.6	0.0	0.0	50.0	69.2
Females										
16–19	1.6	1.0	19.4	18.4	21.9	14.2	46.7	52.4	10.4	14.0
20–24	5.2	2.1	25.7	30.0	50.5	42.8	9.1	10.5	9.5	14.6
25–34	5.8	2.6	18.1	24.7	70.8	57.5	2.2	4.5	3.1	10.7
35–44	4.2	5.0	22.2	25.4	69.5	58.6	2.4	1.8	1.8	9.2
45–54	7.6	7.7	19.9	24.8	70.2	56.3	0.0	1.8	2.3	9.5
55–64	11.9	6.5	28.6	27.8	54.8	55.6	0.0	0.9	4.8	9.3
65 and over	5.3	3.9	26.3	23.1	52.6	65.4	0.0	0.0	15.8	7.7
Total	6.5	5.0	35.7	37.0	25.5	21.3	17.7	14.2	14.7	22.5

Source: Author's calculations based on CPS tapes for May of 1974 and 1984. Figures are rounded.

performed extraordinarily well, while the North Central States have fared poorly. California's economy has done well, while Alabama, Mississippi, and Louisiana have suffered significant increases in unemployment.

The data reveal significant volatility in the pattern of state unemployment rates. The correlation between 1970 and 1985 state unemployment rates was 0.54. Somewhat surprisingly, the correlation between unemployment rates in the mid-1970s and 1985 was significantly lower. For example, the correlation between unemployment rates in 1976 and 1985 was only 0.03, and the correlation between unemployment rates in 1978 and 1985 was 0.33. That volatility over the past fifteen years indicates that regional information has the potential to illuminate the causes of the observed increase in normal unemployment.[28]

9.2.1 Employment Opportunities and Unemployment

One explanation for regional unemployment differentials is differences in industrial composition. For example, the problems of the North Central area are often attributed to its heavy reliance on manufacturing, while the strength of the New England economy is explained by the growth in its "high-tech" industries. To the extent that regional differences in unemployment reflect only differences in industrial composition, however, they can explain only a little of the observed increase in aggregate unemployment.

In order to explore the importance of such composition effects in explaining differences in state unemployment rates, I used direct information from the CPS to compute adjusted state unemployment rates that control for differences in demographic, educational, industrial, and occupational composition among states. I used data from the May CPS for selected years to estimate an equation relating an individual's employment status to his age, sex, and marital characteristics, two-digit industry, one-digit occupation, educational attainment, and his state of residence.[29] Using the coefficients on the state dummies, I constructed adjusted unemployment rates and then normalized them so that average adjusted unemployment would equal average unemployment as officially reported for the entire year.

Table 9.9 presents both actual and adjusted unemployment rates for each state for 1984, the most recent year for which it was possible to compute adjusted unemployment rates. The striking feature of the data is the similarity between the actual and adjusted unemployment rates. The correlation of the two variables is 0.84. While the adjustments go in the expected direction, reducing unemployment in the Rust Belt states, for

Table 9.9
Actual and adjusted state unemployment rates, 1984 (percent)

State and region	Actual rate	Adjusted rate[a]
New England		
Maine	6.1	6.6
New Hampshire	4.3	6.2
Vermont	5.2	6.8
Massachusetts	4.8	5.6
Rhode Island	5.3	6.9
Connecticut	4.6	5.8
Mid-Atlantic		
New York	7.2	6.4
New Jersey	6.2	6.7
Pennsylvania	9.1	8.2
East North Central		
Ohio	9.4	9.0
Indiana	8.6	7.7
Illinois	9.1	9.2
Michigan	11.2	10.0
Wisconsin	7.3	8.0
West North Central		
Minnesota	6.3	5.2
Iowa	7.0	7.9
Missouri	7.2	8.0
North Dakota	5.1	6.5
South Dakota	4.3	5.1
Nebraska	4.4	4.6
Kansas	5.2	6.6
South Atlantic		
Delaware	6.2	6.4
Maryland	5.4	6.3
District of Columbia	9.0	8.2
Virginia	5.0	6.0
West Virginia	15.0	15.6
North Carolina	6.7	5.5
South Carolina	7.1	5.1
Georgia	6.0	5.2
Florida	6.3	6.2
East South Central		
Kentucky	9.3	8.8
Tennessee	8.6	8.1
Alabama	11.1	7.8
Mississippi	10.8	7.7

Table 9.9 (continued)

State and region	Actual rate	Adjusted rate[a]
West South Central		
Arkansas	8.9	8.3
Louisiana	10.0	9.6
Oklahoma	7.0	6.9
Texas	5.9	4.9
Mountain		
Montana	7.4	8.5
Idaho	7.2	7.2
Wyoming	6.3	8.9
Colorado	5.6	6.7
New Mexico	7.5	8.3
Arizona	5.0	5.3
Utah	6.5	7.8
Nevada	7.8	7.2
Pacific		
Washington	9.5	8.4
Oregon	9.4	9.6
California	7.8	6.8
Alaska	10.0	9.3
Hawaii	5.6	4.3

Sources: Actual unemployment rates are from U.S. Bureau of the Census, *Statistical Abstract of the United States, 1986* (GPO, 1986), p. 409. Adjusted unemployment rates were calculated by the author using the May 1984 CPS.
a. Adjusted unemployment rates are computed relative to Washington, D.C., and are then scaled so that the average adjusted unemployment rate equals the national average unemployment rate.

example, by recognizing the poor performance of manufacturing in recent years, they are not large. Before adjustment for industry and occupation, the difference between the unemployment rate in Massachusetts and that in Ohio was 4.6 percentage points; after adjustment, the difference fell to 3.4 points. Only a relatively small fraction of differences in unemployment rates among states can be explained by differences in the characteristics of workers or jobs. This conclusion is robust. It holds for other years, for changes as well as levels of unemployment, and for employment as well.

This finding suggests that much of the difference in unemployment rates reflects differences across states in the performance of given industries rather than differences in the industrial composition of states. Or it could reflect differences in labor market conditions that influence the willingness to supply labor. Table 9.10 presents estimates of the relationship between employment growth, its components, and changes in unemployment over

Table 9.10
Employment growth and changes in unemployment, various periods, 1970–85[a]

Interval	Percentage change in total employment	Employment change decomposed	
		Change in high-wage employment as a percentage of total employment	Change in non-high-wage employment as a percentage of total employment
1970–85	−0.017 (0.008)	—	—
1975–85	−0.035 (0.026)	−0.151 (0.047)	0.037 (0.035)
1976–85	−0.073 (0.027)	−0.167 (0.045)	0.000 (0.038)
1977–85	−0.083 (0.026)	−0.168 (0.044)	−0.002 (0.043)
1978–85	−0.087 (0.026)	−0.145 (0.045)	−0.025 (0.046)
1979–85	−0.082 (0.029)	−0.144 (0.051)	−0.017 (0.053)
1980–85	−0.057 (0.032)	−0.139 (0.057)	0.004 (0.047)
1981–85	−0.083 (0.038)	−0.147 (0.064)	−0.036 (0.049)
1982–85	−0.150 (0.054)	−0.326 (0.074)	−0.049 (0.059)
1983–85	−0.126 (0.062)	−0.260 (0.096)	−0.076 (0.066)
1984–85	−0.227 (0.062)	−0.182 (0.134)	−0.232 (0.062)

Source: Author's calculations using data from BLS, *Employment and Earnings*, various issues.
a. Dependent variable is the change in unemployment, regressed on a constant and the percentage change in employment of nonagricultural wage and salary workers (first column) and alternatively as the percentage change decomposed into high-wage and non-high-wage employment (last two columns). High-wage employment is defined as employment in manufacturing, mining, construction, and transportation and public utilities. Standard errors are in parentheses.

various sample periods. The first column of the table presents evidence on the relationship between overall employment growth and unemployment. While the relationship has the expected negative sign, it is surprisingly weak. For example, during 1970–85, a hypothetical state that experienced a 30%, or 2% a year, growth in employment would have enjoyed only a 0.5 percentage point decline in unemployment. Over shorter periods, the relationship between employment growth and changes in unemployment is somewhat tighter but still not strong. Between 1981 and 1985, a state that experienced an extra 2% a year of employment growth would have seen its unemployment rate decline by only 0.7%.[30]

The empirical finding that changes in state unemployment rates are only weakly related to total employment growth is vividly illustrated by Massachusetts, which in 1985 had the nation's lowest unemployment rate. While the "Massachusetts Miracle" has been widely discussed, the data in table 9.11 reveal that employment growth in Massachusetts has actually been below national employment growth over the past decade despite the state's 5.5 percentage point reduction in its unemployment rate.[31] In an arithmetic sense, the apparent success of the Massachusetts economy is less the result of job creation than of circumstances that led to relatively slow labor force growth.

Table 9.11

Employment growth and unemployment in Massachusetts and the United States, various periods, 1976–85 (percent except where otherwise indicated)

Period	Change in unemployment (percentage points)	Change in employment	Change in ratio of high-wage employment to total employment[a]
Massachusetts			
1976–80	−3.9	9.7	7.2
1980–85	−1.6	8.4	0.3
1976–85	−5.5	18.9	7.5
United States			
1976–80	−0.6	11.9	3.2
1980–85	0.1	7.9	−0.5
1976–85	−0.5	20.7	2.7

Source: Data for the United States are from BLS, *Handbook of Labor Statistics* (June 1985), and, for 1984 and 1985, from *Employment and Earnings*, vol. 33 (January 1986). Massachusetts data are from *Statistical Abstract of the United States, 1986* and earlier issues.

a. High-wage employment is defined as employment in manufacturing, mining, construction, and transportation and public utilities.

While the relationship between total employment growth and changes in unemployment is weak, the second and third columns of table 9.10 indicate that the relationship between growth in employment in high-wage industries—manufacturing, construction, mining, and public utilities— and unemployment is significantly stronger than the relationship between overall employment growth or growth in low-wage industries and unemployment.[32] The estimates in the last two columns come from separate regressions in which the decomposed employment change is substituted for the total. Creating or avoiding the loss of "good" high-wage jobs appears to be more potent in reducing unemployment than creating low-wage jobs. Further estimates not reported here that allow for a nonlinear relationship between changes in high-wage employment and unemployment suggest that the loss of high-wage jobs has an especially large impact on unemployment. During 1979–85, a fairly representative period, every one hundred high-wage jobs that were lost raised unemployment by twenty-five workers. In contrast, the creation of high-wage jobs had only a minor impact on unemployment. The data in table 9.10 also reveal that over periods longer than a single year, there is essentially no relationship between growth in low-wage employment and unemployment.

As table 9.11 indicates, while Massachusetts did not experience unusual growth in total employment, its high-wage employment growth exceeded that of the rest of the country—though not by enough to account for the extraordinary performance of its economy.

These findings on the relationship between changes in employment and unemployment are instructive. They suggest that in analyzing recent changes in unemployment in the United States, it is not enough to focus on the determination of the total level of employment.[33] It is also necessary to examine the composition of employment growth and to consider the incentives individuals may have to remain unemployed.

9.2.2 What Is Involuntary Unemployment?

As countless analysts have pointed out, the notion of involuntary unemployment involves important logical difficulties. The argument usually goes something like this: virtually everyone counted as unemployed could find some type of job at some wage; even if not, the option of self-employment is surely open; in the sense that there is some option open to all the unemployed, there is a voluntary component to all unemployment.[34] Careful critics of the concept of involuntary unemployment are quick to stress that labeling unemployment as voluntary does not make it benign or socially inconsequential. But they do stress that a proper analysis of its causes requires recognizing its voluntary element.

The standard response to this line of argument is usually to conjure up images of the Great Depression, to highlight the personal and social costs of unemployment, and then to take refuge in some notion that unemployment is involuntary only when "reasonable" jobs are not available. Without some specification of what is meant by a "reasonable" job, the concept of involuntary unemployment is vague, but, at the same time, it does seem to capture an important aspect of what many see happening over the course of cyclical fluctuations.

Perhaps the most coherent set of attempts to justify the concept of involuntary unemployment relies on some notion of segmented labor markets.[35] Where employed workers of a given ability do not receive equal compensation, a meaningful definition of involuntary unemployment is possible. A worker may be defined as involuntarily unemployed if he is unable to get a job at a wage that other workers of his ability are receiving, even if he could get an alternative lower-wage job. If labor markets are segmented so that there are differences in employed workers' compensation unrelated to differences in their ability, it is possible to observe unemployment that has both voluntary and involuntary aspects. It is voluntary in the sense that unemployed workers decline some opportunities to work. But it is involuntary in the sense that others with the same ability as the unemployed are working at wages the unemployed would be willing to accept. Segmented labor markets raise another possibility as well. Some of the unemployed may prefer low-wage jobs to being unemployed, but choose to remain unemployed in order to queue for high-wage jobs.

Any explanation of involuntary unemployment that relies on labor market segmentation must account for the differences in the wages of equally skilled workers in different industries. More specifically, it must explain why high-wage employers who face an excess supply of labor do not reduce wages. A convincing segmented-market interpretation of unemployment should also be able to explain why workers would choose to remain unemployed in order to wait for high-wage jobs, rather than wait while working at lower-paying positions. I take up these issues in turn.

There are three broad classes of explanations for the failure of high-wage employers to reduce their wages in the face of an excess supply of labor. The most obvious is that there are institutional impediments that make it impossible. Unions are one such impediment; regulations are another.[36] But even in the absence of these institutions, there are substantial differentials in the wages different types of employers pay to similar workers.[37] A second class of explanations for wage differentials—labeled efficiency wage theories—holds that firms find it profitable over some range to increase their wages even in the face of an excess supply of labor. By paying higher wages, firms enhance productivity through improved work-force morale, reduced turnover and hiring costs, and increased work-er effort.[38] A third class of explanations—insider-outsider theories—involves the notion of rent sharing between workers and firms. Because hiring and training new workers is costly, incumbent workers have lever-age and so are able to capture a share of the rents that firms earn. Firms are therefore unable to reduce wages even in the face of an excess supply of labor. An important piece of evidence to this effect is that high-wage industries and high-wage firms tend to pay all types of workers high wages.[39]

All three classes of explanations for the failure of high-wage employers to reduce wages when labor supply is excessive support the plausibility of segmented labor markets and thus explain the existence of involuntary unemployment as I have defined it. But on the arguments developed so far, unemployment exists only because the unemployed prefer remaining un-employed to accepting work in low-wage industries. Given the general empirical finding that labor supply is relatively inelastic, it is unlikely that a large number of workers will be willing to work at high- but not low-wage jobs. A more compelling explanation of involuntary unemployment would explain why workers choose to forgo low-wage work in order to seek high-wage work.

In their paper on unemployment in less developed countries, Harris and Todaro offered a very plausible answer to this question. They explained that the high-wage jobs were in the city while the low-wage jobs were in rural areas. It was thus impossible to queue for a high-wage job while holding a low-wage job. The market equilibrated when unemployment in the city was sufficiently high and the chance of getting a high-wage job in the city sufficiently small that workers would opt for the certainty of a low-wage job in the country.

Such an explanation is not plausible for developed economies. Perhaps the most plausible explanation for what has been called "transitional unem-ployment" is that workers who have lost high-wage jobs find it difficult to accept their fate and so prefer remaining unemployed to acknowledging the permanence of their loss by taking a low-wage job.[40] In a society where status is highly bound up with one's occupation, it is to be expected that workers who lose attractive high-wage jobs will be reluctant to accept lesser jobs.

Also, there are fixed costs for workers as well as firms in entering an employment relationship, so that workers who expect to return to high-wage jobs in a relatively short time may find it difficult or undesirable, or both, to take a job at a low-wage firm. Something of this sort must lie behind firms' reluctance to hire "overqualified workers." The unemployed may also feel that accepting a low-wage job suggests to potential high-wage employers that they are not qualified for better jobs and so reduces their chance of getting them. Finally, in some circumstances it may be more efficient to search while remaining unemployed than while working.

While the idea of transitional unemployment can easily be criticized by pointing to the costs to workers of remaining unemployed, the empirical observation that total employment growth in a given state has only a very limited impact on unemployment does suggest that a theory of transitional unemployment is preferable to simple theories based on wage rigidities. If involuntary unemployment were caused by rigid wages, one would expect it to be sharply reduced by movements in the demand for labor, and thus employment, in a given state. The fact that it is not makes it worthwhile at least to explore labor supply aspects of the determination of unemployment. The empirical finding that reductions in high-wage employment increase unemployment and that this impact is not easily offset by growth in low-wage employment suggests that the transitional unemployment suffered by persons losing high-wage jobs is significant.

9.2.3 Unions and Unemployment

To understand the causes of the high and rising normal level of unemployment, it may be desirable to focus on the factors influencing the extent of "transitional unemployment." Without embracing any theory of the cause of transitional unemployment, the preceding discussion suggests that its extent is likely to be determined by the size of the wage differentials between high- and low-wage jobs, the availability of high-wage jobs, and the costs, pecuniary and nonpecuniary, of remaining unemployed. Although all these factors are difficult to quantify, it is a reasonable conjecture that in areas where the level of unionization is high, ceteris paribus, there should be more transitional unemployment. This is especially the case when, as in recent years, the economy is subjected to large intersectoral shocks. High and rising union wage premiums are likely to cause job losses in the unionized sector of the economy and also to make those who lose high-wage jobs more reluctant to accept alternative low-wage employment. The empirical work presented in table 9.12 examines the conjecture that unions increase unemployment.

In investigating the relationship between unionization and unemployment, the critical empirical problem is eliminating other factors that may be correlated with both. Most obviously, the high-wage sector of the economy tends to be more highly unionized than other parts of the economy and in recent years has suffered high unemployment. I address this issue in several ways. First, I estimate the relationship between unionization and both actual unemployment rates and the unemployment rates adjusted for changes in the composition of the labor force, as described earlier. Because the results are broadly similar for the two concepts and because data on official unemployment are available over a longer time span, only results using official unemployment are reported. Second, in several of the specifications reported in table 9.12, I control for the share of the high-wage sector (or alternatively the share of manufacturing) in total employment and for regions in estimating the effect of unionization on unemployment. Third, I treat unionization as endogenous and use the presence of absence of a right-to-work law as an instrument. Nineteen states have such laws, almost all of which were put in place before 1960, so it is plausible to take the presence of a right-to-work law as exogenous. A number of investigators have found that right-to-work laws have a significant effect on union coverage.[41]

The results in table 9.12 support several conclusions. First, there is a clear and substantively significant impact of unionization on state unemployment rates. The estimates for 1985, controlling for both the region and the share of employment in high-wage industries, suggest that an increase of 10 percentage points in a state's unionization rate increases its unemployment rate by 1.2 percentage points. Because there are substantial regional differences in the degree of unionization (in 1982, Texas, with 12.5% of its work force unionized, was the fortieth most unionized state, while Pennsylvania, with 27.0%, ranked tenth), those differences can account for quantitatively important regional variations in the extent of unemployment. Second, there is suggestive evidence that the impact of unionization on unemployment has increased over time. The estimated equation for the change in unemployment between 1970 and 1985, holding constant the

Table 9.12
Unionization and state unemployment rates, 1970–85[a]

Year	Intercept	Union	Share in high-wage industries	Region dummies	Instrumental variables	R^2
1970	3.43 (0.493)	0.044 (0.019)	—	No	No	0.096
1970	4.97 (0.681)	0.059 (0.023)	−0.063 (0.022)	No	No	0.231
1970	5.55 (1.06)	0.053 (0.028)	−0.027 (0.036)	Yes	No	0.540
1970	3.23 (0.784)	0.053 (0.032)	—	No	Yes	0.093
1970	5.18 (1.35)	0.048 (0.041)	—	Yes	Yes	0.561
1985	5.45 (0.750)	0.085 (0.036)	—	No	No	0.309
1985	4.59 (1.62)	0.081 (0.038)	0.035 (0.053)	No	No	0.099
1985	3.46 (2.01)	0.117 (0.045)	0.042 (0.057)	Yes	No	0.554
1985	6.31 (1.20)	0.040 (0.061)	—	No	Yes	0.073
1985	3.60 (2.60)	0.145 (0.085)	—	Yes	Yes	0.549
1970–85	1.67 (0.666)	0.039 (0.026)	—	No	No	0.044
1970–85	0.10 (0.805)	−0.009 (0.027)	0.106 (0.027)	No	No	0.323
1970–85	−1.57 (1.22)	0.062 (0.033)	0.034 (1.47)	Yes	No	0.609
1970–85	3.05 (1.11)	−0.019 (0.045)	—	No	Yes	−0.054
1970–85	−0.77 (1.73)	0.063 (0.053)	—	Yes	Yes	0.585

Source: Author's calculations based on data from the following sources. Unemployment and manufacturing employment data for 1970 are from U.S. Bureau of the Census, *Census of Population, 1970*, vol. 1, *Characteristics of the Population*, section 1, *U.S. Summary* (GPO, 1972), pp. 1–496. Unionization rates for 1970 are from BLS, *Directory of National Unions and Employee Associations 1979*, BLS Bulletin 2079 (September 1980), p. 109. Unemployment and manufacturing employment for 1985 are from *Employment and Earnings*, vol. 33 (January 1986). Unionization rates used in 1985 regressions are 1982 rates obtained from Leo Troy and Neil Sheflin, *Union Sourcebook* (West Orange, New Jersey, Industrial Relations Data and Information Services, 1985), table 7.2, p. 7-4, as no more recent unionization rates could be obtained.

a. Dependent variable is the unemployment rate regressed on a constant and the level of unionization and, where indicated, the percent of workers in high-wage industries (manufacturing, construction, mining, and transportation and public utilities), region dummies, and a dummy instrumental variable for a state with a right-to-work law. Regional divisions correspond to the nine U.S. Census divisions. The regression excludes the District of Columbia since no independent unionization figures for D.C. were published in 1970. Standard errors are in parentheses.

high-wage share of employment and region, suggests that a state with a 20% unionization rate, approximately the sample average, experienced an increase in unemployment of 1.2 percentage points relative to a hypothetical state that had no unions. In this sense, a significant part of the observed increase in normal unemployment in recent years may be attributed to the effects of unions.[42]

In their widely read book *What Do Unions Do?* Richard Freeman and James Medoff estimate that highly unionized states have on average an unemployment rate that is 1 percentage point higher than that of "low" union states.[43] That finding parallels the one reported here. But they report being unable to find any relationship between unionization and the fraction of the population employed in a state, and they infer from that that unions may draw workers into the labor force but that they do not reduce employment. My own findings differ. Table 9.13 reports estimates of the impact of unionization on the employment ratio. While the impact is estimated less precisely than the impact of unionization on the state unemployment rates in table 9.12, the results strongly corroborate the conclusions reached using unemployment data. In fact, in most specifications, the impact of unionization on the employment ratio is greater than its impact on the unemployment rate. For example, when the region and the share of employment in high-wage industries are controlled for, the data suggest that in 1985 an increase of 10 percentage points in the fraction of the work force that was unionized would reduce the employment ratio by almost 4%. Likewise, in most but not all specifications, the impact of unionization on the employment ratio increased by more between 1970 and 1985 than did the impact of unionization on unemployment.

In results not reported here, I have explored the robustness of these conclusions in a number of ways. First, I have estimated the relationship between unionization, unemployment, and the employment ratio using data for every year between 1970 and 1985. The data confirm the upward trend in the impact of unionization. In fact, the trend appears more dramatic when results for the early 1970s are compared with those for the early 1980s. Second, I have estimated the effects of unions on unemployment rates separately for male and female workers. The results indicate that unions have a somewhat greater impact on male unemployment. Third, I have reestimated the equations after combining smaller states into larger units as was done by the CPS in the early 1970s. The reestimate has little impact on the results. Further corroboration for the conclusions reached here comes from the work of other investigators using data on metropolitan areas rather than states. For example, Edward Montgomery, using data

Table 9.13
Unionization and state employment ratios, 1970–85[a]

Year	Intercept	Union	Share in high-wage industries	Region dummies	Instrumental variables	R^2
1970	4.021 (0.027)	−0.024 (0.107)	—	No	No	0.001
1970	4.024 (0.040)	0.081 (0.133)	−0.139 (0.132)	No	No	0.032
1970	4.170 (0.064)	−0.329 (0.169)	0.025 (0.213)	Yes	No	0.393
1970	3.998 (0.043)	0.075 (0.177)	—	No	Yes	−0.017
1970	4.170 (0.088)	−0.379 (0.267)	—	Yes	Yes	0.315
1985	4.123 (0.029)	−0.193 (0.139)	—	No	No	0.038
1985	4.192 (0.061)	−0.193 (0.143)	−0.258 (0.200)	No	No	0.071
1985	4.175 (0.083)	−0.363 (0.188)	0.042 (0.237)	Yes	No	0.451
1985	4.098 (0.046)	−0.063 (0.232)	—	No	Yes	0.021
1985	4.192 (0.106)	−0.387 (0.349)	—	Yes	Yes	0.447
1970–85	0.114 (0.021)	−0.186 (0.082)	—	No	No	0.096
1970–85	0.171 (0.029)	−0.116 (0.098)	−0.252 (0.097)	No	No	0.252
1970–85	0.055 (0.044)	0.021 (0.118)	−0.145 (0.147)	Yes	No	0.577
1970–85	0.100 (0.033)	−0.128 (0.137)	—	No	Yes	0.087
1970–85	0.000 (0.062)	0.083 (0.188)	—	Yes	Yes	0.487

Source: Author's calculations using data from the following sources. Manufacturing employment data for 1970 are from *Census of Population, 1970, U.S. Summary*, pp. 1–469. Labor force participation data are from the same volume, pp. 1–350. Unionization rates for 1970 are from *Directory of National Unions and Employee Associations, 1979*, p. 109. Employment data for 1985 were obtained from *Employment and Earnings*, vol. 33 (January 1986). Population by state is the average of the 1984 population over age 14 and the 1984 population over age 18 multiplied by the growth rate of total population between 1984 and 1985. Unionization rates used in 1985 regressions are 1982 rates obtained from Troy and Sheflin, *Union Sourcebook*, since no more recent unionization rates could be obtained.

a. Dependent variable is the log of the employment ratio regressed on a constant, the level of unionization, and, where indicated, the percent of workers in high-wage industries (manufacturing, construction, mining, and transportation and public utilities), regional dummies, and a dummy instrumental variable for a state with a right-to-work law. Regional divisions correspond to the nine U.S. Census divisions. The regression excludes the District of Columbia since no independent unionization figures for D.C. were published in 1970. Standard errors are in parentheses.

on forty-four standard metropolitan statistical areas in 1983, finds a statistically significant, though not substantially large, negative impact of unionization on employment.[44]

The conclusion that the impact of unions on unemployment has been increasing is not surprising given that the spread in wages between unionized and nonunionized workers has also increased, at least until recently. Table 9.14 presents some information on changes in the employment cost index for unionized and nonunionized workers during 1973–85 and shows that union wage premiums increased during the 1970s and have declined somewhat, but not enough to reverse their previous increase, during the 1980s. Analyses using survey data on the wages of individuals also suggest that union wage premiums rose during the 1970s but find less evidence of a decline in the 1980s than is suggested by newspaper headlines and the employment cost index.[45]

The coincidence of rising union wage premiums and an increasing impact of unionization on state unemployment rates, along with the widely observed decline in employment growth in unionized firms, makes it plausible that union power has accounted for a significant part of the increase in normal unemployment in recent years. The fact that the loss of unionized jobs resulted in increased unemployment despite the rapid creation of jobs

Table 9.14
Annual percentage changes in the employment cost index, by union status, 1973–85

Year	Employment cost index		Cumulative difference
	Union	Nonunion	
1973[a]	5.7	5.5	0.2
1974[a]	7.5	8.0	−0.3
1975[a]	8.6	6.0	2.3
1976	8.1	6.8	3.6
1977	7.6	6.6	4.6
1978	8.0	7.6	5.0
1979	9.0	8.5	5.5
1980	10.9	8.0	6.6
1981	9.6	8.0	8.2
1982	6.5	6.1	8.6
1983	4.6	5.2	8.0
1984	3.4	4.5	6.9
1985	3.6	5.1	5.4

Source: Richard B. Freeman, "In Search of Union Wage Concessions in Standard Data Sets," *Industrial Relations*, vol. 25 (Spring 1986), table 4, p. 139.
a. Estimated from changes in major contract settlements.

in the low-wage service sector provides some support for the "transitional" theory of unemployment advocated here.

9.2.4 Further Evidence on Transitional Unemployment

The discussion so far suggests that increasing union wage premiums during the 1970s contributed to the rising rate of normal unemployment by causing an increase in transitional unemployment. Transitional unemployment is a likely concomitant of any increase in the importance of noncompetitive wage differentials, whether caused by unions or by the efficiency wage and rent sharing considerations discussed above.

Table 9.15, which is drawn from the work of Linda Bell and Richard Freeman, presents several different estimates of the extent of wage dispersion in the economy during 1970–85. Each of the measures indicates that wage dispersion has increased.[46] Rising wage dispersion does not necessarily indicate an increase in the importance of noncompetitive wage dif-

Table 9.15
Dispersion in wages and compensation, 1970–85 (standard deviation of log)

Year	Average hourly earnings in manufacturing	National income and product accounts compensation[a]	Census of manufacturers wages[a]
1970	0.215	0.255	0.221
1971	0.226	0.266	0.222
1972	0.237	0.278	0.237
1973	0.240	0.280	0.242
1974	0.241	0.285	0.240
1975	0.253	0.303	0.247
1976	0.257	0.311	0.252
1977	0.258	0.316	0.260
1978	0.267	0.319	0.269
1979	0.270	0.324	0.279
1980	0.270	0.335	0.282
1981	0.277	0.339	n.a.
1982	0.282	0.349	n.a.
1983	0.286	n.a.	n.a.
1984	0.291	n.a.	n.a.
1985	0.293	n.a.	n.a.

Source: Linda Ann Bell and Richard B. Freeman, "Does a Flexible Industry Wage Structure Increase Employment?: The U.S. Experience," in Linda Ann Bell, "Essays on Labor Market Efficiency" (Ph.D. dissertation, Harvard University, May 1986), table 1, p. 51.
a. n.a. = not available.

ferentials. It could occur because increases in the demand for labor in high-wage industries moved firms along upward-sloping short-run labor supply curves. However, using several different data sources, Bell and Freeman find that the correlation across industries between employment growth and wage growth over the decade of the 1970s was negative, which suggests that shocks in the wage-setting process that moved firms along their labor demand curves predominated. Without invoking the considerations leading to labor market segmentation, noted above, it is difficult to account for these shocks.

It is likely that efficiency wage or rent-sharing considerations led to increases in noncompetitive wage differentials during the 1970s. This inference is supported by evidence that the gap between the wages paid by small firms and those paid by large firms increased during the 1970s even after adjustment for unionization.[47] Given the empirical evidence presented above regarding the impact of unionization on employment, it seems plausible that the general increase in labor market segmentation over the past fifteen years has tended to raise the normal rate of unemployment, though the proposition is difficult to test.

Finally, the transitional unemployment explanation for rising unemployment is also consistent with the information on the nature of the increase in unemployment presented in the first part of this paper. It is most plausibly job losers who would wait to regain high-wage jobs. Investing in waiting for a high-wage job makes much more sense for mature married men, who as a group have a very low employment turnover rate, than for other demographic groups that have much higher turnover rates. Persons losing high-wage jobs are most likely to experience protracted spells of unemployment. Sectoral shocks leading to the loss of high-wage jobs would also lead to plant shutdowns, reducing capacity and thereby raising capacity utilization. In addition, sectoral shocks that hit at high-wage industries could easily account for the change in the vacancies-unemployment relationship, if job losers were reluctant to accept low-wage employment in expanding sectors.

9.3 Conclusions

The analysis in this paper suggests that the rise in normal unemployment over the past twenty years represents a serious problem. The additional unemployment is concentrated among mature married men who have lost jobs and are likely to be out of work for periods of six months or more. Increased unemployment cannot be convincingly dismissed as the consequence of marginal labor force attachment or measurement problems in the CPS. Nor is it simply the result of cyclical weakness in the economy. Persistently high unemployment has coincided with relatively high vacancy and capacity utilization rates.

These conclusions have important implications for economic policy. First, they suggest that while high unemployment is a serious problem, expansionary aggregate demand policies are unlikely to be able to reduce it to the levels of the 1950s and 1960s without creating excessive inflationary pressures, unless they reverse the structural changes that have taken place in recent years. Increased union wage premiums and wage dispersion more generally mean that in equilibrium more people will lose high-wage jobs and choose to remain unemployed longer than was previously the case. The latter effect is magnified by the increasing tendency for the unemployed to be in families with other working members. Between 1977 and 1985, the share of unemployed married males who had another family member working full time increased from 37.4% to 43.6%.

Second, while expansionary policies are not likely to reduce the equilibrium unemployment rate, stable fiscal and monetary policies can probably make a significant contribution. Since workers losing high-wage jobs are the ones most likely to choose transitional unemployment over taking a low-wage job, policies that temporarily contract the high-wage sector of the economy are likely to create structural unemployment. There may be important asymmetries between the effects of expansionary and contractionary policies. Policies that hurt the high-wage sector may create much more transitional unemployment than policies that promote it can alleviate if new high-wage jobs are taken by workers other than those previously laid off.

The recent fiscal-monetary mix and the associated squeeze on the high-wage manufacturing sector are instructive. When the manufacturing sector is squeezed, unemployment increases sharply as those who lose jobs wait to get them back. The eventual abnormal increase in manufacturing output that will be necessary to service the trade debt the United States is now incurring is unlikely to reduce unemployment by as much as the contraction increased it.

I am grateful to David Cutler and Louis Sheiner for extremely capable research assistance and useful discussions. Larry Katz and Jim Poterba provided helpful comments on an earlier draft of this paper. I have benefited even more than usual from the comments of members of the Brookings Panel. The National Science Foundation provided financial support. A data appendix is available from the author on request.

Notes

1. Hall (1970). The title of this paper is patterned after Hall's title. The differences reflect increases in unemployment over the past fifteen years and some doubts about just how close the American economy currently is to full employment.

2. Congressional Budget Office (August 1986).

3. See Medoff (1983) for an earlier treatment of changes in the relationship between unemployment and vacancies. As Abraham (1986) emphasizes, measuring vacancies is not an easy problem. The index used here is the Conference Board Help-Wanted Index adjusted as suggested by Abraham for changes in competition in the newspaper industry and the occupational composition of the labor force.

4. See Perry (1970).

5. For calculations of the natural rate of unemployment and potential GNP that rely heavily on demographically adjusted unemployment rates, see Gordon (1982).

6. The categories are men and women aged 16 to 19, 20 to 24, 25 to 34, 35 to 44, 45 to 54, 55 to 64, and 65 and over.

7. The schooling adjustment is calculated using data for March of each year because questions on educational attainment are asked only in the March CPS.

8. The industry adjustment is not strictly parallel to the others since it is an adjustment to the unemployment rate of experienced workers. This noncomparability is inevitable given that new entrants to the labor force cannot meaningfully be assigned an industry.

9. See Wachter (1977). Wachter forecast, on the basis of demographic considerations, a significant decline in the natural rate of unemployment in the early 1980s.

10. The adjustment is not independent of the previous adjustment for changes in the age-sex composition of the labor force. It also reflects increases in the share of women in the labor force and to some extent reflects changes in the age structure of the labor force. The rise in the proportion of single men noted in the text is particularly striking in light of the decline in the share of teenagers and young men in the labor force.

11. Solow (1976) made this point.

12. For the clearest and most persuasive statement of this view see Hall's comment on Medoff (1983). I consider the argument in more detail later.

13. Age effects may be at work here. It is likely that high school drop-outs in the labor force are on average much younger than people receiving less than eight years of schooling. The issue cannot be investigated using published tabulations.

14. Clark and Summers (1979b). We show that many reentrants have relatively recent work experience and report durations of unemployment very close to the

total time since they last worked. The traditional picture of housewives reentering the labor force after their children have grown up is grossly inconsistent with the facts regarding reentrant unemployment.

15. The consistency of individuals' reported unemployment duration from month to month is examined in Poterba and Summers (1984a, b).

16. This finding is probably a consequence of measurement error in the CPS survey. See Poterba and Summers (1986).

17. For discussion of alternative concepts of the duration of unemployment, see Salant (1977), Akerloff and Main (1980), and Clark and Summers (1979b).

18. Clark and Summers (1979b), table 4.

19. See, for example, Baily (1982), Hall's Comment on Medoff (1983), Burtless (1983), and Akerlof and Yellen (August 1985).

20. For a discussion of these points stressing the ambiguity inherent in the distinction between being unemployed and not being in the labor force, see Clark and Summers (1979b).

21. It would be desirable to examine the quit and lay-off rates in conjunction with other labor market indicators. Unfortunately, publication of these turnover data was discontinued after 1981. As Baily (1982) argued, their behavior up until 1981 does not mirror that of the official unemployment rate.

22. Burtless (1983).

23. My calculation differs slightly from that of Akerlof and Yellen (August 1985) because I used reported labor force participation from the Work Experience Survey as the denominator in calculating the Work Experience Survey unemployment rate rather than using labor force data from the CPS as they did. My procedure reduces somewhat the differential between the two series.

24. The precise estimate depends on what adjustment is made for the changes in the CPS insititued in 1967 after the Gordon Commission report. See President's Commission to Appraise Employment and Unemployment Statistics (1962).

25. See Hall's comment on Medoff (1983) and Hall (July 1978).

26. A phone call to the Bureau of Labor Statistics did not succeed in eliciting any information about the nature of the answers categorized as "other" beyond the observation that it included persons labeling themselves as retired.

27. Studies exploring aspects of the geographic distribution of unemployment include Hall (1972), Medoff (1983), and Marston (February 1985) among many others. The view of geogrpahic differences in unemployment put forward here parallels, in some respects, that of Hall and Marston.

28. U.S. Department of Labor, Bureau of Labor Statistics (September 1986) and earlier issues.

29. The variables included in the equation used to construct adjusted state unemployment rates were age, sex, age-sex, marital status-sex, education, education squared, education-sex, education squared-sex, race, center city status, one-digit occupation, two-digit industry, and state dummies.

30. Employment growth will fail to lead to equal percentage reductions in unemployment if it is associated either with population growth or with increases in labor force participation. Results not reported here indicate that employment growth rates are strongly associated with population growth across states and only weakly associated with changes in labor force participation.

31. For a comprehensive discussion of the Massachusetts experience, see Ladd and Ferguson (1986).

32. See Krueger and Summers (1988) for an examination of the level of wages in different industries controlling for the different characteristics of their workers. We estimate wage premiums of 12% for manufacturing, 12% for construction, 25% for mining, and 25% for public utilities. Very similar results are obtained using data on workers who change industries.

33. Increasing unemployment in Europe has been associated with a cessation of job creation distinguishing it sharply from the United States.

34. For perhaps the best-known recent attack on the concept of involuntary unemployment, see Lucas (May 1978).

35. For arguments along the lines sketched here, see Harris and Todaro (March 1970), Hall (1975), McDonald and Solow (November 1985), and Bulow and Summers (July 1986).

36. For the importance of regulation, see Hall (1975); for the effects of unions, see McDonald and Solow (November 1985).

37. This point has been recognized by institutional labor economists for many years. A recent review of the evidence on wage differentials may be found in Krueger and Summers (1988). Similar conclusions are reached in Dickens and Katz (1987).

38. For an excellent summary of various efficiency wage theories and a strong argument for their relavance to macroeconomics, see Stiglitz (1986). For a survey of some of the relevant empirical literature, see Katz (1986).

39. This finding is reported by Dickens and Katz (1987) and by Groshen (1986).

40. I borrow the term "transitional unemployment" from McDonald and Solow (November 1985). I use it to refer to the unemployment of workers transiting in both directions between the high- and low-wage sectors of the economy.

41. See, for example, Farber (1986).

42. The increase is partially offset by the decline in union coverage of about 4 percentage points between 1970 and 1982. The coefficient estimates for 1985

imply that the decline in union membership reduced the unemployment rate by about 0.5 percentage point. Of course, to the extent that union coverage declined because union members were laid off, the decline in union membership may, over a long transition period, actually have further increased unemployment.

43. Freeman and Medoff (1984).

44. Montgomery (1986).

45. See Freeman (Spring 1986) and Linneman and Wachter (May 1986).

46. Bell and Freeman (May 1986).

47. Gerris (1983).

10 Beyond the Natural Rate Hypothesis

with Olivier J. Blanchard

In a well-known essay, Thomas Sargent (1983) treated the disinflationary policies of Britain's Thatcher government as a useful natural experiment for contrasting two alternative macroeconomic theories. On the classical view, considered by Sargent, disinflation, if credible, is achievable at little cost in unemployment. On the alternative Keynesian view, even credible disinflation is likely to increase unemployment for some time because of the inflationary momentum caused by overlapping price and wage decisions. The results from the Thatcher experiment and from similar experiments conducted in the rest of Europe are now in, and the conclusion is clear: Events have proved both theories wrong. They have been proved wrong in their common presumption that once disinflation dynamics were over, economies would be back to their stable "natural" rate of unemployment.

Consider Britain as an example. Nine years after the onset of disinflationary policies backed by two landslide election victories and significant liberalizations in labor and product markets, and five years after the rate of wage inflation stopped declining, both theories surely would have predicted that unemployment would now have returned at least to its previous level. The reality is very different. The unemployment rate in Britain was 5% when disinflationary policies were commenced in 1979. Over the last four years it has averaged 11.6% and stands at 10% today. While unemployment in Britain is at least declining, the situation in the rest of Europe is grimmer: The OECD actually predicts an increase in the unemployment rate for OECD Europe from 11% in 1987 to 11.2% in 1988.

This paper argues that the European experience of the 1980s poses a profound challenge to standard Keynesian and classical theories of macroeconomic fluctuations. Required is a theory of unemployment in which unemployment, far from returning to a stable "natural rate" over time, is strongly dependent on history. We refer to such an equilibrium as a "fragile equilibrium" because of its sensitive dependence on current and past events.

Developing a theory of fragile equilibrium, we argue, involves questioning and perhaps discarding traditional presumptions about the slopes of labor demand and supply curves.

Section 10.1 briefly reviews macroeconomic developments in Britain over the last ten years, highlighting the inability of standard theories to make useful contact with what has happened. Section 10.2 describes the type of fragile equilibrium theory that is necessary to understand the European experience. Section 10.3 speculates on factors that may lead to fragile equilibria, focusing on possible reasons why labor demand curves may slope upward or labor supply curves may slope downward. Section 10.4 concludes by commenting on the policy implications of the results.

10.1 Standard Theories Cannot Account for the European Experience

Our broad interest is in the dramatic increases in unemployment that has occurred in almost every European country. But we narrow our focus to the United Kingdom for two reasons.[1] First, Britain is often thought to manifest the most advanced case of Eurosclerosis. Second, as emphasized by Sargent, Mrs. Thatcher's election represented a significant structural change in policy. There can be no denying that disinflationary policies encountered credibility problems at the outset, but policy surely became credible after Mrs. Thatcher's second landslide victory.

Standard theories suggest that the high current rate of unemployment could be the result of either structural factors that changed the natural rate of unemployment or cyclical factors that have temporarily driven the British unemployment rate above its normal level. Since at this late date disinflationary policies are surely credible, classical theories suggest that the source of high unemployment must be sought in structural factors, which have increased the equilibrium unemployment rate to its current level. But this line of reasoning runs into two central difficulties.

First, Britain has many structural problems, but it is hard to see how they have gotten worse over the past decade. The last eight years have witnessed the most resolutely conservative government since the second world war, three major Parliamentary acts attacking union power, a generalized attack on the welfare state, and countless ministerial paeans to the free market. The factors stressed by those who see structural factors as a primary cause of high unemployment have all moved in the right direction. Yet more man years of unemployment were suffered in Britian between 1979 and 1987 than in the entire 1939 to 1979 period.

Second, the timing evidence is also difficult to square with the view that structural changes are the cause of high British unemployment. Unemployment increased by 5 percentage points between 1980 and 1982 during which time industrial production plummeted as real interest rates and the pound soared. The origins of the rise in British unemployment in disinflationary policy are clear enough. The mystery is why unemployment has not recovered.

This leads naturally to the second standard explanation for a high unemployment rate: cyclical disturbances that have driven the unemployment rate above its natural level. Keynesian explanations for cyclical contraction are not lacking: For instance, monetary contraction at the beginning of the decade was followed by a period of fiscal austerity leading to today's high unemployment rate. The basic difficulty with this argument is that although unemployment is very high, in most other respects the British economy does not appear to be in recession.

Inflation should have been decreasing sharply if the unemployment rate was far above the natural rate. But CPI inflation in Britain stands at 4.5% for 1987, compared to 5% to 1984, and the rate of growth of nominal wages has more than kept pace with the CPI.[2] Furthermore positive GNP growth since 1982—British real GNP has grown at more than a 3% annual rate over the last three years—has prompted widespread characterizations in Britain of the current period as the longest expansion since the war.

Labor market indicators that normally move cyclically, the rate of permanent layoffs, the overtime rate, and rate at which workers are "stood off" ("temporarily laid off" in the American terminology) all suggest a strong not a weak labor market.[3] At the beginning of 1987, for example, 34% of manufacturing workers worked overtime, just equal to the figure at cyclical peaks in 1974 and 1977, and significantly above the 26% overtime figure in 1981 and the 29% figure observed during the recessions in 1973 and 1976. Similarly less than 1% of the work force was "stood off" during 1986. This rate is comparable to the rate observed during periods of expansion but less than half the rate observed during any previous recession.

The "normality" of the British labor market even in the face of very high unemployment is further evidenced by the data on workers' attitude toward the possibility of unemployment. In June of 1985, 45% of those who were employed thought they could find a job quickly if they became unemployed compared to 40% in September of 1977 when the unemployment rate was only half as high. Similarly the fraction of the employed population regarding their job as safe declined only mildly from 71% to 61% over the same period.

We conclude that it is difficult to account for the British experience within the standard paradigms. In many respects the British labor market appears to be in equilibrium. Yet unemployment has doubled in the presence of structural changes that, if anything, should have worked to reduce it.

10.2 The Need for Theories of Fragile Equilibrium

Almost any theory of the determination of wages and employment can be reduced to the intersection of two shifting loci in wage-employment space. Abusing the language somewhat, we will refer to those loci as demand and supply. Labor demand may, for example, refer to the equilibrium locus of price and employment decisions taken by monopolistically competitive firms given the nominal wage. Labor supply may refer to the set of employment and nominal wage decisions resulting from bargaining between unions and firms given the price level.[4]

Put simply, standard theories of equilibrium unemployment imply sharply sloped downward-sloping labor demand curves and upward-sloping labor supply curves, leading to a sharply defined X diagram with a unique equilibrium. They carry the implication that small shocks, small shifts in supply or demand curves, have small effects on equilibrium unemployment. They also usually imply that this unique equilibrium is stable and that the dynamic effects of transitory shocks on equilibrium unemployment do not last very long. But, as we have just argued, these implications are precisely why standard theories cannot explain the current European experience and why we have to look for alternatives.

A physical analogy is useful here. Consider a ball on a hilly surface. If the surface is bowl shaped, there will be a single uniquely and sharply determined equilibrium position for the ball—at the bottom of the bowl. This is the view implicit in the natural rate hypothesis. But the European experience suggests other possibilities. If the surface contains two pronounced valleys, is extremely flat, or contains many mild depressions, the ball's equilibrium position will not be uniquely or sharply determined but will depend sensitively on just how the ball is shocked. We use the term "fragile equilibria" to refer to situations of this type—where equilibrium outcomes are very sensitive to shocks and may be history dependent.

Returning to labor supply and demand curves, the natural way to think about fragile equilibria in unemployment is to think about economic mechanisms that can give rise either to upward-sloping demand curves or downward-sloping supply curves. Such schedules allow for the possibility of multiple equilibria, unstable equilibria, and equilibria that are extremely sensitive to small changes in initial conditions. Even if supply and demand curves have the conventional slopes, equilibria will appear fragile if the curves are flat and intersect at a narrow angle. In this case small movements in either schedule will have large effects on equilibrium unemployment.

Research on multiple equilibria (e.g., Diamond 1982) and on hysteresis (e.g., Blanchard and Summers 1986) suggests mechanisms that may generate equilibrium unemployment rates that depend sensitively on the shocks an economy has experienced. As the example of the ball finding a position on a hilly surface suggests, the distinctions between these different possibilities is less important than their common implication that unemployment equilibria are likely to be fragile.

10.3 Some Fragile Equilibrium Theories

Modifying the classic labor supply, labor demand determination of employment to make employment equilibria fragile requires either adducing considerations that make labor supply potentially downward sloping or labor demand upward sloping. This section suggests a number of mechanisms that can do the job.

Downward-Sloping Labor Supply

In Blanchard and Summers (1986, 1987) we built on the work of Gregory (1986) in advancing the argument that there is a tendency for the equilibrium unemployment rate to track the actual unemployment rate because unions bargain only on behalf of their incumbent members. In the simplest case where union members simply set wages to ensure the employment of their current members but not to permit the firm to do any hiring, the wage-setting relation and the labor demand curve will coincide, allowing for a continuum of equilibria and hystereses. Even apart from this extreme case, as long as the employed play an important role in wage setting, lower employment may breed greater not lesser aggressiveness in wage setting. As employment decreases, real wage demands by the employed workers will increase, leading to a labor supply curve that is downward sloping in wage-employment space.

There is a different way of generating very similar effects, which has been suggested by Minford. Suppose that unemployment undermines the work ethic. This may arise because of the direct effects on workers' attitudes of prolonged unemployment, because the stigma associated with unemployment declines in a high unemployment society (British libraries in the Midlands make available pamphlets with the title "Leaving School: What You Should Know About Social Security Benefits"), or because of the policy changes unemployment brings about. The Thatcher government stopped requiring unemployment insurance recipients to regularly appear at job centers because there was not enough room to accommodate them. In each of these cases a reduction in employment may work to raise the wages that firms must pay to attract labor, again generating a downward-sloping labor demand schedule.

These interpretations of events in Europe would lead one to expect unemployment to be concentrated among outsiders, new entrants or workers who have been unemployed for a long time. One would expect the employed to feel relatively secure about their jobs and overtime rather than additional hiring to be used for short-term fluctuations, all of which fits well the current situation. One would also expect the short-term unemployed to have more influence on wage bargaining than the long-term unemployed, and this also seems to be the case (Layard and Nickell 1985).

A difficulty shared however by both lines of explanation is that to the extent that they imply movements along a downward-sloping demand curve, one would have expected real wages to have increased as firms moved up their labor demand. But by almost any measure of trend productivity growth, real wages have fallen, not risen, relative to productivity, following the disinflation that began in 1980. This suggests that they omit some important labor demand side element from the story.

Upward-Sloping Labor Demand

Writing from different perspectives, many authors, including Weitzman (1982), Diamond (1982), Howitt and McAfee (1987), and Blanchard and Summers (1987), have recognized that increasing returns provide a natural explanation for why the labor demand curve relating the real wages of workers and the firm's employment decision might slope upward over some range. Essentially the idea is that with increasing returns the marginal revenue product of labor increases with the level of employment. This may be because of physical increasing returns in the production process arising from fixed costs as in Weitzman, the improved matches between employees and employers suggested by Diamond's search model and explored in Howitt and McAfee, or the "fiscal increasing returns" arising from the fall in tax rates when increases in employment raise the tax base available to finance a fixed or increasing level of government spending, as discussed in our earlier paper.

Evidence on the role of physical increasing returns is hard to adduce. The strong performance of labor productivity in British manufacturing over the last five years certainly does not give strong support to this argument, though aggregate productivity growth in Europe as in the rest of the world has been slower during the 1980s, when employment growth has been poor, than during previous periods, when employment grew rapidly. The case for fiscal increasing returns is stronger. We demonstrated in our earlier paper that it was likely that once tax effects were recognized, increases in employment in Europe would be associated with increases in workers' take-home pay. This suggests an upward-sloping labor demand curve in the aftertax wage-employment space.

There is a second mechanism that may generate an upward-sloping labor demand curve. Discussions of European labor markets invariably stress the adverse effects of rules that preclude firms from laying off workers. But the importance of those rules depends very much on such factors as the growth rate of demand facing firms, the quit (or natural attrition) rate, and the degree of uncertainty facing firms. The lower the growth rate or the lower the quit rate, for example, the more likely a firm is to be constrained by those rules, and the greater the shadow cost that they impose. This suggests a mechanism through which high unemployment may increase firm's labor costs, leading to an upward-sloping labor demand curve. As unemployment increases, workers are more reluctant to change jobs, and the quit rate decreases. This increases the shadow cost of firing restrictions. If the effect of unemployment on quits and the effect of reduced quits on the shadow cost of labor are both sufficiently strong, an upward-sloping demand curve for labor will result.

Evidence on this mechanism is also difficult to obtain. Surveys of firms suggest that the importance of firing restrictions varies across European countries, with the restrictions playing a minor role in Britain. Turning to direct evidence, there are no data on quits (versus layoffs) in most European countries, including Britain. For Italy, where data are available, the quit rate in the industrial sector has decreased from an average 14% during 1965 to 1973 to an average of 6.5% for 1980 to 1985. This is a substantial decrease, especially when one takes into account that at such low levels of quit rates, the workers who quit are unlikely to be those that the firm would want to fire. The effect of the attrition rate on shadow cost of labor is also uncertain. Recent theoretical research (Bentolila and Bertola 1987) has derived the relation between the shadow cost of labor and the hiring and firing costs. This research suggests that at least for firms that have low rates of growth, decreases in the quit rate can substantially decrease average employment.

10.4 Conclusions

We believe that understanding unemployment in Europe will require economists to dispense with the natural rate hypothesis that underlies much of both Keynesian and classical macroeconomics. Theories of fragile equilibria are necessary to come to grips with events in Europe. We have suggested some elements that may go into the construction of these theories.

Our focus has been on unemployment equilibria. Drawing supply and demand curves with varying slopes and specifying dynamics, the reader will have no difficulty constructing examples in which equilibria exhibit a variety of stability properties. One possibility is suggested by each of the mechanisms considered above and is intriguing enough to warrant mention. Each of them suggests that transitory deviations may leave the equilibrium rate unchanged, but prolonged deviations may lead to a change in that rate. Union members who lose jobs are unlikely to be disfranchised immediately. It takes time for unemployment's stigma to diminish. Increasing returns effects will only come into play with significant lags as firms enter or exit industries and governments adapt tax rules. Irreversibilities in employment will weigh heavily on firms only when they expect a very long-lasting contraction in demand.

What is the policy implication of the view that European unemployment equilibria are fragile and that current high levels of unemployment are largely the legacy of past policies? Without much needed theoretical and empirical work isolating the reasons why equilibria are fragile, it is difficult to draw firm conclusions. There are clearly two logical possibilities. It may be more difficult to decrease than to increase equilibrium unemployment. If so, there may be relatively little that macroeconomic policy can do to restore full employment. On the other hand, just as the adverse shocks of the late 1970s and early 1980s had a durable impact, policies that sharply increased the demand for labor might have the lasting effect of increasing employment. Resolving the issue will be impossible until economists are willing to move beyond the natural rate hypothesis in thinking about European unemployment.

Notes

1. For a detailed discussion of European experience, see Lawrence and Schultze (1987).

2. More formal estimates of noninflationary unemployment rates (NAIRU) confirm that in most countries, NAIRU and actual unemployment rates are close to each other.

3. Summers (1988) develops the argument in this paragraph in more detail.

4. This is, for example, the structure of the model constructed by Layard and Nickell (1986) to study unemployment in the United Kingdom.

References

Abowd, J., and A. Zellner, "Application of Adjustment Techniques to U.S. Gross Flow Data," in *Proceedings of the Conference on Gross Flows in Labor Force Statistics* (1985), Washington, D.C.: U.S. Government Printing Office.

Abowd, J., and A. Zellner, "Estimating Gross Labor Force Flows," *Journal of Economic and Business Statistics* 3 (1985), 254–283.

Akerlof, G., and B. Main, "Unemployment Spells and Unemployment Experience," *American Economic Reivew* 70 (1980), 885–893.

Akerlof, G., and B. Main "An Experience Weighted Measure of Employment Durations," *American Economic Review* (December 1981), 1003–1011.

Akerlof, G., and J. Yellen, "Unemployment through the Filter of Memory," *Quarterly Journal of Economics* 100 (August 1985), 747–773.

Alchian, A., "Information Costs, Pricing, and Resource Unemployment," in Phelps (ed.), *Microeconomic Foundations*, 27–52.

Altonji, J., "Does the Labor Market Clear? A Test under Alternative Expectations Assumptions," Mimeo (1980).

Altonji, J., "The Intertemporal Substitution Model of Labor Market Fluctuations: An Empirical Analysis," *Review of Economic Studies* 49 (1982).

Ashenfelter, O., and R. Smith, "Compliance with the Minimum Wage Law," Technical Analysis Paper 19A (April 1974), Department of Labor, Office of the Assistant Secretary for Policy, Evaluation and Research.

Azariadis, C., "Implicit Contracts and Underemployment Equilibria," *Journal of Political Economy* 83 (December 1975), 1183–1202.

Bailar, B., "The Effects of Rotation Group Bias on Estimates from Panel Surveys," *Journal of the American Statistical Association* 70 (March 1975), 23–30.

Baily, M., "The Labor Market in the 1930s," in Tobin (ed.), *Macroeconomics, Prices, and Quantities* (1983), Washington, D.C.: The Brookings Institution, 21–62.

Baily, M., "Wages and Employment under Uncertain Demand," *Review of Economic Studies* 41 (January 1974), 37–50.

Baily, M., "Labor Market Performance, Competition, and Inflation," in Baily (ed.) *Workers, Jobs, and Inflation* (1982), Washington, D.C.: The Brookings Institution, 15–44.

Baily, M., and J. Tobin, "Macroeconomic Effects of Selective Public Employment and Wages Subsidies," *Brookings Papers on Economic Activity* 2 (1977), 511–541.

Bancroft, G., and S. Garfinkle, "Job Mobility in 1961," *Monthly Labor Review* 86 (August 1963), 897–906.

Barker, A., P. Lewis, and M. McCann, "Trade Unions and the Organisation of the Unemployed," *British Journal of Industrial Relations* 3 (1984), 391–404.

Barret, N., and R. Morgenstern, "Why Do Blacks and Women Have High Unemployment Rates?" *Journal of Human Resources* 9 (Fall 1974), 456.

Barro, R., "Long-Term Contracting, Sticky Prices, and Monetary Policy," *Journal of Monetary Economics* 3 (July 1977), 305–316.

Barro, R., "A Capital Market in an Equilibrium Business Cycle Model," *Econometrica* 48 (September 1980), 1393–1417.

Barron, J., and W. Mellow, "Search Effort in the Labor Market," *Journal of Human Resources* (forthcoming).

Barth, P., "Unemployment and Labor Force Participation," *Southern Economic Journal* (1968), 375–382.

Bell, L., and R. Freeman, "Does a Flexible Industry Wage Structure Increase Employment?: The U.S. Experience," in Bell, "Essays on Labor Market Efficiency" (May 1986), Ph.D. dissertation, Harvard.

Ben-Porath, Y., "Labor Force Participation Rates and the Supply of Labor," *Journal of Political Economy* 81 (May–June 1973).

Bentolila, S., and G. Bertola, "Hiring Costs, Firing Costs and European Employment," Mimeo, MIT, 1987.

Bishop, Y., S. Feinberg, and P. Holland, *Discrete Multivariate Analysis: Theory and Practice* (1975), Cambridge, MA: MIT Press.

Blanchard, O., and L. Summers, "Perspectives on High World Real Interest Rates," *Brookings Papers on Economic Activity* 2 (1984), 273–334.

Blanchard, O., and L. Summers, "Fiscal Policy, Real Wages and European Unemployment," Mimeo, (June 1986) Harvard.

Blanchard, O., and L. Summers, "Hysteresis and the European Unemployment Problem," in S. Fischer (ed.), *NBER Macroeconomics Annual* 1 (1986), Cambridge: MIT Press.

Blanchard, O., and L. Summers, "Hysteresis and the European Unemployment Problem," in S. Fischer (ed.), *NBER Macroeconomics Annual I* (1986), 15–78.

Blanchard, O., and L. Summers, "Fiscal Increasing Returns, Real Wages, and European Unemployment," *European Economic Review* (1987).

Blanchard, O., and L. Summers, "Hysteresis in Unemployment," *European Economic Review* (1987).

Blinder, A., *Toward an Economic Theory of Income Distribution* (1974), Cambridge: MIT Press.

Blinder, A., and S. Fischer, "Inventories, Rational Expectations, and the Business Cycle," Working Paper (1980), NBER.

Bowen, W., and T. Finnegan, *The Economics of Labor Force Participation* (1969), Princeton: Princeton University Press.

Bradshaw, T., and J. Scholl, "The Extent of Job Search During Layoff," *Brookings Papers on Economic Activity* 2 (1976), 515–524.

Bruno, M., and J. Sachs, *The Economics of Worldwide Stagflation* (1985), Oxford: Basil Blackwell.

Buiter, W., "A Guide to Public Sector Debt and Deficits," *Economic Policy* 1 (November 1985), 13–60.

Bulow, J., and L. Summers, "A Theory of Dual Labor Markets with Application to Industrial Policy, Discrimination and Keynesian Unemployment," *Journal of Labor Economics* 4 (July 1986), 376–414.

Bureau of the Census, *The Current Population Survey Reinterview Program: January 1961 through December 1966*, Technical Paper No. 19 (1969), Washington, D.C.: U.S. Government Printing Office.

Bureau of Labor Statistics, *Jobseeking Methods Used by American Workers*, Bulletin 1886 (1975), 7.

Burtless, G., "Why Is Insured Unemployment So Low?" *Brookings Papers on Economic Activity* 1 (1983), 225–249.

Campbell, J., and G. Mankiw, "Are Output Fluctuations Transitory?" Mimeo (1985), Harvard.

Chamberlain, G., "The Use of Panel Data in Econometrics," Unpublished (1978).

Clark, K., and L. Summers, "Social Insurance, Unemployment and Labor Force Participation" (1978), Department of Labor, Office of the Assistant Secretary for Policy, Evaluation and Research.

Clark, K., and L. Summers, "The Demographic Composition of Cyclical Variations in Employment," Technical Analysis Paper 61 (January 1979), Department of Labor, Office of the Assistant Secretary for Policy, Evaluation and Research.

Clark, K., and L. Summers, "Labor Market Dynamics and Unemployment: A Reconsideration," *Brookings Papers on Economic Activity* (1979), 13−60.

Clark, K., and L. Summers, "Labor Force Transitions and Unemployment," *Brookings Papers on Economic Activity* 1 (1979), 13−60.

Clark, K., and L. Summers, "Demographic Differences in Cyclical Employment Variation," *Journal of Human Resources* 16 (Winter 1981), 61−79.

Clark, K., and L. Summers, "Labor Force Participation: Timing and Persistence," *Review of Economic Studies* 49 (1982), 825−844.

Clark, K., and L. Summers, "The Dynamics of Youth Unemployment," in Freeman and Wise (eds.), *The Youth Labor Market Problem: Its Nature, Causes and Consequences* (1982), Chicago: University of Chicago Press, 199−235.

Coe, D., and F. Gagliardi, "Nominal Wage Determination in Ten OCED Countries," Working Paper 19 (March 1985), OECD Economics and Statistics Department.

Darby, M., J. Hattiwanger, and M. Plant, "Unemployment Rate Dynamics and Persistent Unemployment Under Rational Expectations," *American Economic Review* 75 (1985), 614−637.

Deming, W., and F. Stephan, "On a Least Squares Adjustment of a Sampled Frequency Table When the Expected Marginal Totals Are Known," *Annals of Mathematical Statistics* 11 (1940), 427−444.

Dernberg, T., and K. Strand, "Hidden Unemployment 1953−62: A Quantitative Analysis by Age and Sex," *American Economic Review* 56 (March 1966) 71−95.

Diamond, P., "Aggregate Demand in Search Equilibrium," *Journal of Political Economy* 90 (October 1982), 881−894.

Dickens, W., and L. Katz, "Inter-industry Wage Differences and Theories of Wage Determination," (1987), NBER Working Paper No. 2271.

Dickens, W., and L. Katz, "Inter-industry Wage Differences and Industry Characteristics," in K. Lang and J. Leonard (eds.), *Unemployment and the Structure of Labor Market* (1987), Oxford: Blackwell, 48−89.

Dornbusch, R., and S. Fischer, *Macroeconomics* (1978), New York: McGraw-Hill.

Dornbusch R., et al., "Macroeconomic Prospects and Policies of the European Community," Discussion Paper 1 (1983), Brussels: Center for European Policy Studies [reprinted in O. Blanchard, R. Dornbusch, and R. Layard (eds.) *Restoring Europe's Prosperity* (1986) Cambridge, MA: MIT Press, 1−32].

Drazen, A., "On Permanent Effects of Transitory Phenomena in a Simple Growth Model," *Economics Letters* 3 (1979), 25−30.

Efron, B., *The Jackknife, the Bootstrap, and Other Resampling Plans* (1982), Philadelphia: Society for Industrial and Applied Mathematics.

Ellwood, D., "Teenage Unemployment: Permanent Scars or Temporary Blemishes?" in R. Freeman and D. Wise (eds.), *The Youth Labor Market Problem: Its Nature, Sources and Consequences* (1982), Chicago: University of Chicago Press-NBER.

Employment and Earnings 21 (1975), 159–160.

Employment and Training Report of the President (1978), 201.

Farber, H., "Right-to-Work Laws and the Extent of Unionization," *Journal of Labor Economics* 2 (July 1984), 319–352.

Farber, H., "The Analysis of Union Behavior," in O. L. Ashenfelter and R. Layard (eds.), *Handbook of Labor Economics*, vol. 2 (1986), Amsterdam: North-Holland.

Feldstein, M., "The Economics of the New Unemployment," *Public Interest* (Fall 1973).

Feldstein, M., "Lowering the Permanent Rate of Unemployment," Study prepared for the use of the Joint Economic Committee, 93rd Cong. 1st Sess. (1973), Washington, D.C.: Government Printing Office.

Feldstein, M., "The Importance of Temporary Layoffs: An Empirical Analysis," *Brookings Papers on Economic Activity* 3 (1975), 725–745.

Feldstein, M., "The Temporary Layoffs in the Theory of Unemployment," *Journal of Political Economy* 84 (October 1976), 937–957.

Feldstein, M., "The Private and Social Costs of Unemployment," *American Economic Review* 68 (May 1978, *Papers and Proceedings 1977*), 155–158.

Feldstein, M., "The Effect of Unemployment Insurance on Temporary Layoff Unemployment," *American Economic Review* 68 (December 1978), 834–846.

Feldstein, M., and D. Frisch, "Corporate Tax Integration: The Estimated Effects on Capital Accumulation and Tax Distribution of Two Integration Proposals," *National Tax Journal* 30 (March 1977), 37–52.

Feldstein, M., and B. Wright, "High Unemployment Groups in Tight Labor Markets," Discussion Paper 488 (June 1976), HIER.

Fischer, S., "Long Term Contracts, Rational Expectations and the Optimal Money Supply Rule," *Journal of Political Economy* 85 (February 1977), 191–205.

Fleisher, B., and G. Rhodes, "Unemployment and the Labor Force Participation of Married Men and Women: A Simultaneous Model," *Reivew of Economics and Statistics*, 398–406.

Flinn, C., and J. Heckman, "Models for the Analysis of Labor Market Dynamics," in R. Basmann and G. Rhodes (eds.), *Advances in Econometrics*, Greenwich, CT: JAI Press.

Freeman, R., "Individual Mobility and Union Voice in the Labor Market," *American Economic Review* (May 1976), 361–368.

Freeman, R., "Quits, Separations, and Job Tenure: The Exit-Voice Tradeoff," Unpublished (1977).

Freeman, R., "The Exit-Voice Tradeoff in the Labor Market: Unionism, Job Tenure, Quits, and Separations," *Quarterly Journal of Economics* (June 1980), 643−674.

Freeman R., "In Search of Union Wage Concessions in Standard Data Sets," *Industrial Relations* 25 (Spring 1986), 131−145.

Freeman, R., and J. Medoff, "Why Do Youth Unemployment Rates Differ across Labor Market Surveys?" in Freeman and Wise (eds.) *The Youth Labor Market Problem: It Nature, Causes and Consequences* (1982a), Chicago: University of Chicago Press, 1867−1960.

Freeman, R., "Economic Determinants of the Geographic and Individual Variation in Labor Market Positions of Young Persons," in Freeman and Wise (eds.), *The Youth Labor Market Problem: Its Nature, Causes and Consequences* (1982b), Chicago: University of Chicago Press, 115−154.

Freeman, R., and J. Medoff, "The Youth Labor Market Problem in the United States: An Overview," in Freeman and Wise (eds.), *The Youth Labor Market Problem: Its Nature, Causes and Consequences* (1982c), Chicago: University of Chicago Press, 35−74.

Freeman, R., and J. Medoff, *"What Do Unions Do?"* (1984), New York: Basic Books, 120−121.

Friedman, B., Comment on "After Keynesian Macroeconomics" by R. Lucas and T. Sargent, in *After the Phillips Curve: Persistence of High Inflation and High Unemployment* (1978), Federal Reserve Bank of Boston.

Friedman, M., *Price Theory: A Provisional Text* (1962), Aldine.

Friedman, M., "The Role of Monetary Policy," *American Economic Review* 58 (March 1968), 1−17.

Fuller, W., and T. Chua, "A Model of Multinominal Response Error," Report prepared for the U.S. Bureau of Census (April 1983).

Fuller, W., and T. Chua, "Gross Change Estimation in the Presence of Response Error," in *Proceedings of the Conference on Gross Flows in Labor Force Statistics* (1985), Washington, D.C.: U.S. Government Printing Office.

Gerris, N., "The Changing Size Wage Effect" (1983), Undergraduate thesis, Harvard.

Ghez, G., and G. Becker, *The Allocation of Time and Goods Over the Life Cycle* (1975), NBER.

Gordon, R., "The Welfare Cost of Higher Unemployment," *Brookings Papers on Economic Activity* 1 (1973), 133−195.

Gordon, R., "Inflation, Flexible Exchange Rates, and the Natural Rate of Unemployment," in Baily (ed.), *Workers, Jobs and Inflation* (1982), Washington, D.C.: The Brookings Institution, 89–152.

Gordon, R., "A Century of Evidence on Wage and Price Stickiness in the United States, the United Kingdom and Japan," in J. Tobin (ed.), *Macroeconomics, Prices and Quantities* (1983), Washington, D.C.: Brookings Institution, 85–120.

Gordon, R., and J. Wilcox, "Monetarist Interpretations of the Great Depression, An Evaluation and a Critique," in K. Brunner (ed.), *The Great Depression Revisited* (1981), Martinus Nijhoff, 49–207.

Gottfries, N., and H. Horn, "Wage Formation and the Persistence of Unemployment," Institute for International Economic Studies Working Paper 347 (1986), Stockholm.

Graham, D., "Estimation, Interpretation, and Use of Response Error Measurements," Mimeo (1979), Washington, D.C.: U.S. Department of Commerce.

Gramlich, E., "Impact of Minimum Wages on Other Wages, Employment, and Family Incomes," *Brookings Papers on Economic Activity* 2 (1976), 409–451.

Gregory, R., "Wage Policy and Unemployment in Australia," *Economica* 53, supplement (1986).

Groshen, L., "Sources of within Industry Wage Dispersion: Do Wages Vary By Employer?" (1986) Ph.D. dissertation, Harvard.

Grubb, D., "The OECD Data Set," Working Paper 615 (1984) LSE Center for Labor Economics.

Gustman, A., "Analyzing the Relation of Unemployment Insurance to Unemployment," in R. Ehrenberg (ed.), *Research in Labor Economics*, vol. 5 (1982), Greenwich, CT: JAI Press, 69–114.

Hall, R., "Why Is the Unemployment Rate So High at Full Employment?" *Brookings Papers on Economic Activity* 3 (1970), 369–402.

Hall, R., "Turnover in the Labor Force," *Brookings Papers on Economic Activity* 3 (1972), 709–756.

Hall, R., "The Rigidity of Wages and the Persistence of Unemployment," *Brookings Papers on Economic Activity* (1973), 301–350.

Hall, R., "The Phillips Curve and Macroeconomic Policy," *Carnegie Rochester Conference on Economic Policy* 1 (1976), 127–148.

Hall, R., "The Nature and Measurement of Unemployment," Working Paper 252 (July 1978); NBER.

Hall, R., "A Theory of the Natural Unemployment Rate and the Duration of Unemployment," *Journal of Monetary Economics* 5 (1979), 153–169.

Hall, R., "Employment Fluctuations and Wage Rigidity," *Brookings Papers on Economic Activity* 1 (1980), 91–141.

Hall, R., "Labor Supply and Aggregate Fluctuations," Carnegie Rochester Conference 12 (1980), 7–34.

Hall, R., Comment on Medoff's "U.S. Labor Markets," *Brookings Papers on Economic Activity* 1 (1983), 121–123.

Hamermesh, D., "Entitlement Effects, Unemployment Insurance and Employment Decisions," *Economic Inquiry* 17 (July 1979), 317–332.

Hargraves-Heap, S., "Choosing the Wrong Natural Rate, Accelerating Inflation or Decelerating Unemployment and Growth," *Economic Journal* 90 (September), 611–620.

Harris, J., and M. Todaro, "Migration, Unemployment and Development: A Two Sector Analysis," *American Economic Review* 60 (March 1979), 126–143.

Heckman, J., "The Common Structure of Statistical Models of Truncation, Sample Selection and Limited Dependent Variables and a Simple Estimator for Such Models," *Annals of Economic and Social Measurement* 5 (Fall 1976), 475–492.

Heckman, J., "Statistical Models for Discrete Panel Data Developed and Applied to Test the Hypothesis of True State Dependence against the Hypothesis of Spurious State Dependence," Unpublished (1978).

Hilaski, H., "The Status of Research on Gross Changes in the Labor Force," *Employment and Earnings* 15 (October 1968), 6–13.

Holt, C., et al., "Manpower Proposals for Phase III," *Brookings Papers on Economic Activity* 3 (1971), 703–722.

Houthakker, H., and L. Taylor, *Consumer Demand in the U.S.: Analysis and Projections*, (1970).

Howitt, P., and R. P. McAfee, "Costly Search and Recruiting," *International Economic Review* 33 (February 1987), 89–107.

Kaitz, H., "Analysing the Length of Spells of Unemployment," *Monthly Labor Review* 93 (November 1970), 11–20.

Katz, L., "Efficiency Wage Theories: A Partial Evaluation," in S. Fischer (ed.), *NBER Macroeconomics Annual* 1 (1986), Cambridge, MA: MIT Press, 235–289.

Kaufman R., "On Britain's Competitive Sector," *British Journal of Industrial Relations*, (March 1984).

Kiefer, N., and G. Neumann, "An Empirical Job-Search Model, with a Test of the Constant Reservation-Wage Hypothesis," *Journal of Political Economy* 87 (February 1979), 89–107.

Krueger, A., and L. Summers, "Efficiency Wages and the Wage Structure," Working Paper 1952 (1986), NBER.

Krueger, A., and L. Summers, "Reflections on the Inter-industry Wage Structure," in K. Lang and J. Leonard (eds.), *Unemployment and the Structure of the Labor Market* (1987), Oxford: Blackwell, 17−47.

Kydland, F., and E. Prescott, "Time to Build and Aggregate Fluctuations," *Econometrica* 50 (January 1982), 1345−1370.

Ladd, H., and R. Ferguson, "Massachusetts' Economic Development: A Case Study," Working Paper (1986), Kennedy School of Government, Harvard.

Lancaster, T., "Econometric Methods for the Duration of Unemployment," *Econometrica* 47 (1979), 935−956.

Lawrence, R., and C. Schultze, *Barriers to European Growth: A Transatlantic View* (1987), Washingtons D.C.: The Brookings Institution.

Layard, R., "Youth Unemployment in Britain and the U.S. Compared," in Freeman and Wise (eds.), *The Youth Labor Market Problem: Its Nature, Causes and Consequences* (1982), Chicago: University of Chicago Press.

Layard, R., and S. Nickell, "Unemployment in Britain," *Economica* (Special Issue on Unemployment) (1985).

Layard, L., and S. Nickell, "The Performance of the British Labor Market," Paper presented at the Chelwood Gate Conference on the British Economy (May 1986a).

Layard, R., and S. Nickell "Unemployment in Britain," *Economica* 53, supplement (1986b).

Layard, R., S, Nickell, and R. Jackman, "On Vacancies," LSE Center for Discussion Paper 165 (August 1984), LSE Center for Labor Economics.

Layard, R., et al., "Europe: the Case for Unsustainable Growth," 8/9 (May 1984) Center for European Policy Studies [reprinted in O. Blanchard, R. Dornbusch, and R. Layard (eds.), *Restoring Europe's Prosperity* (1986), Cambridge, MA: MIT Press 33−94].

Leuchtenburg, W., *Franklin D. Roosevelt and the New Deal* (1963), New York: Harper & Row.

Lilien, D., "The Cyclical Pattern of Temporary Layoffs in United States Manufacturing" (1977), Ph.D. dissertation, MIT.

Lindbeck, A., and D. Snower, "Involuntary Unemployment as an Insider-Outsider Dilemma," in W. Beckerman (ed.), *Wage Rigidity, Employment, and Economic Policy* (1986a), London: Duckworth.

Lindbeck, A., and D. Snower, "Wage Setting, Unemployment and Insider-Outsider Relations," *American Economic Review, Papers and Proceedings* (May 1986b), 235−239.

Lindbeck, A., and D. Snower, "Cooperation, Harassment and Involuntary Unemployment," Working Paper 321 (1986c), Institute for International Economic Studies, Stockholm.

Linneman, P., and M. Wachter, "Rising Union Premiums and the Declining Boundaries Among Noncompeting Groups," *American Economic Review* 76 (May 1986, Papers and Proceedings 1985), 103–108.

Lippman, S., and J. McCall, "The Economics of Job Search: A Survey," *Economic Inquiry* 14 (June 1976), 155–189.

Long, C., *The Labor Force Under Changing Income and Employment* (1958), Princeton: Princeton University Press.

Lucas, R. "International Evidence on Output-Inflation Tradeoffs," *American Economic Review*, 316–334.

Lucas, R., "An Equilibrium Model of the Business Cycle," *Journal of Political Economy* (1975), 1113–1144.

Lucas, R., "Unemployment Policy," *American Economic Review* 68 (May 1978, Papers and Proceedings 1977), 353–357.

Lucas, R., and L. Rapping, "Real Wages, Employment, and Inflation," *Journal of Political Economy* (1969), 721–754.

Mankiw, N., "The Permanent income Hypothesis and the Real Interest Rate." *Economic Letters* 7 (1981), 307–311.

Mankiw, N., "Hall's Consumption Hypothesis and Durable Goods," *Journal of Monetary Economics* (1982).

Mankiw N., J. Rotemberg, and L. Summers, "Intertemporal Substitution in Macroeconomics," *Quarterly Journal of Economics* (February 1985), 179–198. Chapter 6 in this book.

Marston, S., "Employment Instability and High Unemployment Rates," *Brookings Papers on Economic Activity* 1 (1976), 169–203.

Marston, S., "Unemployment Insurance and Voluntary Employment," Report to the National Commission on Unemployment Compensation (October 1979), Washington, D.C.: NCUC.

Marston, S., "Two Views of the Geographic Distribution of Unemployment," *Quarterly Journal of Economics* 100 (February 1985), 57–79.

McCallum, B., "Rational Expectations and the Estimation of Economic Models: An Alternative Procedure," *International Economic Review* (1976), 484–490.

McDonald, I., and R. Solow, "Wage Bargaining and Unemployment," *American Economic Review* 71 (December 1981), 896–908.

McDonald, I., and R. Solow, "Wages and Employment in a Segmented Labor Market," *Quarterly Journal of Economics* 100 (November 1985), 1115–1141.

McFadden D., "Conditional Logit Analysis of Qualitative Choice Behavior," in P. Zarembka (ed.), *Frontiers in Econometrics* (1974), New York: Academic Press, 105–42.

Medoff, J., "Layoffs and Alternatives under Trade Unions in U.S. Manufacturing," *American Economic Review* (1979), 380–395.

Medoff, J., "U.S. Labor Markets: Imbalance, Wage Growth, and Productivity in the 1970s," *Brookings Papers on Economic Activity* 1 (1983), 87–120.

Mincer, J., "Labor Force Participation of Married Women," in H. Lewis (ed.), *Aspects of Labor Economics* (1963), Princeton: Princeton University Press.

Mincer, J., "Labor Force Participation and Unemployment: A Review of Recent Evidence," in R. Gordon (ed.), *Prosperity and Unemployment* (1966), New York: Wiley.

Minford, P., *Unemployment: Cause and Cure* (1982), Oxford: Martin Robertson.

Mitchell, B., *Depression Decade: From New Era through New Deal* (1947), New York: Holt, Rinehart.

Montgomery, E., "The Impact of Regional Difference in Unionism on Employment," *Economic Review of the Federal Reserve Bank of Cleveland* 1 (1986), 2–11.

Monthly Labor Review (May 1944).

Mortenson, D., "Job Search, the Duration of Unemployment, and the Phillips Curve," *American Economic Review* 60 (December 1970), 847–862.

Mortenson, D., "Unemployment Insurance and Job Search Decisions," *Industrial and Labor Relations Review* 30 (July 1977), 505–517.

National Commission on Employment and Unemployment Statistics, *Counting the Labor Force: Preliminary Draft Report of the National Commission on Employment and Unemployment Statistics* (January 1979), 65–66.

Nelson, R., and C. Plosser, "Trends and Random Walks in Economic Time Series: Some Evidence and Implications," *Journal of Monetary Economics* 10 (September 1982), 139–162.

Nickell, S., "A Review of *Unemployment: Cause and Cure* by Patrick Minford with David Davies, Michael Peel and Alison Prague," Discussion Paper 185, LSE Center for Labor Economics.

Nickell, S., "Why Is Wage Inflation in Britain So High?" Mimeo (1986), Oxford.

OECD, *Employment Outlook* (1984).

Okun, A., "Upward Mobility in a High Pressure Economy," *Brookings Papers on Economic Activity* 1 (1973), 207–252.

Oswald, A., "The Economic Theory of Trade Unions: An Introductory Survey," *Scandinavian Journal of Economics* 87 (1985), 163–193.

Perry, G., "Changing Labor Markets and Inflation," *Brookings Papers on Economic Activity* 3 (1970), 411–441.

Perry, G., "Unemployment Flows in the U.S. Labor Market," *Brookings Papers on Economic Activity* 2 (1972), 245–278.

Perry, G., "Potential Output and Productivity," *Brookings Papers on Economic Activity* 1 (1977), 11–47.

Phelps, E., *Inflation Policy and Unemployment Theory* (1972), New York: Norton.

Phelps, E., et al., *Microeconomic Foundations of Employment and Inflation Theory* (1970), New York: Norton.

Pollak, R., "Endogenous Tastes in Demand and Welfare Analysis," *American Economic Review* (1978).

Poterba, J., and L. Summers, "Multinominal Logit with Errors in Classification," Mimeo (1982), MIT.

Poterba, J., and L. Summers, "Survey Response Variation in the Current Population Survey," *Monthly Labor Review* (March 1984a), 31–37.

Poterba, J., and L. Summers, "Response Variation in the CPS: Caveats for the Unemployment Analyst," *Monthly Labor Review* 107 (March 1984b), 37–43.

Poterba, J., and L. Summers, "Reporting Errors and Labor Market Dynamics," *Econometrica* 54 (November 1986). Chapter 3 in this book.

President's Commission to Appraise Employment and Unemployment Statistics, *Measuring Employment and Unemployment* (1962), Washington, D.C.: U.S. Government Printing Office.

Romer, C., "Spurious Volatility in Historical Unemployment Data," *Journal of Political Economy* 94 (February 1986), 1–37.

Rosenfeld, C., "Job Search of the Unemployed, May 1976," *Monthly Labor Review,* (November 1977).

Sachs, J., "Real Wages and Unemployment in the OECD Countries," *Brookings Papers on Economic Activity* 1 (1983), 255–289.

Sachs, J., "Wages, Profits and Macroeconomic Adjustment: A Comparative Study," *Brookings Papers on Economic Activity* 2 (1979), 263–319.

Sachs, J., "High Unemployment in Europe," Mimeo (1985) Harvard.

Salant, S., "Search Theory and Duration Data: A Theory of Sorts," *Quarterly Journal of Economics* 91 (1977), 39–57.

Salop, S., "Systematic Job Search and Unemployment," *Review of Economic Studies* 40 (April 1973), 191–201.

Samuelson, P., *The Collected Scientific Papers of Paul A. Samuelson II* (1966), Cambridge, MA: MIT Press.

Sargent, T., *Macroeconomic Theory* (1980).

Sargent, T., "Stopping Moderate Inflations: The Methods of Poincare and Thatcher," in R. Dornbusch and M. Simonsen (eds.), *Inflation, Debt and Indexation* (1983), Cambridge, MA: MIT Press, 54–99.

Schmeisser, J. "Hiring in a Low Wage Labor Market," Unpublished senior honors thesis (1979), Department of Economics, Harvard.

Schreiner, I., "Reinterview Results from the CPS Independent Reconciliation Experiment," Unpublished (1980), Washington, D.C.: Bureau of the Census.

Slichter, S., "Notes on the Structure of Wages," *Review of Economics and Statistics* 31 (1950), 283–288.

Smith, R., "Dynamic Determinants of Labor Force Participation: Some Evidence from Gross Change Data," Working Paper (1973) Washington, D.C.: The Urban Institute.

Smith, R., "A Simulation Model of the Demographic Composition of Employment, Unemployment and Labor Force Participation," in R. Ehrenberg (ed.) *Research in Labor Economics* (1977), Greenwich, CT: JAI Press 259–303.

Smith, R., and J. Vanski, "Gross Change Data: The Neglected Data Base," in National Commission on Employment and Unemployment, *Counting the Labor Force* (appendix to vol. II) (1979), Washington, D.C.: U.S. Government Printing Office.

Smith, R., and J. Vanski, "The Volatility of the Teenage Labor Market: Labor Force Entry, Exit, and Unemployment Flows," Prepared for presentation at the Conference on Employment Statistics and Youth (February 1979), U.S. Department of Labor.

Smith, R., J. Vanski, and C. Holt, "Recession and the Employment of Demographic Groups," *Brookings Papers on Economic Activity* 3 (1974), 737–758.

Solow, R., "Macro-policy and Full Employment," in Eli Ginzberg (ed.), *Jobs for Americans* (1976), New York: Prentice-Hall 46–48.

Stasny, E., "Estimating Gross Flows in Labor Force Participation Using Data from the Canadian Labor Force Survey," Ph.D. dissertation, Department of Statistics, Carnegie-Mellon.

Stasny, E., and S. Feinberg, "Some Stochastic Models for Estimating Gross Flows in the Presence of Nonrandom Response," *Conference on Gross Flows in Labor Force Statistics* (1985), Washington, D.C.: U.S. Government Printing Office.

Stigler, G., "The Economics of Information," *Journal of Political Economy* 69 (June 1961), 213–225.

Stiglitz, J., "Theories of Wage Rigidity," in Butkiewicz, Koford, and Miller (eds.) *Keynes' Economic Legacy: Contemporary Economic Theories* (1986), New York: Praeger, 153–206.

Summers, J., "The Phillips Curve: Employment Ratio vs. Unemployment Rate" (1978).

Summers, L., "Tax Policy, the Rate of Return and Savings," Working Paper 995 (1982), NBER.

Summers, L., "Why Is the Unemployment Rate So Very High Near Full Employment?" *Brookings Papers on Economic Activity* 2 (1986), 339–383. Chapter 9 in this book.

Summers, L., "Hysteresis and British Unemployment," Employment Institute Pamphlet (1988), London.

Taylor, J., "Staggered Wage Setting in a Macro Model," *American Economic Review* 69 (May 1979), 108–113.

Tella, A., "Labor Force Sensitivity to Employment by Age, Sex," *Industrial Relations* 4 (February 1965), 69–83.

Thurow, L., *Generating Inequality* (1976).

Tobin, J., "Inflation and Unemployment," *American Economic Review* 62 (March 1972), 1–18.

Toikka, R, W. Scanlon, and C. Holt, "Extensions of a Structural Model of the Demographic Labor Market," in R. Ehrenber (ed.), *Research in Labor Economics I* (1977), Greenwich, CT: JAI Press, 305–332.

U.S. Department of Labor, *Unemployment Insurance Statistics* (March 1978).

U.S. Department of Labor, Bureau of Labor Statistics, *Geographic Profile of Employment and Unemployment, 1985* (September 1986) and earlier issues.

U.S. Department of Labor, Employment and Training Administration, Unemployment Insurance Service, *Comparison of State Unemployment Insurance Laws* (1978), Washington, D.C.: U.S. Government Printing Office, 3–28.

Vanski, J., "Recession and the Employment of Demographic Groups: Adjustments to Gross Change Data," in Holt, C. et al. (eds.) *Labor Markets, Inflation, and Manpower Policies*, Final Report to the Department of Labor (1975), Washington, D.C.: The Urban Institute.

Wachter, M., "A Labor Supply Model for Secondary Workers," *Review of Economics and Statistics* 54 (May 1972), 141–151.

Wachter, M., "Intermediate Swings in Labor Force Participation," *Brookings Papers on Economic Activity* 2 (1977), 545–574.

Weitzman, M., "Increasing Returns and the Foundations of Unemployment Theory," *Economic Journal* 92 (December 1982), 787–804.

Weitzman, M., *The Share Economy* (1984), Cambridge, MA: Harvard University Press.

Woltman, H., and I. Shreiner, "Possible Effects of Response Variance on the Gross Changes Data," Memo (11 May 1979), Washington, D.C.: Bureau of the Census.

Woytinsky, W., "Three aspects of Labor Dynamics" (1942), Washington, D.C.: Social Science Research Council.

Yatchew, A., "Heterogeneity and State Dependence in Labor Supply," Unpublished (1977).

Index